SERVICE MANAGEMENT AND MARKETING

SERVICE MANAGEMENT AND MARKETING

A CUSTOMER RELATIONSHIP MANAGEMENT APPROACH

Second edition

Christian Grönroos

Hanken
Swedish School of Economics and Business Administration
Finland

JOHN WILEY & SONS, LTD
Chichester • New York • Weinheim • Brisbane • Singapore • Toronto

Published by John Wiley & Sons, Ltd,
            Baffins Lane, Chichester,
            West Sussex PO19 1UD, England

            National   01243 779777
            International   (+44) 1243 779777
            e-mail (for orders and customer service enquiries):
            cs-books@wiley.co.uk
            Visit our Home Page on http://www.wiley.co.uk
                    or http://www.wiley.com

Reprinted February 2001, August 2001

Other Wiley Editorial Offices

John Wiley & Sons, Inc., 605 Third Avenue,
New York, NY 10158-0012, USA

WILEY-VCH Verlag GmbH, Pappelallee 3,
D-69469 Weinheim, Germany

Jacaranda Wiley Ltd, 33 Park Road, Milton,
Queensland 4064, Australia

John Wiley & Sons (Asia) Pte Ltd, 2 Clementi Loop #02-01,
Jin Xing Distripark, Singapore 129809

John Wiley & Sons (Canada) Ltd, 22 Worcester Road,
Rexdale, Ontario M9W 1L1, Canada

Library of Congress Cataloging-in-Publication Data

Grönroos, Christian, 1947–
      Service management and marketing : a customer relationship management approach
   / c by Christian Grönroos.—2nd ed.
      p. cm.
      Includes bibliographical references and index.
      ISBN 0-471-72034-8 (alk. paper)
      1. Service industries—Marketing. 2. Customer services. I. Title.

   HD9980.5 .G776 2000
   658.8—dc21
                                                                          00–032093

British Library Cataloguing in Publication Data

A catalogue record for this book is available from the British Library

ISBN 0-471-72034-8

Typeset in 10/12pt Palatino by Mayhew Typesetting, Rhayader, Powys
Printed and bound in Great Britain by Antony Rowe, Chippenham
This book is printed on acid-free paper responsibly manufactured from sustainable
forestry of which at least two trees are planted for each one used in paper production.

CONTENTS

PREFACE

This book is on the *service perspective* in business. It is not only about how to manage service firms from a market-oriented point of view. Rather it offers a management perspective for any type of organization—service firms, manufacturers of physical goods, organizations in the public sector—which is helpful in situations where the organization's core solution to customer problems (a service or a physical product) is not enough to create a sustainable competitive advantage. The firm has to look for other sources of developing such an advantage. Understanding the internal value-generating processes of customers—for example, ultimate consumers, end users, suppliers, and distributors—and how to develop a total integrated offering which serves these value-generating processes offer a perspective which suits the competitive situation of most firms today. This is the service perspective. The core solution, be that of a service or a physical good, is integrated with a number of services into a total offering which best can be described as a service offering.

Firms compete with services, not physical products. Service firms have always done so, but today this goes for all firms with few exceptions. This competitive situation can be described as service competition. A firm, which cannot manage service competition, will have problems surviving. Service competition can be defined as a situation where the core solution of a firm—a service or a physical good—is a prerequisite only for a competitive advantage, but where firms compete with a number of services surrounding the core solution. In order to be able to do this successfully the firm has to view its business and its customer relationships from a service perspective.

As services are inherently relational, managing customers out of service perspective benefits from a customer relationship management approach. There are always relationships between a service organization and its customers. The key issue is whether the firm wants to make use of these relationships in the way it manages customers or not, and whether a given customer wants to be in an actively managed relationship with a supplier or service provider, or not. Hence, in this book a customer relationship management approach is taken. It should be noted that customer relationship management (CRM) is not treated in the narrow sense here, which is often the case in the field of information technology. Instead it is used to describe how the whole relationship between a firm and its customers, with all its various contacts, interactive processes and communication elements, is managed. In this way CRM is viewed more or less as a synonym to relationship marketing.

As this book addresses how the relationships between a firm and its customers are managed in service competition, it automatically takes a customer-oriented approach. Using a traditional terminology this may be described as a marketing approach. That is why the title of this book is *Service Management and Marketing*. However, the term marketing may not be the best one to describe the kind of customer management approach needed in service competition, where a long-term perspective to customer relationship management most often has to be taken. Marketing as a term is too much related to the times when obtaining customers was the only, or most important, task in customer management. When keeping and growing customers has become the critical issue, marketing does not describe this phenomenon in the best possible way. It is too much associated with getting out to the market, not with staying there. Although the term marketing is used in this book to describe the phenomenon of managing customers, it is good to remember that marketing as a term is not more than a hundred years old, whereas the underlying phenomenon is as old as trade and commerce. We do not have to continue using a term, like marketing, in the future, which appears to become more and more inappropriate.

A decade ago I published a book with the same title as the one of the present book. That is why this book is labeled as a second edition. In reality, although the basic topic, how to manage a firm in service competition, is the same, this is a totally new book. Some material, of course, remains from the previous one, but new chapters have been added and most of the old chapters have been updated and totally rewritten, based on the research that has taken place during the last ten years.

The first three chapters describe the basic perspective of the book, i.e. service as a perspective, the customer relationship management and relationship marketing approach, and the nature of service consumption and usage and how this affects customer relationships. In the two following chapters the nature of service quality, quality management and measurement models in services are presented and illustrated. In this context relationship quality issues are also discussed.

In Chapter 6 the profit potential of services and the return on service and relationships are analyzed. The concepts of relationship costs and customer perceived value are analyzed, and the links between perceived quality and profitability of customer relationships are explored. In the following chapter the development of service offerings is discussed, and the model of the augmented service offering, which is geared to how customers perceive the quality of services, is presented. In Chapter 8 the characteristics of a service-based strategy are discussed, and the pitfalls of using traditional guidelines from manufacturing are described. Finally, as a conclusion, some principles of service management are put forward.

In Chapter 9 the productivity issue in service organizations is developed. Productivity is a manufacturing-related concept which has been frequently used by service firms, but which nevertheless has been studied only to a very limited extent from a service perspective. Traditional manufacturing-based productivity concepts are too simplistic to be used as such in services. They often lead managers astray and direct decision making in a dangerous direction. Therefore, a concept of service productivity is developed and presented in this chapter.

In Chapter 10 the issue of marketing is addressed. Since understanding services is very much related to understanding which benefits customers appreciate, a market or customer orientation is implicit in service management. However, marketing is not a function for marketing specialists only. Instead a marketing attitude of mind has to be instilled in all parts of the organization, where a large number of part-time marketers, frequently outnumbering the marketing specialists or full-time marketers, have a decisive impact on the quality perception of customers and on their future purchasing behavior. In the following two chapters the issues of communication from a totally integrated marketing communications perspective and of brand and image management are analyzed.

In Chapter 13 organizational issues are discussed. It is observed that in a service and relationship context marketing cannot be organized in the same way as is traditionally done. Marketing cannot be delegated to one separate department only, but in order to achieve a good marketing impact new solutions are needed. Because marketing is the responsibility of the whole organization, dominating marketing departments may create or at least widen the gap between marketing and operations, and other functions in a firm.

In the following chapters internal marketing and the development of a service culture are discussed. Internal marketing is an umbrella concept for a range of internal activities in an organization aimed at enhancing a service culture and maintaining a service orientation among its employees. Internal relationships influence the external relationships of a firm. Therefore, internal marketing is geared towards the relationship approach to managing customers. Internal marketing is one means, among others, to create and reinforce a corporate culture where giving good service to internal as well as external customers is considered a natural way of life in the organization. The characteristics of such a culture are analyzed in the chapter on service culture.

Chapter 16 offers a conclusion to the book. Service management and marketing is viewed as the management of the processes of enabling, giving and keeping promises to customers and other partners in an integrated way. In the concluding section, six rules of service and a number of barriers which makes it difficult to follow these rules are discussed as guidelines for management to cope with the challenges of service competition.

Finally, I would like to acknowledge everyone who over the years has encouraged and supported me in my research and in my book projects. They are too many to mention. Colleagues in academia all over the world have contributed to this process, and therefore also to this book. However, business executives have been equally influential, both in terms of encouragement and input in the development of my thoughts on service management and marketing, relationship marketing, customer relationship management, and related fields. This book has greatly benefited from supportive comments and constructive criticism by a number of reviewers of the manuscript. Thank you for your help.

I especially would like to acknowledge David Bowen, Ray Fisk, Peter Murphy, Kaj Storbacka and Steve Worthington who have contributed short case illustrations to the book. I appreciate your support very much. I would also like to thank Marie-Paule Sheard who has developed the supplementary materials for lecturers adopting this book for their course. If you wish to request these materials, please contact the publisher at the following email address: college@wiley.co.uk I also appreciate the continuous support that Steve Hardman from John Wiley & Sons has provided me with throughout this process. Last but not least I would like to acknowledge the support I have received from my family throughout this endeavor.

Please note that "he" and "his" have been used in this book to mean "he/she" and "his/her." This is intended to ensure that the text flows more smoothly and is not meant to be sexist.

Christian Grönroos
Degerö, Finland

Chapter 1

THE SERVICE AND RELATIONSHIP IMPERATIVE: MANAGING IN SERVICE COMPETITION

Everyone faces service competition. No one can escape from it.

The Role of Services

The Western world has experienced a post-industrial service economy for over two decades. This is not the situation in all parts of the world. In industrialized countries the value created by the service sector as a percentage of GDP in current prices rose from 53 per cent in 1960 to 66 per cent in 1995. In the European Union it rose from 47 to 68 per cent, and in the USA from 57 to 72 per cent, and it keeps rising.[1] However, the "service sector" has for a long time counted for over 50 per cent of gross national product or total employment in developed countries. In several countries this percentage is closer to 100 than 50. However, quoting statistics is largely irrelevant, because they are compiled based on the industrial era, where the creation of wealth in a society was due to that society's capability to produce manufactured goods in efficiently functioning factories. Services were considered add-ons, something that was necessary but which did not add much value for the society. What in official statistics was not included in manufacturing, the industrial sector or the agricultural sector was put together in what was called the service sector. This included financial services, transportation, hospitality services, professional services, and services provided by the public sector. Official statistics on the importance of services to society were vastly understated.

Today services are still defined in this outdated way. The reason why this is an anachronistic way of defining the amount and importance of services in a society is the fact that it views services *as something provided by a certain type of organization*. This is misleading, giving managers in businesses as well as high-level political and economic decision-makers the wrong signal about the importance of services, and also about the impact of services on the development of competitiveness between firms and on wealth in a society. There are two reasons why this is misleading:

- it neglects the *hidden services* of manufacturers and agriculture; and
- it views services as a "sector" of the economy, not as a *perspective* on how to create a competitive advantage.

These two issues are interrelated. All goods manufacturers today offer a number of services to their customers. For example, one of the leading firms in the elevator manufacturing business, the Kone Corporation, has claimed for over a decade that more than half of their total turnover comes from repair, maintenance and modernization services. Schindler, another major player in the same business, recently claimed that only eight per cent of their workforce was engaged in manufacturing jobs, while the rest were in services. Orio Giarini[2] states that "for each product we buy, be it an automobile or a carpet, the pure cost of production or of manufacturing is very seldom higher than 20 per cent." The rest of the value ("production" costs) of manufactured products is accounted for by various types of services. For a manufacturer the service functions or components that contribute to total costs can be described as belonging to five categories:[3]

- before manufacturing (e.g. research and development, design, financing);
- during manufacturing (e.g. financing, quality control, safety, maintenance);
- selling (e.g. logistics, distribution networks, information);
- during consumption and usage (e.g. maintenance, leasing, information, customer training, software upgrading, complaints handling, invoicing); and
- after consumption and usage (e.g. waste management, recycling).

Providing information, upgrading software, handling logistics and offering engineering and other types of professional services are examples of services that are offered and invoiced by manufacturers either separately or as part of a total package including physical product components. For most manufacturers, these and other types of services form a substantial part of their total invoicing. These services are often outsourced. However, regardless of whether they have been outsourced or managed internally, firms have started to see their strategic value in the package they offer to customers, and moreover, can see their potential for the development and maintenance of a sustainable competitive advantage. These services can be labelled *hidden services*, because in statistics they are registered as part of manufacturing's contribution to GNP and employment.

Service functions of course form the core area of firms, such as banks, insurance companies, transportation firms, health care organizations, hotels and restaurants, but here also a number of physical goods components are involved.

Non-Billable Hidden Services

Even the discussion in the previous section of the importance of services for manufacturers is based on a restricted view of the role of services in customer relationships, since it only includes service components that can be invoiced and calculated as part of total turnover, *billable services* being offered to customers. In reality, these form only a part of the service offered to customers. For example, all customers, individual consumers as well as organizations, note the way a firm handles invoicing, takes care of quality problems, mistakes and service failures, manages complaints, offers documentation and directions for the use of goods and services, offers customer training on how to use machines, equipment and software, handles queries and answers questions and e-mails, pays attention to customers and their special requests and wishes, keeps promises and delivers promptly, etc. The clarity and accuracy of invoices, speed and efficiency in managing failures and complaints, the attention that employees show customers and the promptness with which actions are taken all influence a customer's perception of the value of being a customer of a given supplier or service provider. They either make it easier or more troublesome to be a customer and also frequently help the customer to save money (these issues will be discussed in subsequent chapters). The customer orientation of these services contributes to making it worthwhile for customers to continue purchasing from the same firm, and prevents customers from considering alternative options. Hence, these normally *non-billable* types of service components also contribute to the creation of a competitive advantage.

The problem with non-billable services such as invoicing, complaints handling, documentation and customer training is that they are seldom perceived as services by management, and therefore are frequently not designed and managed as value-enhancing services to customers. Instead they are managed as administrative routines with internal efficiency criteria and cost consideration as the main guidelines. As a result, customers generally do not perceive most of these as support and value-creating activities. As will be discussed later on in this book, the development of value-enhancing services out of such administrative routines in customer relationships is a powerful way of setting apart a firm from its competitors and of creating a sustainable competitive advantage. Thus, these types of service elements are also *hidden services*, too seldom seen as services by managers and never seen as such by economists and statisticians.

A Customer Perspective

Customers do not buy goods or services, they buy the benefits goods and services provide them with.[4] *They buy offerings consisting of goods, services, information, personal attention and other components.*[5] Such offerings render *services* to them, and *it is this customer-perceived service of an offering that creates value for them.*[6] In the final analysis firms always offer a service to customers, regardless of what they produce.[7] The value of goods and services to customers is not produced in factories or in the back offices of service firms, although the discussion of how value is created in firms often implies this. Instead, *value is created in customers' value-generating processes*, when individual consumers or industrial users make use of the solution or package they have purchased.[8] Before that moment only resources, such as physical products, services, information, employees, technology, systems, know-how and the customers themselves, exist and wait to be used. In service contexts customers' value-generating processes and the process where the service is created (which is normally called the service production and delivery process) take place to a large extent simultaneously. Physical products are first produced and only afterwards consumed or used by customers and create value for them in those consumption or usage processes.

Customers are looking for solutions or packages which they can use so that value is created for them. Consequently, firms should provide customers with solutions consisting of all the components required to function in a value-creating way in customers' own value-generating processes. A high-quality production machine does not help a customer create value unless maintenance and repair tasks are taken care of in a skilful and timely manner, and a delicious restaurant meal does not create value in a customer's lunch break process if it is served too slowly.

This discussion leads to the following conclusion: customers do not look for goods or services *per se*; they look for solutions that serve their own value-generating processes. To take this one step further, whatever customers buy should function as a service for them. Sometimes this service requirement can be offset by a low price. Sometimes it can be offset by imaginary factors surrounding the physical product or service; for example when consumers choose button-fly jeans over jeans with zippers that are much easier to use because of their brand name. Sometimes a technologically advanced core solution is preferred, although it may be difficult or expensive to use. When firms choose a strategic perspective they should carefully analyze their customers' value-generating processes and know what their customers want. Generally speaking, customers always benefit from firms which consider a service perspective; however, for various reasons this is not always the case.

The Service Perspective

This section will discuss what a service perspective means, and in the following section this perspective will be contrasted with three other strategic perspectives.

In addition to professional advice, logistics and other services that are viewed as services to customers, the various kinds of billable and non-billable *hidden services* provide effective means of competition and, as has been concluded in previous sections, are a powerful source of competitive advantage. In order to make use of these potential open and hidden services, management has to view the business from a *service perspective*. One has to realize that providing customers with a large variety of services in addition to the core product, whether that is physical goods or services, is a way of outperforming competitors with the same quality and price of core products. Such a situation is normal in modern competition. It is difficult to build a competitive advantage based on a company's core product, unless the firm has a sustainable technological advantage or continuously lower costs. Many firms fall into the trap of competing with low prices, which sometimes may be effective, but most often is a way of giving away the revenue that is needed to create and maintain a sustainable advantage over the competition. Price is never a sustainable advantage. As soon as a competitor can offer a lower price, the customer will be gone.

Every firm, regardless of whether its core product is a physical good or a service, or whether the firm is operating on consumer markets or business-to-business markets, has the option of taking a service perspective. This will enable management to see different possibilities than compared with other strategic perspectives. In the next section the service perspective will be contrasted with three other perspectives.

The Service Perspective Compared to Other Strategic Perspectives

Firms can choose from a number of strategic perspectives, of which a service perspective is one. For example, four major strategic perspectives can be distinguished as follows:

- a service perspective;
- a core product perspective;
- a price perspective; and
- an image perspective.

First, the three comparison perspectives will be briefly described, followed by the service perspective.

A *core product perspective* is a traditional scientific management-based approach[9] where the quality of the core solution is considered to be the main source of competitive advantage. A firm that, for example, has a sustainable technological advantage can benefit from applying such a perspective. The core product is supposed to be the sole or major carrier of value for customers. In such cases, services are necessary elements in customer relationships, but their role is not strategic. A firm which adopts a core product perspective without having a technological advantage often falls into the price trap. As the core product does not distinguish the package as it is supposed to do, customers are persuaded to buy because the price is lower than that of the competitors. In the long run, this is not a sustainable strategy.

Taking a *price perspective* means that the firm considers a continuously low price to be the major means of competition. If a sustainable cost advantage can be achieved and maintained, this is a possible perspective to take. The firm may still obtain an acceptable profit margin so that it can invest in its future. However, if the cost advantage is lost, a strategic approach based on a price perspective becomes dangerous. Prices are pressed further down by the competition, and the firm loses its chance to develop for the future.

An *image perspective* will make the firm use predominantly means of marketing communications to create imaginary values in addition to the value of the core product. For some types of goods and services; for example, fashion products such as designer clothes and perfumes, some consumer packaged goods such as soft drinks, and some services such as fast-food restaurants, an image approach has been effective. Such a strategic approach requires there to be an attractive and functioning core product as a starting point. The package also easily becomes very dependent on the imaginary extras created by the firm's marketing strategy. If the firm stops reinforcing them, the offering may eventually deteriorate to just another physical product or service in the marketplace. Therefore, pursuing a strategy based on an image perspective demands continuous heavy investment in marketing communication. If the firm cannot afford this, the product (consisting of a core physical good or service and a weakening support) will lose its attractiveness and competitors who can continue to invest extensively in marketing communication will take over.

A *service perspective* means that the role of service components in customer relationships is seen as strategic. The core solution, whether a physical good or a service, has to be good enough to provide a competitive advantage, but this is not enough for success in the marketplace, or in the Internet-based marketspace. What creates a sustainable competitive advantage is the development of every element of the customer relationship, including all types of services discussed in the previous section, into one overall package. The driving force is the service perspective, according to which customers are served with goods and services of a core solution, additional separately billable services and other non-billable services, such as invoicing, complaints handling, advice and personal attention, information and other value-enhancing components. This situation can be described as *service competition*.[10] This is a *competitive situation where the core solution is the prerequisite for success, but where the management of a number of services, together with the core solution, forms a Total Service Offering and determines whether or not the firm will be successful*. This book is about how to manage an organization and its customer relationships in service competition.

The central requirement of management in service competition is to appreciate the service perspective as a strategic approach and to understand how to manage the firm in order to develop a total service offering. This is called *service management*, and can be seen as an alternative management approach to scientific management, geared to the demands of service competition.[11] Service management as a management focus will be discussed in detail in a subsequent chapter.

A firm can choose any one of the perspectives discussed above. Following this choice it will develop a strategic approach which differs from the approach that would have been taken if another strategic perspective had been adopted. Choosing one strategic perspective does not mean that aspects of the other perspectives are not important. However, the choice of a perspective determines the way a firm will develop resources and competencies. For example, choosing a service perspective as the main strategy does not mean that less attention than otherwise will be paid to production technologies and the technical quality of the core solution. On the contrary, because of strong competition in most industries and in most markets, firms are required to develop a better core product platform for a service-based competitive advantage. Elements from other perspectives will, however, always be geared to the requirements of the dominating perspective. The fine tuning of a strategic approach varies, of course, but Table 1.1 shows in a simplified way the strategic orientation of the four strategic perspectives.

A Customer Relationship Management Perspective

Services are inherently relational. A service encounter, where a customer, for example, is a restaurant guest or makes a telephone call, is a process. In this process the service provider is always present, interacting with the customer on a

TABLE 1.1 Characteristics of strategic perspectives

Strategic perspective	Characteristic of a corresponding strategic approach
Service perspective	The firm takes the view that an enhanced offering is required to support the customer's value-generating processes, and that the core solution (a physical product, service or combination of goods and services) is not sufficient to differentiate the offering from those of competitors. Physical product components, service components, information, personal attention and other elements of customer relationships are combined into a *total service offering*. The offering is labeled a service offering, although the core solution may be based on a physical product, because all elements of the offering are combined to provide a value-generating service for customers. Developing such a total service package is seen to be of strategic importance and therefore given highest priority by management. *Hidden services*, both billable and non-billable, are considered part of this offering and supportive to the customer's value-creating processes. Price is considered less important for customers than long-term costs. A firm that adopts a service perspective will consider itself a *service business*.
Core product perspective	The firm concentrates on the development of the core solution, whether this is a physical product or a service, as the main provider of value for the customer's value-creating processes (the customer's use of solutions to create value for himself or for an organizational user). Additional services may be considered necessary but not of strategic importance, and therefore they have a low level of priority. *Hidden services*, especially non-billable ones, are not recognized as value-enhancing services. The firm differentiates its package from others through providing an excellent core solution.
Price perspective	The firm takes the view that price is the dominating purchasing criterion of its customers, and that being able to offer a low price is a necessity for survival in the marketplace. Price is seen as the main contribution to the customer's value-creating processes. The provision of additional services is not considered value-enhancing and is therefore of lower priority than the capability to offer a low-price solution. Price is considered more value-enhancing than the long-term cost effects of a solution. The firm is differentiating its offering by being the cheapest alternative available, or one of the cheapest.
Image perspective	The firm differentiates its offering by creating imaginary extras (a brand image) around its core product. Such extras are mainly created in the minds of customers by advertising and marketing. The core solution is seen as a starting point for the development of customer value, but the brand image that is created by marketing is considered to be the major contribution to the customer's value-creating processes.

broad base, as in a restaurant, or providing the process infrastructure, as a telephone operator does. Even a single encounter includes elements by which a relationship between the service provider and the customer can be built. If several encounters follow each other in a continuous or discrete fashion, a relationship may emerge. If a customer feels that there is something special and valuable in his contacts with a given firm, a relationship may develop. Perceived relationships are not enough to make customers loyal, but they are a central part of loyalty, and loyal customers are normally, but not always,[12] profitable customers. Hence, at least as a ground rule, managing relationships with customers is a profitable approach for service firms and manufacturers providing services as part of their package.

Relationship marketing has emerged, or rather re-emerged, as a marketing paradigm.[13] Managing customer relationships is seen as an alternative to focusing on transactions or exchanges of goods and services for money. Firms choosing a service perspective as their strategic approach almost inevitably have to focus on relationships with their customers and other stakeholders, such as suppliers, distributors, financial institutions and shareholders. Thus, *understanding relationship marketing or marketing based on customer relationship management becomes a necessity for understanding how to manage a firm in service competition.* Hence, the approach to managing in service competition taken in this book is geared towards customer relationship management as a dominating marketing perspective. In the next chapter this approach will be discussed in detail.

The Importance of Intellectual Capital

Ever since the interest in service marketing research started to grow more than two decades ago, everyone, academics and practitioners alike, has claimed that employees form the most important resource of a firm. Without knowledgeable, skilful, motivated people committed to good service the firm will not perform well. In spite of this, in reality employees have been treated as before; that is, as a cost that can and should be eliminated as soon as possible. By and large, the declaration of the critical importance of employees has remained lip service. And as Reichheld observes, during the previous decade the high turnover of employees, due to downsizing and sometimes forced early retirement, has had a negative effect on the *intellectual capital* of firms.[14]

Intellectual capital can be defined, for example, as all the assets of a firm except those in the balance sheet, or the total value of a firm minus its book value.[15] Most of this capital is due to people: managers, supervisors and other employees throughout an organization, as well as network partners and customers in consumer as well as business-to-business markets. The new, more comprehensive ways of taking into account the assets of a firm[16] have clearly pinpointed the long-term value of intellectual capital as at least an equally important determinant of success as short-term financial capital.[17] However, as the long-term success of a firm eventually is dependant on its financial performance, the intellectual capital has to be managed so that it is turned into economic results. As Gummesson says, *"the issue is to recognize the long-term importance of intellectual capital for the generation of financial capital, and to gradually convert intellectual capital into financial capital."*[18]

Intellectual capital can be divided into *individual* and *structural* capital.[19] Individual capital consists of employees, network partners and customers with their individual knowledge, behavior and network of relationships. Structural capital is part of company culture that can be retrieved and used by a newly appointed employee. It is embedded in the corporate culture and thus transferable to new people, employees, network partners and customers alike. Individual capital is destroyed when a person leaves a firm, whereas the structural capital stays and can be utilized in the future.

For service providers, as for any type of organization, it is critical to keep the individual intellectual capital on a managerial as well as on an operational level, or to transfer as much of it as possible to structural capital. Some can be stored in databases, but a substantial part of it cannot be secured when an employee or a customer leaves. A vital part of the intellectual capital is of course knowledge, which can be either *migratory* or *embedded knowledge*.[20] Embedded knowledge is part of structural capital. Knowledge, not pure information, that can be found in databases and put to use by almost anyone, is an example of such knowledge. Embedded knowledge is also stored in images and brands as well as in strong relationships with network partners and customers which are not dependent on a given employee. The more embedded knowledge there is, the better off the firm is. The more migratory knowledge there is, the more vulnerable the firm is to employee turnover, because when employees leave this kind of knowledge migrates with them.

In conclusion, employees on a managerial as well as on an operational level are critical to the success of service providers, as they are to any firm. Keeping skilful, motivated and committed employees is of vital importance. However, *knowledgeable and demanding customers and network partners are also a valuable asset* that has to be treasured. They not only, as customers, bring the service provider business and, as network partners, make it possible to provide customers with competitive solutions, but they also support the development of new ideas, service concepts, solutions, technologies and operational systems by sharing their requirements, visions and knowledge, and simply by being demanding.

Shareholder Value and the Service and Relationship Perspective

As a ground rule the service perspective requires a customer relationship management approach. Value is created for customers in long-term customer relationships. In a going concern situation where the firm is well managed and customers are provided with the quality and value they are looking for, profits should be continuously accumulating, and the firm can be expected to produce value for its owners and shareholders on a continuous basis. However, when times are turbulent and strategic or other changes have to be made, it may take time before customer relationships have been developed so that the results in terms of profits and shareholder value are seen to rise. In situations like this, shareholders and owners have to be patient. Shareholders who are looking for quick growth in volume and profit prioritize short-term sales over the develop-ment of long-term relationships. The long-term relationships with customers and partnerships with suppliers, distributors and other network partners that may be needed, cannot be established in a sustainable way if the firm has shareholders who are reacting on quarterly results and, in so doing, make management focus on short-term value-creating decisions.[21]

In the final analysis, shareholder value comes from profitable customer relationships, not from the stock exchange. However, many investors are blinded by the opportunity of making short-term profits, without realizing that this probably damages the firm's chances of making money in the long term. Therefore, the firm also has to manage its relationships with shareholders, and with financial institutions and stock analysts who advise shareholders on

investment decisions. The firm should, if possible, deliberately look for responsible shareholders who are committed to long-term growth and profit. Long-term
shareholders are a critical asset for firms that want to develop their capability to
cope with service competition and manage customer relationships successfully.[22]

Managing relationships with shareholders may be as critical to long-term
success, and sometimes more critical, as the management of relationships with
customers, employees and other network partners. According to Reichheld, US
firms lose half of their investors and owners in just one year, they lose half of
their customers in five years and half of their employees in four years.[23] At least
as far as shareholders and customers are concerned, the situation may be similar
in Europe and Australasia. As one option, Reichheld even suggests that firms
should withdraw from the stock market and become private companies.[24]
Indeed, there are examples of large and successful firms that have chosen this
option. Ingvar Kamprad, the founder and president of the IKEA furniture chain
operating in a large number of countries, has said that he could not think of
introducing his firm on the stock market with investors crying out for short-term
profits when his goal is to develop a growing and sustainable business.[25] It could
not be said in a clearer way.

The Logic of Service Competition

Service competition is nothing new. Service firms such as banks, hotels, restaurants and transportation firms have always faced the situation where competing
with services is critical to success. They have not always realized what this
requires of them, and therefore, for example, may have fallen into a price trap or
over-emphasized marketing communication. However, firms in more and more
industries, regardless of whether they are traditionally categorized as service or
manufacturing industries, now find themselves in a situation where the core
product only offers a starting point for the development of a competing advantage, but does not guarantee a competitive advantage any more. In such a
situation a service perspective offers an approach to the strategic reorientation of
the firm. The development of the core product into a service offering including
value-enhancing billable and non-billable service components may make the firm
competitive again. *Service competition* has become a reality for most firms. Without adopting a *service competition logic* such firms will be in trouble.

There are at least three reasons for the need to focus on services. The demand
for adopting a service perspective, and thus for learning how to cope with service
competition, is partly *customer-driven*, partly *competition-driven*, and partly
technology-driven. First, customers in a greater number of markets demand more
than a mere technical solution to a problem provided by a service firm or a
manufacturer. Customers are gradually becoming more sophisticated, more
informed and, consequently, more demanding. By and large, they are looking for
more comfort, fewer problems, lower additional costs and less trouble caused by
the use of goods and services; in short, they are looking for better value. Secondly,
this demand by customers is constantly enhanced by competition, which is
becoming more fierce and increasingly global. In the pursuit of more valuable
offerings for their customers, firms turn to services, and thus force competitors to

appreciate the importance of services too. Third, technological developments, especially in the area of information technology, enable firms to create new services more easily. An early example of this was the just-in-time approach to logistics, which to be successfully implemented required high-power computerized information systems. More recently, the development of the Internet and electronic commerce has also made it possible to create new services. The Internet is a highly relational tool, making it possible for firms to develop interactive and relationship-building contacts with their customers, thus enhancing the value of their core solution. The emergence of mobile commerce will reinforce this trend. By and large, new information technology often makes it easier to maintain relationships with customers, as well as creating new ways of doing so.[26]

When new elements are added to the goods and service components of customer relationships, these relationships are expanded. Traditionally, marketing and sales organized in marketing and sales departments have been responsible for customer relationships. The other departments of the firm were involved only to a limited extent. As the relationship grows in scope, more functions are in immediate contact with customers: for example, bank tellers and ATMs, service technicians involved in the technical service and maintenance of machines and equipment, telephone receptionists, call center and contact center systems, people in R&D departments. Responsibility for developing and maintaining customer relationships, which is normally called marketing, is no longer solely related to the marketing department and the marketing director. In the organizational structure this new shared responsibility for the customer has to be recognized and accepted.

Finally, management has to intellectually accept this change to service competition and base its decisions and its involvement in implementing decisions on this new form of competition. The technical solution, irrespective of whether it is provided by a physical good or a service, is not the key to success any more. Services, understood in a broad sense as billable and non-billable service components, are in customer relationships the values with which firms compete. The technical solution is more or less taken for granted by customers.

The *post-industrial economy* has been given different labels: information economy, knowledge-based economy, service economy, even the new economy. Of course, the label used is not important. It is the content of this post-industrial economy that is important. In the author's opinion, because a service perspective is imperative in this economy, a service-oriented terminology should be used. Information and knowledge are nothing new. They have always existed, although new technological solutions make it possible to compile, store, disseminate and retrieve data in ways which make more information more instantly available to more people than ever before. In the best case this also contributes favorably to the level of knowledge. Services are not new either. However, it is not the growing amount of information or increased level of knowledge *per se* that are important in the post-industrial economy. The challenge for firms is to be able to *use* information and knowledge to develop more *customer-oriented* and *value-enhancing services* for their customers and to create *total service offerings* out of physical products or services. If a label other than post-industrial economy is chosen it would be *service economy*. In such an economy information and knowledge are only fuel for development. This economy is fairly new now, but it will not remain a new economy for ever.

Marketing: The Last Untouched Business Process

During the past 20 years firms and most of their business functions and processes have undergone a substantial change. Through automation, process re-engineering, total quality management and just-in-time logistics, manufacturing, operations, warehousing and deliveries have been developed, and the productivity of these processes has been improved in such a dramatic way that a person who knew how these functions and processes looked half a century ago would not believe his eyes today. Moreover, management and administrative routines and processes have also changed in a remarkable way through the introduction of computerized systems, information technology, extranets and intranets and, following downsizing, re-engineering and outsourcing efforts. As reported by Sheth and Sisodia,[27] from 1947 to the mid-1990s manufacturing and operations costs have decreased from 50 to 30 per cent of total costs, and during the same period management and administrative costs have decreased from 30 to 20 per cent of total costs. Meanwhile, marketing's share of total costs has increased from 20 per cent in the 1940s to 50 per cent in the 1990s.

Increased competition is one explanation of this huge relative growth of marketing costs but, more importantly, this upward trend is due to the fact that there have been no major productivity gains in marketing during this 50-year period. Furthermore, since it has been acceptable to claim that the return on marketing costs cannot be calculated in any meaningful way, attempts to improve the productivity of marketing have been few. In addition, because of the generally accepted view that money used for the marketing of goods and services is a cost, not an investment in customers, this astonishingly unbusiness-like treatment of marketing can be understood, if not applauded.

The development of service competition and the need to take a relationship approach to the management of customers will put pressure on the efficient and effective use of marketing resources. First, as will be demonstrated throughout this book, if customers are to be attracted and kept profitably in the future, marketing resources and manufacturing and operations resources; and resources for human resource management and administrative processes and routines cannot be kept apart any more. The resources used for these different processes are to a large extent the same. Intelligent use of resources, for example, for operations, logistics, maintenance and technical service will make these processes productive, and at the same time their use as marketing resources will automatically be efficient and effective. However, "intelligent use" is not the same as in the industrial era when, for example, manufacturing and operations resources, and other traditionally non-marketing resources could be separated from resources used for marketing. As will be shown in this book, a *new business logic* is needed in order for firms to cope with service competition and to help them use resources in an intelligent way.

Second, in many situations, marketing resources—for example for mass communication, sales negotiations and other traditional separable marketing activities—will be needed. Most customer management—in other words, marketing activities—will take place in manufacturing and operations, logistics, invoicing, complaints handling and other departments which traditionally have had no or limited contact with marketing. Moreover, these marketing activities will not be in the hands of full-time marketing specialists, but will be taken care of by the very people who, at the same time as they make a marketing impact on the customer, take care of the regular tasks related to, for example, operations, deliveries, maintenance, technical services, or customer training. This will also have a positive effect on the efficient and effective use of total marketing resources.

Finally, the growth of information technology-based interactions with customers, electronic commerce, mobile commerce and the extended use of the Internet, extranets and intranets in the management of relationships with customers can have a positive effect on the costs of customer relationship management; in other words, on the costs of marketing. However, the service competition logic, which affects Internet-based customer interaction as well as electronic commerce, must be understood and recognized by firms. Otherwise there is an obvious risk that too many firms will add a layer of IT resources on top of old business resources and the result will be the opposite of the desired effect.

In conclusion, the introduction of service competition offers a long overdue opportunity for firms to analyze the return on their investments in customers and on the management of customers—in other words, to analyze how efficiently and effectively the firm's total marketing resources, processes and activities are used. However, with an old business logic from the days of the industrial era still haunting many firms, this cannot be done. The opportunity will be lost. With the new service competition logic of the post-industrial society this will be possible.

The Problem with using Terms Originating in Manufacturing

In research into services people have always been confronted with a situation where the much older manufacturing-oriented research has already developed well-manifested terms and concepts for similar phenomena and processes. In the service management and marketing literature a number of terms that do not exactly fit the requirements of services are used.

Marketing as a term refers to a function and is therefore less appropriate for situations where managing customers is a process to which most of the organization contributes. In most firms, to people outside the group of marketing and sales specialists, marketing is an awkward function and people have ambiguous feelings about it. Psychologically, marketing is a miscredited concept that is difficult to sell to non-marketing people. However, the term "marketing" is still used to describe the phenomenon of managing customers in situations when this is not a function anymore, but instead the process of ongoing management of customer relationships. From time to time the term marketing is used in this sense. However, in due course this term will be abandoned in situations where managing customer relationships is the basis for marketing. The *phenomenon* of managing customers will not of course lose its importance.

When describing service competition and how to manage services, other terms are also less suitable. For example, the process where services emerge for customers, often in interactions with other customers, has traditionally been called "service production" or "service production and delivery." Both the production term and the delivery term come from manufacturing, and neither fits service contexts well. "Production" is the process of producing products. Services are processes by themselves. The process is the service, although it also leads to a service outcome. However, no products in the sense of physical products are created. "Delivery" means that an outcome of a production process, a physical product, is moved from the place of production or storage to the place of use or sale. Services are not delivered in that sense. In this book the term *service process* is used to denote the process in which the service is emerging for, and perceived by, customers, often in interactions with customers. Sometimes for the sake of those readers who may not be used to this term the phrase *service production process* is also added.

Perhaps the most problematic manufacturing-oriented term in service management is the term "productivity." In manufacturing it refers to how efficiently labor, raw materials and other inputs into a production process are transformed into ready-made outputs, or physical products. Although the use of the terms *product* and *production* fit service contexts badly, they only sometimes guide managers in the wrong direction. However, the term "productivity" always misguides management. The productivity concept and all related measurement instruments are based on a *constant-quality assumption*, which is true in traditional manufacturing at least, but does not make any sense in a service context. Therefore, Chapter 9 is devoted to a discussion of a service-oriented productivity concept and how to understand and manage service productivity. Again, productivity is a misleading term, but as there is no alternative available we use the phrase *service productivity* hoping that the reader will realize that this is something different from manufacturing-oriented productivity, although it describes and ultimately measures the same thing; how effectively the creation of value for customers takes place within a firm.

The Objective and Approach of this Book

The main objective of this book is to describe the nature and scope of market-oriented management in service competition in an in-depth and innovative way. It takes a management approach and a strategy focus; therefore, tactical issues and instruments are only discussed briefly. Instead, the strategic issues of market-oriented management in service competition are discussed in greater detail. It is not a what-to-do book, but a *how to think* and *what to think* book. Topics such as personal selling and pricing, which are typical parts of standard textbooks, are not addressed here, other than as parts of larger strategic issues.

The definition of service competition has been briefly touched upon already in this chapter. But what is *market-oriented management*, and what is the difference between market-oriented management and marketing management? Briefly, market-oriented management is what is needed when the competitive advantage of a firm is built upon customer relationships, including a wide variety of customer contacts consisting of physical products and services as core solutions, as well as a host of billable and non-billable services. The nature of billable and non-billable services, or *hidden services*, has been discussed already in this chapter. In a context where success in the marketplace is based on successful transactions or exchanges of goods and services for money with anonymous customers, marketing seen as a function alongside other business functions has been the accepted way of managing customers; and it was effective. However, when customers' perception of the quality and value of a firm's products and the trustworthiness and reliability of this firm is dependent on a host of activities and interactive contacts in ongoing customer relationships, no separate function can successfully guarantee that customers will be satisfied with the quality and value they receive and will be interested in continuing and deepening the relationship. Managing customers becomes a process, one where most business functions become involved. Therefore, all areas of the firm have to be managed with a *customer focus*, that is in a market-oriented manner. *Market-oriented management* is a way of expressing the need to radiate an appreciation for the customers' needs, value systems and internal processes throughout the organization. Hence, in service and relationship contexts, market-oriented management is a more appropriate term than marketing management. However, as discussed in the previous section, perhaps because it is shorter, from time to time we still use the term "marketing" instead of "market-oriented management."

Although this book is based on international research into various areas of service management and marketing, it is geared to the service-oriented marketing school of thought which has internationally been labeled the *Nordic School*.[28] The main characteristic of this school of thought is the notion that, in service contexts, marketing decisions cannot be separated from overall management and the management of other business functions. Neither top management decisions nor decisions concerning any business functions can be made without considering the external implications of such decisions; that is, without taking into account the customer or marketing consequences. On a research-oriented note, the Nordic School has encouraged qualitative research and conceptual development, rather than jumping into theory testing when there is no theory to test, although theory testing and quantitative research approaches have of course been discussed when appropriate. The position of the Nordic School has always been that the sound development of context-oriented theories is a prerequisite for any meaningful testing of theories. No quantum leaps are made based on quantitative testing of pre-existing theories; only conceptual work can provide new perspectives suited to new or changing conditions.

This book is not a service marketing text, although it is intended to be used for the development of marketing knowledge or, rather, market-oriented management knowledge. The notion that it is not a traditional marketing text follows from the fact that in service competition marketing cannot remain only a separate function but instead it becomes everybody's business. This means that marketing becomes a top management issue, much more so than it is normally thought to be. As soon as a substantial part of the management of customers—that is of the total marketing process—is handled and managed outside a marketing department, and thus marketing becomes an interfunctional and interdepartmental issue, the person in charge has to be above the level of the department. Managing a marketing department has always been the responsibility of the head of that department. However, managing customers today is a much larger issue and thus *the responsibility of top management*.

This book is intended for people who, as students or practitioners, are interested in how to cope with service competition in a customer-oriented manner. It is not a book about market-oriented management and managing customers in service firms only. It is equally intended for manufacturers of physical goods operating in business-to-business or consumer markets, because the importance of service to success is constantly growing for such firms. Finally, because services and relationships are interrelated, the present book is equally based on customer relationship management and relationship marketing as it is on service management and managing customers in service contexts.

Two decades ago, the co-chair of the first of a long series of conferences on the marketing of services in North America, William R. George, now retired Professor of Marketing from Villanova University, said in a plenary speech that he waited for the day when standard marketing textbooks would be based on a service perspective, perhaps with a chapter about special characteristics of consumer goods marketing towards the end of the book. Today, marketing based on the traditional context of consumer goods still dominates most marketing texts but now, around the turn of the millennium, the scale is tipping over. The importance of service marketing has already been extended far beyond what is traditionally termed service industries and the service sector. In fact, it can be argued that *everybody* is in services. The service perspective has slowly won more ground, and will soon in the form of service management take over and become the norm.[29] Because the service perspective requires that marketing becomes a top management issue, and not remain an issue for a separate department, in the post-industrial society, service management is a more appropriate concept than service marketing.[30]

Further Reading

Ames, B.C. & Hlavacek, J.D. (1984) *Managerial Marketing for Industrial Firms*. Toronto: Random House.

Badarocco, Jr., J.L. (1991) *The Knowledge Link: How Firms Compete through Strategic Alliances*. Boston, MA: Harvard Business School Press.

Berry, L.L. & Parasuraman, A. (1993) Building a New Academic Field—The Case of Services Marketing. *Journal of Retailing*, **69**(1), pp. 13–60.

Edvinsson, L. & Malone, M.S. (1997) *Intellectual Capital*. New York: Harper Collins.

Giarini, O. (1999/2000) The Globalisation of Services in Economic Theory and Economic Practice: Some Key Issues. *Progress Newsletter* (Research Programme on the Service Economy, Geneva), 30, December–January, Annex II.

Griffiths, A. (2000) The Structure of all Industry and Services. In Blois, K. (ed.), *The Oxford Textbook of Marketing*. Oxford: Oxford University Press, pp. 69–102.

Grönroos, C. (1990) *Service Management and Marketing. Managing Moments of Truth in Service Competition*. Lexington, MA: Lexington Books.

Grönroos, C. (1990b) Service Management: A Management Focus for Service Competition. *International Journal of Service Industry Management*, **1**(1), pp. 6–14.

Grönroos, C. (2000) Service Reflections: Service Marketing Comes of Age. In Swartz, Teresa A. & Iacobucci, D. (eds), *Handbook of Services Marketing & Management*. Thousand Oaks, CA: Sage Publications, pp. 13–16.

Grönroos, C. & Gummesson, E. (1985) The Nordic School of Service Marketing. In Grönroos, C. & Gummesson, E. (eds), *Service Marketing—Nordic School Perspectives*. Stockholm University, Sweden, pp. 6–11.

Gummesson, E. (1999) *Total Relationship Marketing. Rethinking Marketing Management: From 4Ps to 30Rs*. Oxford: Butterworth Heinemann.

Gummesson, E. (1999b) Total Relationship Marketing: Experimenting with a Synthesis of Research Frontiers. *Australasian Marketing Journal*, 7(1), pp. 72–85.

Gummesson, E. (1999/2000) Return on Relationships (ROR): Building the Future with Intellectual Capital. *2nd WWW Conference on Relationship Marketing*. MCB University Press and Monash University, 15 November 1999–15 February 2000 (http://www.mcb.co.uk/services/conferen/nov99/rm/paper5.html).

Gummesson, E., Lehtinen, U. & Grönroos, C. (1997) Comment on the Nordic Perspectives on Relationship Marketing. *European Journal of Marketing*, **31**(1–2), pp. 10–16.

Kaplan, R.S. & Norton, D.P. (1996) *The Balanced Scorecard*. Boston, MA: Harvard Business School Press.

Levitt, T. (1969) *The Marketing Mode. Pathways to Corporate Growth*. New York: McGraw-Hill.

Levitt, T. (1980) Marketing Success Through Differentiation—Of Anything. *Harvard Business Review*, January–February, pp. 83–91.

Levitt, T. (1981) The Industrialization of Service. *Harvard Business Review*, September–October, pp. 63–74.

Normann, R. & Ramírez, R. (1993) From Value Chain to Value Constellation. *Harvard Business Review*, July–August, pp. 65–77.

Reichheld, F.F. (1996) *The Loyalty Effect. The Hidden Force Behind Growth, Profits, and Lasting Value*. Boston, MA: Harvard Business School Press.

Sheth, J.N. & Sisodia, R.S. (1995) Improving Marketing Productivity. In *Marketing Encyclopedia*, Lincolnwood, IL: NTC Business Books, pp. 217–237.

Sisodia, R.S. & Wolfe, D.B. (2000) Information Technology. Its Role in Building, Maintaining, and Enhancing Relationships. In Sheth, J.N. & Parvatiyar, A. (eds), *Handbook of Relationship Marketing*. Thousand Oaks, CA: Sage Publications, pp. 525–563.

Storbacka, K. (1994) *The Nature of Customer Relationship Profitability—Analysis of Relationships and Customer Bases in Retail Banking*. Helsinki/Helsingfors: Swedish School of Economics, Finland/CERS Center for Relationship Marketing and Service Management.

Taylor, F.W. (1947) *Scientific Management*. London: Harper & Row (a volume of two papers originally published in 1903 and 1911, and a written testimony for a Special House Committee in the US in 1912).

Webster, Jr., F.E. (1984) *Industrial Marketing Strategy*. 2nd edition. New York: John Wiley & Sons.

Notes

1 Griffiths, A., The Structure of All Industry and Services. In Blois, K., *The Oxford Textbook of Marketing*. Oxford University Press, 2000, pp. 69–102.

2 Giarini, O., The Globalisation of Services in Economic Theory and Economic Practice: Some Key Issues. *Progress Newsletter* (Research Programme on the Service Economy, Geneva), 30, December 1999–January 2000, p. 3.

3 Giarini, *op.cit*.

4 This, of course, is not a new finding. See Levitt, T., Marketing Success Through Differentiation—Of Anything. *Harvard Business Review*, January–February 1980, pp. 83–91. Levitt's observations regarding how customers perceive the value of offerings and what benefits they are looking for have been widely cited, but other than that they have generally been ignored in marketing research and practice.

5 This is not a new observation either. Especially in industrial marketing, the need for developing packages consisting of goods and services was pointed out long ago. See, for example, Ames, B.C. & Hlavacek, J.D., *Managerial Marketing for Industrial Firms*. Toronto: Random House, 1984, and Webster, Jr., F.E., *Industrial Marketing Strategy*. 2nd edition. New York: John Wiley & Sons, 1984. This, too, has been widely neglected in practice.

6 Gummesson, E., *Total Relationship Marketing. Rethinking Marketing Management: From 4Ps to 30Rs*. Oxford: Butterworth Heinemann, 1999.

7   This is by no means a new observation. In 1981 Levitt observed that "distinguishing between companies according to whether they market services or goods has only limited utility . . . Everybody sells intangibles in the market place, no matter what is produced in the factory" (p. 94). However, this 20-year-old wisdom does not seem to have penetrated the mainstream marketing and management theories. See Levitt, T., The Industrialization of Service. *Harvard Business Review*, September–October 1981, pp. 63–74. Levitt's classical observation that people do not buy "quarter-inch drills but quarter-inch holes" (p. 343) has been widely cited, but not understood very well. See Levitt, T., *The Marketing Mode. Pathways to Corporate Growth*. New York: McGraw-Hill, 1969.

8   Normann, R. & Ramírez, R., From Value Chain to Value Constellation. *Harvard Business Review*, July–August 1993, pp. 65–77.

9   Taylor, F.W., *Scientific Management*. London: Harper & Row, 1947 (a volume of two papers originally published in 1903 and 1911, and a written testimony for a Special House Committee in the US in 1912).

10 Grönroos, C., *Service Management and Marketing. Managing Moments of Truth in Service Competition*. Lexington, MA: Lexington Books, 1990.

11 Grönroos, C., Service Management: A Management Focus for Service Competition. *International Journal of Service Industry Management*, **1**(1), 1990b, pp. 6–14.

12 See Storbacka, K., *The Nature of Customer Relationship Profitability—Analysis of Relationships and Customer Bases in Retail Banking*. Helsinki/Helsingfors: Swedish School of Economics Finland/CERS Center for Relationship Marketing and Service Management, 1994.

13 Gummesson, *op.cit.*

14 Reichheld, F.F., *The Loyalty Effect. The Hidden Force Behind Growth, Profits, and Lasting Value*. Boston, MA: Harvard Business School Press, 1996.

15 Gummesson, 1999, *op.cit.*

16 The most notable of these is the balanced scorecard, which in its original form includes four categories of capital, financial, customer, internal business process, and learning and growth. See Kaplan, R.S. & Norton, D.P., *The Balanced Scorecard*. Boston, MA: Harvard Business School Press, 1996.

17 Edvinsson, L. & Malone, M.S., *Intellectual Capital*. New York: Harper Collins, 1997.

18 Gummesson, E., Total Relationship Marketing: Experimenting with a Synthesis of Research Frontiers. *Australasian Marketing Journal*, **7**(1), 1999b, p. 81.

19 Gummesson, 1999b, *op.cit.*

20 Badarocco, Jr., J.L., *The Knowledge Link: How Firms Compete through Strategic Alliances*. Boston, MA: Harvard Business School Press, 1991.

21 Reichheld, *op.cit.*

22 Reichheld, *op.cit.*, and Gummesson 1999, *op.cit.*

23 Reichheld, *op.cit.*, p. 1.

24 Reichheld, *op.cit.*

25 Gummesson, E., Return on Relationships (ROR): Building the Future with Intellectual Capital. *2nd WWW Conference on Relationship Marketing*. MCB University Press and Monash University, 15 November 1999–15 February 2000 (http://www.mcb.co.uk/services/conferen/nov99/rm/paper5.html).

26 Sisodia, R.S. & Wolfe, D.B., Information Technology. Its Role in Building, Maintaining, and Enhancing Relationships. In Sheth, J.N. & Parvatiyar, A. (eds), *Handbook of Relationship Marketing*. Thousand Oaks, CA: Sage Publications, 2000, pp. 525–563.

27 Sheth, J.N. & Sisodia, R.S., Improving Marketing Productivity. In *Marketing Encyclopedia*, Lincolnwood, IL: NTC Business Books, 1995, pp. 217–237.

28 See Berry, L.L. & Parasuraman, A., Building a New Academic Field—The Case of Services Marketing. *Journal of Retailing*, **69**(1), 1993, pp. 13–60, where the Nordic School is described as one of three main approaches to service marketing research. For a detailed discussion of the content and scope of the Nordic School perspective, see Grönroos 1990b, *op.cit.*, Gummesson, E., Lehtinen, U. & Grönroos, C., Comment on the Nordic Perspectives on Relationship Marketing. *European Journal of Marketing*, **31**(1–2), 1997, pp. 10–16, and Grönroos, C. & Gummesson, E., The Nordic School of Service Marketing. In Grönroos, C. & Gummesson, E. (eds), *Service Marketing—Nordic School Perspectives*. Stockholm University, Sweden, 1985, pp. 6–11.

29 We have elaborated on this argument in Grönroos, C., Service Reflections: Service Marketing Comes of Age. In Swartz, T.A. & Iacobucci, D. (eds), *Handbook of Services Marketing & Management*. Thousand Oaks, CA: Sage Publications, 2000, pp. 13–16.

30 In Scandinavia the term *service management* has dominated since the 1980s, and the use of this term has spread throughout the rest of Europe and to Australasia. It also seems to come in use in Latin America. In North America the expression *services marketing and management* won some ground in the 1990s.

Chapter 2

MANAGING CUSTOMER RELATIONSHIPS: AN ALTERNATIVE PARADIGM IN MANAGEMENT AND MARKETING

All business is based on relationships. The firm only has to make them visible and meaningful for its customers— provided that the customers want that.

Introduction

In this chapter the relationship marketing perspective, or marketing based on customer relationship management, is discussed. The nature of relationship marketing (as compared with transaction marketing) and the strategic and tactical characteristics of a relationship approach to marketing are discussed, along with what a relationship is and which customers are interested in relationships. The importance to service management of a relationship perspective in marketing is also described. After having read the chapter the reader should have acquired an understanding of what is meant by relationship marketing as a perspective and how and when relationship marketing can be implemented.

Exchange and Relationships as Core Marketing Phenomena

Since the 1970s the *exchange* of value, for example physical products, for money has been considered the core phenomenon in marketing. According to this view, marketing is planned and implemented to facilitate the exchange of products for money. This basic view of the meaning of marketing has, naturally, had the effect that standard marketing models and concepts have to a large extent been geared towards the task of creating exchanges. As a consequence, the major focus of marketing programs has been to make customers buy, regardless of whether they are old or new customers. A smaller—sometimes only a marginal—part of the marketing budget has explicitly been directed towards old customers and the management of already established customer relationships.

In the literature this form of marketing has often been labeled *transaction marketing*, that is the focus is to create purchases and singular exchanges (or transactions). Marketing has become campaign-dominated to a certain extent where the goal is predominantly to offer goods or services for sale. Price often becomes an important argument. The marketer tries to win customers over and over again, regardless of whether they have made purchases before or not. Campaigns may also be designed to develop or support the image of goods and services, but even then the focus is more on facilitating purchases than on the maintenance of existing customer relationships. This transactional approach to marketing may function very well in situations where a firm needs new customers. However, today more and more firms are in a situation where keeping the customers they have is equally, or even more, important than getting new customers. In that situation a marketing approach that overwhelmingly focuses on getting customers does not seem very appropriate or effective.

The exchange phenomenon was first studied in the context of consumer goods, where the marketing mix management approach and its 4P model became central elements. In situations where markets are growing and the exchange does not demand any considerable interactions between the customer and producer of the products to be exchanged, this transaction-oriented marketing approach has been successful, and still is. As markets mature, at the same time as competition increases and in many contexts becomes increasingly global, winning customers as the main or dominating focus of marketing is too limited.

In the context of consumer goods there is one major limitation which has made a transaction orientation almost a necessity. This is the fact that normally markets are large and no interactions exist between the producer and consumers of consumer goods. Identifying individual existing customers and focusing on them has been difficult, often impossible. However, here the development of information technology, database techniques, etc. is removing this limitation. For service firms as well as for companies marketing to business markets this limitation for identifying customers and maintaining a relationship with them does not exist, and never has existed. Continuous interactions with customers have always occurred. The development of information technology and automated operational systems in services has narrowed the scope of these interactions, but they still exist.

Since the 1970s a new marketing approach has emerged based on the notion that *interactions* between service providers or suppliers of goods and industrial buyers and their customers—*buyer–seller interactions*—are important elements in marketing, because the way these interactions are managed has an impact on the purchasing behavior of customers. In Europe this new direction of marketing thought was initiated very early in service marketing research by the Nordic School of service management and marketing[1] and in industrial marketing by the IMP (Industrial Marketing and Purchasing) Group.[2] Both these research groups originated in Scandinavia and Northern Europe, but have won international recognition and support.[3]

The focus on interactions between producer and customer, which in addition often are ongoing, either on a continuous or discrete basis, makes it possible for the marketer to view the customer not only as someone who from time to time buys from the firm, but as a relationship partner. This alternative view is based on the notion that it is not exchanges *per se* that are the core of marketing, but that exchanges take place in ongoing *relationships* between parties in the market-place—and now also in the virtual marketspace facilitated by the Internet—provided that relationships are managed in such a way that customers, private customers and business customers alike, receive the quality and value with which they are satisfied. Thus, according to this view, *relationships between parties* are considered the core phenomenon in marketing. Continuous purchases and cross-sales opportunities, exchanges or transactions, follow from well-managed relationships. This is called a *relationship perspective*,[4] in contrast to the *exchange perspective*. Singular transactions are not seen as most important in marketing; rather, relationships which are considered to facilitate and support exchanges or transactions are most important.

Relationships in Service Contexts

It is natural that relationships are given a central place in the development of marketing models and concepts to be used in service contexts.[5] When producing services, in service firms, manufacturers of physical goods, or organizations in the public sector, contact with customers always occurs. The customer always has to interact with the service provider in some way. These interactions may take a long time, such as in restaurants or air transportation, or a short time, such as in ordering theater tickets over the telephone. The contacts may also be indirect, such as when talking with someone on the telephone, where the telephone operator creates and facilitates the infrastructure and technology so that the service can be produced and used. In some areas, such as management consulting, the service process is continuous for a long period of time, including a large number of contacts and interactions.

In all cases mentioned above, the service process leads to some form of co-operation between customer and service provider. A customer relationship emerges. If this relationship is not satisfactory to the customer, the exchange of value for money stops. The customer turns to another service provider. This view of the customer relationship, where the customer interacts in some way with the service provider, is characteristic of all kinds of services. Hence, in a service context there are always relationships between the customer and the service provider which can be used as a basis for marketing, if the firm chooses to do so and provided that the customer is interested.

Although services, and therefore the marketing of services, is based on relationships, there are sometimes situations where the customer does not want this relationship to be emphasized. The important thing to keep in mind is that services are inherently relationship-oriented.

Why has the Relationship Perspective been Re-emphasized?

Relationship marketing and an emphasis on the management of customer rela-tionships in business is not a new phenomenon.[6] This perspective has been discussed in the marketing literature over the last 10 to 15 years. The term *relationship marketing* was introduced in the service marketing literature by Leonard Berry in 1983;[7] the interest in a relationship orientation in marketing is about 10 years older than that. However, the relationship perspective in business is much older, and older than the exchange perspective in marketing. The relationship orientation is probably as old as the history of trade and commerce.

As Sheth and Parvatiyar[8] have shown, historically, trade and commerce was more relationship-oriented than not. Following the Industrial Revolution, however, the relationship perspective lost much of its position. The industrial era changed the game plan, and middlemen became more powerful in the distribution chain. When mass production was made possible by new production methods and the increasing wealth of the quickly growing middle class led to mass consumption, mass distribution and mass marketing was needed. The traditional ties between producers and manufacturers and consumers and users were broken, and new ways to take the factory outputs to customers who were geographically far away were introduced on a large scale. In service contexts the ties between the producer of services, the service provider, and the consumer were not broken. However, especially after World War II, the consumer goods-oriented marketing models that dominated marketing were largely adapted by service firms as well. This has led to a situation where service firms used their marketing budgets for mass marketing and the facilitation of exchanges, instead of spending marketing money on the management of ongoing interactions with their customers. In the Western world at least, service firms generally developed a growing reputation for bad service and poor quality.

Of course, there are always exceptions, firms that continued to base their marketing programs on the management of customer relationships, and service firms known for good service. The general trend was, nevertheless, an orientation towards mass marketing and the facilitation of exchanges. And this was not a bad strategy for most firms at the time, because markets were growing, demand was often greater than supply, and there was less competition than today.

The mass marketing approach is now less effective and less profitable. More and more markets are mature and oversupplied. New customers are more and more difficult to find. Therefore, it is becoming increasingly important to keep a firm's existing customers. In many businesses, customers become profitable only after they have remained customers for some time. For example, for some insurance services it may take several years before a customer becomes profitable. At the same time customers are better and better informed. It has become much easier to get information about existing market options. Customers are, by and large, also more sophisticated and often demand more than before.

If customers perceive that they get lower quality, less value or worse service than a competitor seems to be able to offer, and they do not feel that they can trust their supplier or service provider, why should they stay? A low price may keep the customer for some time, but in the long run sales and marketing geared towards making the customer interested in more exchanges will not be very effective. In cases like this, the firm should probably concentrate on managing the whole customer relationship including the quality and value of their goods and service and their level of overall service to the customer. In this way the customer

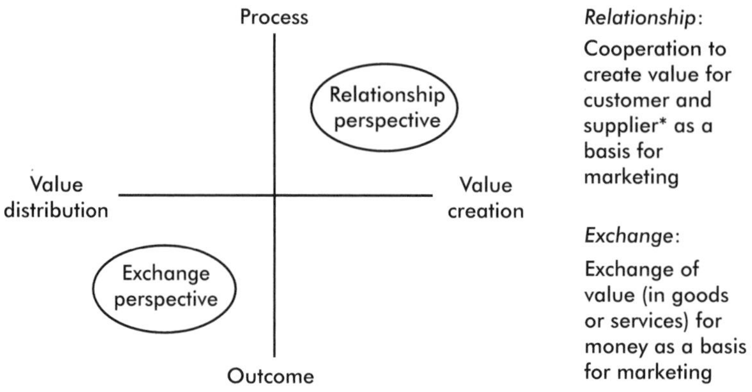

Process

Relationship perspective

Relationship:
Cooperation to create value for customer and supplier* as a basis for marketing

Value distribution

Value creation

Exchange perspective

Exchange:
Exchange of value (in goods or services) for money as a basis for marketing

Outcome

* A service provider or manufacturer of physical goods

FIGURE 2.1   The exchange versus the relationship perspective in the marketing process. Source: *International Business Review*, 4(4), Sheth, J.N. & Parvatiyar, A., The Evolution of Relationship Marketing, p. 412. Copyright 1995, with permission from Elsevier Science.

may be kept. Keeping existing customers may have a positive profitability impact in situations where it is difficult and/or expensive to find new customers to replace the profitable ones who have been lost.

Differences between the Exchange and Relationship Perspectives

The process of *creating value for customers* is different in a relationship-oriented perspective than an exchange- or transaction-oriented perspective.[9] This is illustrated in Figure 2.1.

In traditional marketing models based on the exchange perspective, value for customers is created by the firm, basically in a factory or in the back office of a service firm, and embedded in a product, which is distributed to customers. This means that marketing is preoccupied with the *distribution of value* that has been preproduced for customers. This also means that it is the *outcome of a production process* that is the focus of marketing programs, although marketing of course has a responsibility for carrying out proper market research so that value-creating products are developed and produced. In conclusion, the focus of marketing is to effectively distribute or deliver a preproduced value to customers. The 4P model of the marketing mix is clearly based on this fundamental requirement of the exchange perspective.

As is illustrated in Figure 2.1, the situation is quite different according to the relationship perspective. Value is not preproduced in a factory or a back office. Another way of saying this is that value for customers is not embedded in products. Products are only facilitators of value. Instead, *value for customers is created throughout the relationship by the customer, partly in interactions between the customer and the supplier or service provider*. The focus is not on the products but on

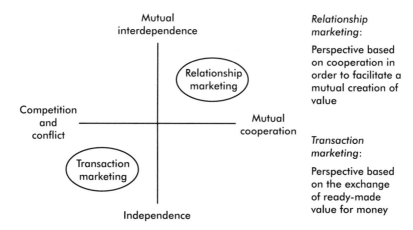

FIGURE 2.2   Inherent values in relationship and transaction marketing. Source: *International Business Review*, **4**(4)., Sheth, J.N. & Parvatiyar, A., The Evolution of Relationship Marketing, p. 400. Copyright 1995, with permission from Elsevier Science.

the customers' *value-creating processes* where value emerges for customers and is perceived by them. In conclusion, according to the relationship perspective, the focus of marketing is to facilitate and support the customers' consumption and usage processes throughout the relationship, in which value for customers is created by the customers and in interactions with the supplier or service provider. This means that marketing is inherent in most business functions involved in this process.

To sum up, according to a relationship perspective, the focus of marketing is *value creation* rather than value distribution, and the facilitation and support of a value-creating process rather than simply distributing ready-made value to customers.

This shift of focus leads to considerable changes in the approach and content of marketing. This is illustrated in Figure 2.2. The exchange-based transaction marketing approach is based on a notion of mass markets where individual customers are anonymous. The goal is to make customers choose one particular brand over competing brands. This easily creates a situation of *competition* between the marketer and the customer, where the customer is seen as someone the marketer does something *to*, instead of does something *for*.[10] The two parties have conflicting interests. The starting point is that the customer does not want to buy; he or she has to be persuaded to do so. This mindset seems to characterize transaction marketing to an overwhelming degree. In contrast, in relationship marketing, which is based on value creation in interactions between the supplier or service provider and the customer, *cooperation* is required to create the value that the customer is looking for. Of course, this does not mean that conflicts could not exist; however, co-operation is the driving force, not conflicts.

In transaction marketing situations customers, as unidentified members of a segment, are exposed to a number of competing products, and they are supposed to make *independent choices* from among the available options. In relationship marketing, where interactions and co-operation exist at some level, the customer and the supplier or service provider are not totally isolated from each other. The choice of what to buy in a relationship depends to some extent on mutual influences in the interactions. There is an *interdependence* between the two parties.

In transaction marketing the customer is seen as an antagonist who has to be persuaded to choose a particular option, whereas in relationship marketing the customer is seen instead as a resource together with whom the firm can create a valued solution that fulfils the customer's needs and solves his problems.

In situations where there are a limited number of customers and/or where continuous interactions with customers occur, a relationship approach is relatively easy to adopt, if this is considered profitable and appreciated by the customers. This is the case in many business-to-business markets and in service markets. When a firm has mass markets with limited direct contact with its customers, a relationship approach is less obvious, but it may still be profitable and it is certainly possible; for example, through the development of information technology and interactive media.

As a basis for our discussion of relationship marketing we use the following definition:[11]

> (The purpose of) . . . marketing is to identify and establish, maintain and enhance, and when necessary terminate relationships with customers (and other parties) so that the objectives regarding economic and other variables of all parties are met. This is achieved through a mutual exchange and fulfillment of promises.

In this chapter this definition will not be elaborated upon. The issue will be returned to in Chapter 10, where other definitions will also be discussed.

Once Upon A Time: A Case of Relationship Marketing

In a village in ancient China there was a young rice merchant, Ming Hua.[12] He was one of six rice merchants in that village. He was sitting in his store waiting for customers, but business was not good.

One day Ming Hua realized that he had to think more about the villagers and their needs and desires, and not just distribute rice to those who came into his store. He understood that he had to provide the villagers with more value and something different from what other merchants offered them. He decided to develop a record of his customers' eating habits and ordering periods and to start delivering rice to them. To begin with Ming Hua walked around the village and knocked on the doors of his customers' houses asking:

- how many members were there in the household;
- how many bowls of rice they cooked on any given day; and
- the size of the rice jar in the household.

Then he offered every customer

- free home delivery; and
- a service to replenish the household's rice jar automatically at regular intervals.

For example, in one household with four persons, every person would consume on average two bowls of rice a day, and therefore the household would need eight bowls of rice every day for their meals. From his records Ming Hua could see that the rice jar of that particular household contained rice for 60 bowls, or approximately one bag of rice, and that a full jar would last for 15 days. Consequently, he offered to deliver a bag of rice every 15 days to this house.

By establishing these records and developing these new services Ming Hua managed to create more extensive and deeper relationships with the villagers, first with his old customers, then with other villagers. Eventually the size of his business increased and he had to employ more people: one person to keep records of customers, one to take care of book-keeping, one to sell over the counter in the store, and two to take care of deliveries. Ming Hua spent his time visiting villagers and handling contacts with his suppliers, a limited number of rice farmers whom he knew well. Meanwhile his business prospered.

Strategic and Tactical Elements of a Relationship Strategy

The story about Ming Hua, the rice merchant, demonstrates how he, through what today would be called a relationship marketing strategy or a marketing strategy based on customer relationship management, changed his role from a transaction-oriented channel member to a value-enhancing relationship manager. In that way he created a competitive advantage over rivals who continued to pursue a traditional strategy. As can be seen from this case story, three *tactical elements* of a relationship strategy are included:[13]

- to *seek direct contacts with customers* and other business partners (such as rice farmers);
- to *build a database* covering necessary information about customers and others; and
- to *develop a customer-oriented service system.*

Three important *strategic requirements* of a relationship strategy can also be distinguished:[14]

- to redefine the business as a *service business* and the key competitive element as *service competition* (competing with a total service offering, not just the sale of rice alone);
- to look at the organization from a *process management perspective* and not from a functionalistic perspective (to manage the process of creating value for the villagers, not only distributing rice); and
- to establish *partnerships* and a *network* to handle the whole service process (close contacts with well-known rice farmers).

The three strategic requirements set the strategic base for the successful management of relationships. The three tactical elements are required to successfully implement customer relationship management. In the next sections the strategic requirements then the tactical elements will be discussed in some detail.

Defining the Firm as a Service Business

A key requirement in a relationship marketing strategy is that a manufacturer, wholesaler, retailer, service firm or supplier knows the long-term needs and desires of their customers better, and offers added value on top of the technical solutions imbedded in consumer goods, industrial equipment or services. A service firm is by definition a service business, but this service notion applies to any type of firm that wants to adopt a relationship marketing strategy. *Customers do not only look for goods or services, they demand a much more holistic service offering* including everything from information about how to best use a product, to delivering, installing, updating, repairing, maintaining and correcting solutions they have bought. And they demand all this, and much more, to be delivered in a friendly, trustworthy and timely manner.

In a customer relationship that goes beyond a single transaction of goods or services, the product itself as a technical solution involving goods, services or industrial equipment becomes just one element in the *total, ongoing service offering*. For a manufacturer, the physical good is a core element of his service offering, because it is a prerequisite for a successful offering. For a service firm it is a service. In today's competitive situation this core is very seldom enough to produce successful results and a lasting position in the marketplace. What counts is the ability of the firm, regardless of its position in the distribution channel, to manage the additional elements of the offering better than its competitors. Moreover, the core product is less often the reason for dissatisfaction than the elements surrounding the core. For example, when buying a car, the car is seldom the reason for customer dissatisfaction; the after-sales service is the main reason. Or in a restaurant, the meal may be good but poor service is the reason for dissatisfaction. In other words, competing with the core product is not enough; competing with the total package, where the core product is only one element, or rather one service, of the total service offering, is what counts. The transition from the product as the dominating element of the offering to management of human resources, technology, knowledge and time in order for the firm to create successful market offerings is evident.

In Figure 2.3 the thick black arrow from the factory or back office of a service firm out toward the customer demonstrates the traditional product-oriented approach, where the factory (and the management of what takes place in the factory) is considered the key to success in the marketplace. Services are con-sidered add-ons to the factory output. In service firms interactions in the service process are considered less important to the customer than what is produced in the back office. This management approach is based on a factory or back office focus. Although this approach to management has been highly successful in the past, it does not reflect the current competitive situation, where a new manage-ment perspective is needed. As indicated by the second arrow in the figure from the customer toward the factory or back office, the various service elements of the firm are the first elements of the output of the firm that the customer sees and perceives. These service processes create added value for the customer, whereas the factory or back office output is only a prerequisite for value.

A growing number of industries, manufacturers and service firms now face a competitive situation for which we have coined the term *service competition*. They

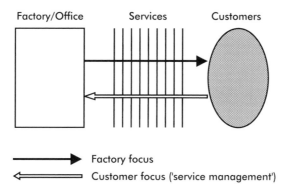

FIGURE 2.3   A customer focus: the firm as a service business. Source: Adapted from Grönroos, C., Relationship Marketing Logic. *Asia-Australia Marketing Journal*, **4**(1), 1996, p. 13.

have to understand the nature of *service management* as a new management approach geared to the demands of the new competitive situation. *The solution to customer problems seen as a total service offering thus becomes a service.* When service competition is the key to success for everybody and the product has to be defined as a service, *every business is a service business.*

A Process Management Perspective

An ongoing relationship with customers where customers look for value in the total service offering, requires internal collaboration among departments that are responsible for different elements of the offering, such as the core product (goods or services), advertising the product, delivering the product, taking care of complaints and rectifying mistakes and quality faults, maintaining the product, billing routines, product documentation, etc. The whole chain of activities has to be co-ordinated and managed as a total process. Moreover, from profitability and productivity perspectives only activities that produce value for customers should be carried out. Other resources and activities should be excluded from the process. In a traditional functionalistic organizational setting this cannot be achieved. Therefore, *relationship marketing, for the same reasons as modern management principles, requires a process management approach.*

A process management perspective is very different from the functionalistic management approach. A functionalistic organization allows for suboptimization, because every activity and corresponding department within a company is more oriented towards specialization within departments than collaboration between them. As indicated in Figure 2.4, the various departments do not necessarily direct their efforts toward the demands and expectations of the customers. This creates subvalues but not total value. Customers do not look for a combination of suboptimized outputs of different departments of a supplier that is not supporting a total value for them. For example, an outstanding technical solution and a cost-effective transportation system may be optimal from the supplier's point of view, but for the customer it is often

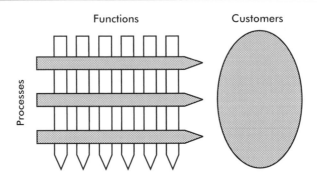

FIGURE 2.4   A process focus: the firm as a value-generating operation. Source: Grönroos, C., Relationship Marketing Logic. *Asia-Australia Marketing Journal*, **4**(1), 1996, p. 14.

equivalent to an unreliable supplier. An unreliable supplier equals low value for the customer.

Project and task force organizations are first attempts to break free from the straitjacket of a functionalistic organization, so that the various departments are geared towards working according to the horizontal arrows in the figure. However, in order to be able to produce maximum total value in a co-ordinated relationship with customers, the firm should strive to go further. A process management approach should be taken to the whole operation of the firm. In such an approach traditional departmental boundaries are torn down and the workflow (including traditional sales and marketing activities, production, administration and distribution activities with a host of customer contact activities involved) is organized and managed as a value-creating process that enables and strengthens relationship-building and management.

Partnerships and Networks

As relationship marketing is based on co-operation, firms will not view each other from a win–lose perspective but will rather benefit from a win–win situation, where the parties involved will be best off as partners. Furthermore, frequently manufacturing and service firms will find that they cannot by themselves supply customers with a total offering needed, and that it is too expensive to acquire the necessary additional knowledge and resources to produce the required elements of the offering themselves. Hence, it may be more effective and profitable to find a partner who can offer the complementary elements of the offering needed to develop a successful relationship with a customer. *Partnerships and networks of firms are formed horizontally and vertically in the distribution channel and in the supply chain.* Although firms compete with each other, they may sometimes find it effective and profitable to collaborate in some areas to serve mutual customers. This of course demands the existence of one key ingredient of relationship marketing; *trust* between the parties in a network. Otherwise they will not feel committed to the mutual cause.

The next sections turn to the tactical elements of relationship marketing.

Seeking Direct Contacts with Customers

Relationship marketing is based on a notion of trusting co-operation with known customers. Hence, firms have to get to know their customers much better than has normally been the case. In an extreme situation, which is quite possible in many consumer service markets such as household insurance and industrial markets such as merchant banking, a firm can treat each customer individually. At the other extreme of consumer goods to mass markets, customers cannot be identified in the same way. However, the manufacturer or retailer should develop systems that provide them with as much information about their customers as possible so that, for example, advertising campaigns, sales contacts and complaint situations can be made as relationship-oriented as possible. Modern information technology provides the firm with ample opportunities to develop ways of showing a customer that he is known and valued. Also, traditional advertising campaigns become too expensive and ineffective if they are not directed towards customers so that a dialog can be initiated. One-way market communication costs too much and produces too little.

Regardless of how close a firm can get to the situation of knowing and treating customers as individuals, one should always use face-to-face contacts with customers or means provided by information technology to get as close as possible to customers.

Developing a Customer Database

Traditionally, marketing operates with limited and incomplete information about customers. In order to pursue a relationship marketing strategy a firm cannot let such ignorance last. A database consisting of *customer information files* has to be established.[15] If such a database does not exist, customer contacts will only be handled partially in a relationship-oriented manner. If the person involved in a particular interaction with a customer has first-hand information about the customer and knows the person he is in contact with, the interaction may go well. However, in many situations, for example, staff who answer customers' phone calls, meet customers at a reception desk or make maintenance calls will not personally know the customer. A well-prepared, updated, easily retrievable and easy-to-read customer information file is needed in such cases to make it possible for the employee to pursue a relationship-oriented customer contact. In addition, a good database will be an effective support for cross-sales and new product offerings.

In addition to their primary use to maintain customer relationships, databases can be used for a variety of marketing activities, such as segmenting the customer base, tailoring marketing activities, generating profiles of customer types, supporting service activities and identifying likely purchasers.

A customer information file for relationship marketing purposes should also include profitability information, so that one knows the long-term profitability of customers in the database. If such long-term profitability information is lacking, the firm may easily include segments of unprofitable customers in its customer base.

Creating a Customer-oriented Service System

Successful relationship marketing demands that the firm defines its business as a service business and understands how to create and manage a total service offering, i.e. manage service competition. The value-generating processes of the organization thus have to be designed to make it possible to serve customers and produce and deliver a total service offering. In other words, the firm has to know and practice *service management*. The philosophy and principles of service management are in many respects different from those of a traditional management philosophy. In a later chapter we will discuss such differences. Four types of resources are central to the development of a successful service system; employees, technology, customers and time.

Customers take a much more active role than they normally do. The perceived quality of the service package partly depends on the impact of the customer. The service system is increasingly built upon *technology*. Computerized systems and information technology used in design, production, administration, service and maintenance have to be designed from a customer-oriented perspective, and not only from internal production and productivity-oriented viewpoints. The success of relationship marketing is highly dependent on the attitudes, commitment and performance of the *employees*. If they are not committed to their role as true service employees and are not motivated to perform in a customer-oriented fashion, the strategy fails. Hence, success in the external marketplace requires success internally in motivating employees and making them committed to the pursuit of a relationship marketing strategy. Relationship marketing is, therefore, highly dependent on a well-organized and continuous *internal marketing* process. Internal marketing will be discussed in some detail in Chapter 14. *Time* is also a critical resource. Customers have to feel that the time they spend on their relationship with a supplier or service firm is not wasted. Badly managed time creates extra costs for all parties in a relationship.

What is a Relationship?

Relationship marketing is based on managing customer relationships (as well as relationships with other parties). However, in much of the literature on the subject the questions "what is a relationship?" or "when do we know that a relationship has developed?" are not discussed.

One thing is quite clear, although it does not seem to be obvious to many practitioners of relationship marketing: a relationship with a customer has not been established only because the marketer has said it has. Far too often marketers state that they have turned to relationship marketing and believe that their marketing efforts are relationship-oriented, without making sure that the customers see it in the same way. In reality, if one asks the customers, much of what marketing practitioners call relationship marketing has very little to do with customer relationship management.[16] A firm may provide more tailor-made direct mail, membership of a loyalty club or the like, but for the customer this may mean the same slow service and uninterested service personnel, no or late response to e-mails or phone calls, or slow complaints handling. The customer may benefit from improved direct mail and membership in a loyalty club, but this is absolutely not relationship marketing, and no relationship has developed. A relationship can develop only when all, or at least most, important customer contacts and interactions are relationship-oriented.

One way of defining when a relationship has developed is to measure how many times a given customer has made purchases from the same firm. If there has been a number of continuous purchases, or a contract has been effective for a certain period of time, one might say that a relationship with this customer has developed. And of course, repetitive purchases by a customer can be a sign of the development of a relationship between the firm and this customer. This measure is not a good way of assessing whether a relationship has developed or not, but it can be used as one way of doing it. However, it should not be used alone, because there are many reasons for a customer to continue buying from one supplier or service provider for some time without perceiving that he has a relationship with that firm. Low prices may be one such reason. When a competitor offers a better price, the customer will turn to that firm. Convenient location may be another such reason. For example, a supermarket may be conveniently placed on a person's way home from work and is therefore patronized by him.

There are a number of other *bonds* that keep a customer attached to a firm, even though the customer does not feel that there is any relationship with that firm. If these bonds are removed, there is a high likelihood that such a customer will be lost. Such bonds may, for example, be technological, geographical or knowledge-based in nature, or they may be of some other type.

Therefore, it is important that one has some other conception of what a relationship is. A relationship is by and large related to an attitude. A person or a group of people feel that there is something that ties them to another party. Whatever this glue is, it should not be possible to break it easily. This feeling does not develop out of nothing. *It has to be earned* by the supplier or service provider. The relationship is earned by the way relationship marketing is implemented. Hence, a firm should create interaction and communication processes that facilitate a relationship, but it is the customer, not the firm, who determines whether or not a relationship has developed.

The following attitude-oriented description of a relationship may be useful for an understanding of a relationship: *A relationship has developed when a customer perceives that a mutual way of thinking exists between customer and supplier or service provider.*[17]

From the customer's point of view this can be stated in another way: "I am not there for the supplier only, the supplier is there for me as well." A mutual way of thinking means that there is two-way commitment. The firm should understand its customers and continuously demonstrate this by actions. Loyalty does not only mean that the customer should stay loyal to the firm, but that the latter should stay loyal to the former as well. This mutual way of thinking develops over time. This development process includes *interactions* between the supplier or service provider and the customer and *communication* between them. Inter-action includes all sorts of exchanges of goods, services, information, admin-istrative routines; in fact any contact that occurs between the two parties. Communication takes place as part of all interactions, but in addition, a series of separate planned communication efforts, such as direct mail, advertising, sales negotiation, etc. take place. Interaction and communication activities and processes continue over time and become integrated into one value-creating relationship process. If they do not develop in that way, a relationship will not emerge. In Chapter 11 we shall go into these interaction and communication issues in more detail.

It is of course not an easy task to measure whether or not a relationship has emerged based on this description. However, the marketer should measure the existence of a relationship on this level as well. Even though an ideal measurement instrument cannot be developed, this is not an excuse for not trying to create an instrument that comes as close as possible.

The inherent mutuality in the relationship perspective creates a *win–win* situation, where both parties should gain something. This goes for consumer markets as well as business-to-business markets. Effective collaboration in a long-term relationship between a supplier or service provider and a customer can continue only if the parties involved feel like "winners," or at least feel that they continuously gain more from the situation than from any other option available.[18] This requires that all parties view each other as partners. The marketer must not view the customer as an outsider who should be persuaded to choose the seller's solution whatever it takes. An adversarial situation where the marketer aims at doing something *to* the customer and not *with* and *for* the customer, which is far too common in much marketing practice, is not part of the relationship marketing perspective. Hence, correctly understood and implemented relationship marketing can foster mechanisms which create ethical values in an organization and support ethical decision-making.[19]

When is the Customer a Customer?

In a transactional approach to marketing the customer is considered a customer when he (or the buying organization) is the target of marketing and sales efforts. According to the relationship marketing perspective the situation is different. A relationship is an ongoing process. From time to time exchanges or transactions of goods, services, information and other utilities for money take place, but the relationship exists all the time, including in between such exchanges. Customers should continuously feel that the other party is there to help and support them, not just when they make a purchase. Hence, *once a relationship has been established, customers are customers on a continuous basis—and they should be treated as such regardless of whether at any given point in time they are making a purchase or not.* Firms which understand this and perform like this treat their customers as *relational customers*.

For several years a Scandinavian airline showed that they understood the meaning of their most valued customers, holders of the most prestigious frequent traveler cards and hence the most frequent users of the airline's service, and regarded them as *relational customers*. Such card holders were invited to use the airline's lounges regardless of whether they traveled on a flight operated by this airline or not. Customers felt that they were respected as relational customers and frequent users of the airline's service. It is not always possible to use a given firm's services all the time. There may be no suitable flight to the passenger's destination, the flight may have been fully booked, or perhaps the passenger just wanted to see how a competitor was doing. As all frequent travelers know, access to airport lounges is a real value-adding service. For some reason, this policy was sudddenly abolished. "Why should we bear the extra costs of serving other airline's customers?" may have been the question asked by somebody in a top management position. Customers are no longer customers unless they are making purchases. Only a decision-maker obsessed with costs and uninformed about the importance of customer relationship management and the meaning of the relationship perspective in marketing can ask such a question. The result is that customers now know that they are no longer relational customers but are treated as valued passengers only when they actually use the airline's services.

To sum up, customers of a firm are also customers when they do not purchase and consume/use services, or goods, marketed by that firm. They should therefore be treated as *relational customers*; that is, valued customers important to the firm. Unless customers are treated in this way the firm does not show a genuine *relational intent*, even though it knows about the importance of relation-ship marketing and customer relationship management in theory.

Are all Customers Interested in Relationships?

It is always possible to take a relationship approach, regardless of whether the core of a product is a service, a solution for industrial users, or consumer goods. It may not always be a profitable strategy for a firm to be relationship-oriented, although it seems to be this in an increasing number of situations. However, not all customers will be interested in forming relationships with suppliers or service providers.

Customers, individual customers and organizational users, can be seen as interested in either a relational or transactional contact with a firm. Regarding different types of goods and services and industrial solutions, the same indi-vidual or organization will probably take a different interest. Thus, in a given marketing situation the customer is either in a *relational mode* or in a *transactional mode*.[20] Some customers who, for example, buy books from Amazon.com or any other bookstore on the Internet welcome continuous information about new books that fit their past purchasing history. Others only get annoyed by such messages showing up in their e-mail inbox.

Furthermore, consumers or users in an relational mode can either be in an *active* or a *passive* relational mode.[21] For example, marketers of canned juice can provide e-mail addresses, or fax or telephone numbers on the can, so that cus-tomers have an opportunity to get in contact with the firm, give feedback, make suggestions, file complaints, etc. Or for the same reason a hotel chain can include an e-mail contact on their Web site. Customers in an active relational mode seek contact, whereas customers in a passive relational mode are satisfied with the understanding that, if needed, the firm will be there for them. They will not make use of the contact opportunity, but if it is missing they will nevertheless feel disappointed. For customers in a passive relational mode, a relationship-oriented

TABLE 2.1   Relational and transactional customers

Customer Mode	Customers' Expectations and Reactions
Transactional mode	Transactional customers are looking for solutions to their needs at an acceptable price, and they do not appreciate contacts from the supplier or service provider in between purchases.
Active relational mode	Active relational customers are looking for opportunities to interact with the supplier or service provider in order to get additional value. A lack of such contacts makes them disappointed, because the value inherent in the relationship is missing.
Passive relational mode	Passive relational customers are looking for the knowledge that they could contact the supplier or service provider if they wanted to. In this sense they too are seeking contact, but they seldom respond to invitations to interact.

marketing strategy is important, although it may not seem so. In Table 2.1 the different customer modes are summarized.

Customer Benefits in a Relationship

Why people enter a relational mode and choose to react favorably to a relationship marketing approach by a firm is a topic that has not been studied very much. It could be that the primary reason is to reduce choice. After having found a reliable relationship partner other alternatives are less attractive for the customer in a relative sense and thus do not have to be considered on a regular basis.[22] Another reason that has been mentioned is that by entering a relationship customers can more effectively fulfill goals that they had earlier committed to or tentatively committed to. Goals may, of course, be very different, such as profitability, cost reduction, comfort, health or self-esteem. Furthermore, it has been suggested that some customers may sometimes feel that being involved in a relationship is an end in itself.[23]

In a study of the benefits for customers of maintaining a relationship with a service provider, Gwinner, Gremler, and Bitner[24] concluded that benefits can be of three types:

- *confidence*: reduced anxiety, faith in the service provider, feeling of trustworthiness of the service provider;
- *social benefits*: personal recognition by employees, customer being familiar with employees, the development of friendship with employees; and
- *special treatment*: extra services, special prices, higher priority than other customers.

The *confidence* types of special relational benefits were considered most important by customers across all categories of services studied. This means that the best that can be achieved by a firm that adopts a relationship marketing strategy is to make its customers feel more secure by their choice than they would feel by patronizing any other firm. In this way *cognitive dissonance*, or a feeling of having made a less optimal choice after all, can be minimized or altogether eliminated.

Clearly, confidence benefits are key results of well-functioning long-term relationships.

The other types of relational benefits are also important. Wherever interpersonal contacts exist, *social benefits* can be developed. Such contacts should be enhanced so that customers, for example, have a sense of "my own contact employee" or in some other way feel that there is a special connection to employees. Clearly, this also has a positive effect on the *confidence* type of relational benefits. Although *special treatments* also were considered important by customers, their role was found to be less important in this study.

Customers and providers of services are different, and relationships are different. Managers should realize that, although the types of customer benefits of a relationship found in the study referred to here may be universal, other kinds of benefits may also exist in any given situation. However, the important implication for managers is that building and maintaining relationships with customers does create benefits on top of the value of the core solution offered to those customers. This means that the relationship itself adds to the total value perceived by customers. In Chapter 6 this issue will be discussed in more detail. On the other hand, as we have observed previously, not all customers are relational customers who appreciate such relational benefits.

Trust, Commitment and Attraction

In relationship marketing literature the concepts of trust, commitment and attraction play an important role. However, in spite of numerous studies, especially of trust and commitment, it is not clear how these concepts function. One reason for this may be the effect of other variables in the customer relationship, such as bonds between a customer and a supplier or service provider, or boredom and curiosity on the part of the customer. In this section we shall briefly discuss these issues.

Trust in another party can, for example, be described as one party's expectation that the other party will behave in a certain predictable way in a given situation. If the other party does not behave in the expected way, the trusting party (for example the customer), will experience more negative outcomes than they otherwise would.[25] Another commonly cited definition of trust states that trust is a willingness to rely on a business partner in whom one has confidence.[26] There is a substantial discussion in the literature about what constitutes trust. The trust concept can be divided into four subcategories, which may develop from different sources:[27]

- generalized trust;
- system trust;
- personality-based trust;
- process-based trust.

Generalized trust is derived from social norms. For example, a customer knows that a large supplier can be expected to stay in business and offer the same components and parts in the future due to its size and reputation, he therefore trusts this supplier to be the continuous source of the components that he is looking for. *System trust* depends on laws, industry regulations and contracts but also on the professionalism of the other party. If a customer, for example, has entered into a long-term contract with a supplier, the customer trusts that the supplier will perform according to expectations. A service supplier known for outstanding professional skills will also make a customer feel comfortable with his choice of business partner. *Personality-based trust* is based on the human tendency to rely upon another person to behave in a predictable way according to expectations because of personality traits. If a person considers that he can rely upon the word or statement of another person representing a supplier or service provider, trust exists and the customer is prepared to continue a business relationship with that other party. Finally, *process-based trust* follows from experience of business and contacts that have taken place over time in an ongoing relationship between two parties. A customer who has been doing business with a service provider for some time and is pleased with the results is inclined to trust that service provider.

As can be seen from the four sources of trust discussed above, trust partly depends on *past experiences* from interacting with another party; partly on other factors, such as *contracts, regulations, and social norms* on the one hand, and *personality factors* on the other hand, which can be expected to make the other party in a relationship behave in a predictable way according to expectations. Regardless of the reason for trust in a specific situation, the existence of trust in a relationship is a kind of insurance against risks and unexpected behavior in the future.

When pursuing a relationship marketing strategy the supplier or service provider should be concerned for the welfare of its customers.[28] The marketer should want to meet and preferably exceed the expectations of his customers and be anxious to help customers find the best solutions to their problems.

Commitment means that one party in a relationship feels motivated to some extent to do business with an other party. Commitment has also been defined as an enduring desire to maintain a valued relationship.[29] A customer is committed to a supplier, for example because the latter has proved to be trustworthy and has shown that it is able to offer solutions that successfully support the value-generating processes of the customer. A manufacturer may feel committed to a repair and maintenance provider who has consistently proved that it can offer skilful and timely service of its production machines. If the service provider has taken extra trouble to do so, for example in spite of excess demand for its services at some point in time, the sense of commitment is even deeper. In the definition of a relationship in an earlier section of this chapter, commitment had a central position.

A third key concept in relationship marketing is *attraction*.[30] This means that there should be something that makes a supplier interesting to a given customer, or the other way round. Attraction can be based on, for example, *financial, technological*, or *social* factors. A globally operating certified accountant will probably find a large firm with affiliations in several countries an attractive potential customer which offers large financial opportunities. In the same way a supplier of the latest technology for a manufacturing process is an attractive partner for a manufacturing firm. Even social contacts that are highly appreciated may form a source of attraction that can lead to a business relationship. If attraction between two parties exists, there is a basis for a relationship to develop. If attraction is lacking, the parties will probably not start doing business with each other.

The relation between trust, commitment and attraction and the development of commercial relationships is not clear. However, it seems as if the existence of trust in a business partner and commitment to that partner (probably in consumer as well as in business-to business markets) may be more important for customers who see more value in the relationship itself. Such relationship-oriented customers may appreciate the existence of trust and commitment more than being satisfied with every single exchange in an ongoing relationship, whereas customers who are more transactionally-oriented demand that every transaction should be satisfactory. However, although this sounds logical, one should keep in mind that the research that supports this conclusion is limited.[31]

Long-term relationships should increase business between two parties. It is, however, not clear that this always is the case. There may also be negative effects of long-standing relationships that makes customers look for alternative solutions. Curiosity or boredom may be such reasons. The customer wants to experience other alternatives for a change. There may also be good reason for customers to look for alternatives. Overlong relationships with one supplier or service provider may create a certain blindness. The customer may not see, for example, new technologies or new financial opportunities developed by competing suppliers. The existing relationship partner may not have been able to follow the developments that have taken place, and as a consequence the customer is locked up with a low-quality or old-fashioned supplier. The trust and commitment in the relationship partner has remained, but the customer has not observed that the financial or technological attraction that initially may have been the reason for the relationship to start to develop does not exist any more. In relationships, customers must always be aware of this risk. It has sometimes been called "the dark side of a relationship."[32]

What Relationship Marketing is and What it is Not

Chapter 10 discusses marketing based on a relationship strategy. It is, however, important to realize from the beginning what a relationship perspective and relationship marketing are and, especially, what relationship marketing is not.

As the discussion in the previous section demonstrated, relationship marketing is based on a distinct view of the relationship between a firm and a customer. It is not a number of tools that can be included in the marketing mix toolbox. Instead it is a perspective of how value is created for customers (value creation together with customers rather than the distribution of ready-made value) and how the relationship between the firm and a customer can be characterized (co-operation and interdependence rather than conflict and independent choices). Thus, relationship marketing is first and foremost a *perspective* of how the firm can relate to its customers and other parties, which has an impact on how the business is developed and customers are managed. According to this perspective, *marketing is seen as the management of customer relationships* (and of relationships with suppliers, distributors and other network partners as well as financial institutions and other parties).[33] Of course, relationship marketing requires tools, activities and processes that support and facilitate the management of customer relationships. Many of these are traditional external marketing tools, such as advertising, direct mail and other marketing communications activities as well as price. However, the ongoing management of relationships requires that activities and functions that have previously not been considered part of marketing, such as invoicing, claims handling, maintenance, interactions between the customer and service employees, etc. become part of the implementation of relationship marketing.

Gummesson points out some of the central aspects of the relationship perspective by saying that relationship marketing ". . . is marketing based on relationships, networks and interactions, recognizing that marketing is embedded in the total management of the network of the selling organization, the market and the society. It is directed to long term win–win relationships with individual customers and other stakeholders, and value is jointly created between the parties involved. It transcends the boundaries between specialist functions and disciplines."[34]

In fact, if customer relationship management is to be successfully handled, there has to be an aspect of marketing thinking in all business functions, and this may be one of the key aspects of the relationship perspective. Of course, this does not mean that marketing is more important than other aspects of management, but it means that the consequences for customers of all actions and investments have to be taken into account wherever in the organization they are initiated, planned and implemented, not only the consequences of traditional marketing efforts managed by a marketing department. A *marketing attitude of mind* is required throughout the organization.

This is what the relationship perspective in marketing means. However, what is *not* relationship marketing? First of all, it is not only a set of tools. It is not a new way of using direct mail or direct marketing. It is not a loyalty program. These may all be useful means of implementing a relationship marketing strategy, but they are not relationship marketing. In practice, the use of such tools alone is unfortunately often labeled relationship marketing, which has miscredited relationship marketing to some extent.[35] Unfortunately, there frequently seems to be a gap between relationship marketing as a new perspective or a theory and the way it is practiced.[36] The easiest way of doing something that is new and looks relationship-oriented is to implement a loyalty program or make communication efforts more dialog-like. But even though this is relatively easy to do—it can even be totally planned and implemented by an outside agency or consultant—it does not make the firm's overall marketing approach relationship-oriented. This requires a strategic orientation which is geared towards a relationship perspective, and when implemented it demands far more than a few relationship-looking activities or programs.

In conclusion, *relationship marketing is not only a new or improved way of communicating with customers; it is much more than that.* Although improved communication with customers using planned means of marketing communication is an essential element, the management of activities related to the facilitation, management and everyday handling of interactions with customers may be much more critical to successfully implemented relationship marketing. As we have said before, the integration of interactions and communication makes relationship marketing, not communication alone.

The relationship marketing philosophy relies on co-operation and a trusting relationship with customers and other stakeholders and network partners instead of an adversarial approach to customers; on collaboration within the company instead of specialization of roles and the division of labor only; and on the notion of marketing as a market-oriented management approach, with part-time marketers spread throughout the organization, rather than as a separate role for specialists only.

Summary and Questions for Discussion

In this chapter the nature of the relationship marketing perspective was described, and the importance of such a perspective to services was discussed. Strategic and tactical elements of a relationship marketing strategy and market-ing based on customer relationship management were also discussed in some detail. In the final parts of the chapter, relationships, who decides when a relationship has been established, and which customers are interested in rela-tionships with suppliers or service providers were discussed. Which customers can benefit from relationship marketing was also briefly covered.

Questions for discussion

1. How does a relationship marketing strategy differ from a transactional marketing strategy?
2. What is the nature of a relationship marketing perspective compared to a marketing perspective geared to facilitating transactions or exchanges?
3. Which are the three strategic requirements for the implementation of relationship marketing and what challenges for an organization are created by them?
4. Which are the three tactical elements of a relationship marketing approach?
5. When can customers be expected to be interested in a relationship marketing approach? Why may they not be interested?
6. What benefits do customers in any given industry look for that can be offered by a relationship marketing strategy?
7. How is the relationship marketing concept misused by marketers?

Further Reading

Bagozzi, R.P. (1995) Reflections on Relationship Marketing in Consumer Markets. *Journal of the Academy of Marketing Science*, **23**(4), pp. 272–277.

Berry, L.L. (1983) Relationship Marketing. In Berry, L.L., Shostack, G.L. & Upah, G.D. (eds), *Emerging Perspectives on Services Marketing*. Chicago, Ill.: American Marketing Association.

Berry, L.L. (1995) Relationship Marketing of Services—Growing Interests, Emerging Perspectives. *Journal of the Academy of Marketing Science*, **23**(4), pp. 237–245.

Berry, L.L. & Parasuraman, A. (1993) Building a New Academic Field—the Case of Services Marketing. *Journal of Retailing*, **69**(1), pp. 13–60.

Bitner, M.J. (1995) Building Service Relationships: It's All about Services. *Journal of the Academy of Marketing Science*, **23**(4), pp. 57–71.

Buttle, F. (1996) Relationship Marketing. In Buttle, F. (ed.), *Relationship Marketing. Theory and Practice*. London: Paul Chapman Publishing, pp. 1–16.

Dixon, D.F. & Blois, K.J. (1983) *Some Limitations of the 4Ps as a Paradigm for Marketing*. Marketing Education Group Annual Conference, Cranfield Institute of Technology, UK.

Fournier, S., Dobscha, S. & Mick, D.G. (1998) Preventing the Premature Death of Relationship Marketing. *Harvard Business Review*, January–February, pp. 42–51.

Garbarino, E. & Johnson, M.A. (1999) The Different Roles of Satisfaction, Trust, and Commitment in Customer Relationships. *Journal of Marketing*, **63**, April, pp. 70–87.

Grayson, K. & Ambler, T. (1999) The Dark Side of Long-Term Relationships in Marketing Services. *Journal of Marketing Research*, **36**, February, pp. 132–141.

Grönroos, C. (1990) *Service Management and Marketing. Managing Moments of Truth in Service Competition*. Lexington, MA: Lexington Books.

Grönroos, C. (1996) Relationship Marketing Logic. *Asia-Australia Marketing Journal*, **4**(1), pp. 7–18.

Grönroos, C. (1997) Value-driven Relational Marketing: from Products to Resources and Competencies. *Journal of Marketing Management*, **13**(5), pp. 407–420.

Grönroos, C. & Gummesson, E. (1985) The Nordic School of Services—An Introduction. In Grönroos, C. & Gummesson, E. (eds), *Service Marketing—Nordic School Perspectives*. Series R:2, University of Stockholm, Sweden, pp. 6–11.

Gummesson, E. (1999) *Total Relationship Marketing. Rethinking Marketing Management: From 4Ps to 30Rs*. Oxford: Butterworth-Heinemann.

Gummesson, E. (2000) Internal Marketing in the Light of Relationship Marketing and Virtual Organizations. In Lewis, B. & Varey, R. (eds), *Internal Marketing*. London: Routledge.

Gwinner, K.P., Gremler, D.D. & Bitner, M.J. (1998) Relational Benefits in Service Industries: The Customer's Perspective. *Journal of the Academy of Marketing Science*, **26**(2), pp. 101–114.

Halinen, A. (1997) *Relationship Marketing in Professional Services: A Study of Agency–Client Dynamics in the Advertising Sector*. New York: Routledge.

Håkansson, H. (1982) *International Marketing and Purchasing of Industrial Goods*. New York: John Wiley & Sons.

Håkansson, H. & Snehota, I. (1995) *Developing Relationships in Business Markets*. London: Routledge.

Johnson, D.S. & Grayson, K. (2000) Sources and Dimensions of Trust in Service Relationships. In Swartz, T.A. & Iacobucci, D. (eds), *Handbook of Services Marketing & Management*. Thousand Oaks, CA: Sage Publications, pp. 357–370.

Kavall, S.G., Tzokas, N.X. & Saren, M.J. (1999) Relationship Marketing as an Ethical Approach: Philosophical and Managerial Considerations. *Management Decision*, **37**(7), pp. 573–581.

Lane, C. & Bachmann, R. (1996) The Social Contruction of Trust: Supplier Relations in Britain and Germany. *Organizational Studies*, **17**, pp. 365–395.

Möller, K. and Halinen-Kaila, A. (2000) Relationship Market Theory: Its Roots and Direction. *Journal of Marketing Management*, Special Millennium Issue, **16**(1–3), pp. 29–54.

Moorman, C., Deshpandé, R. & Zaltman, G. (1993) Factors Affecting Trust in Market Relationships. *Journal of Marketing*, **57** January, pp. 81–101.

Moorman, C., Zaltman, G. & Deshpandé, R. (1992) Relationships Between Providers and Users of Market Research: The Dynamics of Trust Within and Between Organizations. *Journal of Marketing Research*, **29**, August, pp. 314–329.

Schurr, P.H. & Ozanne, J.L. (1985) Influence on Exchange Processes: Buyers' Preconceptions of a Seller's Trustworthiness and Bargaining Thoughts. *Journal of Consumer Research*, **11**, March, pp. 939–953.

Sheth, J.N. & Parvatiyar, A. (1995) The Evolution of Relationship Marketing. *International Business Review*, **4**(4), pp. 397–418.

Sheth, J.N. & Parvatiyar, A. (1995b) Relationship Marketing in Consumer Markets: Antecedents and Consequences. *Journal of the Academy of Marketing Science*, **23**(4), pp. 255–271.

Vavra, T.G. (1994) The Database Marketing Imperative. *Marketing Management*, **2**(1), pp. 47–57.

Webster, Jr., F.E. (1994) Executing the New Marketing Concept. *Marketing Management*, **3**(1), pp. 9–18.

Zineldin, M. (2000) *Total Relationship Management*. Lund, Sweden: Studentlitteratur.

Notes

1   See Grönroos, C. & Gummesson, E., The Nordic School of Services—An Introduction. In Grönroos, C. & Gummesson, E. (eds), *Service Marketing—Nordic School Perspectives*. Series R:2, University of Stockholm, Sweden, 1985, pp. 6–11, and Grönroos, C., *Service Management and Marketing. Managing the Moments of Truth in Service Competition*. Lexington, MA: Lexington Books, 1990.

2   Håkansson, H. & Snehota, I., *Developing Relationships in Business Markets*. London: Routledge, 1995, and Håkansson, H. (ed.), *International Marketing and Purchasing of Industrial Goods*. New York: John Wiley & Sons, 1982.

3   Berry, L.L. & Parasuraman, A., Building a New Academic Field—the Case of Services Marketing. *Journal of Retailing*, **69**(1), 1993, pp. 13–60.

4   The relationship perspective has its roots in at least five research streams, *service marketing*, *business marketing*, especially the interaction and network approach, *total quality management*, *marketing channels* and *direct and database marketing*. See Gummeson, E., *Total Relationship Marketing. Rethinking Marketing Management: From 4Ps to 30Rs*. Oxford: Butterworth-Heinemannn, 1999, and Möller, K. and Halinen-Kaila, A., Relationship Marketing Theory: Its Roots and Direction. *Journal of Marketing Management*, Special Millennium Issue, **16**(1–3), 2000, pp. 29–54.

5   Grönroos, C., *Service Management and Marketing. Managing Moments of Truth in Service Competition*. Lexington, MA: Lexington Books, 1990, and Bitner, M.J., Building Service Relationships: It's All about Services. *Journal of the Academy of Marketing Science*, **23**(4), 1995, pp. 57–71.

6   See Berry, L.L., Relationship Marketing of Services—Growing Interests, Emerging Perspectives. *Journal of the Academy of Marketing Science*, **23**(4), 1995, pp. 237–245, Sheth, J.N. & Parvatiyar, A., The Evolution of Relationship Marketing. *International Business Review*, **4**(4), 1995, pp. 397–418, and Grönroos, C., Relationship Marketing Logic. *Asia-Australia Marketing Journal*, **4**(1), 1996, pp. 7–18.

7   Berry, L.L., Relationship Marketing. In Berry, L.L., Shostack, G.L. & Upah, G.D. (eds), *Emerging Perspectives on Services Marketing*. Chicago, IL: American Marketing Association, 1983.

8   Sheth & Parvatiyar, *op.cit.*

9   Sheth & Parvatiyar, *op.cit.*

10 See Dixon, D.F. & Blois, K.J., *Some Limitations of the 4Ps as a Paradigm for Marketing*. Marketing Education Group Annual Conference, Cranfield Institute of Technology, UK, July 1983.

11 This definition is further developed from definitions presented in, for example, Grönroos 1990, *op.cit.*, and Grönroos, C., Value-driven Relational Marketing: From Products to Resources and Competencies. *Journal of Marketing Management*, **13**(5), 1997, pp. 407–420.

12 I was told the story of Ming Hua, the Chinese rice merchant, by a student attending a course on service management which I was teaching in an executive program at Thammasat University in Bangkok. This story is a true relationship marketing case, which demonstrates the ingredients of a relationship perspective and also shows that relationship marketing is not new.

13 Grönroos 1996, *op.cit.*

14 Grönroos 1996, *op.cit.*

15 See Vavra, T.G., The Database Marketing Imperative. *Marketing Management*, **2**(1), 1994, pp. 47–57, where the author describes how and by whom customer information files should be developed and what they should consist of.

16 A discussion of the misuse of the relationship marketing concept can be found in Fournier, S., Dobscha, S. & Mick, D.G., Preventing the Premature Death of Relationship Marketing. *Harvard Business Review*, January–February 1998, pp. 42–51.

17 This description is adapted from a definition used by Håkan Håkansson and Ivan Snehota in a discussion of relationships in business-to-business context. They, however, interpret the definition in a somewhat different way. See Håkansson & Snehota, *op.cit.*

18 Gummesson, E., Internal Marketing in the Light of Relationship Marketing and Virtual Organizations. In Lewis, B. & Varey, R. (eds), *Internal Marketing*. London: Routledge, 2000 (forthcoming).

19 Kavall, S.G., Tzokas, N.X. & Saren, M.J., Relationship Marketing as an Ethical Approach: Philosophical and Managerial Considerations. *Management Decision*, **37**(7), 1999, pp. 573–581.

20 Grönroos, C., Value-driven Relational Marketing: From Products to Resources and Competencies. *Journal of Marketing Management*, **13**(5), 1997, pp. 407–420.

21 Grönroos 1997, *op.cit.*

22 Sheth, J.N. & Parvatiyar, A., Relationship Marketing in Consumer Markets: Antecedents and Consequences. *Journal of the Academy of Marketing Science*, **23**(4), 1995b, pp. 255–271.

23 Bagozzi, R.P., Reflections on Relationship Marketing in Consumer Markets. *Journal of the Academy of Marketing Science*, **23**(1), 1995, pp. 272–277.

24 Gwinner, K.P., Gremler, D.D. & Bitner, M.J., Relational Benefits in Service Industries: The Customer's Perspective. *Journal of the Academy of Marketing Science*, **26**(2), 1998, pp. 101–114.

25 See Schurr, P.H. & Ozanne, J.L., Influence on Exchange Processes: Buyers' Preconceptions of a Seller's Trustworthiness and Bargaining Thoughts. *Journal of Consumer Research*, **11**, March 1985, pp. 939–953, and Johnson, D.S. & Grayson, K., Sources and Dimensions of Trust in Service Relationships. In Swartz, T.A. & Iacobucci, D. (eds), *Handbook of Services Marketing & Management*. Thousand Oaks, CA: Sage Publications, 2000, pp. 357–370.

26 Moorman, C., Deshpandé, R. & Zaltman, G., Factors Affecting Trust in Market Relationships. *Journal of Marketing*, **57**, January 1993, pp. 81–101.

27 Johnson & Grayson, *op.cit.*, and Lane, C. & Bachmann R., The Social Contruction of Trust: Supplier Relations in Britain and Germany. *Organizational Studies*, **17**, 1996, pp. 365–395.

28 Buttle, F., Relationship Marketing. In Buttle, F. (ed.), *Relationship Marketing. Theory and Practice.* London, Paul Chapman Publishing, 1996, pp. 1–16.

29 Moorman, C., Zaltman, G. & Deshpandé, R., Relationships Between Providers and Users of Market Research: The Dynamics of Trust Within and Between Organizations. *Journal of Marketing Research*, **29**, August 1992, pp. 314–329.

30 Halinen, A., *Relationship Marketing in Professional Services: A Study of Agency-Client Dynamics in the Advertising Sector.* New York: Routledge, 1997.

31 See Garbarino, E. & Johnson, M.A., The Different Roles of Satisfaction, Trust, and Commitment in Customer Relationships. *Journal of Marketing*, **63**, April 1999, pp. 70–87, who studied satisfaction, trust and commitment as mediating constructs between attitudes and future purchasing intentions in a repertory theater environment.

32 Grayson, K. & Ambler, T., The Dark Side of Long-Term Relationships in Marketing Services. *Journal of Marketing Research*, **36**, February 1999, pp. 132–141. See also Moorman, Zaltman & Deshpandé, *op.cit.*

33 See Zineldin, 2000.

34 Gummesson, *op.cit.*, p. 24.

35 See Fournier *et al.*, *op.cit.*

36 Kavall *et al.*, *op.cit.*, and Fournier *et al.*, *op.cit.*

Chapter 3

THE NATURE OF SERVICES AND SERVICE CONSUMPTION, AND ITS MARKETING CONSEQUENCES

*Goods and services merge—
but on the conditions of
services.*

Introduction

In this chapter the nature and characteristics of services are discussed. The consequences of the process of how services are consumed and used as well as the difference between process consumption and outcome consumption are also covered. Finally, the effects of process consumption which characterizes services and the content and scope of marketing is described. After having read this chapter the reader should understand the nature of services and of service consumption as compared to the consumption or use of physical products, as well as the scope and content of marketing in service contexts.

What is a Service? An Attempt to Define the Phenomenon

A service is a complicated phenomenon. The word has many meanings, ranging from personal service to service as a product. The term can be even broader in scope. A machine, or almost any physical product, can be turned into a service to a customer if the seller makes efforts to tailor the solution to meet the most detailed demands of that customer. A machine is still a physical good, of course, but the way of treating the customer with an appropriately designed machine is a service. Sir John Harvey-Jones, former chairman of ICI, said over a decade ago, referring to some successful firms in the chemical industry, that they had developed an ability to provide a chemical service to customers, rather than selling chemical products.[1] Since then a growing number of manufacturing firms have changed their focus and claimed at least that they are becoming service businesses.

Moreover, as we have discussed previously, there is a variety of administratively managed activities, such as invoicing and handling claims, which in reality are services to the customer. Because of the passive way in which they are handled, they remain "hidden services" for customers. In fact, they are usually taken care of in such a way that they are perceived not as services but rather as nuisances. Obviously, this offers several opportunities to create a competitive advantage for organizations that can innovatively develop and make use of such "hidden services."

In the 1960s, 70s and 80s a range of definitions of services was suggested. These definitions focus upon the service phenomenon, and mainly include only those services rendered by so-called service firms.[2] As a criticism of the variety of definitions suggested, Gummesson, referring to an unindentified source, put forward the following definition: "A service is something which can be bought and sold but which you cannot drop on your feet."[3]

Although this definition in a way criticizes attempts to find a definition that could be agreed upon by everyone, it points out one of the basic characteristics of services; that is, that they can be exchanged although they often cannot be experienced in a tangible sense.

Since the 1980s much less discussion of how to define services has taken place, and no ultimate definition has been agreed upon. Nevertheless, in 1990 the following definition[4] was reluctantly proposed (here slightly modified):

> A service is a process consisting of a series of more or less intangible activities that normally, but not necessarily always, take place in interactions between the customer and service employees and/or physical resources or goods and/or systems of the service provider, which are provided as solutions to customer problems.

Most often a service does involve interactions of some sort with the service provider. However, there are situations where the customer as an individual does not interact with the service firm. For example, when a plumber using the main keys of an apartment complex goes into an apartment to fix a leak when the tenant is out, there are no immediate interactions between the plumber, his physical resources or systems of operating and the customer. On the other hand, many situations where interactions do not seem to be present nevertheless do involve interactions. For instance, when a car problem is taken care of at a garage, the customer is not present and interacting with anybody or anything. However, when the car is taken in by the garage and later delivered to the customer, interactions occur. These interactions are part of the service, as will be shown later on. Moreover, they may be extremely critical as to how the customer perceives the garage. The customer probably cannot properly evaluate the job done in the garage, but can, however, evaluate the garage based on the interactions that occur at both ends of the service process. Consequently, in services, interactions are usually present and of substantial importance, although the parties involved are not always aware of this. Furthermore, services are not things, they are processes or activities, and these activities are intangible in nature.

Since 1990 the importance of information technology to services has increased dramatically. Systems indicated in the definition of services are more and more based on IT and Internet-related solutions.

However, there does seem to be an increasing awareness among researchers, and certainly among practitioners, that it is probably impossible and even unnecessary, to continue to debate service definitions. It is submitted that instead of a definition it may be more productive to take more or less common characteristics of services and an understanding of the nature of service consumption as a starting point for the development of an understanding of how to manage and market services. The next section will discuss characteristics of services.

Some Common Characteristics of Services

A whole range of characteristics of services has been suggested and discussed in the literature. Usually services are compared with physical goods. In Table 3.1 we have summarized the most frequently mentioned characteristics of services and physical goods.

For most services, *three* basic characteristics can be identified.

1. Services are *processes* consisting of *activities* or a *series of activities* rather than *things*.
2. Services are at least to some extent *produced and consumed simultaneously*.
3. The customer *participates in the service production process* at least to some extent.

The specific models and concepts of service management and marketing follow from the fact that the customer is present to a certain degree in the service process, where the service is produced and delivered to him, and that the customer also participates in the process and perceives how the process functions at the same time as the process develops. One of the reasons that understanding service management is now of interest to manufacturers of goods is that customers are now more involved in various processes of the manufacturer such as the design of goods, modular production, delivery, maintenance, helpdesk functions, information share and a host of other processes which in today's competitive environment have become important for the creation of a competitive advantage. All these activities bring the manufacturing of goods and service management closer to each other.

TABLE 3.1   Differences between services and physical goods

Physical Goods	Services
Tangible	Intangible
Homogeneous	Heterogeneous
Production and distribution separated from consumption	Production, distribution and consumption simultaneous processes
A thing	An activity or process
Core value produced in factory	Core value produced in buyer–seller interactions
Customers do not (normally) participate in the production process	Customers participate in production
Can be kept in stock	Cannot be kept in stock
Transfer of ownership	No transfer of ownership

By far the most important characteristic of services is their *process* nature. Services are processes consisting of a series of activities where a number of different types of resources—people as well as other kinds of resources—are used, often in direct interactions with the customer, so that a solution is found to a customer's problem. Because the customer participates in the process, the process, especially the part in which the customer is participating, becomes part of the solution. Most other characteristics follow from the process characteristic. In later sections we shall go into the consequences for management and marketing of this process nature of services.

Because a service is not a thing but *processes* consisting of a *series of activities*—which are *produced and consumed simultaneously* (this is also called the "inseparability" characteristic)—it is difficult to manage quality control and to do marketing in the traditional sense, since there is no preproduced quality to control before the service is sold and consumed. Of course, situations vary, depending on what kind of service is being considered. A hair stylist's service is obviously almost totally produced when the customer is present and receives the service. When delivering goods, only part of the service process (or service production process) is experienced and, thus, simultaneously consumed by the customer. Most of the process is invisible. However, in both cases, one should realize that *it is the visible part of the service process that matters in the customer's mind*. As far as the rest is concerned, he can only experience the result; but the visible activities are experienced and evaluated in every detail. Quality control and marketing must therefore take place at the time and place of simultaneous service production and consumption. If the firm relies on traditional quality control and marketing approaches, the part of the service process where the customer is involved may go uncontrolled and include negative marketing experiences for the customer.

The third basic characteristic of services points out that the customer is not only a receiver of the service; the customer participates in the service process as a production resource as well. Because of this and the previous characteristics it is not possible to keep services in stock in the same way goods are. If an airplane leaves the airport half-full, the empty seats cannot be sold the next day; they are lost. Instead, capacity planning becomes a critical issue. Even though services cannot be kept in stock, one can try to *keep customers in stock*. For example, if a restaurant is full, it is always possible to try to keep the customer waiting in the bar until there is a free table.

In much of the service literature *intangibility* is said to be the most important characteristic of a service. However, physical goods are not always tangible either in the minds of customers. A pound of tomatoes or a car may be perceived in a subjective and intangible way. Hence, the intangibility characteristic does not distinguish services from physical goods as clearly as is usually stated in the literature.[5]

However, intangibility is a characteristic of services. A service is normally perceived in a subjective manner. When services are described by customers, words such as "experience," "trust," "feeling," and "security" are used. These are highly abstract ways of formulating what a service is. The reason for this, of course, lies in the intangible nature of services. However, many services include highly tangible elements as well: for example, the food in a restaurant, the documents used by a forwarding company, the spare parts used by a repair shop. The essence of a service, however, is the intangibility of the phenomenon itself. The intangibility characteristic is probably the most often cited criterion of services. Because of the high degree of intangibility, it is frequently difficult for the customer to evaluate a service. How do you give a distinct value to "trust," or to a "feeling," for example? Therefore, it is often suggested in the literature that one should make a service more tangible for the customer by using concrete, physical evidence, such as plastic cards (in banking) and various kinds of documents (in the travel business).

Furthermore, many definitions of services imply that services do not result in *ownership* of anything. Normally this is true. When we use the services of an airline, we are entitled, for example, to be transported from one place to another, but when we arrive at our destination, there is nothing left but the remaining part of the ticket and the boarding card. When we withdraw money from our checking account we may feel that the bank's service resulted in our ownership of the withdrawn money. After the service process, we undoubtedly have the sum of money in our hands and we own it. However, the bank's service did not create this ownership. We, of course, owned the money all the time. The bank just took care of it for us for some time and used it in exchange for interest. On the other hand, retailing is a service, and after using the services of, say, a grocery store, the customer undoubtedly owns the groceries. And the goods, the assortment of groceries as well as the individual goods, are part of the service offered to the marketplace. In this case, the consumption of the service of the service firm, the grocery store, does result in the ownership of tangible goods.

Finally, because of the impact of people, personnel, customers or both, on the production and delivery process, a "*heterogeneity*" aspect follows from the basic characteristics. A service to one customer is not exactly the same as the "same" service to the next customer. If nothing else, the social relationship in the two situations is different. And the service a customer receives by using an ATM may differ from the "same" service received by the next customer because, for instance, the second person has a problem understanding the instructions on the screen. The heterogeneity of services creates one of the major problems in service management; that is, how to maintain an evenly perceived quality of the services produced and rendered to customers.

Classification Schemes for Services

In many publications from the early days of service marketing research, services were classified in a number of different ways.[6] Here we are only going to discuss two classifications:

- high-touch/high-tech services;
- discretely/continuously rendered services.

First, services can be divided into *high-touch* or *high-tech* services. High-touch services are mostly dependent on people in the service process producing the service, whereas high-tech services are predominantly based on the use of automated systems, information technology and other types of physical resources. This is of course an important distinction to make. However, one should always remember that high-touch also includes physical resources and technology-based systems that have to be managed and integrated into the service process in a customer-oriented fashion. While high-tech services, such as telecommunications or Internet shopping, by and large are technology-based, in critical moments, such as complaints situations or technology failures, or in built-in contacts with service employees representing, for example, helpdesk operations, the high-touch characteristic of the technology-based service takes over. In fact, one can say that high-tech services are often even more dependent on the service orientation and customer-consciousness of its personnel than high-touch services, because human interactions occur so seldom and when they occur they do so in critical situations. If these high-touch interactions of the high-tech service process fail, there are fewer opportunities to recover the mistake than in high-touch service processes. In these cases high-touch contacts are true moments of truth for a firm.

Second, based on the nature of the relationship with customers, services can be divided into *continuously rendered services* and *discrete transactions*. Services such as industrial cleaning, security services, goods deliveries, banking, etc. involve a continuous flow of interactions between the customer and the service provider. This creates ample opportunity for the development of valued relationships with customers. For providers of discretely used services, such as hair stylists, many types of firms in the hospitality industry, providers of *ad hoc* repair services to equipment and so on, it is often more difficult to create a relationship that customers appreciate and value. However, as we know from many hair stylists, hotels and restaurants and other providers of discretely used services, this is possible and is considered a profitable strategy. Firms that offer services which are used on a continuous basis cannot afford to lose customers, because the cost of finding new customers is often too high. On the other hand, firms offering services that are used in a discrete fashion may also develop a profitable business based on transaction-oriented strategies, although a relationship orientation is probably to be recommended in most cases.

Understanding these and other classifications of services is of course important for management. The models and concepts of service management and marketing discussed in this book are intended to be useful for all types of service firms and manufacturers for which service competition is important, and therefore useful for high-touch as well as for high-tech services and for continuously rendered services as well as for discretely used services. However, all services are in some respect unique, and when developing strategies and implementing them this should be taken into consideration.

The Consumption of Services: Process and Outcome Consumption

In order to understand service management and the marketing of services it is critical that one realizes that the consumption of a service is *process consumption* rather than *outcome consumption*. The consumer or user perceives the service process (or service production process) as part of the service consumption, not simply the outcome of that process, as in traditional marketing of physical goods. When consuming a physical product, customers make use of the product itself; that is they consume the outcome of the production process. In contrast, when consuming services customers perceive the process of producing the service to a greater or smaller degree, but always to a critical extent, as well as taking part in the process. The consumption process leads to an outcome for the customer, which is the result of the service process. Thus, the consumption of the service process is a critical part of the service experience.

As service quality research demonstrates, perception of the process is important for the perception of the total quality of a service, even though a satisfactory outcome is necessary and a prerequisite for good quality. In many situations the service firm cannot differentiate its outcomes from those of its competitors. Withdrawing a given sum of money from a checking account leads to the same result; the customer gets the requested amount, regardless of which bank is rendering the service. Flying from one place to another takes the passenger to the destination, regardless of which airline he patronizes. In some situations customers take the quality of an outcome for granted, but in other situations it is difficult for a customer to evaluate the quality of the outcome of the service process. For example, it is difficult to evaluate whether an Internet Web site provided by one firm is better than that which another firm could have offered. However, in every situation customers take part in the service processes and interact with the employees, physical resources, technologies and system of the service provider to some extent. The process easily distinguishes one service from another. Because of this inseparability of the service process and the consumption of a service, the process can be characterized as an *open process*. Hence, regardless of how the customer perceives the outcome of a service process, service consumption is basically *process consumption*.

In Figure 3.1 the nature of the consumption of physical goods (outcome consumption) and of the consumption of services (process consumption) is illustrated. The relationships between production, consumption and marketing is shown in the figure. In the case of outcome consumption of physical goods, which is illustrated in the upper part of the figure, production and consumption are processes that are separated from each other in time and space. The traditional role of marketing, which is geared towards the requirements of consumer goods, follows from this situation. A bridge between production and consumption that closes the gap between these two processes is needed. This bridge has, since the early twentieth century, been labeled marketing.

In the lower part of the figure, process consumption of services is illustrated. Production and consumption are simultaneous processes with interactions between the consumer and the production resources—people, physical resources, operational systems, information technology, etc.—of the service provider. The obvious conclusion that can be drawn from this is that *there is no gap between production and consumption that needs to be closed by a separate activity or function*. There is no room for marketing's traditional bridge-building role in this situation. This can be considered to be the essence of service marketing. Marketing has to be included into the system in a different way than in tradi-tional models of consumer goods marketing. *The heart of marketing services is how*

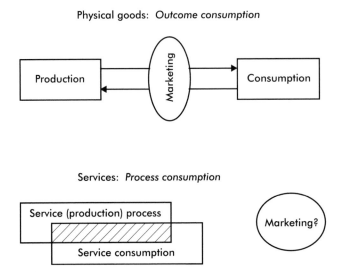

FIGURE 3.1   The nature of consumption of physical goods and services and the role of marketing

the service (production) process and service consumption process match each other, so that consumers and users perceive good service quality and value, and are willing to continue the relationship with the service provider.[7] Of course, some activities of a bridge-building nature remain. For example, market research, as well as efforts to create an interest among potential customers in the service provider and its service offerings and to create trial purchases, is still required. However, the major part of marketing, managing the firm's customer relationships and other market relationships, becomes an integral part of the simultaneous service production and service consumption processes.

Thus service consumption and production have interfaces that are always critical to customers' perception of the service and consequently to their long-term purchasing behavior. For example, in the bank and airline examples used earlier, the location and security of an ATM or the interaction process in a bank as well as the check-in, in-flight, and luggage claim processes in an airline experience have a decisive effect on customers' perception of the service and its quality. Hence, for the long-term success of a service firm the customer orientation of the service processes is crucial. If the process fails from the customers' point of view, no traditional marketing efforts, and frequently not even a good outcome of the service process, will make them stay with a company in the long run, if they can find an alternative.

It is interesting to observe that in the production of a variety of physical goods, everything from automobiles and computers to jeans and dolls, customers can be drawn into the planning of goods and the manufacturing processes of the factory, through the use of modern information technology and the Internet, and modern design and modular production techniques. This enables *mass customization* and interactions between the manufacturer and marketer on the one hand and the customer on the other.[8] Dell Computers offers customized PCs,

Levi Strauss makes jeans to order, and Mattel offers customized "friends of Barbie's" dolls. One can get a customer-ordered BMW, and even made-to-order vitamin pills.[9] In manufacturing in general this is the case both for consumer markets and business-to-business markets. With the introduction of digitization many more manufactured goods can be mass-customized more easily. In such situations the customers' interactions with the production process become part of their consumption process, and the consumption of the physical product becomes partly process consumption. What the firm offers in a situation like this is a factory-related service element in the solution to customer problems. The physical goods become more and more service-oriented, and service marketing knowledge and a service management framework are required to successfully manage the business.

Thus it seems inevitable that understanding service processes is becoming an imperative for all types of businesses, not only for what used to be called service businesses.

Managing Customers in a Physical Goods Context: The Traditional Goods Marketing Triangle

In this and the following section we shall explore how the role of marketing differs between a physical goods and a service context. As a means of illustration we use a marketing triangle. This way of illustrating the field of marketing is adapted from Philip Kotler,[10] who uses it to illustrate the holistic concept of marketing suggested by the Nordic School approach to service marketing and management. This triangle's sides represent *giving promises*, *keeping promises* and *enabling promises*.

A physical product, in the traditional sense, is the result of how various resources, such as people, technologies, raw materials, knowledge and information, have been managed in a factory to incorporate a number of features that customers in target markets are looking for. The production process can be characterized as a *closed process*, where the customer takes no direct part. Thus a product evolves as a preproduced package of resources and features ready to be exchanged. The task of marketing (including sales) is to find out what product features the customers are interested in and to give promises about such features to a segment of potential customers through external marketing activities such as sales and advertising campaigns and to take the product to locations where customers are willing to purchase it. If the product includes features that customers want, it will fulfil the promises that have been given to the customers. This marketing situation is illustrated in the *product marketing triangle* in Figure 3.2.

In the figure the three key parts of marketing in a physical good or product context are shown. These are the firm, represented by a marketing and/or sales department, the market, and the product. Normally, marketing (including sales) is the responsibility of a department (or departments) of specialists or full-time marketers (and salespeople). Customers are viewed in terms of markets of

FIGURE 3.2   The product marketing triangle. Source: Grönroos, C., Relationship Marketing Logic. *Asia-Australia Marketing Journal*, **4**(1), 1996, p. 9.

relatively anonymous individuals. The market offering is a preproduced physical product. Along the sides of the triangle three key functions of marketing are displayed, to *give promises*, to *fulfill promises*, and to *enable promises*. Promises are normally given through mass marketing and in business-to-business contexts, as well as through sales. Promises are fulfilled through a number of product features and enabled through the process of continuous product development based on market research performed by full-time marketers and the technological capabilities of the firm. Marketing is very much directed towards giving promises through external marketing campaigns. The value customers are looking for is guaranteed by appropriate product features, and the existence of a product with the appropriate features will make sure that promises given are also kept.

Managing Customers in a Service Context: The Service Marketing Triangle

For a service firm, the scope and content of marketing become more complicated. The notion of a preproduced product with features that customers are looking for is too limited to be useful here. Also, in the context of business-to-business marketing the traditional product construct is too restrictive, because a customer relationship often includes many more elements than physical goods, normally various types of service processes.

In many cases what the customer wants and expects is not known in detail at the beginning of the service process (service production process) or, consequently, what resources are needed, to what extent and in what configuration they should be used. For example, the service requirements of a machine that has been delivered to a customer may vary; the need to provide training of the customer's personnel and the need to handle claims may vary; a bank customer may only realize what his needs actually are during interactions with a teller or a loan officer. Thus, the firm has to adjust its resources and its ways of using its resources accordingly.

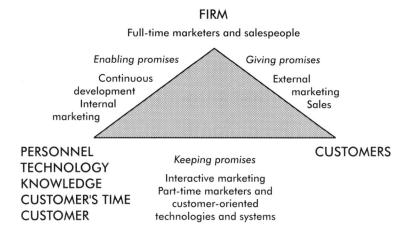

FIGURE 3.3 The service marketing triangle. Source: Grönroos, C., Relationship Marketing Logic. *Asia-Australia Marketing Journal*, **4**(1), 1996, p. 10.

In Figure 3.3, the *service marketing triangle*, marketing in a service context is illustrated in the same way as product marketing was in Figure 3.2. As can be seen, most elements in the figure are different.

The most important change from the goods marketing situation is the fact that the *preproduced product is missing*. In process consumption, no preproduced bundle of features that constitutes a product can be present. Only service concepts and preparations for a service process can be made beforehand and partly prepared services can exist. In many service contexts, such as fast-food restaurants or automobile rental services, physical product elements with specific features are also present as integral parts of the service process. These product elements are sometimes, as in the case of car rental, preproduced, and sometimes (as in the case of the hamburger in a fast-food operation) they are partly preproduced, partly made to order. However, such physical products have no meaning as such, unless they fit the service process. They become one type of resource among many other types that have to be integrated into a functioning service process. A bundle of different types of resources creates value for customers when these resources are used in their presence and in interactions with them. Even if service firms try to create products out of the resources available, they cannot come up with more than a standardized plan to guide the ways of using existing resources in the simultaneous service production and service consumption processes. Customer-perceived value follows from a successful and customer-oriented management of resources relative to customer sacrifice, not from a preproduced bundle of features.

The firm may still have a centralized marketing and sales staff, the full-time marketers, but they do not represent all the marketers and salespeople of the firm. In most cases the service firm has direct contact with its customers, and information about each and every customer can be obtained on an individual basis. This is beneficial because, in many cases, customers (business-to-business customers and individual consumers and households alike), like to be treated much more individually than before.

In Figure 3.3 the resources of a firm are shown divided into five groups: personnel, technology, knowledge, customer's time and the customer. Many of the *people* representing the firm create value for customers in various service processes, such as deliveries, customer training, claims handling, service and maintenance, etc. and some are directly engaged in sales and cross-sales activities. Thus, they are involved in marketing. Gummesson has called these customer contact service employees *part-time marketers*.[11] In many service firms they outnumber the full-time marketers. In addition, they have customer contacts during the crucial moments of truth when the service is produced for the customer, often together with the customer, something that full-time marketers seldom have.

In addition to part-time marketers, other types of resource influence the quality and value perceived by the customer and are hence important from a marketing perspective. *Technologies*, the *knowledge* that employees have and that is embedded in technical solutions, and the firm's way of managing the *customer's time* are such resources. Physical product elements in the service process can, for example, be viewed as technological resources. Moreover, the *customers* themselves as individual consumers or as users representing organizations often become a value-generating resource. The impact of customers on the final development or design of a technical solution or on the timeliness of a service activity may be critical to the value perceived by them.

In summary, from the customers' point of view, in process consumption the solutions to their problems are formed by a *set of resources* needed to create a good customer-perceived service quality and value. In addition, the firm must have *competencies* to acquire and/or develop the resources needed and to manage and implement the service process in a way that creates value for each customer. Thus, a *governing system* is needed for the integration of the various types of resources and for the management of the service processes. In the service marketing literature, the way these resources are managed and implemented in interactions with the customers is called the *interactive marketing* function. We shall return to this concept in Chapter 10.

Promises given by sales and external marketing are fulfilled through the use of all types of resources. In order to prepare an appropriate set of resources continuous product development in its traditional form is not enough, because the service process encompasses a large part of the activities of the service firm. Instead, to enable the fulfillment of promises, continuous *resource development* including *internal marketing* and a continuous development of the competencies and the resource structure of the firm are needed.

Service Management and Marketing: A Case of a Missing Product

The conclusion of the discussion in the previous sections is that *service firms*, or *service organizations of manufacturing firms, do not have products (understood as preproduced bundles of resources and features); they only have processes to offer their customers*. Of course, these processes also lead to an outcome that is important for the customer. However, as the outcome of, for example, a management consultancy assignment process or hotel accommodation cannot exist without the process, and because from the customers' perspective the process is an open process, it is fruitful to view the outcome as a part of the process. Both the process and its outcome have an impact on customer perception of the quality of a service and consequently on customer-perceived value.

A major challenge for service providers is, therefore, to develop innovative ways of managing processes as solutions to customer problems. The value that a firm can offer is not embedded in the resources used in the service process, but it emerges in customers' consumption or usage processes, when they use these resources in interaction with the service provider in order to achieve an outcome for themselves. Models and concepts of service management—perceived service quality, customer perceived value, service production systems, internal marketing and other models and concepts—have been developed to help managers cope with this challenge.

A Case Study: The Missing Product in an Elevator Repair and Maintenance Firm

In the final section of this chapter a case study of a firm providing elevator repair and maintenance services will be presented as an illustration of how the missing product of a service provider has been replaced by a quality-generating service system to promote enduring customer relationships. The case company is a large elevator manufacturer, and repair and maintenance provider operating globally. Its repair and maintenance business had, however, been unprofitable for some time and it had problems in maintaining its customer relationships.

To find out the reason behind the loss of customers, a large-scale survey was conducted among the firm's customers. The questionnaire was based on the assumption that the company offered a product that could be described as the result of repair and maintenance activities. This quantitative study indicated that the repair and maintenance service of the firm was low quality and that its prices were considered high. This result led to great consternation among top management and the marketing and sales group, because they knew that the firm as a major service provider had by far the best trained service technicians, the best possible instruments for diagnosing problems, the best tools and equipment for taking care of any repair and maintenance job, and the widest possible assortment of spare parts. Everybody in the firm considered it to have the best service on the market, and they could not understand that the customers considered the quality of the repair and maintenance services to be low. High prices were easier to understand because, being a large company, it had high overhead costs and had to maintain a high price level.

Because top management had difficulty in accepting the results of the study, a second, qualitative study was initiated. One hundred former customers, mostly representing business customers such as office buildings and institutions but also residential buildings, were interviewed in an unstructured fashion. The main interview question could be phrased as "What went wrong?"

In spite of some variations in results, the average lost customer expressed the following opinion:

We realize that you have the best capabilities on the market to repair and maintain elevators, and in most cases you do a good job. However, we do not feel comfortable with the way you are doing the job. We cannot trust your service technicians to start doing the repair or maintenance task according to what has been promised, and quite often you do not give exact promises about when the job will start. Although some of your people are attentive and show an interest in our concerns regarding the elevator and its problems, most of them could not care less about us as people and the need for information that we sometimes have. Sometimes we do not even recognize them as your employees. Quite often the service technician just leaves a job unfinished and we do not know why or when he will be back to finish it. Because we cannot always trust your way of doing the job and because it is therefore complicated for us to be your customers, we think that the quality of your services is low and that we, therefore, pay too much for them.

The implications of the second study were quite obvious. Top management and the marketing and sales group thought that the company had ready-made products to be delivered to their repair and maintenance customers (more or less equaling the outcome of repair and maintenance), whereas the customers considered the company to be offering processes. Furthermore, although the customers recognized that the processes had to include a successful outcome, their concerns regarding the repair and main-tenance services and their quality were associated with the process and with problems occurring in the process.

The second study helped management to understand that the object of the elevator repair and maintenance business was the service process, and that it really was a case of a missing product. It was realized that the solution to the customers' problems consisted of the outcome of the service process as well as of the process itself. Moreover, the customers clearly indicated that the outcome had to be of an acceptable quality, but when this was the case the outcome (the successful result of the repair and maintenance process) was obvious to the customers and the service process became the issue. Both the outcome and the process have to be carefully planned and well implemented, if the repair and maintenance service is to be considered good. Both the outcome and the service process have to be of good quality. It turned out that the former was perceived by the customers as a prerequisite, and in the final analysis it was the quality of the process that counted.

Clearly the firm thought that it was offering and delivering preproduced products to its repair and maintenance customers, whereas the customers considered the package to be quite different. They saw a process which created quality and value for them, and no ready-made solution. Although the outcome of the service process had to be good, it was the quality of the service process and the value provided by it that determined whether or not the repair and maintenance service was considered good. This case will be continued in Chapter 13. In that context the actions taken to improve the perceived quality of the service as a process will be discussed.

Summary and Questions for Discussion

This chapter discussed the characteristics of services and observed that their processes form their major feature. The difference between process consumption and outcome consumption was analyzed, and it was concluded that the consumption or use of services can be characterized as process consumption. Finally, the consequences for marketing of the process nature of services was discussed at some length. It was concluded that the scope of marketing is different in services than in physical goods.

Questions for discussion

1. Why is the process nature of services their most important feature? What other characteristics of services can be identified?
2. What impact does the process nature and other characteristics of services have on the scope and content of marketing?
3. What are the differences between outcome consumption and process consumption?
4. What are the major managerial consequences of the fact that services to a critical extent are consumed at the same time as they are produced?

Further Reading

Grönroos, C. (1990) *Service Management and Marketing. Managing the Moments of Truth in Service Competition*. Lexington, MA: Lexington Books.

Grönroos, C. (2000) Service Reflections: Service Marketing Comes of Age. In Swartz, T.A. & Iacobucci, D. (eds), *Handbook of Services Marketing & Management*. Thousand Oaks, CA: Sage Publications, pp. 13–16.

Gummesson, E. (1987) Lip Services—A Neglected Area in Services Marketing. *Journal of Services Marketing*, **2**(1), pp. 19–24.

Gummesson, E. (1999) *Total Relationship Marketing. Rethinking Marketing Management: From 4Ps to 30Rs*. London: Butterworth Heinemann.

Harvey-Jones, J. (1989) *Making It Happen. Reflections on Leadership*. Glasgow: Fontana/Collins.

Kotler, P. (1994) *Marketing Management. Analysis, Planning, Implementation and Control*. 8th edition. Englewood Cliffs, N.J.

Lovelock, C.H. (1983) Classifying Services to Gain Strategic Marketing Insights. *Journal of Marketing*, **47**(3), pp. 9–20.

Lovelock, C.H. (1991) *Services Marketing*. Englewood Cliffs, NJ: Prentice-Hall.

Peppers, D. & Rogers, M. (1997) *Enterprise One-to-One*. London: Currency/Doubleday.

Schonfeld, E. (1998) The Customized, Digitized, Have-it-Your-Way Economy. *Fortune*, September 28, pp. 69–74.

Zeithaml, V.A. & Bitner, M.J. (2000) *Services Marketing. Integrating Customer Focus Across the Firm*. 2nd edition. New York: McGraw-Hill.

Notes

1   Harvey-Jones, J., *Making It Happen. Reflections on Leadership*. Glasgow: Fontana/Collins, 1989.
2   A range of such definitions is discussed in Grönroos, C., *Service Management and Marketing. Managing the Moments of Truth in Service Competition*. Lexington, MA: Lexington Books, 1990.
3   Gummesson, E., Lip Services—A Neglected Area in Services Marketing. *Journal of Services Marketing*, 1, 1987.
4   Grönroos 1990, *op.cit.*
5   See, for example, Zeithaml, V.A. & Bitner, M.J., *Services Marketing. Integrating Customer Focus Across the Firm*. 2nd edition. New York: McGraw-Hill, 2000, and Lovelock, C.H., *Services*

Marketing. Englewood Cliffs, NJ: Prentice-Hall, 1991. Since the early 1980s it has become a habit to say that intangibility, inseparability, heterogeneity and perishability are *the* characteristics of services. This is repeated in almost every context without any discussion of the underpinning logic. Intangibility is most often mentioned as the most characteristic feature of services, which clearly is a highly questionable statement.

6   A comprehensive discussion of classification schemes can be found in Lovelock, C.H., Classifying Services to Gain Strategic Marketing Insights. *Journal of Marketing*, **47**(3), 1983, pp. 9–20. See also Grönroos 1990, *op.cit.*

7   See Grönroos, C., Service Reflections: Service Marketing Comes of Age. In Swartz, T.A. & Iacobucci, D. (eds), *Handbook of Services Marketing & Management*. Thousand Oaks, CA: Sage Publications, 2000, pp. 13–16.

8   Peppers, D. & Rogers, M., *Enterprise One-to-One*. London: Currency/Doubleday, 1997.

9   See Schonfeld, E., The Customized, Digitized, Have-it-Your-Way Economy. *Fortune*, September 28, 1998, pp. 69–74.

10 Kotler, P., *Marketing Management. Analysis, Planning, Implementation and Control.* 8th edition. Englewood Cliffs, N.J., 1994. However, he only included people in his triangle model and omitted the physical resource (technology and systems) elements of the Nordic School approach to service marketing.

11 See, for example, Gummesson, E., *Total Relationship Marketing. Rethinking Marketing Management: From 4Ps to 30Rs*. London: Butterworth Heinemann, 1999.

Chapter 4

SERVICE AND RELATIONSHIP QUALITY

An acceptable outcome is an absolute necessity for good perceived quality, but an excellent service process creates a distinct and sustainable competitive edge.

Introduction

Based on the discussion of the characteristics of services and service consumption, and on the customer relationship management approach to marketing in the previous chapters, this chapter discusses how the quality of services is perceived in service encounters as well as in ongoing relationships. The *Perceived Service Quality Model* is presented as a basic model of the perception of total service quality. The characteristics and determinants of good service quality, such as the *Seven Criteria of Good Perceived Service Quality*, are then discussed, followed by a description of instruments for measuring perceived service quality. Attribute-based approaches, such as the SERVQUAL instrument, are presented as well as the *critical incident* approach to measuring quality. In the latter part of the chapter dynamic approaches to understanding service quality in a relationship context are presented. After having read the chapter, the reader should understand the nature of perceived service quality and the determinants or criteria of service quality as well as know how to measure perceived service quality. The reader should also understand how perceived service quality develops into relationship quality in a long-term relationship context.

Research into Service Quality

Chapter 3 illustrated the complexity of most services. Consequently, the quality of services has to be very complex, too. The quality of goods is traditionally related to the technical specifications of the goods, although, even in a goods context, a firm using an image strategy, for example, tries to add to the quality of their goods component by creating imaginative extra value for their customers using, for example, fashion, status, or lifestyle aspects.

Services that are a series of processes, where production and consumption cannot be totally separated, and where the customer often actively participates in the production process, are bound to be perceived as extremely complex. However, in order to develop service management and marketing models, it is important to understand what customers are really looking for and what they evaluate.

When the service provider understands how services will be evaluated by the users, it will be possible to identify ways of managing these evaluations and influencing them in a desired direction. The relationship between the service concept, the service offered to customers, and customer benefits has to be clarified.

Interest in service quality emerged in the late 1970s. Ever since, the topic has attracted substantial attention among researchers and practitioners. Grönroos introduced a service-oriented approach to quality (in English) in 1982 with the concept of *Perceived Service Quality* and the model of total perceived service quality.[1] This approach is based on research into consumer behavior and the effects of expectations concerning goods performance on post-consumption evaluations. The perceived service quality approach with its *disconfirmation construct* (that is, it measures how well experiences of the service process and its outcome meet expectations) still forms the foundation of most ongoing service quality research.[2]

The focus of the research into service quality has varied over the years. The original Perceived Quality Model was developed to help managers and researchers understand what constitutes a service in the minds of customers. Features of a service emerge during the simultaneous service production and consumption processes. The Perceived Service Quality model was introduced as a conceptual framework which describes how customers perceive the "features" of a service. In the same way as a marketer of physical goods needs to know how customers perceive the quality of product features, the service marketer has to assess how customers perceive the quality of the "service features" implied by the perceived service quality framework. Once this is known, normal customer satisfaction studies can be conducted to find out how satisfied customers are with a certain service.

In addition to research into service quality, there is also an existing quality management establishment with roots that go a long way back in the twentieth century. During the 1990s this took the form of total quality management and various attempts to earn quality certificates. However, this quality movement is overwhelmingly devoted to issues related to goods quality. Because of the characteristics of services, much of the goods-related quality know-how is not directly applicable in service organizations.

Of course, on the other hand, much of this is useful for services, too. This should not be forgotten, although this chapter concentrates on what is unique to quality and quality management in service contexts.

Quality is What Customers Perceive

Too often improving quality is mentioned as an internal goal without any explicit references to what is meant by service quality. To talk about better quality without defining it, how it is perceived by customers, and how it can be improved and enhanced is of limited value. Very often this is only paying lip service to service quality improvement. In service quality literature it is noted that the quality of a particular product or service is *whatever the customer perceives it to be.*

There is always a risk that, when quality is defined too narrowly, quality programs become too narrow in scope. For example, the technical specification of a service, or a product, is frequently considered the only or the most important feature of the perceived quality. The more technology-oriented the firm is, the bigger this risk tends to be. In reality, customers often perceive quality as a much broader concept and, moreover, aspects other than technical ones frequently dominate the quality experience. Within firms, one has to define quality in the same way customers do, otherwise, in quality programs, the wrong actions may be taken and money and time may be poorly invested. It should always be remembered that *what counts is quality as it is perceived by customers.*

Quality Dimensions: What and How

Services are more or less subjectively experienced processes where production and consumption activities take place simultaneously. Interactions, including a series of moments of truth between the customer and the service provider, occur. What happens in these interactions, so-called *buyer–seller interactions* or *service encounters*, will obviously have a critical impact on the perceived service.

Basically, the quality of a service as it is perceived by customers has two dimensions; a *technical* or *outcome dimension* and a *functional* or *process-related dimension*. The hotel guest will be provided with a room and a bed to sleep in, the consumer of a restaurant's services will get a meal, the airline passenger will be transported from one place to another, the client of a business consultant may get a new organization scheme, a factory may get its goods transported from its warehouse to a customer, the bank customer may be granted a loan, the servicing of a machine may be taken care of by the manufacturer, a claim by a unsatisfied customer may be settled by a retail store, and so on. All of these outcomes of service processes are obviously part of the quality experience.

What customers receive in their interactions with a firm is clearly important to them and their quality evaluation. Internally, this is often thought of as *the quality* of the service delivered. However, this is not the whole truth. It is merely *one* quality dimension, called the *Technical Quality of the outcome* of the service production process. In service management literature the term "outcome quality" has also been used for this dimension. It is *what* the customer is left with, when the service production process and its buyer–seller interactions are over. Frequently, but by no means always, this dimension can be measured relatively objectively by customers, because of its characteristic as a technical solution to a problem.

However, as there are a number of interactions between the service provider and the customer, including various series of moments of truth, the technical quality dimension will not count for the total quality which the customer perceives he has received. The customer will obviously also be influenced by the way in which the technical quality—the outcome or end result of the process—is transferred to him. The accessibility of ATM, a Web site, a restaurant or a business consultant, the appearance and behavior of waiting staff, bank staff, travel agency representatives, bus drivers, cabin attendants, repairmen and service and maintenance technicians, and how these service employees perform their tasks, what they say, and how they do it also influence the customer's view of the service. The way in which telecommunications technologies function; for example when making a phone call using a given mobile phone operator or the trustworthiness of an Internet store also have an impact on the process experience.

Furthermore, the more often customers accept self-service activities or other production-related routines they are expected to perform themselves, the better they will, probably, regard the service. Also, other customers simultaneously consuming the same or similar services may influence the way in which a given customer will perceive a service. Other customers may cause long queues, or disturb the customer; on the other hand, they may have a positive impact on the atmosphere of the buyer–seller interactions in these service encounters.

In summary, the customer is also influenced by *how* he receives the service and how he experiences the simultaneous production and consumption process. This is another quality dimension, which is closely related to how the moments of truth of the service encounters themselves are taken care of and how the service provider functions. Therefore, this is called the *Functional Quality of the process*. In the literature this dimension is also labeled "process quality." Hence, as illustrated in Figure 4.1, we have two basic quality dimensions, namely, *What* the customer receives and *How* the customer receives it; the technical result or outcome of the process (technical quality) and the functional dimension of the process (functional quality). It is easy to see that the functional quality dimension cannot be evaluated as objectively as the technical dimension; frequently it is perceived very subjectively.

Usually the service provider cannot hide behind brand names or distributors. In most cases the customers will be able to see the firm, its resources, and its operating methods. *Company and/or local image* is therefore of utmost importance to most services. It can affect the perception of quality in various ways. If the provider is good in the minds of the customers; that is, if it has a favorable image, minor mistakes will probably be forgiven. If mistakes often occur, the image will be damaged. If the image is negative, the impact of any mistake will often be considerably greater than it otherwise would be. As far as the quality perception is concerned, image can be viewed as a filter.

The two quality dimensions, that is, *What* and *How*, are not only valid for services. The technical solution for a customer—provided by, for example, a machine or another good—is part of the overall technical quality perceived by this customer. But attempts to tailor the machine according to the specific demands of a customer is an additional value of a functional nature and therefore part of the overall functional quality which this customer experiences.

Various services such as deliveries, logistics and materials administration, technical service, claims handling, and customer training provide added value, which is partly of a technical nature (that is, adds to technical quality) and partly of a functional nature (that is, adds to functional quality). For example, if a claim

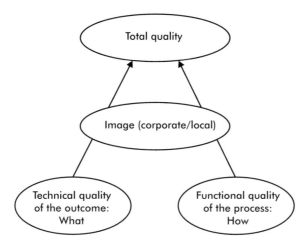

FIGURE 4.1 Two service quality dimensions

is settled with satisfactory results for the customer, the outcome of the claims handling process has good technical quality. The customer would be less satisfied if it had been, for instance, complicated and time-consuming to get results. In such a case, the functional quality of the claims handling process has been low and *total perceived quality* lower than it otherwise would have been.

Additional Dimensions

Recent research has suggested that the two basic quality dimensions could be extended to others. Rust and Oliver discussed the need for explicitly recognizing the physical environment of the service encounter as a third dimension.[3] Thus, the *where* of the service quality perception would be added to the *what* and *how*. In the Perceived Service Quality model the service processes include the environment of the process, and thus the *functional quality* perception is influenced by elements of the physical environment. The *where* aspect is considered to be part of the *how* dimension, which is logical because the perception of the process clearly is dependent on the context of that process. For example, shabby decor influences the perception of the service process in a restaurant. However, as a way of increasing the clarity of the model, a distinction between "how" and "where" could very well be made. Hence, a third basic dimension (not counting image) would be introduced into the model. This dimension could, for example, be labeled *Serviscape Quality*, using the term "serviscape"[4] introduced by Bitner to describe various elements of the physical environment of the service encounter.

The economic consequence is another aspect of perceived service quality that Holmlund has suggested in a business-to-business context.[5] *Economic Quality* would denote the perceived economic consequences of a certain solution. It is not directly a question of price or other kinds of sacrifice for a customer, but rather the perception of the possible economic consequences of a solution. In some situations, not only in industrial markets, it may very well be justified to take this aspect of perceived service quality into account.

Quality and the Competitive Edge

Quality is often considered to be one of the keys to success. The competitive advantage of a firm is said to depend on the quality, and value, of its goods and services. In service contexts, quality may be the foundation of the competitive edge, but which quality dimension (*what* or *how*) is the vital part of excellent total quality? If this question is not answered correctly, the wrong actions may be taken within a company, and the company would lose its chance to achieve a stronger competitive position.

Too often technical quality considerations are thought of as the paramount quality issues. A technical quality strategy is successful if a firm succeeds in achieving a technical solution that the competition cannot match. Today, this is rarely the case; there are a number of firms that can produce approximately the same technical quality. Creating a technical advantage is difficult because, in many industries, competitors can introduce similar solutions relatively quickly. In services, creating a technical advantage seems to be even more difficult than in manufacturing. For example, in financial services or insurance competitors often launch a similar service in a technical sense in response to competition within weeks or even days. Even when an excellent solution is achieved, the firm may be unsuccessful, if excellent technical quality is counteracted or nullified by badly managed or handled buyer–seller interactions or service encounters; that is, by an unsatisfactory functional quality of the process.

Implementing a service strategy is a possible option for most firms, service firms and manufacturers of physical goods alike. This means, in principle, that improving the buyer–seller interactions becomes the basis for quality programs. Developing the functional quality dimension may add substantial value for the customers and thus create the necessary competitive edge. To state this in a more simplified way, you can beat the competition if you provide your customers with more and better services where functional quality is emphasized. Of course, this does not mean that technical quality issues are not important, and that technical quality improvements are not necessary in service competition.

The technical quality of the outcome of a service process is normally a prerequisite for good quality. It has to be at an acceptable level. The definition of an acceptable level depends on the strategy of a firm and the needs and expectations of its customers. However, once the outcome is good enough, this becomes transparent. Good technical quality alone does not mean that customers perceive that the service quality is good. If customers are to consider total service quality good, functional quality has to be good as well. In a situation where a number of firms are competing with similar outcomes or technical quality, it is the functional quality impact of the service process that counts. In that situation, firms compete with their service processes and the functional quality impact created by them. However, if technical quality fails, total perceived quality fails as well.

The Perceived Service Quality

In previous sections we discussed the two basic quality dimensions—the *what* and the *how*—in the minds of the customer. We also noted that quality is to a large extent perceived subjectively. However, the quality perception process is more complicated. It is not just the experiences of the quality dimensions that determine whether quality is perceived as good, neutral, or bad.

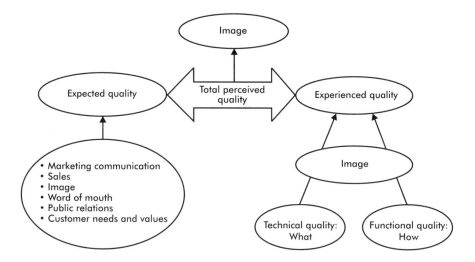

FIGURE 4.2   Total perceived quality

Figure 4.2 illustrates how quality experiences are connected to traditional marketing activities resulting in a *Perceived Service Quality*. When we consider manufacturers of goods providing services as part of their package, it may be more appropriate to talk about *total perceived quality*. Good perceived quality is obtained when the *experienced quality* meets the expectations of the customer; that is, the *expected quality*. If expectations are unrealistic, the total perceived quality will be low, even if the experienced quality measured in an objective way is good. As shown in Figure 4.2, the expected quality is a function of a number of factors, namely marketing communication, word of mouth, company/local image, price, customer needs and values. *Marketing communication* includes advertising, direct mail, sales promotion, Web sites, Internet communication and sales campaigns, which are directly under the control of the firm. The *image* and *word of mouth* factors, as well as public relations, are only indirectly controlled by the firm. External impact on these factors may also occur, but they are basically a function of the previous performance of the firm, supported by, for example, advertising. Finally, the *needs* of the customer as well as the values that determine the choice of customers also have an impact on his expectations.

When quality programs, which may even include functional quality aspects, are implemented, Perceived Service Quality may still be low, or even deteriorate, if, for example, the firm simultaneously runs advertising campaigns that promise too much or are inadequate in some other respect. The level of total perceived quality is not determined simply by the level of technical and functional quality dimensions, but rather by the *gap between the expected and experienced quality*. Consequently, every quality program should involve not only those involved in operations, but those responsible for external marketing and market communication as well.

Image plays a central role in customer perception of service quality, and is as important to a service firm as to any other organization. Hence, it is imperative that image be managed in a proper manner. The issues of how image develops and what causes image problems are not always very well understood. Therefore these issues will be dealt with at length in Chapter 12 on the management of brands and image in services.

Managing Expectations to Secure the Quality Perception

As the Perceived Service Quality model shows, customer expectations have a decisive impact on customers' quality perceptions. If a service provider over-promises, it raises customers' expectations too high and, consequently, customers will perceive that they get low quality. The level of quality may very well still be high, objectively measured, but as customer expectations were not in balance with his experiences, the perceived quality is nevertheless low. Many quality development processes are destroyed by too much promise of improved service, too early. The marketer has to be very careful when designing external marketing campaigns and activities, so that he avoids making promises that cannot be kept. Indeed, it may be wiser to try to keep promises on a lower level than actual customer experiences. In that way customers will at least not be dissatisfied with the quality they perceive. At the same time it allows the service provider to offer its customers unexpected surprises, which much more effectively create loyalty and repurchases than simply satisfactorily perceived quality. We shall return to this issue in the next chapter.

In conclusion, from a marketing point of view it is better to underpromise in order to be sure that the organization can fulfill the promise that has been given. *It is even better to underpromise and overdeliver.*

Managing Expectations: The Sabel Wilderness Hotel Case Study

The Sabel Wilderness Hotel is situated in a large natural park and wilderness area in Scandinavia. Several other hotels operate in the vicinity. The Sabel is a hotel with some 80 beds and is well known for its high standard of service. The hotel has invested in large and well furnished rooms as well as in a cosy restaurant serving local and international dishes. Over the years it has invested substantial sums in training its employees to offer excellent service to the hotel guests in a personal and flexible way. The most recent theme of the managing director's regular meetings with the employees has been service recovery. A support system for service recovery has been developed.

In every customer satisfaction study made over the years the Sabel has been given the best possible rating by most customers. Over 75% of the guests say that they are very satisfied with the hotel overall, and under 5% indicate that they are less than satisfied. Almost all guests who stay at the Sabel and who come back to the national park area make new reservations at the Sabel. However, as the area continuously attracts new visitors, the Sabel has a substantial number of first-time guests every year.

The management of the Sabel was recently offered an opportunity to upgrade the hotel to the highest class in the unofficial rating system used for hotels in the country. However, Mr Leopold, the managing director also directly responsible for marketing and customer service, turned down this offer. He did not want hotel guests to expect the best, although he is convinced that the hotel indeed offers its guests the highest quality service. Says Mr Leopold, "It is much better that guests come to us with lower expectations based on our next-to-highest rating, because then we can always surprise them with better service than they thought they would get." He continues, "I believe it is much better for us to underpromise and overdeliver." According to Leopold, guests perceive that they get a better quality this way, and this has a favorable impact on the image of the Sabel. In addition, it reinforces positive word of mouth behavior.

A Synthesized Model of Perceived Service Quality

As a synthesis of the Perceived Service Quality model and research into service quality in North America, Brogowicz, Delene and Lyth have developed what they call a Synthesized Model of Perceived Service Quality.[6] This model is illustrated in Figure 4.3.

The model is self-explanatory. The perceived service quality is divided into a *technical quality gap* and a *functional quality gap*, which then merge into a *total service quality gap*. The customer experiences influencing these gaps are divided into experiences of a *technical service package* and of a *functional service package*, respectively. These packages are, of course, blended into a *total service package*. The logic of keeping the technical and functional packages apart is clear. It makes the marketers and people responsible for quality think explicitly in terms of *what* is offered and *how* the process is functioning. If this distinction is not constantly kept in mind one could tend to overemphasize the importance of the *what* dimension or the technical services offered and underestimate the *how* dimension or the functional services offered. At the bottom of the figure *human resources* and *physical resources* that influence the two types of packages are listed. At the top of the figure, image and factors which have an impact on expectations are presented.

The Gummesson 4Q Model of Offering Quality

The Gummesson 4Q Model of Offering Quality has been developed based on earlier models combining concepts from the Perceived Service Quality model and goods-oriented quality notions.[7] The model is illustrated in Figure 4.4.

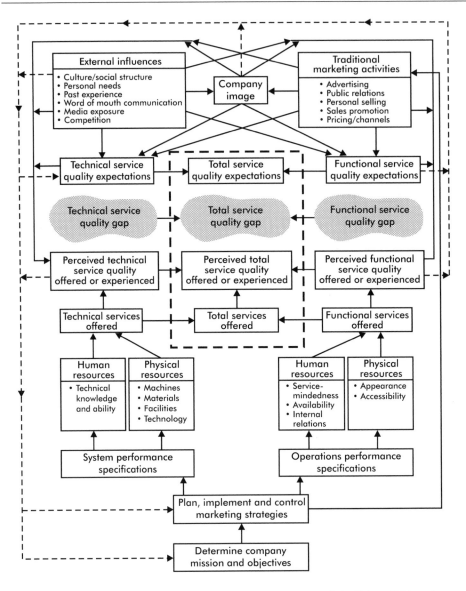

FIGURE 4.3 Synthesized quality model. Source: Brogowicz, A.A., Delene, L.M. and Lyth, D.M., A Synthesised Service Quality Model with Managerial Implications. *The International Journal of Service Industry Management*, **1**(1), 1990, p. 39. Copyright 1990, with permission from MCB University Press.

The starting point for the development of this model was the idea that services and physical goods are integral parts of services offered. Hence, the model combines service and goods elements and is intended to be helpful for developing and managing quality regardless of whether services or physical goods are the core of the offering. As businesses are becoming more and more service businesses and it is difficult to keep goods and services apart, this clearly makes sense.

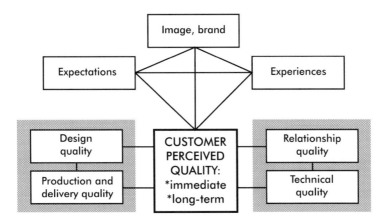

FIGURE 4.4   The Gummesson 4Q Model of Offering Quality. Source: Gummesson, E., *Quality Management in Service Organizations*. New York: ISQA, 1993, p. 229; further revised by Gummesson, 2000.

The model includes *expectations* and *experiences* variables and, in addition, an *image* and a *brand* variable. Image refers to company image as in the Perceived Service Quality model. The brand element adds a new aspect to models of perceived quality. Whereas image is related to customers' view of a firm, *brand refers to the view of a product that is created in the minds of customers*. The term "brand image" is sometimes used for this phenomenon. According to the Gummesson 4Q Model of Offering Quality, customers' perception of the total quality, on the one hand, influences the image of the firm, but on the other hand it also contributes in a decisive way to the brand that is emerging in the minds of the customers (Chapter 12 discusses the brand and image concepts in some detail).

The two first quality concepts in the model are *sources* of quality. *Design quality* refers to how well.the service and goods elements of the product and the combination of them into a functioning package is developed and designed. Design quality errors result in poor performance and negative experiences. *Production and delivery quality* refers to how well the package and its elements are produced and delivered, compared to the design. If there are problems either in production of goods elements or in service processes, or if the delivery of goods does not meet expectations, a quality problem occurs.

The two other quality concepts form the *result* of the goods production and delivery, and of service processes. *Relational quality* refers to how the customer perceives quality during the service processes. Customer-oriented, attentive and empathetic service employees who demonstrate competence and skills contribute favorably to relational quality. Customization of physical goods is another factor that influences this type of quality. Relational quality is closely related to the functional quality dimension. In this model *technical quality* refers to the short-term and long-term benefits of a package. If maintenance of production machines keeps a manufacturer from losing money caused by machine breakdowns, a person's economic security is well covered by an insurance company, or a car performs according to specifications, technical quality is good.

This model clearly points out important dimensions of quality. It takes into account the fact that good quality or quality problems, respectively, can often be traced back to the factory or back office (production quality), or even further back to the design table (design quality). It also incorporates the specific characteristics of the service elements of offerings (delivery and relational quality), and includes the longer-term outcome of these, which is not explicitly included in the Perceived Service Quality model.

The Moments of Truth and Quality

As noted in this chapter, the situations in which the customer meets resources and the service provider's ways of operating are critical to the quality experience. These buyer–seller interactions or service encounters determine the level of the functional quality dimension. In these interactions most or all of the technical quality of the outcome is transferred to the customer. In service management such situations are often called *moments of truth*, to use a term that was introduced into the service management literature by Normann.[8]

The "moments of truth" concept literally means that this is the time and place when and where the service provider has the opportunity to demonstrate to the customer the quality of its services. It is a true *moment of opportunity*. In the next moment the opportunity will be lost, the customer will have gone, and there are no easy ways of adding value to the Perceived Service Quality. The moment of opportunity is gone. If a quality problem has occurred, it is too late to take corrective action. In order to do so, a new moment of truth has to be created. The service provider can, for example, actively contact the customer to correct a mistake or to at least explain why things went wrong. This is, of course, much more troublesome and probably less effective than a well-managed moment of truth.

In reality, the customer will experience a whole series of moments of truth when patronizing a service organization. When using the services of an airline the passenger goes through a number of such moments, beginning with arrival at the airport and ending with baggage claim and transportation away from the airport.

The service process must always be planned and executed so that no badly handled moments of truth take place. If such situations go unmanaged there is a evident risk that unexpected quality problems may occur. In particular, the functional quality of the process will be damaged and cause quality deterioration.

The Effect of Emotions and Mood

Emotions that customers feel when consuming a service have not been included in Perceived Service Quality models, or in models for measuring satisfaction with service quality. However, it is quite obvious that felt emotions, such as anger and depression, guilt or happiness, delight and hopefulness, somehow affect the pure cognitive perception of service processes. Some services, such as theater or an ice hockey game, should arouse emotions, but emotions also form either a filter mediating experiences of the service process, or are variables that influence the experiences alongside cognitively perceived quality elements.

It is important to take affective functions into account in service quality management. The literature does not yet offer clear models. However, managers should always bear in mind the potential effects of emotions on perceived service quality. There have been some minor studies of the effects of emotions on satisfaction with service quality. One such study indicated that negative emotions may have a stronger effect on satisfaction with quality than positive emotions.[9] However, no conclusive guidance for management has yet been found.

Mood is a related concept which may also have a decisive effect on how the quality of a service is perceived. Previous research on consumer behavior has shown that customers' mood—positive or negative—has an effect on their evaluations and behavioral responses to, among other things, service encounters.[10] As with emotions, research into the effects of mood on how service quality is perceived is very scarce. However, based on existing research, it seems that mood may only have a limited impact on how customers perceive service encounters.[11]

How is Service Quality Perceived? Service Quality Attributes

How service quality is perceived has been studied extensively during the past two decades. Most of these studies are based on the disconfirmation notion; that is, quality is perceived through a *comparison between expectations and experiences* over a number of quality attributes. The best-known and most influential studies are the ones by Leonard Berry and his colleagues related to the development of the SERVQUAL instrument. In the following sections we shall discuss this instrument in some detail.

First, one of the earliest studies of aspects of perceived service quality, by British Airways in the 1980s, will be presented. Although this study covered British Airways' airline services only, the results seem generally to be valid. Although this study is old, it still demonstrates some of the key aspects of service quality perceptions. The researchers wanted to find out what airline passengers considered most important in their flying experience.[12] The following four aspects emerged:

1. *Care and concern*: the customer wants to feel that the organization, its employees and its operational systems are devoted to solving his problems.
2. *Spontaneity*: contact employees demonstrate a willingness and readiness to actively approach customers and take care of their problems. They show that they can think for themselves and not just go by the book.
3. *Problem solving*: contact employees are skilled in taking care of their duties and perform according to standards. Moreover, the rest of the organization, including operational support employees and operational systems, are also trained and designed to give good service.

4. *Recovery*: if anything goes wrong, or something unexpected happens, there is someone who is prepared to make a special effort to handle the situation.

Two of these factors, *care and concern* and *problem solving*, were explicitly recognized earlier by British Airways, as they probably would be by most service providers. However, the *spontaneity* and *recovery* issues were new. They had not been thought of in any concrete manner as characteristics of good service. Here again the importance of the functional quality dimension is stressed. Problem solving is the only technical quality factor; the three other factors are process-related.

The British Airways study was conducted in order to assess which attributes of service quality customers appreciate most. No comparison between expectations and real experiences were reported. One strength of this study is that it (with only four aspects, or attributes) demonstrates what is at the heart of customer perceptions of service quality. It also includes the *recovery* issue, which has recently become an important area of research in service management.

Service Quality Determinants and the SERVQUAL Instrument

In the mid-1980s Berry and his colleagues Parasuraman and Zeithaml began to study service quality determinants and how customers evaluate the quality of services based on the Perceived Service Quality concept.[13] In Figure 4.5 the results of their initial study, the 10 service quality determinants, are summarized.

The 10 determinants were found to characterize customers' perception of the service. One of the determinants, *competence*, is clearly related to the technical quality of the outcome, and another, *credibility*, is closely connected to the image aspect of perceived quality. However, it is interesting to observe that the rest of the determinants are more or less related to the process dimension of perceived quality. The importance of the functional quality dimension is very much stressed by these findings.

As a result of a later study the 10 determinants of service quality were decreased to the following five:[14]

1. *Tangibles.* This determinant is related to the appeal of facilities, equipment and material used by a service firm as well as to the appearance of service employees.
2. *Reliability.* This means that the service firm provides its customers with accurate service the first time without making any mistakes and delivers what it has promised to do by the time that has been agreed upon.
3. *Responsiveness.* This means that the employees of a service firm are willing to help customers and respond to their requests as well as to inform customers when service will be provided, and then give prompt service.
4. *Assurance.* This means that employees' behavior will give customers confidence in the firm and that the firm makes customers feel safe. It also means that the employees are always courteous and have the necessary knowledge to respond to customers' questions.

1. *Reliability* involves consistency of performance and dependability:
   - the firm performs the service right the first time
   - accuracy in billing
   - keeping records correctly
   - performing the service at the designated time
2. *Responsiveness* concerns the willingness or readiness of employees to provide service:
   - timeliness of service
   - mailing transaction slips immediately
   - calling the customer back quickly
   - giving prompt service
3. *Competence* means possession of the required skills and knowledge:
   - knowledge and skills of the contact employees
   - knowledge and skills of operational support personnel
   - research capability of the organization
4. *Access* involves approachability and ease of contact:
   - the service is easily accessible by telephone
   - waiting time to receive service is not extensive
   - convenient hours of operation
   - convenient location of service facility
5. *Courtesy* involves politeness, respect, consideration, and friendliness of contact personnel:
   - consideration for the consumer's property
   - clean and neat appearance of contact personnel
6. *Communication* means keeping customers informed in language they can understand and listening to them:
   - explaining the service itself
   - explaining how much the service will cost
   - explaining the trade-offs between service and cost
   - assuring the consumers that a problem will be handled
7. *Credibility* involves trustworthiness, believability, honesty, and having the customer's best interests at heart:
   - company name
   - company reputation
   - personal characteristics of the contact personnel
   - the degree of hard sell involved in interactions
8. *Security* is the freedom from danger, risk, or doubt:
   - physical safety
   - financial security
   - confidentiality
9. *Understanding/Knowing the Customer* involves making the effort to understand the customer's needs:
   - learning the customer's specific requirements
   - providing individualized attention
   - recognizing regular customers
10. *Tangibles* include physical evidence of the service:
    - physical facilities
    - appearance of personnel
    - tools or equipment used to provide the service
    - physical representations of the service (cards, etc.)
    - other customers in the service facility

FIGURE 4.5 Determinants of perceived service quality. Reprinted with permission from the *Jounal of Marketing*, published by the American Marketing Association, Parasuraman, A., Zeithaml, V.A. & Berry, L.L., Fall 1985, p. 47.

5. *Empathy*. This means that the firm understands customers' problems and performs in their best interests as well as giving customers individual personal attention and having convenient operating hours.

SERVQUAL is an instrument for measuring how customers perceive the quality of a service. This instrument is based on the five determinants above and on a comparison between customers' expectations of how the service should be performed and their experiences of how the service is rendered (disconfirmation or confirmation of expectations). Usually 22 attributes are used to describe the five determinants and respondents are asked to state (on a seven-point scale from "Strongly Disagree" to "Strongly Agree") what they expected from the service and how they perceived the service. Based on the discrepancies between expectations and experiences over the 22 attributes, an overall quality score can be calculated. The more this score shows that experiences are below expectation, the lower the perceived quality.[15] However, more important than calculating the overall score may be the scores on the individual attribute scales, perhaps summarized over determinants.

There has been some controversy regarding the use of the SERVQUAL instrument. In many studies the determinants have been reported to be stable over various types of services, but in other studies the set of five standard determinants has not been found. Moreover, sometimes in a factor analysis one set of determinants emerges for expectations and another set for experiences. In addition, the 22 attributes used in the original instrument do not always accurately describe all aspects of a given service.

The SERVQUAL scale should be applied carefully, and the determinants and attributes of the instrument should always be reassessed in any situation, before the instrument is used. Services, as well as markets and cultural environments, are different. It may be necessary to add new aspects of the service to be studied to the original set of determinants and attributes, and sometimes to exclude some from the measurement instrument used. From a managerial point of view, when trying to understand what constitutes a given service, the five determinants, and also the original ten determinants give a valuable starting point for the development of an understanding of what aspects characterize the service that is provided. However, when using a SERVQUAL-type of approach to measuring perceived service quality one should always carefully customize the set of determinants and attributes used to the specific situation at hand.

Finding Service Quality Attributes and Measuring Quality Perceptions

The point has already been made that customers have certain expectations about the kind of performance that is appropriate to a particular service. Certain services are more industrialized and transaction-based, e.g. fast food, ticket sales, and airline check-in desks. Other service encounters are more *ad hoc* and feature more unpredictability, and hence opportunities for customization through situational sensitivity. Performance measurement would appear to lend itself more readily to transaction-based encounters than relationship-based encounters. It is generally agreed that the latter features more opportunities than the former for feedback, adjustment and continuous improvement.

In a recently reported study[16] it was found that if the service employees, through their experience and observations of encounters, were to compile a basic list of significant service attributes they would in turn be able to formulate a simple measurement system that would emulate the process control system of manufacturing. During the study, it became clear that customers did not have undifferentiated or generic service expectations about low-involvement transactional service encounters. The study evidenced a two-step configuration of attributes—*should* values and *could* values—the former being values without which the latter could not effectively operate.

Service employees privately sampled their own performance, using a preset scoring system. Findings indicated that using such simple measuring techniques actually enhanced performance *where the rate of continuous improvement was known*. Where performance was measured and the rate of continuous improvement was not known, performance degraded over time. Of the number of conclusions that this study yielded, the most salient were as follows.

1. That the act of measuring and totaling did indeed enhance subsequent performance.
2. That service providers are motivated by the evidence and not simply by feeling that they have improved their progress.
3. Measurement systems are able to benefit from the measurement effect.
4. A continuous improvement component could be seen to operate.

Source: Unpublished case study teaching material contributed by Peter Murphy, Dundee University, Scotland.

Problems with Expectations/Experiences Measurements and Comparisons

There has been a considerable amount of debate regarding what kind of expectations the real experiences of a given service should be compared to. In the original SERVQUAL instrument, customers were asked what they expected from the service they had consumed, so the expectations and experiences measurements related to the same service. Later the measurement method was changed so that customers were asked what they expected from an excellent or ideal service in the same category as the one they had consumed. The original Perceived Service Quality model from which the expectations/experiences comparison originates in service quality contexts was developed to help managers and researchers understand how customers perceive features of a given service. Hence, the expectations concept in that model is quite clearly related to the same service that is also experienced. Following the original model, the expectations should be measured as the expectations of the service that is consumed.

However, independent of what one wants to know about a given service, different kinds of expectations could be measured. If one wants to assess how good a given service is considered to be compared to the best in its category, expectations of the best-in-the-category service or an ideal service should be measured. On the other hand, if one wants to find out how customers perceive the quality of a given service, both expectations and experiences regarding this particular service should be measured.

There is another problem with measurement instruments that are based on comparisons between expectations and experiences over a number of attributes. This is because there are certain validity problems related to the measurement of expectations. These problems can be summarized in the following three points.[17]

1. If expectations are measured after the service experience or at the same time as the experiences occur, which they for practical reasons often are, then what is measured is not really expectation but something which has been biased by experience.
2. It does not necessarily make sense to measure expectations *prior* to the service experience either, because the expectations which customers have beforehand are perhaps not the expectations with which they will compare their experiences. The customer's experiences of the service process may change his expectations, and altered expectations are ones with which the experiences should be compared to determine the actual quality perception of a customer.
3. Measuring expectations is not a sound way of proceeding in any case, because experiences are perceptions of reality, and inherent in these perceptions are prior expectations. Consequently, if first, one way or the other, expectations are measured and then experiences are measured, then the expectations are *measured twice*.

When measuring perceived service quality, the problems described above are not easy to solve. Theoretically, a comparison of experiences and expectations still makes sense, because expectations clearly influence the perception of quality. Managers need to observe the management of expectations when developing quality programs. However, we may have to find alternative ways of measuring perceived quality.

In her study on the restaurant industry Liljander[18] compared a number of different standards to relate experiences to, expectations being one of them. Her conclusion was that making no comparisons at all seems to be a good approach to measuring perceived service quality. This means that *by measuring experiences only* over a set of appropriate attributes, one can get a good approximation of the perceived quality. In an North American study, based on similar arguments as Liljander's, a measurement instrument called SERVPERF (service performance only) was suggested.[19] Indeed, this may be the best and most valid way of measuring perceived service quality using an attribute approach to measure customers' experiences of the service only. Thus, the researcher develops a set of attributes that describes the service as conclusively as possible and only measures how customers experience the service on scales that measure these attributes. This way of measuring perceived service quality is also much easier to administer and the data is easier to analyze.

Studying Critical Incidents: An Alternative Way of Measuring Service Quality

The measurement methods discussed in the previous sections are based on attributes and quantitative measurement of these attributes. An alternative way of creating an understanding of how customers perceive the quality of a given service is the *critical incident method*. This method has been used a great deal in various studies in the service field.[20]

The methodological approach is to ask respondents, in this case customers with experiences of a given service, to think of situations where the service, or any part of the service process including the outcome of that process, clearly deviated from the normal, either in a favorable or unfavorable way. These are *critical incidents*. Then the respondent is asked to describe, in as much detail as possible, *what happened* and *what made him consider the incident critical*. Finally, the researcher analyzes the descriptions of the critical incidents and the reasons for them in order to find out what kind of quality problems exist and why these problems occur. Favorable quality perceptions and the reasons for them are also categorized in the same fashion.

A study using critical incidents gives the marketer rich material indicating problem areas and strengths as well as what should be developed in order for the firm to improve the perceived quality of its services. One may find out, for example, that a lack of resources, problems with the technical skills of service employees or negative attitudes towards customers seem to be frequently occurring reasons for negative critical incidents, causing a low perception of service quality. If needed, the marketer can use these findings as a basis for further research on actions necessary to improve service quality. Frequently the findings from a critical incident study give direct indications about what actions need to be taken.

Perceived Service Quality Versus Customer Satisfaction

Customer satisfaction with a physical product is often measured using an instrument where a given physical product is described by a set of attributes that reflect key product features. A comparison of experiences with prior expectations is also often made. Probably because the development of measurement models for perceived service quality included similar elements to models for measuring satisfaction with goods features, the question whether there is a difference between service quality and customer satisfaction has been debated in the literature. Furthermore, if there is a difference, the question whether quality is perceived first and then satisfaction; or satisfaction with a service comes first and then leads to a quality perception has also been discussed. This discussion has been extensive and even heated at times; however, it is submitted, it is quite unnecessary.

The Perceived Service Quality model is intended to offer a conceptual framework for understanding the features of a service, including its outcome, process and image dimensions. It is not a measurement model. Instead it should give the researcher and marketer a basis for developing a service offering with a certain quality. In the same way as a customer first perceives the quality of the features of a physical product, and only then, perhaps taking into account price and other sacrifice-related issues, finds out whether or not he is satisfied with the product, a person consuming a service first perceives the quality of the dimensions of the service, and only then, again perhaps considering other issues as well, is either satisfied or not with the quality of that service.

A logical analysis clearly shows that a perception of service quality comes first followed by a perception of satisfaction or dissatisfaction with this quality.

A Summary: The Seven Criteria of Good Perceived Service Quality

There has been a range of studies of service quality conducted in many countries. From them various lists of attributes or factors of good quality can be collated. As was mentioned earlier in the context of the SERVQUAL determinants, such lists are useful as starting points for managers who want to develop an appropriate list of attributes or features that describe a given service. However, in order to make such lists of determinants or factors of good service quality useful for managerial purposes, they have to be short, yet still provide a comprehensive list of aspects of good quality. Figure 4.6 provides such a list. These seven criteria of good perceived service quality are an integration of available studies and conceptual work. Some of these studies have been discussed in this section. One of the seven, *professionalism and skills*, is outcome-related and thus a Technical Quality dimension. Another criterion, *reputation and credibility*, is image-related, thus fulfilling a filtering function. However, four other criteria, *attitudes and behavior*, *accessibility and flexibility*, *reliability and trustworthiness*, and *service recovery*, are clearly process-related and thus represent the Functional Quality dimension. Finally, following the conceptual work by Bitner, Rust and Oliver,[21] the impact of the *serviscape* is introduced as a seventh criterion. This is clearly a process-related, Functional Quality criterion.

These seven criteria of good perceived service quality can be viewed as guidelines based on a solid body of empirical and conceptual research as well as on practical experience. Therefore, they should be useful as managerial principles. Of course, the list is not exhaustive. In various industries and for various customers certain criteria are more important than others. And of course, there may in specific situations be other determinants of good quality that are not covered by these criteria.

The role of *price* in a quality context is not very clear. Normally, however, the price of a service can be viewed in relation to the quality expectations of customers or to their previously perceived service quality. If the price of a service is considered too high, customers will not buy. Price also has an impact on expectations. But in some situations price seems to be a quality criterion. A higher price level may equal a better quality in the minds of customers, especially when the service is highly intangible. In many cases professional services are examples of such services.

---

1. Professionalism and Skills

Customers realize that the service provider, its employees, operational systems, and physical resources have the knowledge and skills required to solve their problems in a professional way (outcome-related criteria).

2. Attitudes and Behavior

Customers feel that the service employees (contact persons) are concerned about them and interested in solving their problems in a friendly and spontaneous way (process-related criteria).

3. Accessibility and Flexibility

Customers feel that the service provider, its location, operating hours, employees, and operational systems are designed and operate so that it is easy to get access to the service and are prepared to adjust to the demands and wishes of the customer in a flexible way (process-related criteria).

4. Reliability and Trustworthiness

Customers know that whatever takes place or has been agreed upon, they can rely on the service provider, its employees and systems, to keep promises and perform with the best interest of the customers at heart (process-related criteria).

5. Service Recovery

Customers realize that whenever something goes wrong or something unpredictable happens the service provider will immediately and actively take action to keep them in control of the situation and find a new, acceptable solution (process-related criteria).

6. Serviscape

Customers feel that the physical surrounding and other aspects of the environment of the service encounter support a positive experience of the service process (process-related criteria).

7. Reputation and Credibility

Customers believe that the service provider's business can be trusted and gives adequate value for money, and that it stands for good performance and values which can be shared by customers and the service provider (image-related criteria).

FIGURE 4.6   The seven criterion of good perceived service quality

Relationship Quality: A Dynamic Approach to Perceived Quality

The Perceived Service Quality model is basically static, although the *image* factor does give the model a dynamic aspect. Most service quality models and instruments are also static. As services are processes and inherently relationship-oriented, clearly customers' quality perceptions develop and undergo change over time as the relationship continues. Even if there is only one single service encounter, this encounter is a process which includes a series of moments of truth and the customer's quality perception develops in a dynamic fashion throughout this interaction process. The need for dynamic models to further develop the understanding of how service quality is perceived by customers was expressed at the beginning of the 1990s.[22] Driven by service quality research an interest in *relationship quality* emerged.[23] Relationship quality can be described as *the dynamics of long-term quality formation in ongoing customer relationships.* In the last part of this chapter models that describe how long-term quality perceptions can be understood and analyzed are described.[24]

From the customer's point of view, relationship quality is their continuously developing quality perception over time. However, as a relationship includes at least two parties, the supplier or service provider and the customer, a quality perception is really developing on both sides. The supplier or service provider forms an impression of the quality of the customer and, especially in business relationships, there may be ongoing reciprocal business developing over time with continuous quality perceptions by both parties related to the two-way exchanges of goods, services, information or other items of value.

A Relationship Framework for the Analysis of Relationship Quality

In services as well as in any commercial relationship between two parties, *interaction* is the key concept. Interactions are the basic phenomena in quality and value creation.[25] The perception of relationship quality occurs in ongoing interactions, which may be either continuous, such as in security and cleaning services, or discrete, such as in bank services or goods transportation. Maria Holmlund has developed a framework for understanding and analyzing ongoing interactions.[26] These interactions may be very different depending on the type of marketing situation involved. Some contacts are between people, some between customers and machines and systems, and some between systems of the supplier and customer, respectively. In every case interactions are involved. The framework is equally valid for describing and analyzing relationships in consumer markets and relationships between organizations.

The framework consists of a continuous flow of *acts*, *episodes* and *sequences*, which form the *relationships*.[27] Figure 4.7 illustrates this *relationship framework*.

Acts are the smallest unit of analysis in the interaction process, Examples of *acts* could include phone calls, plant visits, service calls and hotel registration. In service management literature they are often called moments of truth. Acts may be related to any kind of interaction elements, physical goods, services, information, financial aspects or social contacts.

Interrelated acts form a minor part of a relationship. These are called *episodes* (or *service encounters* to use a concept frequently used in the service management literature) and examples of these include paying bills from a home computer or visiting a bank office to withdraw money, a negotiation, a shipment of goods, or dinner at a hotel restaurant during a stay at that hotel. Every episode includes a series of acts. For example, a shipment may include such acts as the placement of an order by telephone, assembling and packing the products, transporting the products, unpacking them, making a complaint, and sending and paying an invoice.

Interrelated episodes form the next level of analysis in the interaction process, a *sequence*. Sequences can be defined in terms of a time period, a product package, a campaign or a project, or a combination of these. The analysis of a sequence may contain all kind of interactions related to a particular project which may take up to a year or even longer. As an example, in a hotel context a

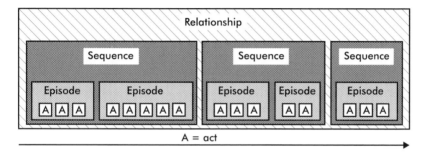

FIGURE 4.7 A relationship framework: interaction levels in a relationship. Source: Holmlund, M., *Perceived Quality in Business Relationships*. Helsinki/Helsingfors: Hanken Swedish School of Economics, Finland/CERS, p. 96.

sequence comprises everything that takes place during one stay at a particular hotel, including episodes such as accommodation, eating in the hotel restaurant and using the hotel's gym or pool. Sequences may naturally overlap, so that episodes belonging to one sequence may also be part of another sequence.

The final and most aggregated level of analysis is the *relationship*. Several sequences form a relationship. Sequences may follow each other directly, may overlap or may follow after longer or shorter intervals depending, for example, on the type of business or on whether the service is of a continuous or discrete nature. This way of dividing the interaction process into several layers on different levels of aggregation gives the marketer a detailed enough instrument to be used in the analysis of interactions between a supplier or service provider and his customers. All different types of elements in the interaction process— goods and service outcomes, service processes, information, social contacts, financial activities, etc.—can be identified and put into their correct perspective in the formation of a relationship over time.

Perceived Quality in a Relationship Framework

The more or less static models of perceived service quality describe how quality is perceived at the episode (or service encounter) level, and the measurement instruments that have been developed measure perceived quality on that level. From a dynamic perspective, quality is perceived at every level of the relationship framework, and thus accumulating to an overall perception of quality at any given point of time. The quality perception at a certain time reflects onto the perception of quality in, for example, single acts and episodes, for example by continuously forming and reforming the customer's image of the service provider. Thus, single acts such as visiting a movie theater's Web site, buying tickets for a certain movie and finally paying for the tickets over the Internet form the episode (or service encounter) of buying cinema tickets. The customer forms a perception of the quality of an act, and this perception, or image, is reflected in the expectations of and perceptions of the next act. Some of these quality perceptions may be good, others neutral or poor. Together these quality perceptions form the perception of the quality of the buying-cinema-ticket-over-the-Internet episode.

Act-level, or *first-level*, quality perception reflects upon the episode-level, or *second-level*, quality perception. However, the dynamics of relationship quality formation then make upper-level quality perceptions (in this case the perceived quality of the Internet ticket purchase) reflect back on the perception of lower-level acts of following episodes. The quality perception of the purchase episode forms customer expectations and the image of the firm, and these influence the perception of following lower-level acts; in this case, the act of picking up tickets at the ticket counter of the movie theater, the comfort of the seat and visibility of the screen from the seat, and the movie experience itself, which together form a second episode. The perceptions of these visit-the-movie-theater-related acts accumulate into the perceived quality of this whole second episode as a second second-level quality perception. According to the relationship quality dynamics, the quality experiences of continuous episodes, some good, some neutral or poor, accumulate into an overall *third-level* quality perception of the whole sequence of going to the movie theater on a particular evening, including buying the tickets over the Internet and going to the movie theater to see the movie. This third-level quality perception then reflects back on continuing lower-level perceptions of episodes and acts in the relationship between a given customer and this particular movie theater in the future.

Finally, the quality perceptions of sequences of episodes accumulate into a *fourth-level* quality perception; that is into *relationship quality*. This quality perception in turn, following the logic of relationship quality dynamics, reflects back on how quality is perceived in the future on lower levels.

The dynamics of relationship quality are schematically illustrated in Figure 4.8. The arrows indicate how perceptions of quality reflect up onto higher levels and then back again in the form of image and expectations. For the sake of clarity, the figure does not show all influences. The grade of shading of the boxes depicting acts, episodes, sequences and the relationship illustrate whether the quality is perceived as good, neutral, or poor. For the sake of simplicity, only a three-grade scale is used here to show the level of the quality perception. As the figure shows, the level of quality may vary and this influences the formation of the quality perception on higher levels. In practical quality management it is of course important to build as much consistency and continuously good quality perceptions as possible into the process, because unfavorable quality experiences always have a negative effect, which in turn will reflect on future quality perceptions.

The strength of this relationship framework with its four levels of analysis is that it enables the supplier or service provider to study in detail the development of a relationship with a customer and also makes it possible to understand and analyze how the development of a series of customer contacts adds to an overall relationship quality. It clarifies the multi-faceted dynamics involved in customers' perceptions of quality. An analysis of the relationship demonstrates the multitude of acts and episodes (service encounters) that contribute to the long-term formation of quality and makes managers more aware of the range of customer contacts which have to be managed from a quality perspective. It shows which acts or episodes are relationship-breaking and which are less critical for the continuation of the relationship. It does not, however, go into the detailed aspects of the dynamics in long-term quality formation. The next section deal with this issue.

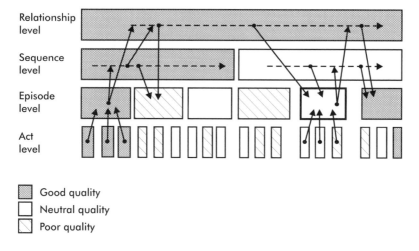

Relationship
level

Sequence
level

Episode
level

Act
level

■ Good quality
□ Neutral quality
▨ Poor quality

FIGURE 4.8   Inherant dynamics in the formation of quality in a relationship. Source: Adapted from Holmlund, M., *Perceived Quality in Business Relationships*. Helsinki/Helsingfors: Hanken Swedish School of Economics, Finland/CERS, p. 160.

The Liljander–Strandvik Model of Relationship Quality

The *Liljander–Strandvik Model of Relationship Quality* includes four important aspects:[28]

- it makes a distinction between episode-level quality (the perceived quality of a service encounter) and relationship-level quality;
- it incorporates satisfaction and customer perceived value in a quality framework;
- it enables an extension of the traditional limited disconfirmation notion used in static models of perceived service quality to include a range of comparison standards; and
- it includes customer behavior variables.

The model is illustrated in Figure 4.9. Concepts used in the model are described in Table 4.1. The lower part of the Liljander–Strandvik model is related to the perception of service quality in a single service encounter (*episode-level quality*). *Episode performance*; that is, the service experienced in one service encounter, can be compared to any *comparison standard*, not only to predictive expectations as is traditionally the case in service quality models (see Table 4.1), or it can be compared to no comparison standards, depending on what seems to generate the most valid result. By comparing the *episode quality* that emerges with the customer's perceived *sacrifice* (such as price, queuing time, lost earnings opportunities and standstill costs) the customer forms his (or the organization's) perception of the *value* for him (or the organization) provided by the episode. This in turn leads to *satisfaction* (or *dissatisfaction*) with the service. The *zone of tolerance* is an accepted variation in performance levels.

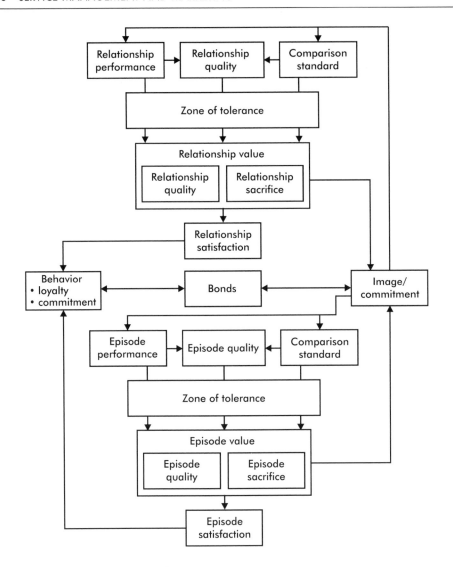

FIGURE 4.9   The Liljander–Strandvik relationship quality model. Source: Adapted from Liljander, V. & Strandvik, T., The Nature of Relationships in Services. In *Advances in Services Marketing and Management*, **4**, Greenwich, CT: The JAI Press, 1995, p. 143.

The satisfaction with a given service encounter (episode) influences the future behavior of the customer. The customer's behavior is dependent on his feelings of loyalty and commitment to the firm. However, there are also other factors that have an impact on behavior. These are *bonds* which exist between the customer and the service provider. Some bonds, such as *legal, economic, technological, geographical* and *time-related* bonds, often constitute barriers to exiting from the relationship. Other bonds, such as *knowledge-related, social, cultural, ideological* and *psychological* bonds, may glue the customer to the service provider in a positive fashion. The ten different types of bonds are described in some detail in Table 4.2.

TABLE 4.1 The Liljander-Strandvik relationship quality model. Source: Adapted from Liljander, V. & Strandvik, T., The Nature of Relationships in Services. In *Advances in Services Marketing and Management*, 4, Greenwich, CT: The JAI Press, 1995, p. 144.

Concept	Episode level	Relationship level
Comparison standard	All comparison standards suggested in the literature (e.g. predictive expectations, brand norm, adequate, product norm, best brand norm, excellent service, ideal, competitor).	All comparison standards suggested in the literature except predictive expectations.
Disconfirmation	Direct or inferred disconfirmation of any comparison standard.	Direct or inferred disconfirmation of any comparison standard except predictive expectations.
Performance	Perceived performance of one particular episode.	Perceived performance across all episodes in the relationship.
Zone of tolerance	The accepted variation in performance levels. A plateau in the quality function.	The accepted accumulation variation in the performance within the relationship.
Quality	Customers' cognitive evaluation of the service of one episode compared to some explicit or implicit comparison standard.	Customers' cognitive evaluation of the service across episodes compared to some explicit or implicit comparison standard.
Sacrifice	Perceived sacrifices (price, etc.) connected to the service episode compared to some explicit or implicit comparison standard.	Perceived sacrifices (price, etc.) across all service episodes in the relationship compared to some explicit or implicit comparison standard.
Value	Episode quality compared to episode sacrifice.	Relationship quality compared to relationship sacrifice.
Satisfaction	Customers' cognitive and affective evaluation based on the personal experience of one service episode.	Customers' cognitive and affective evaluation based on the personal experience across all service episodes within the relationship.
Image	The holistic perception of a service provider that filters performance evaluations and can in itself constitute a comparison standard. It is also the attitudinal component of commitment in a relationship. All types of bonds can affect the image positively or negatively. Image itself is more likely to affect and strengthen the psychological bonds.	
Commitment	Commitment is defined as the parties' intentions to act and their attitude towards interacting with each other. High relationship value will positively affect commitment.	
Behavior	Purchase behavior and communication behavior (word of mouth, complaints). Loyalty which is based also on positive commitment by the customer indicates a stronger relationship than if it is based on mere repetitive purchase behavior. The behavior is also affected by the bonds between the customer and the service provider. By using the same service provider the bonds may be strengthened.	
Bonds	Exit barriers that tie the customer to the service provider and maintain the relationship. These are legal, economic, technological, geographical, time, knowledge, social, cultural, ideological and psychological bonds.	

TABLE 4.2   The Liljander-Strandvik relationship quality model. Source: Adapted from Liljander, V. & Strandvik, T., The Nature of Relationships in Services. In *Advances in Services Marketing and Management*, 4, Greenwich, CT: The JAI Press, 1995, p. 153.

Type of bond	Examples
Legal bond	A contract between the customer and service provider (e.g. telephone company, cable TV, electricity, bank services).
Economic bond	Lack of resources may force the customer to buy a service that fits the customer's budget; price reductions based on relationship.
Technological bond	The purchase of a specific product that requires the use of a specified deal for repairs/maintenance and/or original spare parts from manufacturer or retailer.
Geographical bond	Limited possibilities to buy the service from other than one or a few service providers because of distance and/or lack of transportation.
Time bond	A service provider may be used because of suitable business hours or because of a flexible appointment system. Customers are limited by business hours set by service providers (e.g. child care from 8 am to 4 pm) or employers (office hours and limited lunch hour).
Knowledge bond	The customer may have an established relationship with a doctor who knows the customer's medical history. A customer's relation to a bank teller may be strong because of the teller's knowledge about the customer's business which facilitates the transactions. It also works the other way, so that the customer gains knowledge about the service provider (e.g. the scripts of how to behave are known to the customer which reduces uncertainty.)
Social bond	Social bonds exist when the customer and the service personnel know each other well. Contact is easy, there is mutual trust (services can be handled by phoning the bank, the customer does not have to go there personally).
Cultural bond	Customers may identify themselves with a subculture (e.g. language, country) and therefore relate more strongly to certain companies or products made by certain countries.
Ideological bond	Customers may be inclined to prefer some service providers because of certain personal values (e.g. environmentally friendly products, avoiding companies that exploit nature, support local or national products over imported products).
Psychological bond	The customer is convinced of the superiority of a certain service provider (brand image).

The customer-perceived episode-level value, as well as bonds that exist in the relationship, influence the customer's *image* of the service provider. As in the image concept in the basic Perceived Service Quality model, the image incorporates the customers' old and recent experiences with the firm and builds a bridge to the relationship level of the model. The image functions as a filter when the customer perceives the next episode or service encounter. As in the model of perceived quality described in the previous section, perceptions of quality and value of episodes or service encounters following each other accumulate into perceived quality of the relationship. According to the Liljander–Strandvik model the customer compares the firm's ongoing performance in subsequent service encounters (*relationship performance*) with a comparison standard and, based on that comparison, *relationship quality* emerges. When this quality perception is compared to customer-perceived long-term sacrifice (*relationship sacrifice*) the value of the relationship at a given point in time is perceived (*relationship value*). This affects long-term satisfaction with the service provider (*relationship satisfaction*), which in turn feeds into the image on the one hand and into future behavior (loyalty and commitment) on the other hand.[29]

From a management point of view this model of relationship quality offers a good description of the mechanisms of relationship quality. It demonstrates how customers proceed through the service process over time and shows how they perceive their relationship with a service provider. The model includes several concepts, such as bonds, value and sacrifice, and connections between concepts which help managers understand the process and determine where action should be taken. Some of these concepts will be further discussed in Chapter 6. The major strength of this model is its multi-faceted nature. It demonstrates to managers how perceived quality is formed and accumulates over time as the relationship proceeds, and describes which factors need to be taken into account when managing quality in an ongoing relationship context. It is not a measurement model. It should guide managers towards a comprehensive approach to understanding relationship quality and quality management to make customer-oriented decisions.[30]

The Dynamics of Expectations

The Liljander–Strandvik Model of Relationship Quality implies that a range of comparison standards can be used by customers to compare their experiences of quality attributes. In measurement models this is certainly true, because of the problems involved in measuring expectations in a valid way. As has been noted earlier, it may often be best to use no comparison standard at all, but simply to measure customers' experiences of various quality attributes. However, customers' expectations do theoretically form an important factor influencing perceived service quality both on an episode (service encounter) level and on a relationship level. In order to understand how quality is perceived in an ongoing relationship, one has to understand how expectations develop throughout the relationship. This is important for several reasons. First, it is critical to understand that customers may not expect the same aspects of quality at a later stage in the relationship as they do in the beginning, and why this change has taken place. Second, one has to know the inherent mechanisms of the dynamics of expectations to be able to manage expectations.

Jukka Ojasalo[31] studied the way the quality of professional services develops in a customer relationship over time. Although this study was carried out in the professional services area, the *dynamics of expectations* revealed in the study seem to be valid for any types of service in customer relationships. Figure 4.10 illustrates the expectations model.

In the long-term, three different types of expectations can be identified: *fuzzy*, *explicit* and *implicit* expectations. These can be characterized in the following way:[32]

- *fuzzy expectations* exist when customers expect a service provider to solve a problem but do not have a clear understanding of what should be done;

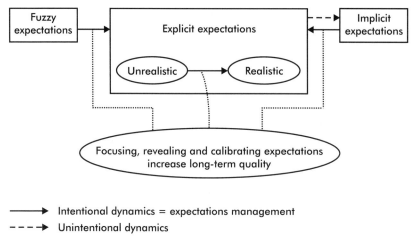

FIGURE 4.10   A dynamic model of expectations. Source: Ojasalo, J., *Quality Dynamics in Professional Services*. Helsinki/Helsingfors: Swedish School of Economics/CERS, Finland, 1999, p. 97.

- *explicit expectations* are clear in customers' minds in advance of the service processes. They can be divided into *realistic* and *unrealistic* expectations;
- *implicit expectations* refer to elements of a service which are so obvious to customers that they do not consciously think about them but take them for granted.

Fuzzy Expectations

It is essential for a service provider to understand which *fuzzy expectations* customers may have, because even though customers cannot consciously formulate such expectations, they still have an impact on satisfaction with quality. Customers may feel that there is a need for service or for a change of their current state in general, but they do not have a clear understanding of what would fulfill this need or change the current situation. They perceive that something is needed, but they do not have a picture of exactly what should be done, and how. Such fuzzy expectations are very real, because customers expect something to be done. If the service rendered by the service provider does not fulfill such fuzzy expectations, customers are disappointed. They feel that something is missing, and they do not understand why they are not satisfied. Fuzzy expectations remain fuzzy.

The service provider should be aware of the existence of such expectations and try to make them surface in the form of explicit expectations. Only then can it be sure that a satisfactory service is delivered. Otherwise the service organization may be faced by unhappy and frustrated customers. The existence of such fuzzy expectations has been recognized for a long time in professional services. For example, see Wittreich's article on a client who wished to purchase marketing communications services or management consultancy services.[33] Similar situations may also occur in other types of service to organizations and individuals alike.

A manufacturing firm that looks for security services does not necessarily understand what needs to be done to provide full security, for example, for its plants. A provider of security services offers a package which seems appropriate but the manufacturer may still feel that more could be done. The customer may not know what could or should be done and cannot make his expectations explicit, but he still expects something more in addition to what is already done. This customer remains unsatisfied. For example, restaurant customers often have unclear, fuzzy expectations about what they want from an evening at a restaurant. They know that they want to have a good time, but not what will make them feel that they are having a good time. If the evening does not offer experiences that fulfill this unspecified wish for a good time, they will leave the restaurant disappointed. In all these examples, fuzzy expectations exist. If the service provider *can make these explicit for the customer and for itself*, there is an opportunity to satisfy the customer.

Explicit Expectations

Customers actively and consciously assume that *explicit expectations* will be met. However, some of these expectations may be unrealistic. For example, a customer who believes that a financial advisor always will be able to manage his funds so that their value grows may one day be very disappointed. It is important for service providers to help customers adjust unrealistic expectations into more realistic ones. If this is done, the likelihood that a service is delivered which will meet customers' expectations will be much higher. In the beginning of a relationship, but of course also as it continues, the service provider should be very careful in what promises it makes. The more vague promises are, the bigger the risk is that customers will form unrealistic explicit expectations. Such "implied-in-fact" promises[34] are extremely dangerous, because the customer is led to believe that the service offered will include features that in fact are not included. Unclear and deliberately vague sales messages easily lead to such "implied-in-fact" promises, and to possibly unrealistic explicit expectations.

Implicit Expectations

Customers take for granted that a service provider will fulfill their *implicit expectations*, because these are so obvious that they are never clearly expressed. Because of this, the service provider may neglect them and not include elements that are required to fulfill such expectations in the service offering. Often customers do not even consciously think about implicit expectations, as long as they are fulfilled. However, the existence of such expectations becomes obvious when they are not met by the service provided, and in that situation dissatisfaction occurs. It is important that service providers make sure that no implicit expectations remain undetected, so that the service offering can be designed to meet all a customer's expectations, not only the explicit ones.

Referring back to Figure 4.10 the thick arrows demonstrate *intentional dynamics*; that is, how the service provider can and should actively manage expectations.

Fuzzy and implicit expectations should be detected and made explicit. Fuzzy expectations become less fuzzy if they are focused on by the service provider. As the relationship continues the service organization knows what to do and the customer learns what to expect. Implicit expectations become explicit if they are not fulfilled. Unrealistic expectations should be detected and customers should be made aware of what is realistic to expect.

The dotted lines in the figure indicate what could be called *unintentional dynamics*; that is, shifts in the nature and range of expectations which take place over time without interference from the service provider as the relationship proceeds.

Customers calibrate fuzzy expectation into explicit ones and unrealistic into realistic expectations as time goes by and they learn what they explicitly need and want as well as accept what it is unrealistic to expect. Of course, the effect of these unintentional dynamics processes is not always positive in the sense that customers accept that unrealistic expectations really are unrealistic. They may shift to another firm which may have the capability to fulfil expectations that were considered unrealistic by the previous service provider.

The dotted arrow in the figure (from explicit expectations towards implicit expectations) demonstrates another type of learning process that creates unintentional expectations dynamics. As customers get used to a certain level of quality in a relationship, some expectations which were originally explicitly expressed become implicit. Customers do not think of them any more and, as long as everything continues as before, no problems occur. However, if the service provider changes something in the service offering—for example, a new service employee takes over a task in the relationship and starts to carry out tasks in a different way than the customer is used to—the customer may become disappointed. The implicit expectation becomes explicit once again.

Summary and Questions for Discussion

In this chapter we first discussed the nature of perceived service quality and presented the *Perceived Service Quality Model* as a basic model of service quality. The *technical quality* (*what*) and *functional quality* (*how*) dimensions of the model as well as *image* as a quality filter were discussed. Extensions of this model (a possible *serviscape*-related *where*) as well as determinants of service quality were then discussed. Measurement approaches, such as the attribute-based SERVQUAL instrument and the *critical incident model*, were presented. In the latter part of the chapter, models of relationship quality and a dynamic approach to managing expectations in service contexts were discussed.

Questions for discussion

1. Why is quality of services understood as perceived quality?
2. Which dimensions of perceived service quality have to be recognized, according to the *Perceived Service Quality model*? Why? Which additional dimensions could be included?

3. Discuss various determinants and criteria of perceived service quality.
4. What are the strengths and weaknesses of the SERVQUAL instrument as a measurement model? What are those of the critical incident approach?
5. Which are the different layers on which quality is formed and perceived in an ongoing relationship context? How does quality develop?
6. Discuss the dynamics of the Liljander–Strandvik Model of Relationship Quality. Which are its strengths and weaknesses for practical use?
7. Discuss how various kinds of *expectations* influence the perception of quality in a relationship context. What are the risks of not clarifying a customer's expections?
8. Discuss how the quality of one or several services offered by your firm, or the quality of any given service, is perceived by a specified group of customers. What problems exist? What needs to be improved?

Further Reading

Albrecht, K. & Zemke, R. (1985) *Service America*. Homewood, IL: Dow Jones-Irwin.

Andreassen, T.W. & Lindestad, B. (1998) The Effect of Corporate Image in the Formation of Customer Loyalty. *Journal of Service Research*, **1**(1), pp. 82–92.

Berry, L.L. & Parasuraman, A. (1991) *Marketing Services. Competing Through Quality*. New York: Free Press.

Bitner, M.J., Booms, B.H. & Tetrault, M.S. (1990) The Service Encounter: Diagnosing Favorable and Unfavorable Incidents. *Journal of Marketing*, **54**, January, pp. 71–84.

Brogowicz, A.A., Delene, L.M. & Lyth, D.M. (1990) A Synthesized Service Quality Model with Managerial Implications. *International Journal of Service Industry Management*, **1**(1), pp. 27–45.

Calonius, H. (1992) The Promise Concept. In Blomqvist, H.C., Grönroos, C. & Lindqvist, L.-J. (eds), *Economics and Marketing. Essays in Honour of Gösta Mickwitz*. Helsinki/Helsingfors: Swedish School of Economics, Finland, pp. 37–56.

Cronin, Jr., J.J. & Taylor, S.A. (1992) Measuring Service Quality: A Reexamination and Extension. *Journal of Marketing*, **56**, July, pp. 55–68.

Cronin, Jr. J.J. & Taylor, S.A. (1994) SERVPERF Versus SERVQUAL: Reconciling Performance-Based and Perceptions-Minus-Expectations Measurement of Service Quality. *Journal of Marketing*, **58**, pp. 125–131.

Edvardsson, B. (1992) Service Breakdowns: A Study of Critical Incidents in an Airline. *International Journal of Service Industry Management*, **3**(4), pp. 17–29.

Fournier, S. (1998) Consumers and Their Brands: Developing Relationship Theory in Consumer Research. *Journal of Consumer Research*, **24**(4), pp. 343–373.

Gardner, M.P. (1985) Mood States and Consumer Behavior: A Critical Review. *Journal of Consumer Research*, **12**, December, pp. 281–300.

Gifford, Jr. D. (1997) Moving Beyond Loyalty. *Harvard Business Review*, **75**, March–April, pp. 9–10.

Grönroos, C. (1978) A Service-Orientated Approach to the Marketing of Services. *European Journal of Marketing*, **12**(8), pp. 588–601.

Grönroos, C. (1982) *Strategic Management and Marketing in the Service Sector*. Helsinki/Helsingfors: Swedish School of Economics, Finland (published in the USA in 1983 by Marketing Science Institute and in the UK in 1984 by Chartwell-Bratt).

Grönroos, C. (1984) A Service Quality Model and Its Marketing Implications. *European Journal of Marketing*, **18**(4), pp. 36–45.

Grönroos, C. (1993) Toward a Third Phase in Service Quality Research: Challenges and Future Directions. In Swartz, T.A., Bowen, D.E. & Brown, S.W. (eds), *Advances in Services Marketing and Management*, Volume 2, 1993, Greenwich, CT: JAI Press, pp. 49–64.

Gummesson, E. (1979) *Models of Professional Service Marketing*. Stockholm, Sweden: Liber/Marketing Technique Center.

Gummesson, E. (1987) *Quality—The Ericsson Approach*. Stockholm, Sweden: Ericsson.

Gummesson, E. (1993) *Quality Management in Service Organizations*. New York: ISQA International Service Quality Association.

Gummesson, E. (1999) Total Relationship Marketing: Experimenting With a Synthesis of Research Frontiers. *Australasian Marketing Journal*, **7**(1), pp. 72–85.

Holmlund, M. (1997) *Perceived Quality in Business Relationships*. Helsinki/Helsingfors: Hanken Swedish School of Economics, Finland/CERS Center for Relationship Marketing and Service Management.

Holmlund, M. & Strandvik, T. (1999) Perception Configuration in Business Relationships. *Management Decision*, **37**(9), pp. 686–696.

Knowles, P.A., Grove, S.J. & Pickett, G.M. (1999) Mood Versus Service Quality Effects on Customers' Responses to Service Organizations and Service Encounters. *Journal of Service Research*, **2**(2), pp. 189–199.

Leuthesser, L. (1997) Supplier Relational Behavior: An Empirical Assessment. *Industrial Marketing Management*, **26**(3), pp. 245–254.

Liljander, V. (1994) Introducing Deserved Service and Equity into Service Quality Models. In Kleinaltenkamp, M. (ed.), *Dienstleistungsmarketing—Konzeptionen und Anwendungen* (Service Marketing—Conceptualization and Implementation). In German. Berlin, Germany: Gabler Edition Wissenschaft, pp. 1–30.

Liljander, V. (1995) *Comparison Standards in Perceived Service Quality*, Helsinki/Helsingfors: Hanken Swedish School of Economics, Finland/CERS Center for Relationship Marketing and Service Management.

Liljander, V. & Strandvik, T. (1995) The Nature of Customer Relationships in Services. In Swartz, T.A., Bowen, D.E. & Brown, S.W. (eds), *Advances in Services Marketing and Management*, **4**, Greenwich, CT: JAI Press, pp. 141–167.

Liljander, V. & Strandvik, T. (1997) Emotions in Service Satisfaction. *International Journal of Service Industry Management*, **8**(2), pp. 148–169.

Murphy, P. (1999) Service Performance Measurement Using Simple Techniques Really Works. *Journal of Marketing Practice: Applied Marketing Science*, **5**(2), pp. 56–73.

Normann, R. (1992) *Service Management*. 2nd edition. New York: John Wiley & Sons.

Ojasalo, J. (1999) *Quality Dynamics in Professional Services*. Helsinki/ Helsingfors; Swedish School of Economics Finland/CERS Center for Relationship Marketing and Service Management.

Parasuraman, A., Berry, L.L. & Zeithaml, V.A. (1991) Refinement and Reassessment of the SERVQUAL Scale. *Journal of Retailing*, **67**(4), pp. 420–450.

Parasuraman, A., Zeithaml, V.A. & Berry, L.L. (1988) SERVQUAL: A Multiple-Item Scale for Measuring Consumer Perceptions of Service Quality. *Journal of Retailing*, **64**, Spring, pp. 12–40.

Rust, R.T. & Oliver, R.L. (1994) Service Quality: Insights and Managerial Implications From the Frontier. In Rust, R.T. & Oliver, R.L. (eds), *Service Quality: New Directions in Theory and Practice*. Thousand Oaks, CA: Sage Publications.

Wittreich, W.J. (1966) How to Buy/Sell Professional Services. *Harvard Business Review*, March–April, pp. 127–138.

Zeithaml, V.A. & Bitner, M.J. (2000) *Services Marketing*. 2nd edition. New York: McGraw-Hill.

Notes

1   Grönroos, C., *Strategic Management and Marketing in the Service Sector*. Helsinki/Helsingfors: Swedish School of Economics Finland, 1982 (published in the USA in 1983 by Marketing Science Institute and in UK in 1984 by Chartwell-Bratt). See also Grönroos, C., A Service Quality Model and Its Marketing Implications. *European Journal of Marketing*, **18**(4), 1984. Evert Gummesson was probably the first service marketing researcher to express the quality of services as perceived quality: in the context of professional services he concludes that "(quality) becomes a matter of subjectively *perceived* quality" (emphasis as in the original publication). See Gummesson, E., *Models of Professional Service Marketing*. Stockholm, Sweden: Liber/Marketing Technique Center, 1979, p. 9.

2   There is, however, some criticism of the use of customers' expectations as the only comparison standard in models and measurements of perceived service quality. See Liljander, V., *Comparison*

Standards in Perceived Service Quality, diss. Helsinki/Helsingfors, Finland: Hanken Swedish School of Economics Finland/CERS, 1995.

3   Rust, R.T. & Oliver, R.L., Service Quality: Insights and Managerial Implications From the Frontier. In Rust, R.T. & Oliver, R.L. (eds), *Service Quality: New Directions in Theory and Practice*. Thousand Oaks, CA: Sage Publications, 1994.

4   Bitner, M.J., Serviscapes: The Impact of Physical Surroundings on Customers and Employees. *Journal of Marketing*, **56**, April 1992, pp. 57–71. The *serviscape* consists of the physical resources, technology and other physical elements surrounding the service process. It helps to create the ambience of the service process. Thus, it is expected to have an impact on the way service employees and customers behave and interact in service encounters.

5   Holmlund, M., *Perceived Quality in Business Relationships*, diss. Helsinki/Helsingfors, Finland: Hanken Swedish School of Economics Finland/CERS, 1997.

6   Brogowicz, A.A., Delene, L.M. & Lyth, D.M., A Synthesised Service Quality Model with Managerial Implications. *International Journal of Service Industry Management*, **1**(1), 1990, pp. 27–45.

7   Gummesson, E., *Quality Management in Service Organizations*. New York: ISQA International Service Quality Association, 1993.

8   Normann, R., *Service Management*. 2nd edition. New York: John Wiley & Sons, 1992.

9   Liljander, V. & Strandvik, T., Emotions in Service Satisfaction. *International Journal of Service Industry Management*, **8**(2), 1997, pp. 148–169.

10   Gardner, M.P., Mood States and Consumer Behavior: A Critical Review. *Journal of Consumer Research*, **12**, December 1985, pp. 281–300.

11   Knowles, P.A., Grove, S.J. & Pickett, G.M., Mood Versus Service Quality Effects on Customers' Responses to Service Organizations and Service Encounters. *Journal of Service Research*, **2**(2), 1999, pp. 189–199.

12   This study was reported in Albrecht, K. & Zemke, R., *Service America*. Homewood, IL: Dow Jones-Irwin, 1985.

13   The conceptual and empirical results of their studies of service quality have been reported in a large number of articles. Key aspects are presented in Berry, L.L. & Parasuraman, A., *Marketing Services. Competing Through Quality*. New York: Free Press, 1992, and in Zeithaml, V.A. & Bitner, M.J., *Services Marketing*. 2nd edition. New York: McGraw-Hill, 2000.

14   Parasuraman, A., Zeithaml, V.A. & Berry, L.L., SERVQUAL: A Multiple-Item Scale for Measuring Consumer Perceptions of Service Quality. *Journal of Retailing*, **64**, Spring 1988, pp. 12–40.

15   A detailed description of the SERVQUAL instrument as well as the attributes used to measure the five determinants can be found in Parasuraman, A., Berry, L.L. & Zeithaml, V.A., Refinement and Reassessment of the SERVQUAL Scale. *Journal of Retailing*, **67**(4), 1991, pp. 420–450.

16   Murphy, P., Service Performance Measurement Using Simple Techniques Really Works. *Journal of Marketing Practice: Applied Marketing Science*, **5**(2), 1999, pp. 56–73.

17   Grönroos, C., Toward a Third Phase in Service Quality Research: Challenges and Future Directions. In Swartz, T.A., Bowen, D.E. & Brown, S.W. (eds), *Advances in Services Marketing and Management*, Volume 2, 1993, Greenwich, CT: JAI Press, 1993, p. 56.

18   Liljander, *op.cit.*

19   Cronin, Jr., J.J. & Taylor, S.A., Measuring Service Quality: A Re-examination and Extension. *Journal of Marketing*, **56**, July 1992, pp. 55–68. See also Cronin, Jr. J.J. & Taylor, S.A., SERVPERF Versus SERVQUAL: Reconciling Performance-Based and Perceptions-Minus-Expectations Measurement of Service Quality. *Journal of Marketing*, **58**, 1994, pp. 125–131.

20   See, for example, Bitner, M.J., Booms, B.H. & Tetrault, M.S., The Service Encounter: Diagnosing Favorable and Unfavorable Incidents. *Journal of Marketing*, **54**, January, 1990, pp. 71–84, and Edvardsson, B., Service Breakdowns: A Study of Critical Incidents in an Airline. *International Journal of Service Industry Management*, **3**(4), 1992, pp. 17–29.

21   Bitner, *op.cit.*, and Rust & Oliver, *op.cit.*

22   Grönroos 1993, *op.cit.*

23   Evert Gummesson introduced the *relationship quality* concept in 1987 as part of a study of quality in an Ericsson Quality program. With this concept he drew attention to the fact that relationships are part of customer perceived quality. See Gummesson, E., *Quality—The Ericsson Approach*. Stockholm, Sweden: Ericsson, 1987.

24   Relationship quality has been studied to a very limited extent. Therefore, general attributes or antecedents of relationship quality cannot be presented. There are some studies that give valuable

indications. From a consumer brand perspective, see Gifford, Jr. D., Moving Beyond Loyalty. *Harvard Business Review*, **75**, March–April 1997, pp. 9–10, and Fournier, S., Consumers and Their Brands: Developing Relationship Theory in Consumer Research. *Journal of Consumer Research*, **24**(4), 1998, pp. 343–373, and from a business relationship perspective, see Leuthesser, L., Supplier Relational Behavior: An Empirical Assessment. *Industrial Marketing Management*, **26**(3), 1997, pp. 245–254.

25   This observation has always been evident in Nordic School research into service marketing, and it has become more and more evident as the relationship aspect of buyer–seller interactions in services and in any types of businesses is studied. See Gummesson, E., Total Relationship Marketing: Experimenting With a Synthesis of Research Frontiers. *Australasian Marketing Journal*, **7**(1), 1999, pp. 72–85, and Grönroos, C., A Service-Orientated Approach to the Marketing of Services. *European Journal of Marketing*, **12**(8), 1978, pp. 588–601.

26   Holmlund 1997, *op.cit.* Although this framework was originally developed in a business-to-business context, it is equally suited for understanding and analyzing relationships in consumer markets.

27   In the context of services the interaction process has been studied in terms of *acts*, *episodes* and *relationships*. According to Liljander and Strandvik an episode is, for example, a visit to a bank office to discuss a loan, whereas an act is the meeting with the loan officer during the visit. Several interactions related to, for example, withdrawal of money, payment of bills, etc. form a relationship. See Liljander, V., Introducing Deserved Service and Equity into Service Quality Models. In Kleinaltenkamp, M. (ed.), *Dienstleistungsmarketing—Konzeptionen und Anwendungen*. In German. Berlin, Germany: Gabler Edition Wissenschaft, 1994, pp. 1–30, and Liljander, V. & Strandvik, T., The Nature of Customer Relationships in Services. In Swartz, T.A., Bowen, D.E. & Brown, S.W. (eds), *Advances in Services Marketing and Management*. Vol. 4, Greenwich, CT: JAI Press, 1995, pp. 141–167. Holmlund has added a *sequence* level and has, based on these concepts, offered a relationship framework. See Holmlund 1997, *op.cit.*

28   Liljander & Strandvik, *op.cit.*

29   Compare also Andreassen, T.W. & Lindestad, B., The Effect of Corporate Image in the Formation of Customer Loyalty. *Journal of Service Research*, **1**(1), 1998, pp. 82–92.

30   In ongoing relationships a two-party situation is formed. When developing instruments for the measurement of relationship quality, especially in business-to-business markets, this fact should be taken into account: the quality perception of both parties in the relationship should be measured. An interesting conceptual foundation for such an instrument is developed in Holmlund, M. & Strandvik, T., Perception Configuration in Business Relationships. *Management Decision*, **37**(9), 2000, pp. 686–696.

31   Ojasalo, J., *Quality Dynamics in Professional Services*. Helsinki/Helsingfors; Swedish School of Economics Finland/CERS, 1999.

32   Ojasalo, *op.cit.*

33   Wittreich, W.J., How to Buy/Sell Professional Services. *Harvard Business Review*, March–April 1966, pp. 127–138.

34   The term "implied-in-fact" promises is used by Henrik Calonius to indicate unclear promises by marketers that create unrealistic expectations. See Calonius, H., The Promise Concept. In Blomqvist, H.C., Grönroos, C. & Lindqvist, L.-J. (eds), *Economics and Marketing. Essays in Honour of Gösta Mickwitz*. Helsinki/Helsingfors: Swedish School of Economics Finland, 1992, pp. 37–56.

Chapter 5

QUALITY MANAGEMENT IN SERVICES

It is important for a firm to manage service quality well, but it is essential for it to manage service failures even better.

Introduction

After discussing the nature of service and relationship quality in Chapter 4, this chapter now turns to various models for the management of quality in service contexts. In this chapter the gap analysis framework and other holistic models for service quality management are discussed. The tolerance zone concept and the shape of the quality function are also described, then quality management in situations where a service failure or another problem has occurred is discussed at some length. Service recovery, as opposed to traditional complaints-handling as well as elements of a service recovery process, are discussed. In addition, the timing of service recovery and various timing strategies are put forward. After having read the chapter the reader should understand how quality can be managed in services; for example, by using the gap analysis approach and following a quality development structure, and he should know how service recovery should be taken care of in situations where a service failure has occurred.

Why Managers Hesitate to Invest in Services and Service Quality

Managers often believe that developing and offering services with 100 per cent quality is impossible. Consequently, the organization accepts that mistakes happen, and failures are allowed. Psychologically, the battle for excellent performance is over before it has even begun.

Tom Gillett, Director of Services of telecommunications firm GTT, used to tell his employees the following anecdote when they argued that in the complex telecommunications business top quality could not be achieved and thus could not be offered to their customers: "Imagine a large international airport with hundreds of take-offs and landings each day. If they accepted a quality level of 99 per cent, they would have a number of accidents every day. That just cannot be allowed to happen. And can you imagine a more difficult and technically complicated service and service production system than that of an airport?" The conclusion is, of course, that if an airport can offer and maintain a 100 per cent quality level, you can do it as well, whatever your business is.

Saying and perhaps even believing that a particular firm's services are so complex and difficult to produce that top quality cannot be achieved is just an excuse for not trying hard enough. True, hard work and long-term effort may be required, but it is never impossible.

Some Reasons Why Quality Improvement Processes Fail

In spite of the obvious benefits of improving quality, many firms which have implemented quality programs feel that these programs did not pay off. Normally, the problem is in a firm's approach to quality enhancement. If it is only considered as a program or project, if a limited time frame is given to the effort, and it is perceived by everybody in the organization, top management and all other employees alike, as simply a tactical issue, the risk of failure is high. For some managers, quality improvement is a matter of time-and-motion studies or investment in machinery or equipment which allows the firm to reduce its labor force. For others, it means a training program, or introducing a new monetary reward system.

While all these elements can be parts of a quality improvement process, as isolated programs they are bound to fail in the long run. The main problem is in the approach. Quality enhancement must not be considered as a program, or even worse a campaign, but has to be an ongoing *process*. A continuous appreciation of the importance of quality and an understanding of how to influence good service quality is required of every individual in the organization, and this has to be constantly maintained by management. Quality, and hence quality improvement and management processes, are strategic issues, which require continuous attention by top management.

How Good Should Quality Be?

A question which is often asked is how good should be the optimal quality of a given service? First of all, the answer depends on the strategy of the firm and the expectations of the customers for whom its services are intended. And these two factors are dependent on each other. A service provider, where strategy is to be the best on the market and cater to customers demanding excellent service, should first create such expectations among its potential customers, and second provide a service quality which is perceived as excellent. The strategy of another firm may be to provide a less demanding target group of customers with service of a lower quality, at a lower price. In this case, the level of service quality can be lower, but the expectations that the customers are given should not deviate from

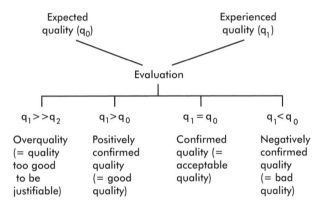

FIGURE 5.1 The quality evaluation options. Reprinted with permission from *Emerging Perspectives on Services Marketing*, published by the American Marketing Association, Berry, L.L., Shostack, G.L. & Upah, G. (eds), 1983.

the real level of quality. If, in this situation, expectations and experiences meet, the perceived quality is still good.

Figure 5.1 illustrates the possible perceived quality outcomes. In principle, there are four possible outcomes—underquality, confirmed quality, positively confirmed quality, and overquality. Good quality, of course, requires that experiences at least equal expectations, or exceed expectations, otherwise the quality expectations of customers are not met. *Acceptable quality* is always required. However, if the firm wants to make its customers really happy with its services, acceptable quality may not be enough.

Positively confirmed quality should, then, be the objective to aim for. There is a danger here, of course. If the perceived quality is too high, the costs of production are probably unnecessarily high. The cost–benefit ratio will be low or may even be negative. Then we have *overquality*, which cannot be justified for economic reasons. Moreover, overquality may simply be perceived by the customer to exceed what is really needed, which in turn can even create bad word of mouth. Overquality may also give the impression that the service is overpriced, even if this is not the case.

There is an often-mentioned ground rule that customers should get a little bit more than they expect. Acceptable quality (confirmed quality where expectations are met but no more) satisfies a customer but does not necessarily make him feel that this is a relationship with a service provider that must not be broken. It does not make the customer talk about his experiences to friends, neighbors and business associates. Positively confirmed quality when expectations are exceeded to some extent, which is sometimes also called *customer delight*, may make customers more interested in continuing the relationship with the service provider, and this also creates good word of mouth benefits. The positively surprised customer remembers the experience and often likes to talk about it.

Critics of this ground rule argue that customers learn from their experiences and the next time their expectations are higher. This will lead to an upward spiral where the firm in the end cannot, profitably at least, produce a quality level which meets the increased level of expectations. However, surprising customers does not necessarily mean providing them with something that raises expectations. Normally the surprise effect can be achieved by a small gesture that does not cost anything and which leads to a similar positive feeling on the part of the customer every time. It is also important to note that the expectations of customers can be exceeded and customers can be surprised regardless of the level of the quality of a given service. The same positive effects on loyalty and on word of mouth can be achieved by small surprises in situations where the level of service quality is low. It does not matter whether the level of expectations is high or low or in between.

Service providers should not, however, provide customers with a surprising effect once, and then revert to a previous quality level. Rust and Oliver call this "hit-and-run delight."[1] According to them, a firm which does this will be worse off than if it had not, because a one-time rise in quality experience will increase expectations, and the next time customers will be dissatisfied. Dissatisfaction causes more negative effects than the positive effects created by one-time surprise. Hence, offering customers more than they expect once only may create higher expectations that damage the firm at the next service encounter, when customers experience a lower-quality service experience. However, when a higher level of experiences is constantly offered, customers may forget the surprise element from one occasion to another. The surprise-creating element may be remembered, but the feeling of surprise it causes is not. Then the same surprising experience can be repeated again, and the same positive quality effect be achieved every time.[2]

Case Study: Go the Extra Mile to Make the Customer's Day

Inspired by the Asian economic crisis in the final years of the 1990s, the Shangri-La Hotel in Bangkok, as seems to be the industry standard among luxury hotels in the region, appears to have downsized out of proportion. In spite of the fact that the number of employees attending to guests during breakfast and happy hour in Horizon Club (the hotel's executive floor) is much less than it was before the crisis and that the employees seemed to be constantly overworked, Ms Tippawan, one of the employees, found the time to show special concern for a guest whom she found out was temporarily ill with a nasty cold and high fever. She insisted that she fetched hot soup from the kitchen for the guest and served it in his room. Said Ms Tippawan, "hot soup in the morning is good for this illness." Every morning she brought a different kind of soup, until the guest was up on his feet again after a few days. By showing this extraordinary care and concern, she made the guest's day, and he was positively surprised every time.

Managing Service Quality: The Gap Analysis Approach

Berry and his colleagues have developed what they call a *Gap Analysis Model*, which is intended to be used for analyzing sources of quality problems and for helping managers understand how service quality can be improved.[3] The model is illustrated in Figure 5.2.

CONSUMER

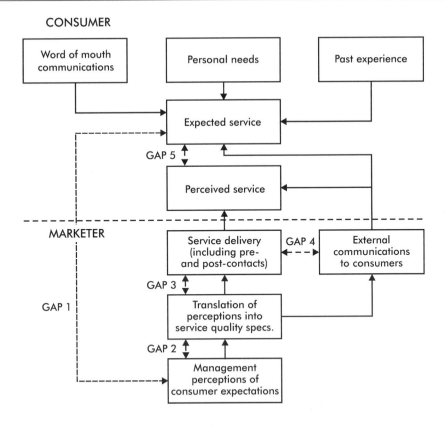

FIGURE 5.2 Conceptual model of service quality—the gap analysis model. Reprinted with permission from the *Journal of Marketing*, published by the American Marketing Association, Zeithaml, V.A., Berry, L.L. & Parasuraman, A., 1988, p. 36.

First of all, the model demonstrates how service quality emerges. The upper part of the model includes phenomena related to the customer, while the lower part shows phenomena related to the service provider. The *expected service* is a function of the customer's *past experience* and *personal needs* and of *word of mouth communication*. It is also influenced by the *market communication* activities of the firm.

The service experienced, which in this model is called the *perceived service*, on the other hand, is the outcome of a series of internal decisions and activities. *Management perceptions of customer expectations* guide decisions about *service quality specifications* to be followed by the organization, when *service delivery* (the execution of the service process), takes place. The customer, of course, experiences the service delivery and production process as a process-related quality component, and the technical solution received by the process as an outcome-related quality component. As is illustrated, *marketing communication* can be expected to influence the perceived service as well as the expected service.

This basic structure demonstrates the steps that have to be considered when analyzing and planning service quality. Possible sources of quality problems can then be detected. In Figure 5.2 five discrepancies between the various elements of the basic structure, so-called *quality gaps*, are illustrated. These quality gaps are the result of inconsistencies in the quality management process. The ultimate gap, that is, the gap between expected and perceived (experienced) service (Gap 5), is, of course, a function of the other gaps that may have occurred in the process. The five gaps, their consequences, and the reasons why they occur are discussed in the next section.

Managing the Quality Gaps

The Management Perception Gap (Gap 1)

This gap means that *management perceives the quality expectations inaccurately*. This gap is due to:

- inaccurate information from market research and demand analyses;
- inaccurately interpreted information about expectations;
- nonexistent demand analysis;
- bad or nonexistent upward information from the firm's interface with its customers to management; and
- too many organizational layers which stop or change the pieces of information that may flow upward from those involved in customer contacts.

There may be various cures. If problems are due to bad management, obviously either a change of management or an improvement in the knowledge of the characteristics of service competition on the part of management is required. Most often, but not always, the latter action is more appropriate, because normally the problems have not occurred because of a genuine lack of competence but rather because of a lack of knowledge or appreciation of the nature and demands of service competition among managers.

Part of any cure is always better research, so that the needs and wishes of customers are better observed and appreciated. The information obtained through market research and from internal flows of information from the customer interface is perhaps not good enough or only partly appropriate. Necessary action to open up or improve the various internal information channels has to be taken in such cases. This may even have implications for the organizational structure of the firm.

The Quality Specification Gap (Gap 2)

This gap means that *service quality specifications are not consistent with management perceptions of quality expectations*. This gap is a result of:

- planning mistakes or insufficient planning procedures;
- bad management of planning;
- lack of clear goal-setting in the organization; and
- insufficient support for planning for service quality from top management.

Depending on the size of the first gap, the potential planning-related problems vary. However, even in a situation where there is enough and sufficiently accurate information on customer expectations, planning of quality specifications may fail. A fairly normal reason for this is a lack of real commitment to service quality among top management, because quality is not considered an issue of highest priority. An obvious cure in such a situation is to change a firm's priorities. Quality as perceived by customers is such a vital success factor today, certainly in service competition, that it is imperative that commitment to quality ranks high on the priority list of management.

Of course, the problem may be in the planning process itself. Those providing the services also have to feel a commitment to the quality specifications. This has to be taken into account in goal-setting and planning routines. Planning from the top without the collaboration of those who actually produce the service should be avoided. Ideally, goals and specifications should be agreed upon by the service providers as well as by the planners and management. Also, it is good to remember that too-rigid specifications damage flexibility and decrease the willingness of employees to take flexible actions involving risks. And this, again, usually damages service quality.

In summary, commitment to service quality among management as well as service providers is far more important in closing the Quality Specification Gap than any too-rigid goal-setting and planning procedure.

The Service Delivery Gap (Gap 3)

This gap means that *quality specifications are not met by performance in the service production and delivery process*. This gap is due to:

- specifications which are too complicated and/or too rigid;
- employees not agreeing with the specifications and therefore not fulfilling them;
- specifications not being in line with the existing corporate culture;
- bad management of service operations;
- lacking or insufficient internal marketing; and
- technology and systems not facilitating performance according to specifications.

The possible problems here are many and varied, and normally the reasons for the existence of a Service Delivery Gap are complicated. There is seldom only one reason, and the cure is, therefore, usually complicated. The reasons for this gap can be divided into three categories: management and supervision, employee perception of specifications and rules/customer needs and wishes, and lack of technological/operational support.

Management- and supervision-related problems may also be varied. For example, supervisors may not be encouraging and supportive of quality behavior, or the supervisory control systems may be in conflict with good service or even with quality specifications. In any organization where control and reward systems are decided upon separately from the planning of quality specifications, which is the case far too often, there is an inherent risk of a Service Delivery Gap occurring. And this risk is not small. Too often non-essential or unimportant activities are controlled, perhaps even rewarded; and activities that contradict quality specifications are encouraged by the control system. They too may even be rewarded. Of course, this puts employees in an extremely awkward position. Control and reward systems partly determine the corporate culture, and goals and specifications that do not fit the existing culture tend not to be well executed. The cure here involves changes in the way managers and supervisors treat their subordinates, and in the way supervisory systems control and reward performance. Larger issues related to the culture of the firm and internal marketing may also have to be attended to. We will return to the issues of internal marketing and corporate culture in Chapters 14 and 15.

From what has been discussed above it follows, among other things, that employees may feel that their role as service providers is ambiguous. We have already mentioned the way in which performance requirements of the specifications, on the one hand, and existing control and reward systems, on the other hand, are in conflict with each other. An awkward situation could also occur for personnel when a customer contact person realizes that a customer, or many customers, requires different behavior on the part of the service provider than that expected according to the company's existing specifications. The service provider knows that the customer is not getting what he expects and may feel that the demands and wishes of the customer are justified and perhaps could be fulfilled, but the service provider is not allowed to perform accordingly. This slowly but surely kills any motivation for quality-enhancing behavior among personnel.

The cure in situations like these is to remove all reasons for ambiguity on the part of the personnel. This may, on the one hand, require changes in the supervisory systems so that they are in line with the quality specifications. It may, on the other hand, also require better employee training, so that they are aware of the limitations for performance due to, for example, strategic considerations or profitability reasons. Here again the issue of internal marketing is critical.

Finally, the skills and attitudes of personnel may cause problems. It may be that the wrong people have been recruited in the first place. The firm may have people who cannot adjust to the specifications and systems that guide operations, however justifiable they are. The cure in this situation is, of course, to improve recruitment processes so that poor decisions can be avoided. Furthermore, the workload perceived by employees may be a problem. There may, for example, be too much paperwork or other administrative tasks involved, so that quality specifications cannot be fulfilled. Because of this, the service provider does not have time to attend to customers as expected.

The cure is to clarify the tasks of all personnel and to find a solution where necessary tasks are dealt with without interfering with quality performance. Finally, the technology or the systems of operating, including decision-making and other routines, may not suit the employees. The problem may be the employees, of course, but it is more probable that technology and operational and administrative systems have been introduced in the wrong way. Perhaps technology and the company's systems do not support quality behavior, or they have not been properly introduced to the employees who are expected to live with them. The cure is either to make proper changes to technology and systems so that they are supportive of the execution of the quality specifications or again to improve training and internal marketing.

The Market Communication Gap (Gap 4)

This gap means that *promises given by market communication activities are not consistent with the service delivered*. This gap is due to:

- market communication planning not being integrated with service operations;
- lacking or insufficient coordination between traditional external marketing and operations;
- the organization failing to perform according to specifications, whereas market communication campaigns follow these specifications; and
- an inherent propensity to exaggerate and, thus, promise too much.

The reasons for the occurrence of a Market Communication Gap can be divided into two categories, namely, the planning and executing of external market communication and operations and a company's propensity to overpromise in all advertising and market communication.

In the first case, the cure is to create a system that coordinates planning and execution of external market communication campaigns with service operations and delivery. For example, every major campaign should be planned in collaboration with those involved in service production and delivery. Two goals can be achieved by this. First, promises in market communication become more accurate and realistic. Second, a greater commitment to what is promised in external campaigns can be achieved, which also has the effect that more can be promised than otherwise would be the case. The second category of problems, overpromising because of the very nature of market communication where superlatives are far too easily used, can only be dealt with by improving planning of market communication. The cure may be better planning procedures, but closer management supervision also helps.

The Perceived Service Quality Gap (Gap 5)

This gap means that *the perceived or experienced service is not consistent with the expected service*. This gap results in:

- negatively confirmed quality (bad quality) and a quality problem;
- bad word of mouth;
- a negative impact on corporate or local image; and
- lost business.

The fifth gap may, of course, also be positive, which leads either to a positively confirmed quality or overquality. If a Perceived Service Quality Gap occurs, the reason for this could be any of those discussed in this section, or any combination of these. Of course, there may also be other reasons in addition to those mentioned here.

The Gap Analysis Model should guide management in finding out where the reason (or reasons) for the quality problem lie and in discovering appropriate ways to close this gap. Gap analysis is a straightforward and appropriate way of identifying inconsistencies between a service provider and customer perceptions of service performance. Addressing these gaps is a logical basis for developing service processes in which expectations and experiences consistently meet. In this way the likelihood of good perceived service quality will be increased.

Managing Tolerance Zones

According to the disconfirmation concept of the Perceived Service Quality model, according to which the experiences of customers are compared to their expectations, customers' expectations of the level of a given service attribute is thought of and measured as one singular level of expectation. No variation in expectations is included. The *Zone of Tolerance* concept has been suggested by Leonard Berry and his colleagues,[4] because they considered the underlying assumption of this concept too simplistic.

The Zone of Tolerance concept assumes that customers do not have expectations of a service attribute on *one* given level. Rather, they can tolerate a variation in the real experiences and still consider them acceptable according to their expectations. This concept implies that customers' expectations exist on two levels, a *desired level* and an *adequate level*. The desired level reflects on what level the service *should* be, whereas the adequate level is what customers believe it *could* be. The latter level is the least acceptable level of the service experience. These two levels of expectations form the borders of customers' *zone of tolerance*. If the real experiences of a customer fall in between these borders, they are tolerated by him and the perceived quality is considered good.

The zone of tolerance can of course vary from customer to customer, and from service attribute to service attribute. It may also, for a given customer, vary from time to time. It is suggested that, in general, it is narrower for outcome-related service features and broader for process-related features. This means that customers generally tolerate more variation in the process (expectations related to the *functional quality* dimension) than in the outcome of the process (expectations related to the *technical quality* dimension). In addition, if a service encounter does not go well and a service failure has to be corrected, the zone of tolerance diminishes, regarding both outcome-related and process-related service features.

Measuring the zone of tolerance of expectations and comparing them to the experiences of customers may give management useful information about where service quality problems exist, and where there is no need for immediate action. For those attributes where the experience measurement falls in between the desired and adequate levels of expectations the level of perceived service quality is at least tolerable. Again, for those attributes where the experience measurement is lower than the adequate level immediate corrections may be required, so that the overall level of perceived service quality does not decrease. It is of course more urgent to take action if such an attribute is considered central to customers' quality perception, than if its impact is only marginal.

The Shape of the Quality Function

In the service quality models it is normally assumed that the quality function is linear; that is, as the performance of a service provider improves, the perceived quality increases at the same pace, and vice versa. In Figure 5.3 this assumption is illustrated at the left of the figure. In reality, this relationship varies between customers and between quality attributes, and probably also between one customer's perception of different service encounters. However, the quality function is probably not linear at all.[5]

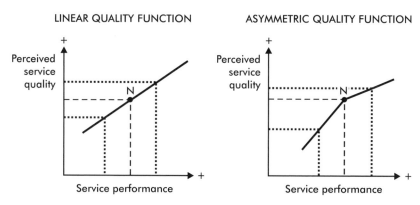

FIGURE 5.3 Linear and assymetric quality functions. Expanded from Strandvik, T., *Tolerance Zones in Perceived Service Quality*. Helsink/Helsingfors: Swedish School of Economics, Finland, 1994, p. 154.

At the right of Figure 5.3 a typical quality function is illustrated. When the service firm performs better than normal (denoted with the letter N in the figure), perceived service quality increases at a lower pace than it decreases when the firm performs below its normal level. This *asymmetric shape of the quality function*[6] means, among other things, that it is easier to make a bad impression when quality deteriorates than it is to please a customer with quality above the normal expected level. Another conclusion is that it is dangerous for a service provider to let its overall performance, or performance on some critical attributes, drop below normal expectations, because the quality perception then decreases quickly. On the other hand it is difficult to increase the quality perception above normal, because the service performance has to be improved (relatively speaking) much more to lead to significant results. As the figure demonstrates, a given increase in service performance has a much smaller effect on the perceived service quality than does a similar decrease.

For example, if an Internet shop responds to a customer's inquiry or order more slowly than this customer considers normal, speeding up the response time can be expected to have a rapid impact on the perceived quality. However, improving perceived quality by answering even faster than this normal level will have a much smaller impact on the customer's quality perception.

Another assumption that is often made in the literature is that all quality attributes are equally important. However, there may be a clear distinction between the effect on perceived quality of different attributes. Customers are perhaps not loss-aversive in relation to all quality attributes as indicated above. Again, there is probably a difference between customers and between various types of services, but generally it seems as if different attributes have a different impact on the quality perception. The main thing is that some attributes may be necessary for a good perception of service quality, but if they are improved then this does not have a significant positive effect on perceived quality. Reliability, functionality and competence could be examples of such *hygiene factors*. Other quality attributes may be *quality-enhancing factors*, where a higher level of performance has a positive effect on the quality perception, whereas there is no significant negative effect once it has reached a certain low level. Friendliness, attentiveness, cleanliness and availability could be examples of such attributes. There may also be quality attributes that influence perceived quality *both ways*. Comfort, communication and courtesy could be examples of such attributes.[7]

For example, the *reliability* of an airline assuring a passenger that he will arrive at the destination on time is an essential hygiene factor. Delays have negative effects on quality perception. Arriving ahead of time probably has no, or a very limited, positive effect. On the other hand, the *friendliness* and *attentiveness* of the in-flight personnel and the cleanliness of restrooms are quality-enhancing factors that linearly increase the quality perception. However, when they have reached a certain low point, passengers will have become so frustrated or annoyed that an even worse performance will not further decrease their quality perception.

Another related way of studying quality attributes is to divide them into *satisfiers* and *dissatisfiers*.[8] According to a major study in the banking industry in the UK,[9] *attentiveness*, *care* and *friendliness* are examples of predominantly satisfying determinants. Good performance on such determinants causes an increase in perceived service quality, whereas poor performance below a certain expectations level does not necessarily have a further damaging effect on quality. *Integrity*, *reliability*, *availability*, and *functionality* are examples of dissatisfiers. Good performance above a certain expectation level on such attributes does not increase the perceived service quality, whereas poorer performance has a negative effect on quality.

In this study *responsiveness* was found to be both a satisfier and dissatisfier. This is a crucial observation, because this quality attribute is often considered to have a decisive impact on satisfaction with quality. The different ways satisfiers and dissatisfiers work are illustrated in Figure 5.4. On the left one can see how changes in the performance level of satisfiers impact perceived quality, whereas the reverse effects of dissatisfiers are shown. The normal expected level of quality attributes is denoted by the letter N.

The research results reported in this section are somewhat contradictory, which may be a result of cultural or industry differences or different ways of measuring quality. However, it is important for managers responsible for service quality to bear in mind that various quality attributes or factors that are

SATISFIERS   DISSATISFIERS

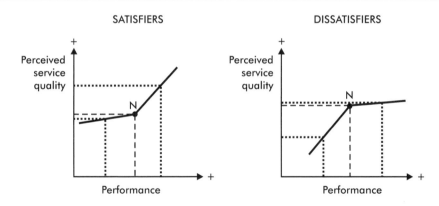

FIGURE 5.4   Service quality attributes: the effect of satisfiers versus dissatisfiers

perceived by customers as part of the quality experience may function in different ways. The examples mentioned are relevant to some services and some customers, and function in this way in some cultures, but in other cases other attributes may function as hygiene, quality-enhancing or two-way factors, and as satisfiers or dissatisfiers. Investing in further improvement of hygiene factors and neglecting investments in quality-enhancing or two-way factors, or investing in dissatisfiers above the acceptable expectations level are clearly ineffective strategies and a waste of money. Such investments are, however, easily made, if one does not have a clear picture of the quality-influencing nature of various quality attributes.

Lessons of Service Quality and Quality Management Research

The models and frameworks of customer perceived service quality and how to manage service quality presented in this chapter demonstrate a number of important lessons learned from research into service quality. Some of these issues have also been focused on in studies of good quality management. The lessons are as follows.

1. *Quality is what customers perceive.* Quality cannot be determined by management alone; it has to be based on customer needs, wishes, and expectations. Moreover, quality is not what is planned in objective measures; instead it is how customers subjectively perceive what is delivered.
2. *Quality cannot be separated from the service process (the production and delivery process).* The outcome of the service production process is only part of the customer perceived service quality. The production and delivery process itself is perceived by customers who also actively participate in this process. Therefore, the perception of the process and of the buyer–seller interactions of this process becomes another part of total quality. From a competitive point of view, this *functional quality* dimension is frequently equally important as, or even more important than, the *technical quality* of the outcome.

3. *Quality is produced locally in a series of moments of truth of service encounters or buyer–seller interactions.* Because of the existence of the important functional quality dimension of total service quality, the buyer–seller interactions, including a number of moments of truth (or moments of opportunity) become a pivotal factor in quality perception. Since buyer–seller interactions take place locally, where the customer meets the service provider, and not in centrally located quality design and planning departments, quality is also produced locally. Therefore, the planning and design of quality has to move out to the local level. Technical quality aspects and the overall design of how to create quality can, of course, be planned centrally, but the interface between the organization and its customers has to be involved in quality management and design as well. Otherwise, well-designed quality may remain a desk product which does not materialize in good customer perceived quality.

4. *Everyone contributes to customer perceived quality.* As quality is created and produced in buyer–seller interactions of service encounters, a large number of employees become involved in the production of quality. Since these customer contact employees who handle customer contacts in order to serve their customers well are dependent on the support of people beyond them in the service process, these "support" people also become responsible for the ultimate customer perceived quality. Hence, most employees contribute to quality. If someone in the customer services department or beyond the direct customer interface fails, quality suffers.

5. *Quality has to be monitored throughout the organization by the whole organization.* As quality is produced by a large number of people and departments throughout the organization, quality performance has to be monitored and assured at the point where a quality contribution is produced. A centrally located quality control and management staff cannot normally do this. The task is overwhelming; and having a separate staff department for this has a negative effect psychologically on the people in the organization. The mere fact that such a department exists can easily draw the attention of those producing quality away from quality assurance. It is easy for other employees to stop worrying about the tricky issue of constantly producing, maintaining and monitoring quality when there is a group of specialists to turn to, and to blame when problems occur. Such a staff function may contribute to quality assurance, monitoring and design if it is perceived by everyone as an internal consultancy function in quality issues. However, the organization itself has to do the job of assuring quality.

6. *External marketing has to be integrated into quality management.* Customer-perceived quality is a function of expectations as well as of real experiences. Therefore, improvement of quality experiences may be counteracted by, say, a marketing campaign that promises improvements or gives customers reason to believe that improvements will be greater than they really are. Customer expectations which are not met by reality will be created. The perceived quality is bad, although improvements, objectively measured, may have taken place. Such negative external marketing effects may have far-reaching consequences, for example, because this creates negative publicity and the image of the firm may be damaged. If marketing campaigns are

planned in collaboration with those responsible for the quality improvement process, these mistakes can be avoided. Hence, external marketing, marketing communication and sales have to be integrated with quality management.

A Service Quality Management Program

In this chapter we have discussed concepts and models of perceived service quality, in order to develop an understanding of how service quality is formed and perceived by customers, as well as an understanding of how important aspects of service quality can be managed. In the present section we will sum up these concepts and models in the form of a management-oriented *Service Quality Management Program*. This program is intended to help management implement a service strategy to respond to the challenges of the constantly increasing service competition. If the organization has decided to pursue a service strategy, the Service Quality Management Program should, for managerial purposes, give adequate guidance in what to do.

The Service Quality Management Program consists of seven *subprograms*. These are:

1. service concept development;
2. customer expectations management program;
3. service outcome management program;
4. internal marketing program;
5. physical environment (serviscape) and physical resources management program;
6. information technology management program;
7. customer participation management program.

These will now be described separately in more detail.

1. *Service concept development*. The establishment of customer-oriented service concepts which guide the management of resources and activities to be used in the service process is, of course, the first task in the service quality development process.
2. *Customer expectations management program*. Traditional external marketing and sales activities should never be planned and implemented in isolation. They should always be related to the experiences the service provider is willing and able to deliver to its customers. Otherwise, there will always be a quality problem, irrespective of the other quality development subprograms. Therefore, managing customer expectations must always be an integral part of any service quality program. This makes, for example, managing external market communication and sales part of quality management.
3. *Service outcome management program*. The outcome of the service process (i.e. what customers get as a technical quality of the service), is part of the total service experience. The outcome of the service production process has to be developed and managed according to the service concepts agreed upon, and the specific needs of the target customers.

4. *Internal marketing program.* As we have demonstrated, the functional quality of the process (i.e. how the service process is perceived by customers) is the key in most cases to an excellent service quality and to achieving a winning competitive edge. Most frequently this quality dimension is predominantly due to the courtesy, flexibility and general service-mindedness of the customer contact employees, and to their ability and willingness to perform in a customer-oriented fashion. Hence, the employees, contact staff, managers and other employee categories have to be considered a first, *internal market* of the service provider. A continuous and strategically backed up internal marketing process is, therefore, a vital part of any quality development and management program.

5. *Physical environment (serviscape) and physical resources management program.* The physical resources, technology, and computing systems of service organizations are too frequently developed according to internal efficiency standards. The external effects of, for example, a computer system failure are seldom taken into account to a proper degree. Consequently, these resources, which constitute a technology base for service production as well as the physical environment for service consumption, may have a negative impact on customers' perception of the service process. Hence, a physical environment and physical resources management program should be part of an overall quality program.

6. *Information technology management program.* Customers make increasing use of information technology-based systems; for example, using a Web site on the Internet, to get access to information, feedback or support from a service firm, to making purchases on the Internet or to use some kind of IT applications as part of a service process. Therefore, the service provider must invest in appropriate information technology and must upgrade software and hardware as technology and applications advances. Hence, an information technology management program is required.

7. *Customer participation management program.* Customers should be advised how to act in the service process, so that they have a favorable impact on the process themselves. The service quality can be destroyed by customers who either do not know what to do or do not want to perform according to the service provider's intentions. Negative effects of fellow customers, causing queues, for example, must also be avoided, if possible. Eliminating unfavorable effects on the service process of a misfit between customer segments and individual customers is also part of a customer participation management program.

Service Recovery: Managing Quality When Service Failures Occur

The real test of the customer orientation of a service provider takes place when a service failure has occurred. Ideally, quality should be high all the time and failures should not occur in the service processes. However, employees make mistakes, systems break down, customers in the service process may cause problems for other customers, or a customer may not know how to participate in the process or may change his mind regarding some aspect of the service during the process. As a consequence, the planned service process will not lead to a good result for the customer. The intended level of quality is not achieved. It is important to realize that such a failure does not always result from mistakes made by the service firm; the customer or customers can also cause service failures. However, regardless of whether the firm, the customer, or something else is to blame, every problematic situation for a customer is an opportunity for the service provider to demonstrate its commitment to service.

Hence, regardless of the reason for a failure, the service provider has to take care of the situation and is responsible for solving the problem in a way that satisfies the customer. Unless this is done, the customer will feel that he received poor quality, and the risk of losing that customer grows. Or if complaining customers feel that their complaint is not handled quickly enough and with enough attention and empathy, the quality of the whole relationship will deteriorate. If there is a quality problem in the service process, the service has to be performed very carefully and accurately the second time.[10] Research shows that service providers are often offered a second chance to create a positive quality perception by customers even though a service process has broken down.[11] The way a firm manages service recovery forms a platform for strengthened or weakened customer relationships. A well-managed recovery has a positive impact on the development of a trusting relationship between a firm and its customer and it also may deepen the customer's commitment towards the service provider.[12]

As discussed in the previous chapter, service recovery is a factor influencing perceived service quality. It is a process-related service criterion which can have a positive effect on functional quality. After a good recovery, satisfaction with services can be increased.[13] It has even been claimed that good service recovery can make angry and frustrated customers more satisfied with service quality than they would have been if no problem had occurred in the first place.[14]

Service Recovery Versus Complaints Handling

Service recovery is a concept that was introduced in the service management literature to help firms manage service failures and complaints in a service-oriented way.[15] The traditional way of handling service or goods-related failures is complaints handling, where customers who have experienced problems are requested to make formal complaints. Such complaints are analyzed and handled by the firm usually in an administrative way. Frequently it seems as if the objective of complaints handling is to make sure that, regardless of who caused the failure, the firm does not have to compensate the customer unless absolutely necessary. Complaints handling has a significant effect on customers' perception of the service orientation of a service firm or a manufacturer, and the complaints handling approach is inherently non-service oriented. *Service recovery is a service-oriented approach to managing the same situations that, in an administrative way, are managed by complaints handling routines.*

For traditional complaints handling *internal efficiency*, keeping costs as low as possible and not compensating a customer unless this cannot be avoided for legal reasons, seems to be the standard. The result is unsatisfied customers and lost business. For service recovery *external efficiency* is the main guideline. *The objective of service recovery is to satisfy customers in spite of a service failure as well as to maintain and possibly improve long-term relationship quality, to retain customers and long-term profitable business rather than short-term cost savings.*

Tax and Brown[16] define service recovery in the following way:

> Service recovery is a process that identifies service failures, effectively resolves customer problems, classifies their root cause(s), and yields data that can be integrated with other measures of performance to assess and improve the service system.

It should be added that problems caused by a service failure or some other problem are usually two-fold; *factual* problems and *emotional* problems. Both have to be attended to by the firm.

In a problematic situation when service recovery is called upon, customers are often frustrated, may have high expectations, and also tend to have a narrower *zone of tolerance* than normal.[17] Service recovery may therefore be risky.[18] It has to be managed well. It seems that the more committed the employees of a firm feel to the visions, strategies and service concepts of the firm, the better their service recovery performance will be. Moreover, empowered employees can be expected to do better in recovery situations; they are inclined to deal quickly and effectively with service failures.[19] It is important that customers who have suffered from a service failure or some other mistake in the service process feel that they are treated fairly by the firm. The service recovery process should therefore be developed and exercised to maximize fairness as perceived by the customer.[20]

Guidelines for Service Recovery

Service recovery is a strategy for managing mistakes, failures and problems in customer relationships. It can be applied by all types of organizations, regardless of the firm's core business. A manufacturer or an organization in the public sector can benefit from this approach in the same way as a service firm, and the customers of any firm will certainly benefit from an organization that takes a service recovery approach instead of a traditional complaints-handling approach to managing mistakes and quality problems. Unlike traditional complaints handling, service recovery offers a service-oriented approach to managing problems. Below is a list of guidelines for the development of an effective service recovery process.

- It is the organization's responsibility to spot service failures and other types of mistakes or quality problems. Customers should only have to notify the firm about the situation or make a complaint if the firm has been unable to do so.
- If formal complaints are required, it should be made as easy as possible for the customer to complain. The complaints procedure should be made as unproblematic and free from bureaucracy as possible. Written complaints should be used only when absolutely necessary, for example for legal reasons

or when large amounts of money are involved. Remember that most customers who are unsatisfied do not bother to complain; they just take their business away without saying what went wrong.

- The organization should take the initiative to inform the customer about the failure or mistake and, in cases where immediate corrections cannot be made, keep the customer up to date about the progress of rectifying the mistake.
- The organization should actively take measures to correct failures and mistakes, and not wait until the customer demands action. Corrections should be made as quickly as possible. Every mistake or failure should be rectified immediately it has occurred if possible.
- The customer should be compensated immediately and, in cases where immediate compensation cannot be given, no unnecessary delays should be allowed. A lost customer, if profitable, has a greater negative effect on long-term profits than an overcompensated, satisfied customer who continues his relationship with the firm and probably also contributes to favorable word of mouth communication.
- If for some reason, legal or otherwise, a customer cannot be compensated for the problem that has occurred, a swift and service-oriented recovery process may still make the customer feel satisfied with the relationship, because a positive functional quality impact has been created in this situation. However, for long-term profitability it may be wise to compensate customers even when they are wrong or have caused the failure themselves. Taking short-term losses for the sake of long-term revenues in strengthened customer relationships often makes sense.
- Emotional reactions, such as anxiety and frustration, which customers often feel because of a service failure or some other mistake, must also be managed, in addition to recovering the failure itself. Such emotions should probably be attended to first.
- Apologizing is important, but is not enough in most situation. Customers must also be compensated for losses they feel they have suffered and the failure must be dealt with.
- To make full use of the potential of successful recovery, a systematic service recovery system should be developed. In such a system empowered employees such as customer contacts, customer-oriented supervisors and managers as support persons, are in a central position.
- Complaints departments and managers of complaints handling departments often only impede customer-oriented service recovery. However, a service recovery manager may be needed to develop and support the recovery system.

A Service Recovery Case Study: The Ritz Carlton Hotel

A group of four executive MBA students from Europe had attended a service marketing seminar at the Ritz Carlton Hotel in Phoenix, Arizona. Before leaving for the airport in the evening, they wanted to spend a few hours of leisure time at the swimming pool of the hotel. However, when coming down to the pool in the mid-afternoon, they were politely told that the pool area was closing, because the area was about to be prepared for an evening reception and dinner. Upon the students' explanation that during their stay at the hotel this was their only time to spend by the pool before returning to the freezing temperature of their home country and that they had very much looked forward to this opportunity, the waiter asked them to wait while he sorted out the situation. After a short while a supervisor arrived and informed the group that the hotel unfortunately did have to close the whole pool area right away to get ready for the evening event in time. However, he added, a limousine waited for them outside the main entrance to take them and their luggage to the Biltmore Hotel, where the pool area would be at their disposal. The limousine was at the Ritz Carlton's expense, of course.

The group was delighted by this solution, and their already favorable perception of the hotel was improved even more. They have also engaged in a considerable amount of positive word of mouth communication.

Service Recovery Processes

Customer contact employees may spot problems and service failures and take action but, as said in the previous section, to make full use of the potential of successful service recovery the firm should develop a *recovery system*. The following guidelines may be helpful in developing such a system.[21]

1. *Calculate costs of failures and mistakes*. Customers who defect because they are dissatisfied have to be replaced by new customers, and in addition they often engage in negative word of mouth. Getting new customers is always several times more expensive than keeping existing customers. Negative word of mouth also has a damaging effect on image. This makes the acquisition of new customers more difficult and expensive. Correcting mistakes and recovering problematic situations add costs that could have been avoided had the service functioned well in the first place. However, management too seldom realizes the financial effects of bad service. Therefore, careful measurements of the costs involved may warn management of the negative financial effects of badly managed service processes. In view of the high cost of losing customers, the need for a service recovery system is easily appreciated and the cost of compensating, and even overcompensating, customers for their losses becomes marginal.

2. *Solicit complaints*. Most customers never tell a firm about problems with services or goods that they have faced. They just disappear to a competitor. It is important to get information about failures that occur, mistakes that are made, systems that do not function in a service-oriented way according to customers and other reasons for poor perceived quality and dissatisfaction. Employees, especially those in contact with customers, should be able to monitor the service processes for mistakes and service failures, so that the firm realizes that there is a problem, if possible even before the customer does. However, many problems are first and perhaps only perceived by the customer. Therefore, it must be made as easy as possible for customers to

complain about quality problems and failures in the service system, because dissatisfied customers form a first-hand source of information regarding what needs to be improved. Sometimes customers can be trained to complain, for example, through pamphlets and other types of written material. Some firms use information technology to help customers inform the firm about a mistake that has occurred.[22] When customers complain, they must be shown respect and attention by the employee to whom they make the complaint.[23]

3. *Identify recovery needs*. Mistakes can happen and failures can occur almost anywhere. However, by carefully analyzing the service process, human resources, systems used in the process and customers' need for information and guidance, it is possible to spot areas with high risk of failures. Situations where one error can lead to a chain reaction (for example a delayed incoming flight) are particularly problematic. Complicated IT systems is another risky area. The introduction of new systems is always critical. By being aware of such areas where the risk for mistakes is especially high, management can prepare the organization for taking care of possible failures.

4. *Recover quickly*. An old rule of thumb says that disappointed customers tell 12 others about their negative experiences, whereas satisfied customers tell much fewer about their positive experiences. The more slowly a problem is attended to and corrected, the more negative word of mouth is created. In addition, the impact of a slow recovery process on a damaged quality perception is much greater than if there is a quick recovery. We shall turn to this aspect of service recovery in the next section.

5. *Train employees*. Customer contact employees must understand why service failures need to be attended to and recovered quickly, and they need to understand and appreciate why they in the front line have a responsibility, *first of all*, for spotting problems, mistakes and customers who seem to become disappointed with the service process or who do not understand how to participate effectively in the process. *Second*, they need to understand and accept their responsibilities for taking action to manage a disappointed customer's frustration and make efforts to quickly correct mistakes and compensate the customer for his losses. Training is required so that employees have the service-oriented perspective needed to take care of problematic situations and also the skills required in these situations. Without this perspective the employees may have a different view of recovery needs than the customers.[24] This is part of internal marketing, which will be discussed at length in Chapter 15.

6. *Empower and enable customer contact employees*. Training gives employees a better understanding of the situation and their central role in service recovery, and also the knowledge and skills for doing the job. However, to handle dissatisfied and frustrated customers, employees need authority to make decisions about what to do and how much to compensate. They also need to know how far their authority goes and when the recovery of a failure has to be handed over to someone else in the organization, or when a formal written complaint needs to be made. Employees have to be *empowered* with authority and *enabled* with access to information, databases and compensation systems, such as vouchers, free tickets or money. In Chapter 15, empowerment and enabling are discussed at length.

TABLE 5.1 Customer expectations when service failures or problems occur. Source: Amended from Zemke, R. (1992) Supporting Service Recovery: Attributes for Excelling at Solving Customers' Problems. In Sheuing, E.E., Gummesson, E. & Little, C.H. (eds), *Selected Papers from the Second Quality in Services (QUIS 2) Conference*. New York: St. John's University and ISQA International Service Quality Association, p. 46.

Action expected	How action should be handled
Apology	Delivered in person, even if the firm did not cause the problem (however, apology is often not enough).
Fair Compensation	Reasonable compensation on the spot from customer contact employee.
Caring Treatment	By showing empathy and treating each customer as an individual; attending to emotional problems.
Value Added Atonement	Customer gets something as a symbol of appreciation of value as customer (sometimes a fair compensation may serve as such a symbol).
Kept Promises About Recovery	Contact employee describes what will happen and when, with confidence that it actually will happen that way (negative information is better than no information or wrong information; it is better to hear once that a flight is 60 minutes delayed than to hear four times that there is a 15 minute delay).

7. *Keep the customer informed.* The customer should always be told that the failure or mistake has been acknowledged and that the recovery process is underway. If a recovery cannot be made on the spot and if the process takes time customers must be kept informed about its progress. Finally, when a problem has been corrected, the customer should be notified about the result but also about what the firm has learnt form the failure and which corrective actions they have taken to improve the service process.

8. *Learn from mistakes.* The firm must have a system for using service recovery experiences in a productive way. Service failures, quality problems and other mistakes can often be traced back to either a structural problem in some process in the organization or to employee attitude. It is important that the firm analyzes the root cause of a problem and corrects the underlying processes or attitudes. Situations that have led to problematic situations must be handled better the next time they occur.[25]

In summary, a system for effective service recovery includes three areas of focus:[26] *constantly monitor service processes to identify problems, solve problems effectively* and *learn from problems and the recovery process*. Table 5.1 shows the necessary recovery steps expected by customers.[27]

Timing of Recovery Processes

In addition to correcting the mistake, quick response and adequate compensation are usually considered crucial elements of service recovery.[28] However, there are as yet no empirical studies on the negative effects of poor timing of recovery efforts, or what can be gained by good timing. This final section of Chapter 5 will discuss some effects on perceived service quality resulting from various timing strategies.[29] The *relationship framework*, including episodes (or service encounters) consisting of singular acts, sequences of interrelated episodes and the overall relationship itself is used to illustrate various timing strategies. The three strategies are labeled *administrative* (a passive approach), *defensive* (an active approach) and *offensive* (a proactive approach), respectively. A lost-luggage situation is used as an example. A family of three is arriving by air to a distant beach resort for four days of vacation. Upon arrival they realize that all their checked-in luggage has been lost. This means that the family does not have more than their traveling clothes at their disposal. The need for service recovery is evident.

An *administrative service recovery* (passive approach to service failures) is shown in the top part of Figure 5.5. The airline agent does the required paper-work and gives the family a standard voucher for a nominal amount of money. The family realizes immediately that this sum will not cover more than a fraction of the purchases necessary to save their vacation. They are informed that if that is the case they will have to make a formal complaint to the airline after their vacation. The recovery of the service failure will thus be taken care of afterwards when this complaint has been duly processed. The recovery is managed as a separate *service sequence* following the *main service sequence* (the vacation consisting of, for example, three *episodes*: flight to the vacation resort, stay at the resort, and flight back). This configuration of the relationship is illustrated in the upper part of Figure 5.5. This way of handling service failure can be labeled *administrative recovery*, because the service failure is not fully recovered at all. Instead the responsibility to seek redress is left to the customer as a separate process (sequence). This type of recovery is similar to traditional complaints handling.

Furthermore, the emotional effects of the failure are not addressed, which will probably negatively influence the customer's perception of the quality of the service. Also, the damage to the perceived service quality caused by the failure is not likely to be diminished, even if the customer is fully compensated after the complaints-handling process.

A *defensive service recovery* (active approach to service failures) is illustrated in the middle part of the figure. Following this timing strategy the airline company suggests to the family that they buy what they need at their own expense and then get their purchases reimbursed at the airline's office after the return trip. In this way the recovery of the failure is managed as a separate recovery episode, but as part of the main service sequence (as part of the vacation). This approach to managing service failures can be called *defensive recovery*, because there is a clear attempt to recover the situation without any formal complaints procedures. In this sense it is an active approach. However, it is defensive, because it leaves the customer to sort out the problem for himself first. The formal recovery is taken care of later, however, as part of the main service sequence.

The emotional problems following the service failure are probably not managed very well in this way either, although they will have less influence on the perceived service quality than the administrative service recovery. As the customer knows from the beginning that he will be able to make the purchases

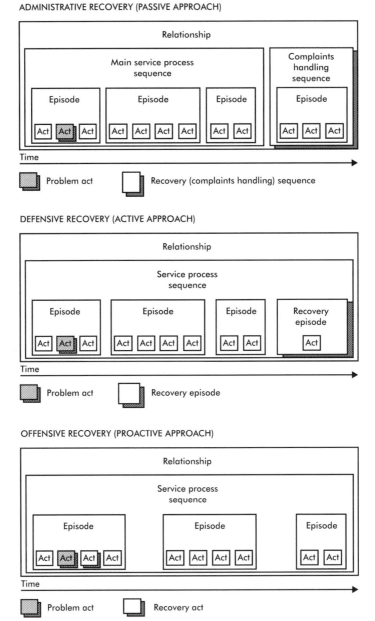

FIGURE 5.5   Timing of service recovery in a relationship framework. Reprinted with permission from *Jazzing into the New Millennium*, published by the American Marketing Association, 1999, pp. 40–42.

required without economic consequences for himself, the intended service quality perception can probably be restored.

An *offensive service recovery* (proactive approach to service failures) is shown at the bottom of the figure. The airline company could also make the recovery of the service failure immediately as part of the episode where the failure occurred. The agent could, for example, offer the family the opportunity to make all the purchases they need at the airline's expense in a number of listed shops at the resort. The firm takes a proactive approach to managing the problems caused by the failure, by removing all additional annoyance and problems. The recovery act becomes part of the episode where the failure took place, although some of the recovery-related activities (buying clothes, for example) are part of a later episode.

In this way the emotional problems caused by the service failure are much more likely to be diminished. The customer is likely to be surprised by the positive way the negative situation is handled by the service provider, and there is even a possibility that the originally intended level of perceived service quality will be exceeded.

Managing Service Failures and Quality Problems: A Summary

As was said earlier, some quality problems and failures cannot be corrected immediately. However, the customer's emotional concerns, anxiety and frustration should always be attended to right away. Most failures can be taken care of and recovered on the spot, if there is a *functioning recovery system* in the firm and if the customer contact employees are *empowered* with authority, knowledge and skills, and *enabled* to perform with easily retrievable information, an appropriate compensation system and, when needed, supportive superiors.

Timing is essential. As a ground rule, the quicker recovery can be made, the better. A quick recovery will make the customer *more satisfied with service quality* than otherwise. In addition, a prompt recovery will *cost the firm less* than a slow recovery or a traditional complaints-handling process. First, the costs of handling recovery, including compensation paid, will probably amount to a smaller sum, and second, quick recovery will increase the likelihood of positive word of mouth and also for customer retention. If customers stay in the relationship, the much higher costs of getting new customers to replace lost ones can be avoided. Patrick Mene, Director of Quality at the Ritz-Carlton Hotel Company, a Malcolm Baldrige Quality Award winning service firm, coined the "1-10-100 rule of service recovery."[30] What costs the firm one pound, euro or dollar to fix immediately will cost 10 tomorrow and 100 later on. This is the financial logic of service recovery in a nutshell.

Summary and Questions for Discussion

In this chapter the reasons why firms hesitate to invest in improved service quality were described. Then quality management models for service organizations were discussed: these included the Gap Analysis model to close gaps in the quality generation processes of the firm, and programs for holistic management of service quality. In the latter part of the chapter service recovery, as an alternative to traditional complaints handling, was described and service recovery processes were discussed.

Questions for discussion

1. Why are managers often hesitant to invest in quality improvements in services?
2. How can reasons for quality problems be traced using the gap analysis framework?
3. Why is the management of quality a holistic issue in service contexts?
4. What are the benefits (for the customer and the firm) of a service recovery approach to handling mistakes or quality problems compared to a traditional complaints-handling system?
5. How could a proactive service recovery system be installed in your organization, or in any given organization?

Further Reading

Andreassen, T.W. (1997) *Dissatisfaction with Services. The Impact of Satisfaction with Service Recovery on Corporate Image and Future Repurchase Intentions*. Stockholm, Sweden: Stockholm University.

Berry, L.L. & Parasuraman, A. (1991) *Marketing Services. Competing Through Quality*. New York: Free Press.

Boshoff, C. & Leong, J. (1998) Empowerment, Attribution and Apologising as Dimensions of Service Quality. *International Journal of Service Industry Management*, **9**(1), pp. 24–47.

Boshoff, C. & Allen, J. (2000) The Influence of Selected Antecedents on Frontline Staff's Perception of Service Recovery Performance. *International Journal of Service Industry Management*, **11**(1), pp. 63–90.

Bowen, D.E. & Lawler III, E.E. (1995) Empowering Service Employees. *Sloan Management Review*, **36**, Summer, pp. 73–84.

de Ruyter, K. & Wetzels, M. (2000) Customer Equity Considerations in Service Recovery: A Cross-industry Perspective. *International Journal of Service Industry Management*, **11**(1), pp. 91–108.

Edvardsson, B. (1992) Service Breakdowns: A Study of Critical Incidents in an Airline. *International Journal of Service Industry Management*, **3**(4), pp. 17–29.

Grönroos, C. (1999) The Role of Service Recovery: Administrative, Defensive and Offensive Management of Service Failures. In Fisk, R. & Glynn, L. (eds), *Jazzing Into the New Millennium. 1999 Servsig Services Research Conference*. Chicago, IL: American Marketing Association, pp. 39–43.

Hart, C.W.L., Heskett, J.L. & Sasser, Jr., W.E. (1990) The Profitable Art of Service Recovery. *Harvard Business Review*, July—August, pp. 148–156.

Johnston, R. (1995) The Determinants of Service Quality: Satisfiers and Dissatisfiers. *International Journal of Service Industry Management*, **6**(5), pp. 53–71.

Johnston, R. & Fern, A. (1999) Service Recovery Strategies for Single and Double Deviation Scenarios. *The Service Industry Journal*, **19**(2), pp. 69–82.

Kelley, S.W. & Davis, M.A. (1994) Antecedents to Customer Expectations for Service Recovery. *Journal of the Academy of Marketing Science*, **22**(1), pp. 52–61.

Lovelock, C.H. (1994) *Product Plus: How Product + Service = Competitive Advantage*. New York: McGraw-Hill.

Parasuraman, A., Berry, L.L. & Zeithaml, V.A. (1991) Refinement and Reassessment of the SERVQUAL Scale. *Journal of Retailing*, **67**(4).

Patlow, C.G. (1993) How Ritz-Carlton Applies "TQM." *The Cornell H.R.A. Quarterly*, August, pp. 16–24.

Roos, I. (1999) *Switching Paths in Customer Relationships*. Helsinki/Helsingfors: Swedish School of Economics Finland/CERS Center for Relationship Marketing and Service Management.

Rust, R.T. & Oliver, R.L. (2000) Should We Delight the Customer? *Journal of the Academy of Marketing Science*, **28**(1), pp. 86–94.

Silvestro, R. & Johnston, R. (1992) The Determinants of Service Quality: Hygiene and Enhancing Factors. In Sheuing, E.E., Gummesson, E. & Little, C.H. (eds), *Selected Papers from the Second Quality in Services (QUIS 2) Conference*, New York: St John's University and ISQA International Service Quality Association, pp. 193–210.

Smith, A.K. & Bolton, R.N. (1998) An Experimental Investigation of Customer Reactions to Service Failure and Recovery Encounters. *Journal of Service Research*, **1**(1), pp. 65–81.

Spreng, R.A., Harrell, R.A. & Mackoy, G.D. (1995) Service Recovery: Impact on Satisfaction and Intentions. *Journal of Services Marketing*, **9**(1), pp. 15–23.

Strandvik, T. (1994) *Tolerance Zones in Perceived Service Quality*. Helsingfors/Helsinki: Swedish School of Economics Finland.

Tax, S.S., Brown, S.W. & Chandrashekaran, M. (1998) Customer Evaluation of Service Complaint Experiences: Implications for Relationship Marketing. *Journal of Marketing*, **62**, April, pp. 60–76.

Tax, S.S. & Brown, S.W. (1998) Recovering and Learning from Service Failure. *Sloan Management Review*, **40**(1), pp. 75–88.

Tax, S.S. & Brown, S.W. (2000) Service Recovery: Research Insights and Practices. In Swartz, T.A. & Iacobucci, D. (eds), *Handbook in Services Marketing & Management*. Thousand Oaks, CA: Sage Publications, pp. 271–285.

Zeithaml, V.A., Berry, L.L. & Parasuraman, A. (1988) Communication and Control Processes in the Delivery of Service Quality. *Journal of Marketing*, **64**, April, pp. 35–49.

Zeithaml, V.A., Berry, L.L. & Parasuraman, A. (1993) The Nature and Determinants of Customer Expectations of Services. *Journal of the Academy of Marketing Science*, **21**(1), pp. 1–12.

Zemke, R. (1992) Supporting Service Recovery: Attributes for Excelling at Solving Customers' Problems. In Sheuing, E.E., Gummesson, E. & Little, C.H. (eds), *Selected Papers from the Second Quality in Services (QUIS 2) Conference*, New York: St. John's University and ISQA International Service Quality Association, pp. 41–46.

Notes

1 Rust, R.T. & Oliver, R.L., Should We Delight the Customer? *Journal of the Academy of Marketing Science*, **28**(1), 2000, pp. 86–94.

2 Rust & Oliver, *op.cit.*

3 The Gap Analysis model as well as reasons for gaps and ways of managing gaps are discussed in Parasuraman, A., Zethaml, V.A. & Berry, L.L., A Conceptual Model of Service Quality and Its Implications for Future Research. *Journal of Marketing*, **61**, Fall 1985 and Zeithaml, V.A., Berry, L.L. & Parasuraman, A., Communication and Control Processes in the Delivery of Service Quality. *Journal of Marketing*, **64**, April 1988.

4 See Berry, L.L. & Parasuraman, A., *Marketing Services. Competing Through Quality*. New York: Free Press, 1991.

5 In a large study of the restaurant industry Tore Strandvik demonstrated that in general customers seem to show a loss aversion. See Strandvik, T., *Tolerance Zones in Perceived Service Quality*. Helsingfors/Helsinki: Swedish School of Economics Finland, 1994.

6 See Strandvik, *op.cit.*

7 This classification of quality attributes and the examples of various types of attributes were suggested by Silvestro and Johnston. See Silvestro, R. & Johnston, R., The Determinants of Service Quality: Hygiene and Enhancing Factors. In Sheuing, E.E., Gummesson, E. & Little, C.H. (eds), *Selected Papers from the Second Quality in Services (QUIS 2) Conference*, New York: St. John's University and ISQA International Service Quality Association, 1992, pp. 193–210.

8 Johnston, R., The Determinants of Service Quality: Satisfiers and Dissatisfiers. *International Journal of Service Industry Management*, **6**(5), 1995, pp. 53–71.

9 Johnston, *op.cit.*

10 This is an expression used in Berry & Parasuraman, *op.cit.*

11 Boshoff, C. & Leong, J., Empowerment, Attribution and Apologising as Dimensions of Service

Quality. *International Journal of Service Industry Management*, **9**(1), 1998, pp. 24–47 and Andreassen, T.W., *Dissatisfaction with Services. The Impact of Satisfaction with Service Recovery on Corporate Image and Future Repurchase Intentions*. Stockholm, Sweden: Stockholm University, 1997.

12 Tax, S.S., Brown, S.W. & Chandrashekaran, M., Customer Evaluation of Service Complaint Experiences: Implications for Relationship Marketing. *Journal of Marketing*, **62**, April, 1998, pp. 60–76.

13 Spreng, R.A., Harrell, R.A. & Mackoy, G.D., Service Recovery: Impact on Satisfaction and Intentions. *Journal of Services Marketing*, **9**(1), 1995, pp. 15–23.

14 Kelley, S.W. & Davis, M.A., Antecedents to Customer Expectations for Service Recovery. *Journal of the Academy of Marketing Science*, **22**(1), 1994, pp. 52–61.

15 An early publication where service recovery was suggested as a way of managing service failures is Hart, C.W.L., Heskett, J.L. & Sasser, Jr., W.E., The Profitable Art of Service Recovery. *Harvard Business Review*, July–August 1990, pp. 148–156.

16 Tax, S.S. & Brown, S.W., Service Recovery: Research Insights and Practices. In Swartz, T.A. & Iacobucci, D. (eds), *Handbook in Services Marketing & Management*, Thousand Oaks, CA: Sage Publications, 2000, p. 272. See also Lovelock, C.H., *Product Plus*. New York: McGraw-Hill, 1994.

17 Tax, Brown & Chandrashekaran 1998, *op.cit*. See also Zeithaml, V.A., Berry, L.L. & Parasuraman, A., The Nature and Determinants of Customer Expectations of Services. *Journal of the Academy of Marketing Science*, **21**(1), 1993, pp. 1–12.

18 Smith, A.K. & Bolton, R.N., An Experimental Investigation of Customer Reactions to Service Failure and Recovery Encounters. *Journal of Service Research*, **1**(1), 1998, pp. 65–81.

19 Boshoff, C. & Allen, J., The Influence of Selected Antecedents on Frontline Staff's Perception of Service Recovery Performance. *International Journal of Service Industry Management*, **11**(1), 2000, pp. 63–90. The authors of this article suggest that managers must be prepared for their staff to make mistakes and that "they must adopt an 'it's better to try and fail than not to try at all' attitude" (p. 82).

20 de Ruyter, K. & Wetzels, M., Customer Equity Considerations in Service Recovery: A Cross-industry Perspective. *International Journal of Service Industry Management*, **11**(1), 2000, pp. 91–108.

21 See Hart, Heskett & Sasser, *op.cit.*, Berry & Parasuraman, *op.cit.* and Tax, S.S. & Brown, S.W., Recovering and Learning from Service Failure. *Sloan Management Review*, **40**(1), 1998, pp. 75–88. In these publications service recovery systems are discussed at length.

22 Tax & Brown, *op.cit.*

23 In a study of the food retailing industry Inger Roos observed that a lack of respect for customers' complaints had a decisive effect on customers' decisions to switch from one shop to another. See Roos, I., *Switching Paths in Customer Relationships*, Helsinki/Helsingfors: Swedish School of Economics Finland, 1999.

24 In a study of the airline industry Edvardsson found a considerable difference between how employees and customer perceived critical incidents in the service process. See Edvardsson, B., Service Breakdowns: A Study of Critical Incidents in an Airline. *International Journal of Service Industry Management*, **3**(4), 1992, pp. 17–29.

25 Bill Marriott, Managing Director of Marriott Corp., says that he demands that his firm not only do whatever is necessary to take care of guests in normal situations, but that employees also track, measure and follow up on how to handle things better in the future. See Bowen, D.E. & Lawler III, E.E., Empowering Service Employees. *Sloan Management Review*, **36**, Summer 1995, pp. 73–84.

26 Compare Berry & Parasuraman, *op.cit.*

27 Zemke, R., Supporting Service Recovery: Attributes for Excelling at Solving Customers' Problems. In Sheuing, E., E., Gummesson, E. & Little, C.H. (eds), *Selected Papers from the Second Quality in Services (QUIS 2) Conference*, New York: St. John's University and ISQA International Service Quality Association, 1992, pp. 41–46.

28 See, for example, Johnston, R. & Fern, A., Service Recovery Strategies for Single and Double Deviation Scenarios. *The Service Industry Journal*, **19**(2), 1999, pp. 69–82.

29 Grönroos, C., The Role of Service Recovery: Administrative, Defensive and Offensive Management of Service Failures. In Fisk, R. & Glynn, L. (eds), *Jazzing Into the New Millennium. 1999 Servsig Services Research Conference*. Chicago, IL: American Marketing Association 1999, pp. 39–43.

30 Patlow, C.G., How Ritz-Carlton Applies "TQM." *The Cornell H.R.A. Quarterly*, August 1993, pp. 16–24.

Chapter 6

RETURN ON SERVICE AND RELATIONSHIPS

Customers look for added value. However, adding value does not require new services in customer relationships, but that existing customer contacts are managed as services for customers.

Introduction

Building on the discussions of perceived service quality and relationship quality in Chapter 4 and quality management in services in Chapter 5 this chapter now turns to the question of whether investing in services in customer relationships can be expected to pay off. The issues of relationship costs and long-term customer sacrifice are discussed, and various approaches to understanding customer perceived value are described. Finally, a model of customer relationship profitability is presented. After having read the chapter, the reader should understand how to justify investments in service quality and in services in customer relationships, and how to quantify the total benefits of a service package in customer relationships as well as how the profitability of customer relationships is calculated.

Why Customers Are Not Prepared to Pay for Improved Service Quality

Service competition is a fact for a growing number of firms and industries. Service firms have always faced service competition, whereas this situation is new for most manufacturing businesses. In spite of this new competitive situation, one often meets the sceptical suspicion that, in the final analysis, developing services and capabilities to cope with service competition will not pay off after all. "Customers are prepared to pay only for the core solution, a physical product or a service," and "For our customers price is the only important factor, so it is no use to invest in services" are arguments which are frequently heard. In some situations, and for some customers, they may of course be true. However, in general they are certainly not valid. Improved service and the development of sustainable customer relationships usually pays off. The problem for most firms is that many customers, individual consumers as well as organizational, do not see how improved services means more value for them. The service provider has to make customers realize the value-enhancing potential of better service.

If customers do not appreciate the value to them of good service and are not willing to pay for service, there can be at least four reasons for this:

- the service provider has not been able to demonstrate to its customers how they can benefit from the service offered in terms of added comfort, support, security and/or lowered costs;
- the service provider has not managed to show the customers that long-term cost effects of a service package are a more important decision-making criterion than price;
- the service offering is not as customer-oriented as it should be and does not offer the favorable benefits that customers are looking for; and
- a particular customer is not interested in value-adding additional services but is only looking for the core solution at as low a price as possible.

In this chapter we discuss how to cope with the first two reasons given above. The third reason is discussed in other chapters throughout this book. The fourth reason is not discussed in this context: a firm that has done its market research carefully enough should realize that such customers are in a transactional mode (see Chapter 2) and they should not be offered a total service offering at all but merely the core solution they want.

The Cost of Improving Service Quality

Managers often feel uncomfortable at customer demands for better quality. They feel that improved service quality does not pay off. Two reasons why the firm cannot improve its quality are normally offered; improving quality costs more than can be achieved in additional revenues and new business, and improving quality means that productivity will suffer, which the organization cannot afford. Managers tend to believe that quality improvements come at the expense of productivity, and vice versa. Caught in this apparent dilemma, they often choose to concentrate on one of these issues.[1] Far too often attention to productivity is given priority, and how to improve quality remains an unsolved problem. In Chapter 9 the issue of productivity in services is discussed in some detail, and it is shown that, although it may be true for some firms, as a general rule productivity and quality do not counteract each other.

Both of these reasons for why quality cannot be improved are cost-related. To improve services and increase their quality requires too much resources and additional costs, and supposedly lowers productivity, which leads to higher costs per unit produced. Both reasons are invalid, and are based on an insufficient understanding of the relationships between quality and productivity on the one hand and the use of resources and the sources of costs and revenues on the other. Efforts to raise quality almost always result in better productivity and efforts to raise productivity can very well pay off through better quality. However, in order to achieve positive results, managers will have to rethink the relationship between costs and revenues, productivity and quality (see Chapter 9). If managers are able to define these relationships, they are probably able to exploit their strengths as far as production effectiveness, employee satisfaction and profitability are concerned.

Quality Does Not Cost: A Lack of Quality Does

The notion that high quality implies higher costs is not based on fact. Normally, it is the other way around. Frequently the more important issue is that a lack of quality costs money. Philip Crosby coined the phrase "quality is free."[2] He based his statement on the notion that firms spend more than 20 per cent of their sales revenue doing things wrong and then having to correct these mistakes.

These are facts from manufacturing. However, service organizations are probably no better. On the contrary, it has been suggested that up to 35 per cent of their operating costs may be due to a lack of quality, having to repeat tasks and correct errors. This, of course, follows from the fact that service quality is a complicated phenomenon and that it is more difficult to monitor and assure quality in service than in manufacturing. Furthermore, manufacturing has a long history of quality control research and a whole collection of quality monitoring techniques, quality assurance and total quality management at its service.

Hence, improving quality by creating customer-oriented and foolproof systems and by training employees well is a way, not to increase costs, but to get rid of unnecessary costs. If we assume that 35 per cent of operating costs are unnecessary, because they are due to bad quality, quality improvement by removing these quality problems would save 35 per cent of these costs. All of this would be visible on the bottom line. However, such an improvement would not go unnoticed by the market, and some new business and additional revenues could be expected to be achieved. This would add even more to the bottom line, thus profits would be boosted by more than 35 per cent of the original operating costs. Furthermore, if the firm spends this 35 per cent on further improving quality, operating costs would remain on the same level as they were originally. This quality improvement process could be expected to bring in more business and perhaps, even probably, enable the firm to get a better price for its services. The effects on the bottom line are obvious.

Better Quality, Higher Customer Retention Rates, More Profits

Services are inherently relationship-oriented. This does not mean that some service providers could not develop their marketing strategy in a transaction-oriented fashion. However, there is always the possibility for the development of customer relationships in services. Relationships between service providers and consumers and users of services normally continue over time. Hence, we start our analysis of return on service and relationships by discussing the effects of good service on customer retention and loyalty,[3] and the economic consequences of longer customer relationships.

What "good service" means is a strategic issue. In many cases it means that the service is excellent in comparison with competing offerings and meets customers' expectations and other comparison standards. If this is the case, good service means that the service is genuinely good. However, in other cases it may mean a lower level of service, because the target group of customers may be looking for a lower quality level, for example because the correspondingly lower price better fits their budget. Then the lower level is "good service" for those customers. For example, a couple spending the evening at a gourmet restaurant consider the quality of the restaurant service good if it meets their expectations of good food, attentive waiting staff, and so on. However, in a relative sense they will consider the quality of the service of a fast-food restaurant equally good, if the performance of such a restaurant meets the different expectations they have when visiting such a restaurant.

The Relationship Between Customer Satisfaction and Repurchases and Loyalty

Even though a positive relationship between satisfaction with service and goods quality, on the one hand, and customers' willingness to continue the relationship or make repurchases, on the other, seems to exist, it is important to realize that this function is normally far from linear. Experiences from Xerox reported by Hart and Johnson[4] (see Figure 6.1) clearly indicate that there is a substantial *zone of indifference* including customers who claim that they are everything from "so-so satisfied" to "satisfied." Only the "very satisfied" customers show a high repurchasing rate and a high propensity for positive word of mouth. As the figure shows, the retention curve rises steeply at this point of the satisfaction scale. Evidence from other types of both goods and services support these observations. Two obvious conclusions can be drawn from this:

- It is not enough to offer the quality of services that keeps customers in this *zone of indifference* as far as repurchasing behavior is concerned; customers have to be offered a service package which makes them *very* satisfied before they will repurchase. Hence, it is important to surprise customers in such a way that their quality perception is satisfactory enough to reinforce loyalty and make them repurchase.
- When reporting results from customer satisfaction and service quality studies, it is extremely important to keep those respondents who report that they are very satisfied apart from those who say that they are simply satisfied. The repurchasing and word of mouth behavior, and therefore also the actions required to ensure enduring customer relationships, are totally different for these two groups of customers (normally, the responses of these two categories of customers are reported jointly in the "satisfied or very satisfied" category. By so doing, the firm loses vital information needed to create profitable customer relationships.)

FIGURE 6.1   The satisfaction/repurchase function. Reprinted with permission from *Marketing Management*, published by the American Marketing Association, Hart, C.W. & Johnson, M.D., 1999, p. 9.

Hart and Johnson[5] draw the conclusion that a firm has to go beyond what normally can be described as good service and acceptable value to create loyalty. The firm must serve customers in such a way that they realize that the firm can be *trusted in every respect at all times*. The performance standard to aim at is what can be labeled not just "zero defects" by customers, but "*zero trust defects*." Customers' trust in the organization must never be betrayed by a negative or even mediocre service encounter, wrong or incomplete information or lack of information, or a malfunctioning physical product—not even once. This offers a huge challenge for firms, because very few firms seem to be completely trusted by customers. However, the benefits to be achieved by firms in terms of a competitive edge and increased, profitable business by improving the quality of their service offerings to create a trusting relationship with their customers are equally huge.

Another interesting conclusion that can be drawn from Figure 6.1 is the effect of customer satisfaction on word of mouth communication. Only very satisfied customers will engage in any substantial positive word-of-mouth endorsements and thus become "unpaid" marketing and sales persons for the firm. On the other hand, very unsatisfied customers can be expected to create substantial negative word of mouth, and thus become "terrorists" reinforcing negative but not totally unsatisfactory experiences by other customers and scaring away potential new customers.

The Relationship Between Customer Loyalty and Profitability

The largest published study of higher customer retention levels following better service quality and how this affects profit is one by Bain & Company from a decade ago. It is still very relevant. In this US study several service industries were studied. The effects on profits through improved customer retention and

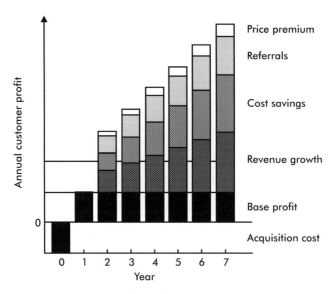

FIGURE 6.2   The profitability effect of loyal customers. Source: Reichheld, F.F., *The Loyalty Effect. The Hidden Forces Behind Growth, Profits, and Lasting Value*. Boston, MA: Harvard Business School Press, 1996.

hence longer relationships with customers are astonishing. It was found, among other things, that the average profit per customer grew constantly over the first five years.

The reasons why the profit per customer increases over time are schematically illustrated in Figure 6.2. The economic effect of customer loyalty can be attributed to the following factors: acquisition costs, revenue growth, cost savings, referrals and price premiums.[6]

The vertical axis in the figure does not have a scale, because the effects on profits of the various factors differ from industry to industry, firm to firm, and even customer to customer. However, the height of the sections gives some general indications of the relative importance of these factors. Every firm should, however, take the time and trouble to study its accounting and reporting system in order to make the necessary calculations of the influence on total profits per customer of these and possibly other profit drivers. It is a time-consuming task, because in most firms the figures needed are not readily available, because revenues and costs are usually registered on a per product basis, not on a per customer basis. These factors are discussed below.

Acquisition costs. The active acquisition of new customers using sales and external marketing efforts is required in most businesses. As a rule of thumb, getting a new customer costs five to six times more than it costs on top of normal service operations (sales calls, providing information about new goods or services, etc.) to keep an existing satisfied customer. In other words, it costs only 15 to 20 per cent of what has to be invested in getting a new customer to keep an existing customer. The economics of customer loyalty are very apparent. These figures of course vary from industry to industry, and situation to situation, but are nevertheless remarkable. In Figure 6.2 the acquisition cost per customer appears as a negative profit effect in the year before the customer relationship starts.

Base profit. In many service industries the price paid by customers during the first year or even first few years does not cover the costs of producing the service. In other cases the price covers costs and produces a profit per customer from the first year. This is the base profit in the figure. After some years, depending on the industry and other factors, the accumulated base profits have covered the initial marketing costs of getting the customer.

Revenue growth. In most situations a long-standing customer will bring more business to the same service provider. This means that, on average, customers can be expected to contribute more to a firm's profits as the relationship grows. The annual revenue per customer increases over the years, thus contributing to growing profits.

Cost savings. As the service provider and the customer learn about each other, about what to expect and how to perform, service processes will be smoother and take less time, and fewer mistakes that have to be corrected will be made. Thus, the average operating costs per customer will decrease, which in turn has a positive impact on profits.

Referrals. Long-standing and satisfied customers will create positive word of mouth communication and recommend the supplier or service provider to friends, neighbors, business associates and others. The customer takes over the role as marketer without any additional costs to the firm. A large number of businesses, especially smaller ones, thrive on good referrals by satisfied customers. In this way new customers are brought in with lower than normal acquisition costs, which has an extra favorable effect on profits.

Premium price. In most business, old customers pay a higher price than newcomers. Discounts that were initially given to new customers do not exist for older customers. In many cases introductory offers decrease prices for new customers. However, the main reason for the premium price effect can be attributed to the fact that long-standing customers realize the value provided by the firm and make cost savings by using the service of a service provider they know well. We shall return to this later in the context of relationship costs. In summary, this value offsets the negative effect of higher prices. Of course, it is not always the case that old customers pay a premium price. Sometimes long-lasting relationships have given the customer a bargaining position based on power or social relationships which keeps prices down. If this happens, a negative profit-eroding effect occurs.

In the study by Bain & Company the economic effects of higher retention rates were calculated in the service industries studied. These results were also quite astonishing. In general, it was found that as the customer defection rate falls (i.e. as customer retention grows), profits increase. The variation between the industries in the study was remarkable. In a bank's branch operations profits improved by 85 per cent as the customer defection rate decreased by five percentage points. Over the service industries in the study the impact on the economic result of a decrease of the defection rate of this magnitude varied between 25 and 85 per cent.[7]

Again, the economics of customer loyalty are quite obvious. Every firm should make similar calculations as the ones reported here. It almost always requires separate studies of the revenue and cost flows, because accounting systems seldom produce the information needed for such calculations. The growth in customer retention rates and customer loyalty is probably not just caused by improved service. However, it is apparent that customer satisfaction with service quality is a central factor here. On the other hand, it is also clear that satisfaction as such does not necessarily create loyal customers. The sacrifice made by customers, in terms of price, comfort, timeliness and costs which may follow from these and other factors, as well as the value customers feel they get, are critical variables affecting loyalty and the length of customer relationships.

In the next sections we shall first discuss how to analyze customer sacrifice and then the customer-perceived value of service in a relationship.

Customer Sacrifice: The Cost of Being a Customer

The view that improved service does not pay off for the service provider or for the customer is expressed quite regularly, as we have seen before. Nevertheless, as a general rule this is not true. Except for special cases, for example with highly transaction-oriented customers, there is always an opportunity to increase customer value and strengthen relationships with customers, *if the service provider understands the nature of service competition and the cost consequences for customers of good and bad service*. One has to realize that bad service creates costs for customers, and good service makes such costs decrease or eliminates them.

The usual problem is that marketers, salespeople and buyers think in terms of short-term exchanges or transactions, and they are therefore preoccupied with short-term sacrifice, or the price to be paid. Because the accounting systems of both the seller and the buyer are normally geared towards registering transactions and not towards following up on costs and revenues caused by suppliers, service providers and customers, neither party realizes the long-term cost effects of bad service; nor do they see the long-term gains of good service. Unnecessary costs caused by bad service and the cost gains of good service occur for the customer as well as for the service provider. In this section we shall concentrate on customer effects. Later on effects on the supplier or service provider will be discussed.

Price is only a part of the total long-term cost of being a customer of a given service provider. *Price*, including discounts and terms of payment, *is a cost component which is perceived in the short run, whereas other cost components are perceived in the long run as the relationship unfolds*. Thus, the total long-term customer sacrifice consists of price and additional costs occurring in the relationship. These additional costs are called *relationship costs*.[8] Hence, it is important to make a distinction between short-term and long-term sacrifice:

1. Short-term customer sacrifice = price
2. Total long-term customer sacrifice = price + relationship costs

Relationship costs are the additional costs on top of price that occur for a customer due to the fact that he has purchased something from a given supplier or service firm and entered into a relationship with this organization. The relationship costs are of three different types:[9]

- direct relationship costs;
- indirect relationship costs;
- psychological costs.

In the following sections these types of relationship costs will be discussed in more detail. Such costs occur in relationships with individual consumers and households as well as in business-to-business relationships. It may be easier to calculate them in the latter type of relationship, but they exist and are perceived by individual consumers too.

Direct Relationship Costs

Direct relationship costs are costs which depend on the internal systems that the customer has to maintain because of the solution offered by the supplier. Such costs consist, for example, of investments in office space, additional equipment, personnel and software and depreciation costs over time. Direct relationship costs can be calculated either as gross or net costs. *Gross direct costs* are the total costs if the customer decides to purchase the solution offered. *Net direct costs* are any additional costs which are less than optimal from the customer's point of view caused by goods, services or solutions consisting of a combination of these and other elements. Both ways of calculating this cost component give the same result. A net calculation may be more useful when comparing two or more competing packages, whereas a gross calculation gives more appropriate information when following up on the total long-term sacrifice in a given relationship with a supplier or service provider.

For example, Xerox once dominated the market in photocopying machines, and offered a service system which was efficient from Xerox's perspective. However, as the Japanese started to introduce photocopying machines which required little servicing, a new standard for optimal service costs was established. Any supplier who provided a solution which required higher service costs caused unnecessary direct relationship costs for the customer. Now, with digitized and computerized office systems there is a move back to favoring Xerox. A classic example of how to manage direct relationship costs is just-in-time logistics. By offering a delivery system which enables a customer to keep a minimum number of items in stock, a supplier can minimize the customer's need to keep capital tied up in inventories and also make it possible for the customer to invest in smaller and probably less expensive facilities. All this decreases the direct relationship costs of being a customer of this particular supplier, and that way the total long-term customer sacrifice also decreases. To take another example, in a relationship where an advertising agency requires the customer to add an additional person to its marketing staff, the extra cost for this person is a direct relationship cost.

A competitor who can offer a just-in-time delivery system that enables the customer to keep an even smaller inventory buffer, or can offer the same advertising services but without requiring the customer to tie up one person in the relationship, helps customers to decrease their long-term direct costs. If everything else is equal, these competing offerings provide more value for customers, because they involve less long-term sacrifice.

Indirect Relationship Costs

Indirect relationship costs caused by a relationship with a given supplier or service firm are due to the amount of time and resources that a customer has to devote to maintaining the relationship in case it does not function as it should. Standstill costs or other quality costs that follow from delays or low-quality repair, maintenance and delivery services or from goods and services that do not function as they are supposed to also cause indirect relationship costs. Complaints always cause such costs. On the other hand, a quick and well-managed service recovery is considered value-enhancing by customers, because it keeps down indirect relationship costs caused by a service failure, mistake or other quality problem.

The less a supplier can be trusted to keep delivery times, or the more problems there are with maintenance services, invoices and other documents, the more resources have to be devoted to the relationship. Documents have to be checked, re-checked, phone calls have to be made, e-mails have to be sent, complaints have to be filed and followed up, more checking is required and more phone calls and e-mails are needed, and so on.

The additional costs caused by this are often significant. Sometimes one or more employees have to spend a considerable amount of time taking care of problems like these, which all are caused by an unreliable supplier or service firm. Temporary personnel may have to be hired or additional personnel added. However, far too often the reasons for these costs go unnoticed by management. The internal report systems seldom show that such additional costs are caused by the poor service of a given supplier; hence, management is not alerted. Another type of indirect relationship costs are standstill costs, and the costs of lost business due to the poor service of a supplier; for example, late deliveries. Such costs can grow very high.

A competitor who provides higher quality service to the buyer creates less pressure, fewer problems and also minimizes standstill costs and other quality costs. Thus, the indirect relationship costs are lower. A company which can demonstrate to the customer that it can provide a service offering at such a quality level that indirect relationship costs are kept to a minimum will be able to show the buyer that in the long run it can provide more value for the customer.

Psychological Costs

Psychological costs are caused when the staff of a firm feel that they cannot trust a supplier or service provider. They worry about the relationship and feel that they have to take action to ensure acceptable service. They feel insecure and lack control. Their mental capacity to perform other tasks is constrained to some extent. They feel that they have to use some of their time to check that everything is in order with the supplier, that deliveries will not be delayed, maintenance will take place as scheduled, and complaints will be attended to in a timely and appropriate way. As a result, decisions are perhaps not taken as promptly as they should be or implemented as swiftly as intended, some tasks may be postponed or even forgotten, etc. This may again lead to indirect costs in the form of increasing overtime, the need for part-time manpower, lost business opportunities, etc. Psychological relationship costs for a customer are not always measurable, but they are always felt by those who suffer from having to cope with suppliers or service firms who provide bad service, and they often create unnecessary additional costs.

Price, Relationship Costs, and Total Long-Term Costs and Sacrifice

From a long-term perspective, price is not the only important cost component. Relationship costs—direct, indirect and psychological—are equally important for the buyer. Frequently, firms do not do this, because they focus on the singular transactions and the cost of singular exchanges. The price becomes the only cost component they consider. Clearly, this is not an effective decision-making criterion in a relationship where long-term cost effects of the performance of the supplier should be taken in account. In Figure 6.3 the formation of total costs in a relationship is schematically illustrated.

The total cost or sacrifice over time may be much higher than price, as is indicated in the figure. Regardless of how high a proportion of total long-term cost is relationship cost, using price as the main or sole criterion for purchasing decisions is always misleading. When a buyer is evaluating the value of competing offerings, the *net present value* of relationship costs that can be expected to occur over time should be calculated. As is illustrated in Figure 6.4, from a long-term perspective a lower-price offering may well lead to higher total long-term costs than a higher-priced product. This should not come as a surprise, because a lower level of service is probably the reason why one competitor is able to offer a lower price. In the end this lower service level will, however, cause added relationship costs. Moreover, additional services that the customer may need over time are normally not included in the price. Hence, the customer will have to pay extra for such services. This is a form of indirect relationship cost. If the customer chooses a higher quality service, such additional service may not have to be purchased separately.

The seller should always calculate what level of relationship cost, both direct and indirect and also psychological, can be expected to occur for a potential customer, to put price in a long-term cost perspective. This is a way of not only helping buyers to make better decisions, but also of justifying a higher price for better service. By carrying out such long-term cost calculations the seller can put a value on the service he provides, which the buyer can understand and appreciate.

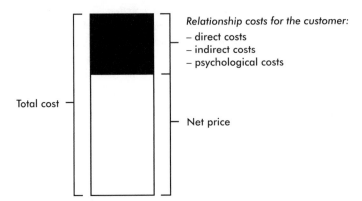

FIGURE 6.3 Relationship costs for the customer and their effect on total costs. Source: Grönroos, C., Facing the Challenge of Service Competition: The Economies of Service. In Kunst, P. & Lemminck, J. (eds), *Quality Management in Services*, 1992, p. 133. Reprodced by permission of Van Gorcum, the Netherlands.

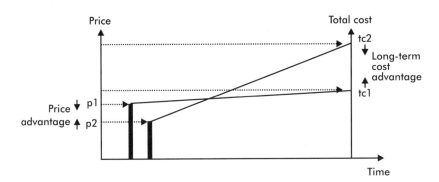

p1 and p2 denote short-term prices of two competing offerings.
tc1 and tc2 denote total long-term costs of these offerings.
(tc2-p2) and (tc1-p1) denote the total relationship costs over time
of the two offerings.

FIGURE 6.4 Price, relationship costs and total long-term costs of two offerings

The Cost of Bad Service: Lost Premium Pricing Opportunities

If a firm offers low-quality service, or an offering where a physical product constitutes the core with additional low quality service, unnecessary relationship costs will be incurred by the customer. However, as is illustrated in Figure 6.5, if a firm's service is high quality, relationship costs for the customer will correspondingly be low.

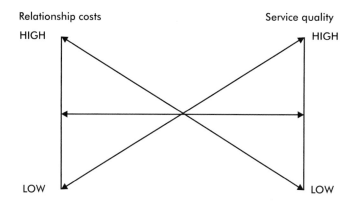

Relationship costs   Service quality
HIGH   HIGH
LOW   LOW

FIGURE 6.5   The relationship between service quality and relationship costs

The less a potential customer thinks in terms of relationship costs and long-term sacrifice, the more important price will be as a decision-making criterion. However, there are firms who claim that they are able to price up to 10 and even 20 per cent above the market price. The reason for this is that these firms understand their customers and have been able to deliver a package which keeps relationship costs at a minimum. Their service lowers any extra long-term costs of being a customer of this particular supplier or service provider. This provides the seller with a well-founded argument for selling his service at a higher price. The argument for a premium price is based on hard facts, i.e. cost savings. The trick is to learn how to calculate these costs and to teach customers to look for the impact of relationships costs on total long-term costs. The lower the relationship costs a firm can guarantee for a buyer, compared to competitors, the more opportunities exist for premium pricing.

If the additional long-term costs of bad service are not perceived by customers in a concrete way (based on facts, references and calculations) it will be difficult to make them pay for better service. In such cases, a lot of opportunities to earn money *both for the buyer and for the seller* are lost. Opportunities to price above the market price will be lost. A firm does not have to price their services 10 or 20 per cent above market price in order to make an increased profit; even one or five per cent may provide the firm with a substantial increase.

Relationship Costs for the Supplier

It is not only for the customer that poor service leads to unnecessary extra costs over time. As illustrated in Figure 6.6, the supplier receives a *net price*, after taking into account any discounts and terms of payment. According to the accounting systems of most firms, the margin between this net price and the *cost of producing* the solution for the customer is the direct economic result of the relationship. However, this is how it looks from a short-term, product-focused and transaction-oriented perspective. In reality, this is far from the truth, a fact

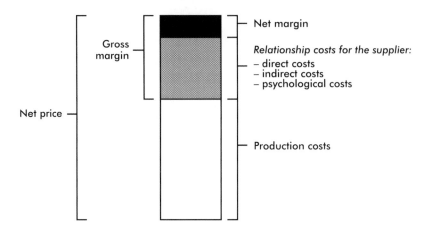

FIGURE 6.6   Relationship costs for the supplier and their profit-destroying effects.
Source: Grönroos, C., Facing the Challenge of Service Competition: The Economies of
Service. In Kunst, P. & Lemminck, J. (eds), *Quality Management in Services*, 1992, p. 133.
Reproduced by permission of Van Gorcum, the Netherlands.

that is immediately obvious when this is studied in the real world of long-term
relationships.

From a customer relationship economics perspective the production costs,
schematically illustrated in the lower part of Figure 6.6, is imaginary. The real
cost of servicing a customer is much higher. To obtain the real cost of maintaining the relationship with a given customer, all other costs caused by the way
the customer is served have to be added. Relationship costs occur for the
supplier or service provider as well, and these costs decrease the *gross margin*
between net price and production cost. If they add too much to production costs,
what should be a good profit unexpectedly turns into a negative *net profit*. Too
much of this is very damaging to a firm. Because of the accounting systems used
in many firms, management may not understand what causes this decrease in
profit level.

Relationship costs for the supplier can be divided into the same types of
costs as relationship costs for the customer. There are the *direct relationship costs*
of maintaining a customer relationship caused, for example, by delivery
systems, invoicing, complaints handling, technical services, customer training,
etc., which the supplier uses. The more complicated, outdated and inefficient
systems are and the more inappropriate the tools and equipment used, the
higher the level of direct relationship costs will be for the supplier. Interest-
ingly, the more inefficient, inappropriate and bureaucratic systems the supplier
uses, *the lower the level of service quality* will be. Of course, the reverse also holds
true.

There are also *indirect relationship costs* for the supplier in a relationship.
Mistakes have to be corrected, complaints have to be attended to, inaccurate
invoices have to be altered, problems have to be looked into, phone calls and e-
mails have to be responded to, and so on. This leads to additional workload, the
need for temporary employees, and possibly the need to employ more personnel,

etc. All these costs are unnecessary and result from less than good service. These costs are also not easily detected and can be attributed to the fact that the firm does not take good care of its customers. However, *firms should always have an account for the costs of bad service rendered, preferably specified per customer or at least customer group.* If this account grows or is frequently added to, management should perceive this as a warning signal. Finally, there are, of course, also *psychological costs* involved.

Excellent Service Pays Off Twice: For Both Parties

The analysis of relationship costs for customers, suppliers and service providers reveals clearly that bad service causes problems and unnecessary costs *for both parties*. Moreover, it shows that by and large it is the same inefficient and untrustworthy service systems that lead to complicated procedures, service failures, quality problems and complaints, thus causing these extra and unnecessary costs. Improving service quality is, therefore, a *win–win strategy* in a customer relationship. Both parties will gain something to improve their profit margin. *Good service pays off twice: for the supplier as well as the customer.* This is illustrated in Table 6.1.

The supplier or service provider has an opportunity to raise prices above market price, and at the same time has considerable cost-saving opportunities, because improved service decreases additional relationship costs for the supplier. On the other hand, the customer can avoid substantial relationship costs if the service rendered is good. Moreover, if customers are satisfied with a given supplier or service provider and feel that they can trust the firm, and perceive that they get good value in the relationship, there is no need to look for alternative suppliers. Thus, the considerable search costs involved in changing supplier and start-up costs resulting from a new business relationship can be avoided. This does not, of course, mean that customers sometimes do not want to check alternative sources of goods and services, just out of interest or to check that their service supplier is keeping up-to-date with new technology. However, in a well-functioning relationship a trusted supplier or service provider frequently has the opportunity to upgrade its solutions to meet or exceed the standard that competitors are offering.

TABLE 6.1 Excellent service pays off twice – for both parties. Source: Grönroos, Christian, Facing the Challenge of Service Competition: The Economies of Service. In Kunst, Paul & Lemmink, Jos, eds., *Quality Management in Services*. Maastricht, the Netherlands: Van Gorcum Assen, 1992, p. 139.

BENEFITS RESULTING FROM GOOD SERVICE	
For the supplier/service provider	For the customer
1. Opportunities to raise prices above the market price	1. Decreasing costs of maintaining the relationship with the supplier
2. Decreasing production costs	2. No search or start-up costs of finding new supplier/service provider

Customer Perceived Value in Relationships

Previous chapters discussed the perceived service quality concept and in this chapter customer perceived sacrifices have been analyzed in terms of short-term sacrifice (price) and long-term sacrifice (relationship cost). In this and the next section we shall take the discussion one step further and analyze how customers perceive value in a relationship. As most services are inherently relational, the value of a service offering will be discussed from a relationship perspective.[10] Such service offerings may include a service or a physical product as its core.

The starting point for understanding value is the observation that *value is perceived by customers in their internal processes and in interactions with suppliers or service providers when consuming or making use of services, goods, information, personal contacts, recovery and other elements of ongoing relationships.* Value is not produced in a factory or in the back office of a service firm.[11] This makes value a complicated concept to understand and manage. However, it is a concept that cannot be ignored.[12] Here approaches to understanding customer perceived value in relationships will be discussed. Based on these approaches, value-destroying elements in a relationship can be detected and eliminated, value-enhancing elements can be spotted and reinforced, and ways of calculating perceived value can be developed.

Customer Perceived Value (CPV) can be described by the following three equations:[13]

$$(1)\ \mathrm{CPV1} = \frac{\text{Episode benefits} + \text{Relationship benefits}}{\text{Episode sacrifice} + \text{Relationship sacrifice}}$$

$$(2)\ \mathrm{CPV2} = \frac{\text{Core solution} + \text{Additional services}}{\text{Price} + \text{Relationship costs}}$$

$$(3)\ \mathrm{CPV3} = \text{Core value} + \text{or} - \text{Added value}$$

The three equations above describe the same value concept from varying angles. By taking them all into account, one finds a deeper perception of how customers perceive value, which factors contribute to this value, and how value can be managed. It should also be observed that this is a matter of perception throughout. For example, the core solution and additional episode and relationship benefits and sacrifice are not absolute terms, but are perceived benefits and sacrifice. The same goes for core solutions and additional services. Even price and relationship costs may also be perceptions.

The first equation (CPV1) demonstrates that value is created by elements in singular episodes or service encounters as well as by perceptions of the relationship itself. This means that inherently value-creating elements exist in a relationship. Such *relationship benefits* may be a feeling of trust in a supplier or service provider, or social and technological bonds that have been established between the parties. The level of such benefits can, of course, be high or low, or somewhere in between, and may vary over time. The point is that such relationship benefits are perceived as true value-creating benefits and not as feelings.

In a similar way, *relationship sacrifice* exists in an ongoing relationship. The customer realizes that some sacrifices are related to a given relationship. For example, being the customer of a certain bank may yield a lower rate of interest on deposits, but the customer may accept this because he trusts the bank and likes the personal attention paid to him (relationship benefits).

Every episode, service encounter or purchase of a physical product produces a benefit (*episode benefit*), and requires a sacrifice (*episode sacrifice*), normally in the form of a price to pay. However, the important thing here is that the value of one service encounter cannot be judged solely on the benefit and sacrifice related to that episode. The benefits and sacrifice involved in the whole relationship also contribute to the total perceived customer value.

The second equation (CPV2) takes a different approach. Benefits for a customer are divided in two parts, the benefit of a *core solution* and of *additional services*. The core solution (a financial transaction, a production machine, or transportation from one place to another) are perceived on a per episode level. In quality terms, the core solution creates the perception of the outcome-related *technical quality* or *what* dimension. Additional services may be related to the episode, such as personal attention, deliveries or meals served during transportation. They may also be part of the continued relationship, such as information support, social calls, or recovery of quality problems or other types of mistakes. In quality terms, such additional services are perceived as the process-related *functional quality* or *how* dimension.

The denominator is divided in a *price* component, which is perceived in the short term, and a *relationship cost* component, which emerges over time as the relationship develops. The sum of price, including discounts and terms of payment, and relationship costs constitutes the total long-term costs or sacrifice in the relationship, and thus equals the sum of episode and relationship sacrifice (see Equation 1).

Customer-perceived value can, of course, be improved by adding benefits; that is, by increasing the nominator of the equation. By providing a better core solution or new additional services, such as consulting services, a firm can improve its value perception in an ongoing customer relationship. However, it is equally important, and sometimes more important, to look at the denominator of the equation (CPV2). By decreasing the sacrifice perceived by a customer, the perceived value also improves.[14] The interesting aspect of decreasing sacrifice is not related to the price component, which should not be lowered, but to the relationship cost component of the equation. By making it easier and more cost-effective for a customer to be involved with a firm, it can also create a positive effect on customer perceived value. This kind of effect is often perceived in a favorable way by customers. In the next section we discuss this issue further in the context of the third customer-perceived value equation (CPV3).

Value and The Management of Value Destroyers

The third equation (CPV3) describing customer perceived value takes yet another approach to the phenomenon. Here value is divided into a *core value* part and an *added value* part. The core value means the benefits of a core solution compared with the price paid for that solution. The added value is created by additional services in the relationship compared with the relationship costs that occur over time.

The interesting thing to observe is the fact that the added value component can be both positive and negative. If it is positive, for example because of quick delivery, attentive and supportive service employees or smoothly handled service recovery, it contributes favorably to total perceived value. However, if additional services cause unnecessary or unexpected relationship costs, the effect of the added value component is negative. Thus it is not an added value, or a negative added value.

Negative added value is created by complicated systems, non-user friendly technology, unfriendly or unskillful employees, late deliveries, incorrect invoices, badly handled complaints, delayed maintenance of equipment, complicated equipment documentation, long queues to get served, etc. If such contacts and processes in the customer relationships are not managed as *services*, but as administrative routines or are focused on internal efficiency only, their effect on customer-perceived value is normally destructive. Even an excellent core value is quickly destroyed by late deliveries, lack of proper support and delayed maintenance, or unfriendly and untrustworthy personnel and a lack of interest in service recovery. Elements in customer relationships—additional services in CPV2—which are not managed as services for the customers, but as administrative routines or in some other customer-aversive fashion, may easily become *value destroyers*. Because they create problems, a bad impression and unnecessary extra costs for customers, they decrease the value of the core solution (core value).

"Adding value" has been a buzzword in management for a long time. However, firms seem to have problems in realizing which services are really valuable for customers and add to their perceived value. "Added value" is almost always treated as something extra or new that is created for customers.[15] However, adding new services to a relationship which *already* includes value destroyers does not make much sense, because these value destroyers spoil the core value of the solution. *A much more effective way of adding value for customers is to improve what is already done for them, instead of creating something new.* By turning customer contacts and processes which are treated as administrative routines, and therefore perhaps create unnecessary and unexpected relationship costs, into services for customers, relationship costs for the customers are eliminated or at least minimized. At the same time the quality of these customer contacts increases. The added value component in Equation CPV3 becomes positive and starts to contribute favorably to total customer perceived value.

Detecting processes and customer contacts in relationships which make the value of the core solution (core value) deteriorate and taking corrective action are essential management tasks. In this way customer-perceived value is improved and the customer relationship will be strengthened. When value destroyers have been removed, if necessary, new value-adding goods or services can be included. However, at that point such extras will probably not be needed any more. Hence, the trick is not to do new things for customers, promarily, but to improve what already exists in the customer relationship.

Managers should define value-creating elements in their customer relationships, and, based on the customer perceived value equations discussed in this section, develop models which in monetary terms represent the worth of the supplier's or service provider's offerings to the customers.[16] Without such models it may be difficult, or even impossible to demonstrate to customers the value of a total service offering and how it develops over time.

Quantifying the Value of a total Service Offering

As previously discussed, a Total Service Offering in a customer relationship consists of goods components, service components, and other components related to, for example, information and personal attention. Service components consist of directly billable services, such as consultancy and maintenance, and services which are not directly billable, i.e. non-services or *hidden services*. Examples of such are invoicing, providing information, call or contact center services and managing complaints. Many of these customer contacts are normally treated as administrative routines, and they are therefore easily turned into *value destroyers* in a customer relationship. In order for the firm to be able to, first, make the customer realize the value of improved services, both billable and non-billable, it has to be able to calculate the *long-term value* of these services to the customer. Second, a *value quantification* of the various components of the total offering is needed, so that the firm can put a price on better service, even on better traditionally non-billable services. In the same manner, improvements of the goods components have to be turned into long-term value for the customer.

In order to quantify the value of a Total Service Offering, the various features that distinguish a given offering from an existing one or from competing alternatives have to be explicitly demonstrated. Such *Offering Features* can be related to goods components, service components, or other components in the customer relationship. As is illustrated in Figure 6.7, both revenue and cost benefits as well as customer investments of each feature must be calculated for a relevant number of time periods (years, months or whatever is most appropriate).

Revenue benefits are sales increases that can be expected to be achieved if a customer chooses the offering. *Cost benefits* are cost savings that follow from the choice of the given offering. Both savings of *direct* and *indirect relationship costs* ought to be included and calculated. Customer *investments* are additional costs that customers have to accept in order to be able to use the offering. Such investments are normally direct relationship costs. Cost benefits are direct relationship costs that can be saved continuously over the whole relationship, whereas customer investments are extra direct costs that normally occur only at the start of the relationship. As the figure demonstrates, revenue benefits, cost benefits and customer investments have to be calculated for each offering feature for each time period. These figures can be calculated based on historical data, sales and revenue forecasts, and calculated anticipated cost effects of the features included. The Total Offering Benefits for each period can be derived, and the *net present value* (NPV) of these total benefits over the whole time span can be calculated using an appropriate interest rate. The total offering benefits and their

OFFERING FEATURES		YEAR				
		1	2	3	4	. . . n
Feature 1:	Revenue benefit Cost benefit Investment					
Feature 1:	Revenue benefit Cost benefit Investment					
Feature 1:	Revenue benefit Cost benefit Investment					
Feature 1:	Revenue benefit Cost benefit Investment					
Total offering benefits						

FIGURE 6.7   Value quantification of the benefits of a total service offering

NPV offer a strong argument in planned marketing communication, development of offers and sales negotiations.

Figure 6.8 shows an example of the quantification of the value of a component in "Salute's Salvation," a manufacturing process over a six-year time period, following the technological upgrading of a previous component ("Salute's Traditional") where a competitor is offering a similar solution at a considerably lower price. The values in the figure represent changes from using the old technology.

Three major Offering Features of "Salute's Salvation" representing value-creating improvements are included. Two features are related to the manufacturing process of the customer: Goods feature 1: Multi-use process component, and Service feature 1: Improved maintenance reliability.

One feature of the offering is related to changes in invoicing routines made by the supplier to make the previously highly internally-focused invoicing procedure a customer-oriented service: Service feature 2: Monthly invoices specified by customer requirements.

The upgraded technology used in "Salute's Salvation" (Goods feature 1) makes it possible for the customer to manufacture several grades of its product without changing the component (the *multi-use feature*). This means that downtime decreases substantially, which can be forecasted to result in additional annual sales and revenues of 30 (annual *revenue benefit* in a currency and magnitude of the reader's choice) over the six-year period (in other situations this can equally well be six one-month periods or ten one-year periods, or any other relevant timespan and scale). The upgraded technology also decreases costs for

OFFERING FEATURES		YEAR					
		1	2	3	4	5	6
Goods features	Revenue benefit	30	30	30	30	30	30
1. Multi-use process component	Cost benefit	20	20	20	20	20	20
	Investment	40	10	0	0	0	0
Service features	Revenue benefit	20	20	20	20	20	20
1. Improved maintenance reliability	Cost benefit	15	15	15	15	15	15
	Investment	25	10	0	0	0	0
2. Monthly customer-specified invoices	Revenue benefit	0	0	0	0	0	0
	Cost benefit	5	5	5	5	5	5
	Investment	0	0	0	0	0	0
Total offering benefits		25	70	90	90	90	90

FIGURE 6.8   Calculation of relationship benefits of a total service offering including goods, service, and other components

changing the component whenever a new product grade is manufactured in the process (thus diminishing *direct relationship costs*). The estimated annual cost savings, based on previous records, are 20 (annual *cost benefit*). The new technology requires substantial new skills among the employees involved in the process (additional *direct relationship costs*). Therefore, initial training costs have to be taken into account: 40 during Year 1, 10 during Year 2, and 0 during the following four years (annual *customer investments*).

The new technology also adds *improved maintenance reliability* to "Salute's Salvation" (Service feature 1). The component requires substantially less maintenance, and the customer can take over follow-up maintenance. First of all, this means that even less downtime will occur, which will lead to additional annual sales and revenues of 20 (annual *revenue benefit*). Furthermore, improved maintenance reliability means lower maintenance costs (diminishing *relationship costs* including both a *direct* and an *indirect* portion), calculated to an annual amount of 15 (annual *cost benefit*). However, the customer will have to invest initially in employee training so that they learn how to handle maintenance-related tasks. These sums are calculated as 25 during Year 1, 10 during Year to 2, and 0 thereafter, because newly hired employees are expected to be trained on the job by more experienced colleagues.

Because the relationship with this customer and others includes the regular shipment of materials in order to strengthen the relationship with its customers the supplier has at the same time developed a new invoicing system, where the invoices are specified according to customer requirements. In addition, instead of sending an invoice for every shipment, which for larger customers may have meant several invoices per month, customers are now invoiced monthly only (Service feature 2: Monthly invoices specified by customer requirements). This is calculated to decrease the customers' cost of handling documents (annual *direct relationship cost*) by 5 every year.

When the revenue and cost benefits are added up and the customer investments subtracted, the Total Offering Benefits for each year can be assessed. In this example they are 25, 70, 90, 90, 90 and 90 for the six years studied. Using the customer's normally applied interest rate the net present value (NPV) of the total benefits of the three new and distinguishing offering benefits can be calculated.

When this NPV is compared with a traditional solution and with the price savings offered by a competitor, the value of improved goods and service features can be put into perspective. A competing offering which does not offer these benefits will have to be priced considerably lower. Another consequence of a value quantification of a Total Service Offering like the one illustrated here is that one can put a price on services. If the total benefits for the customer can be calculated in this way, it is possible to argue for the costs of the improved service which enables the customer to enjoy these benefits. Than a price increase which splits the total savings potential between the supplier and the customer may make sense.

Customer Relationship Profitability

Offering good customer perceived value is critical, because good value will have an positive impact on customer loyalty, which in turn through lower relationship costs and premium pricing opportunities improves a customer's contribution to the firm's profit. However, value is, of course, not the only factor influencing profit. In the following sections a model of customer relationship profitability will be discussed, in order to help managers to understand the mechanisms that make a customer profitable for a firm.

Analyzing the profitability and profit contribution of customers and customer relationships is a problematic task in most firms, for individuals as well as for customer groups. Accounting systems are normally based on products, not customers. For a manufacturer of physical goods, it is possible to calculate revenues, costs, profits and even profitability per product and product group. In a service firm it is much more difficult to do the same, because of the difficulty of measuring and quantifying one unit of service. For both manufacturers and service firms it is almost impossible to find out information about revenues, costs, profits and profitability of customers or customer bases. Separate analysis almost always has to be done, and even then the information registered by the accounting system may not be enough.[17] The tradition of registering cash flow, revenue and cost per product comes from the industrial era, when production was the major bottleneck. In the post-industrial era where customers, and employees, are the bottleneck, customer profitability and registration of cash flows, revenues and costs per customer is more important for strategic as well as tactical management.

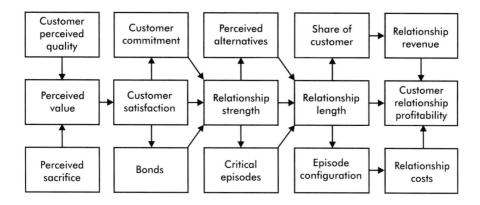

FIGURE 6.9   The customer relationship profitability model: the mechanisms behind profitable customers. Source: Storbacka, K., Strandvik, T. & Grönroos, C., Managing Customer Relationship for Profit: The Dynamics of Relationship Quality. *International Journal of Service Industry Management*, **5**(5), 1994, p. 23.

Figure 6.9 illustrates a *customer relationship profitability* model.[18] This model helps managers to see the mechanisms that make customers more or less profitable. A quick glance at the model demonstrates that the road from *customer perceived value* to customer profitability includes a considerable number of factors, which are areas that have to be planned, managed and monitored if a positive contribution to profit is to be expected. The model is conceptual, and should help managers realize the complicated mechanisms that influence customer profitability. Some of the factors, such as perceived sacrifice, some customer–firm bonds, patronage concentration, relationship length, relationship revenue and relationship cost can be measured in an objective manner using metric scales. Other factors, such as perceived quality and value, satisfaction, commitment, some customer–firm bonds and relationship strength can only be measured using attitudinal scales and/or qualitative data. The objective here is not, however, to develop a calculation model, but to show the reader what to take into consideration and *how to think*.

The *customer relationship profitability* model includes four links as well as factors which influence these links. The four links are:

- from customer perceived value to customer satisfaction;
- from customer satisfaction to relationship strength;
- from relationship strength to relationship length;
- from relationship length to customer relationship profitability.

From value to satisfaction. As discussed earlier in this chapter, the total service offering including core solutions and additional services, how the *quality* of this offering is perceived compared to the *perceived sacrifice* of customers, determines customers' perceptions of the value of this offering and, in ongoing relationships, the value of the relationship. Customers are satisfied with perceived quality provided that the sacrifice involved—price and relationship costs—is not too high. Hence, perceived value determines customer satisfaction.

Customer satisfaction has an effect on two factors that have an impact on the next link in the model. Satisfied customers may become *committed* to the supplier or service provider, because they trust the other party or are pleased with the level of sacrifice involved in the relationship. Customer satisfaction also contributes to the formation of *bonds* between the two parties. Bonds (which can be social, cultural, ideological, psychological, knowledge-based, technological, geographical, time-related, legal or economic) (see the discussion of bonds in Chapter 4), tie customers to the supplier or service provider, because they make it easier, more comfortable or more economical for the customer to continue to patronize the same firm.

From satisfaction to relationship strength. The next link shows how satisfaction has a favorable effect on the strength of a relationship. Strong relationships make customers loyal. Customer satisfaction has a direct impact on *relationship strength*. However, the effect also applies to *customer commitments* and *bonds* between the two parties. The more committed a customer is to a firm and the more bonds that exist between them, the stronger the relationship will be. The model does not say anything about what degree of satisfaction and commitment is required to create relationships of a certain strength, since this varies from case to case. It is important to bear in mind that the degree of satisfaction and commitment and perceived bonds often may have to be quite high to have a definite impact on relationship strength. For example, it seems that customers who claim that they are satisfied with a solution are not always loyal. The percentage of customers who make repeat purchases can be as low as 30 or even lower. However, customers who claim that they are *very* satisfied with a solution seem to have a much stronger relationship with the seller. The repurchase percentage may increase to 80 or above.

Strong relationships influence the number of *alternative solutions* that a customer thinks of. A high relationship strength can be expected to make the customer think less of alternatives to the existing relationship, and vice versa. In addition, a strong relationship will probably include fewer *critical* service encounters or *episodes* (unfavorable incidents). First, customers are satisfied with and feel committed to the relationship, because no or only a few unfavorable incidents have occurred. Second, a strong relationship can be expected to make critical episodes look less unfavorable, provided that such incidents do not occur too often.

From relationship strength to relationship length. In the third link, relationship strength has direct and indirect effects on the *length of a relationship*. The stronger the relationship, the longer it will last. Customers do not see incentives to stop doing business with the same supplier or service provider. At the same time, a strong relationship makes customers perceive that *fewer alternatives exist*, and this lack of alternatives has a positive effect on the length of a relationship. Also, a lack of perceived *critical episodes* has a similar influence.

Longer relationships can be expected to have a favorable effect on two factors which are critical for customers' contribution to profit. In continuing relationships, where customers are satisfied and feel strong ties to the other party, they can be expected to purchase more from this firm. A *patronage concentration* effect thus occurs. The supplier or service provider gets a "larger share of the customer's wallet." In ongoing relationships both parties also learn how to adjust to each other and how to collaborate so that the customer uses the offering in a more effective and personalized way. Fewer mistakes are made, so less recovery is needed. A more cost-efficient *episode configuration* should develop. Moreover, when there is a trusting enduring relationship, the firm can more easily suggest new ways of producing and using a service, moving to, for example, less expensive Internet-based contacts for information and payments. Hence, the service can be produced in a way which ties up less expensive resources without a perceived negative effect on quality and value.

From relationship length to relationship profitability. The final link shows how the length of a relationship influences the profitability of customer relationships. The length of a relationship by itself has a *positive effect on profit*, because costs of customer acquisition can be minimized and in many cases opportunities exist for premium pricing. A higher patronage concentration has a *positive effect* on the *revenue streams* in the relationship with any given customer. In addition, a more cost-efficient episode configuration, where unnecessary elements in relationships, such as answering customer questions and recovering service failures, can be avoided, and less expensive ways of performing a service can be introduced and accepted by customers, has a positive effect on *relationship costs*.

Hence, a stronger relationship can be expected to directly influence customer relationship profitability, and does this indirectly through improved revenue streams, higher relationship revenue, and more cost-efficient service processes and lower relationship costs.

If all favorable effects implied by the model occur, higher perceived service quality compared to customer sacrifice should lead to improved profitability in customer relationships. However, the links are not totally clear-cut; factors external to the model may influence some of the links or factors in an unexpected manner. A customer who introduces a solution, for example, based on new technology, or who aggressively promotes a low price may change the links between the factors in the model. For example, a new much lower price option may make customers perceive episodes in existing relationships in a negative sense, because price may suddenly have become an issue. Or new technology offered by a competitor may untie a technology-based bond. In both cases, a new alternative may suddenly be considered realistic.

Managers must always follow up customer relationships, on individual relationship levels where possible, to monitor how the mechanisms in the model function. What can be measured using hard data should be measured. This requires that accounting systems are adjusted so that data on costs and revenues are available at a customer- or customer-base level. Factors that can be measured only by attitudinal measurement instruments or in qualitative ways should also be monitored.

The Value of Customers

Finally, firms should know the long-term value of their individual customers. The lifetime value of customers should be calculated. When managers have such information they realize that long-term customer relationships are valuable assets. It also helps marketers to realize the importance of keeping existing customers.

The calculation of the customers' value should be based on information on *customers' current contribution to net profit*, not sales figures.[19] For each customer, or for customer groups, the direct costs of producing an offering, including relationship costs occurring for the seller, are deducted from revenues from this customer. What remains after this deduction, the net profit from a customer, should cover the firm's fixed costs.

A customer's contribution to net profit may vary substantially over the life of the relationship. New customers may be unprofitable or their profit contribution may be low, whereas long-standing customers frequently become more profitable as the relationship continues. Such considerations have to be taken into account when calculating the long-term profit contribution of customers. Therefore, it is essential that managers gain as much insight as possible into typical customer life cycles.[20]

The *lifetime value* of a customer relationship or, when individual figures cannot be obtained, the lifetime value of a relationship with a given customer group, can be calculated as the *net present value of the net profits that can be expected over the years*. This lifetime value shows how important each customer is to a supplier or service provider. If such figures are not calculated, the value of existing customers will not be fully appreciated, and the loss of value that follows from departing customers will not be understood. By calculating the lifetime value of customers, managers obtain information on which customer relationships are critical to the firm, which are contributing less to total profitability, and which are not profitable. However, one should always remember that customers who are not profitable at a given time may become profitable in the future, for example as a result of a different episode configuration, increasing disposable income or changing needs.

Analyzing Customer Profitability

Customer-base analyses in which companies specifically focus on determining profitability distributions show that certain parallels can be drawn between companies regardless of industry.

Most companies that have conducted customer profitability analyses have been surprised to discover how large a share of their customer base really is unprofitable. It seems to be the rule, rather than the exception, that more than 30 per cent of customers are unprofitable. This uneven distribution of profits and losses between customers of course leads to a number of strategic and operational problems. A central strategic problem is that customers subsidize each other, i.e. cross-subsidization occurs in the customer base. Cross-subsidization makes a company vulnerable to onslaughts by competitors. Competitors usually try to attract the most profitable customer groups, and if only 30 per cent of a company's customers are profitable, for example, the risk exposure is of course enormous.

Management literature often cites the Pareto rule which claims that 20 per cent of customers account for 80 per cent of profits. This is, however, incorrect. Twenty per cent of customers may indeed account for 80 per cent of volume but, with regard to profit, the distribution can be very different. This is because earnings can be negative of course and this leads to a distribution, which is often very dramatic.

Source: This illustration was developed by Kaj Storbacka, CRM Customer Relationship Management, Ltd.

Segmentation Based on Customer Relationship Profitability

In a relationship context marketers should aim at treating customers on an individual basis. The developing information technology offers the means to do so. However, in some situations it is not financially justified to communicate individually through non-interactive media with each and every customer, or to treat every customer individually. Regardless of this, customer relationship profitability data provides firms with a means of segmenting the existing customer base to direct its marketing and service activities more effectively. It is tempting to consider large customers more interesting from a profitability point of view than small customers, and to consider satisfied customers more profitable than less satisfied ones. Assuming this without knowing it for a fact may turn out to be a dangerous decision-making criterion. As Storbacka[21] has demonstrated in his studies in the retail banking sector, firms can have large groups of very satisfied customers who are unprofitable. These customers are often, but not always, small in terms of volume. Furthermore, large customers in terms of volume may also be unprofitable.[22] Managing a relationship with small and satisfied but unprofitable customers is obviously a different issue demanding different actions compared to handling large and unprofitable customers, or small/profitable and large/profitable customers, respectively.

Figure 6.10 illustrates the segmentation of the customer base of two hypothetical firms based on volume and customer profitability data. The size of the half-circles denote the business volume from the corresponding segment. Both firms clearly manage to serve their medium-sized customers in a profitable way, since segments IV are much larger than the unprofitable segments III. However, most of their small-sized customers are unprofitable, which is indicated by segments I being much larger than segments II. As far as the firms' large customers are concerned, major differences between the two firms can be seen. Firm A obviously has a considerable profitability problem, as segment V is much larger than segment VI. Most firms in Firm A's situation would not realize what the profitability problem was caused by. In the worst case, which unfortunately is common, Firm A would perhaps provide its small and medium-sized customers with a lower service quality to reduce costs, but continue to supply its large customers with the same level of service as before. The profit increase from the small and medium-sized customers would not be substantial, but the risk of losing profitable medium-sized customers due to the lower service quality would increase. However, the unprofitable segment of large customers (V) would

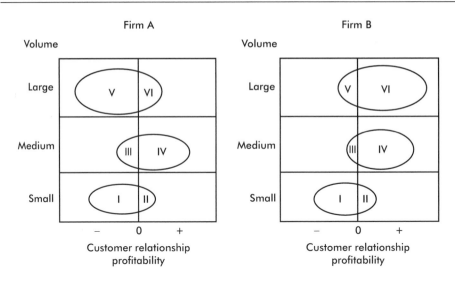

FIGURE 6.10   Segmentation information based on volume and customer
profitability data

remain unprofitable, and only marginal profitability gains would be achieved. In
the worst case, if too many profitable medium-sized customers are lost, total
profitability would decrease. In Firm B totally different actions are called for.
Here the total problem is much smaller. The main action needed is to reconfigure
the service processes for small customers, so that they become profitable.

If one does not know the profitability of different customers or groups of
customers, it is not possible to take proper action. A small but unprofitable
customer should, for example, probably be offered a different and less expensive
service system. For example, using pricing mechanisms, banks have tried to
make their small customers start using less expensive service processes such as
Internet banking or paying bills from their home computers. Large and unprofitable customers probably have to be treated in a different way. However, getting
historical data from a firm's accounting and reporting system is often difficult,
because systems are still geared towards measuring the profitability of products,
not customer profitability. Separate analysis of accounting data is frequently
required, and even then it may be difficult, without making substantial qualified
guesses, to get the information needed.[23]

Summary and Questions for Discussion

In this chapter the issue of return on service and relationships between service
providers and customers was discussed. Sellers have to be able to calculate the
long-term value of their service offerings to make buyers appreciate the value of
services. If such calculations are not made, buyers will frequently consider
service elements in customer relationships to be of limited or no value for them.
The concept of *relationship costs* occurring for customers, suppliers and service
providers was discussed, and it was observed that unnecessary costs are created

for both customers and suppliers due to the same reasons; for example, late deliveries, slow service, failures or quality problems. The profitability of customer relationships was then discussed, and a model of customer relationship profitability was described.

Questions for discussion

1. Why are long-term costs more important to consider than price when making purchasing decisions?
2. What are relationship costs? Why do relationship costs occur? How can such costs be avoided?
3. What is meant by "it is a lack of quality that costs money, rather than adding quality?"
4. What is customer perceived value? How can it be calculated?
5. Develop a customer value model for your business, or for any given business.
6. How can the value of an improved total service package be quantified?
7. Which factors influence the formation of customer relationship profitability?
8. What is customer lifetime value? Why is it important to calculate this?

Case Study

MOM: Strategic Development Based On Customer Base Analysis[24]
By Kaj Storbacka, CRM Customer Relationship Management, Ltd

The Profitability Problem of Major Office Machine (MOM) Ltd

Tom "Jungle" Peterson had been with Major Office Machine Ltd (MOM) for four years when he was appointed Executive Vice President of the business unit selling office equipment and other technical equipment to retailers. In addition to the thrill of promotion, Tom was faced with a serious problem as the business unit had been incurring losses of half a million euros annually for several years. His job was to ensure that the unit at least broke even. His predecessors had tried many different restructuring methods but had all failed. Tom decided to use an alternative method to solve the problem. He decided to start at the customer end and analyze the reasons behind the unprofitable situation.

Tom assembled a team to analyze the situation. The team consisted of an experienced consultant and his assistant, a controller at MOM, and ad hoc members from various departments at MOM who were involved in producing different types of customer encounters.

The development process consisted of three phases.

- *The customer profitability analysis phase.* The aim of this phase was to calculate customer profitability and analyze reasons for the losses.
- *Relationship strategy phase.* The aim of this was to differentiate the offerings and customer relationship processes on the basis of the data obtained from the analysis in order to ensure a satisfactory profit level.

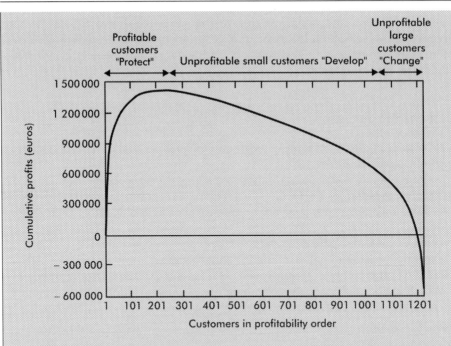

FIGURE 6.11   Case study of MOM: profitability of the customer base (1201 customers).
Source: Storbacka, J.: CRM Customer Relationship Management, Ltd.

- *The implementation phase.* MOM was an established company and had been operating for about 20 years. Tom was well aware that implementing the changes he envisioned would demand a considerable amount of work both within the company and with the customers.

1. The Analysis Phase

The business unit had 1,201 retailers as customers; some belonged to chains, others were large companies, but a large share of the customer base consisted of relatively small retailers. In total the business unit was making an annual loss of about 0.6 million euros.

The analysis team carried out a customer profitability analysis in which all revenue and the total cost mass of the business unit were distributed among customers. The distribution of customer profitability in the business units' customer base is depicted in Figure 6.11 (a so-called *Stobachoff curve*[25].)

The curve is based on the calculation of the profit for each individual customer. The customers are arranged in order of profitability, so that customer 1 is the most profitable and customer 1,201 the least profitable. The profits from each customer are then added together. The curve shows how profit accumulates throughout the customer base.

On the basis of the curve, it was possible for Tom to draw several interesting (and dramatic) conclusions about his customer base:

- As long as the curve rises, profitable customers are added. This makes it possible to determine the number of profitable customers. To Tom's surprise only about 250 out of 1,201 (i.e. 20 per cent) were profitable. They accounted for approximately 1.5 million euros of revenue. These were later called the *Protect* group.
- Out of the unprofitable customers, two groups emerged. The first group consisted of the next 800 customers, who all seemed to be equally unprofitable since an almost straight line emerged between customers numbered 250 to 1,050. Together, these customers created a loss of about 0.75 million euros. Tom found out in the analysis that these were small sales volume customers. These were later called the *Develop* group.
- The final 151 customers, who were the most unprofitable, created a loss of over a million euros. These customers were, to Tom's great surprise, very large and highly valued at MOM. He noticed the "customer profitability paradox:" *only really large customers can be very profitable or very unprofitable!* This group was later called the *change* group.

Tom concluded that his customer base was especially sensitive to attacks from competitors. The company's existence depended on about 250 profitable customers! Also, there had to be serious problems with the strategy of the business unit since it allowed about 100 customers to be extremely unprofitable.

Finding the Profitability Potentials

It is tempting, based on the Stobachoff curve, to draw straightforward, simple conclusions. It might seem attractive to "cut" the curve at around customer number 1,000. Thus, it would seem to be possible to eliminate the most unprofitable customers. Even if the idea of terminating relationships is part of the relationship marketer's arsenal, a more developed analysis rapidly shows that this is not a simple solution to the profitability problems of a customer base. The termination of customer relationships should never be the main solution to improving customer profitability. The reason for this is obvious. Most costs in most businesses these days are fixed costs. When analyzing customer profitability, fixed costs are divided among customers. Even if the most unprofitable customer relationships were terminated, the fixed costs remain, and these, in turn, have to be redistributed to the rest of the customers, leading to the emergence of an identical curve. Terminating customer relationships is thus not an optimal solution.

To work with customer profitability as a calculation exercise is in itself uninteresting. What is interesting is using customer profitability knowledge to identify profitability potentials within the customer base and implement changes which make it possible to benefit from this potential.

The information gathered can be used to conduct simulations of consequences of various changes in the relationships ("what-if"-analyses). You can simulate for example, that you terminate certain relationships and redistribute all costs, raise prices (and assume that some customers will decrease their purchases), invest in marketing and simulate by how much sales have to increase for profitability to reach an acceptable level, etc. These analyses usually show dramatic results. Even small changes in customer purchasing behavior can have dramatic effects if you are able to change the behavior of a large share of the customer base.

To identify profitability potential, you have to analyze the causes of unprofitability. Companies need to ask themselves what aspect of their operations encourages unprofitable behavior. In principle there seem to be three causes of unprofitability.

1. *Work*. Most unprofitable customers are unprofitable because the service provider is investing too much in the relationship in proportion to the revenue derived from it. "Work" includes all activities carried out within the relationship, both for the customer and with the customer. To benefit from the profitability potential, the provider should reduce activities for which it is not compensated. Typical activities, which create large costs, are all types of activities that are performed in connection with the logistics process: order lines, deliveries, after-sales service. Customer service work in terms of sales, technical service, help desk- and call-center activities also results in costs.

2. *Price*. Pricing is a complex issue which is partly determined by the competitive situation, but which in surprisingly many cases includes a large component of creativity. Profitability analyses often indicate that really unprofitable customers are unprofitable because of pricing problems. A reason for this may be the fact that relationships with large customers are less symmetrical, i.e. large customers can negotiate prices which are favorable to them. But even in asymmetric relationships, where the provider's power is greater, the pricing system can lead to unprofitability. In such a case it is often a question of discount systems based on sales volumes. In certain cases the price is so low that the customer is no longer profitable. In other cases corrective actions can include other pricing issues such as the pricing of deliveries, after-sales service, interest on delayed payments and additional fees for small deliveries. In general, of all the measures a provider can take to influence customer purchasing behavior, price is the most powerful. It is therefore important to ensure that pricing leads to the customer behavior that is desired by the provider. A quick analysis often proves that companies lack pricing policies with general principles about how price should influence customer behavior. If a daily newspaper, for example, wants its customers to commit for longer periods, it has to ensure that this is advantageous to the customer from a pricing point of view. In most cases in the newspaper industry, however, it would seem that it is cheapest for the customer to subscribe periodically, taking advantage of the special rates that newspapers offer.

3. *Volume*. Even if volume in itself is not a good indicator of relationship value, it is clear that customers with greater volume are more interesting from the profitability point of view. In most customer bases, all small-volume customers are unprofitable because their volume is not sufficient to cover fixed costs. As a result, many providers have chosen to set volume limits which customers have to reach in order to enter into a relationship with the provider. Alternatively, transaction fees can be imposed in the form of an additional fee, for example, for small deliveries, which ensures that even small deliveries can be sufficiently profitable. Choosing one's customers can thus also be a sound strategy.

Profitability potential can be identified on the basis of the analysis carried out in the Stobachoff curve. The grouping of customers has a direct effect on the profitability potential. Profitability potential includes:

- *Protecting profitable customers.* By protecting these customers a company can ensure that relationships become long-term and that it can maintain the positive cash flow from profitable customers. This creates security and a starting point for further business development.
- *Developing small customers.* This development can often involve both an increase in relationship revenue and a decrease in relationship costs. Revenue can be increased by changing the pricing policy or by setting a minimum volume limit for customers. Changing relationship strategies so that the amount of work invested in each relationship decreases can also cut costs.
- *Changing the behavior of the most unprofitable customers.* These customers, taken individually, are the most interesting since they hold the potential to become very profitable. Individual analyses of the causes behind customer unprofitability can be carried out and individual solutions created for each customer with the aim of changing pricing (to increase relationship revenue) or changing relationship processes to reduce the work done for the customer (and thus cut costs).

All customers have profitability potential and are therefore of interest. Profitable customers are interesting because they constitute the backbone of the provider's cash flow and enable future development of the business. The most unprofitable customers taken individually are interesting since it is possible to rapidly transform them into profitable customers. Customers seldom wish to be unprofitable since they know that this will have adverse effects on the service they receive from the provider. Individual negotiations can therefore lead to dramatic results.

Even small customers are interesting, although perhaps they are more interesting as a group. This is because there are usually many of them and relationships with them are asymmetric. Asymmetry in this context refers to their ability and desire to oppose changes initiated by the provider. Implementing changes in pricing is often easier with small customers. In many of the cases we have observed, the largest profitability potential was found among the small customers.

2. The Relationship Strategy Phase

Existing MOM customer relationships were analyzed with regard to their processes and the activities which MOM performed in these processes.

The analysis showed that MOM was serving its small customers "too well," i.e. that both large and small customers received the same level of service. It was also concluded that customers with the same purchasing volume could differ quite significantly in profitability—and this seemed to be true in most volume classes. To find out why customers with the same volume could vary so much regarding profitability, Tom compared the purchasing behavior of some customers with the help of customer profiles, describing the behavior behind the profitability figures. Tom focused on issues such as

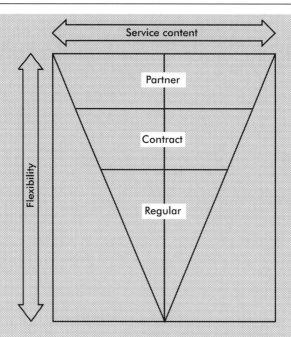

FIGURE 6.12   Relationship strategy dimensions

product mix, number of sales calls, number of calls to the call center, number of orders, number of order lines, number of invoices, credit limit, number of returned products, number of service visits, number of deliveries and after-sales service.

First, Tom discovered that there were differences in the profitability of the different products, i.e. customers who bought products with a better sales margin were naturally more profitable than others. He also noted that some customers enthusiastically used MOM's free services. Service Support, Helpdesk, and Customer Service were functions that demanded a lot of time and work and which cost a great deal. Personal contacts also affected profitability. Tom was forced to admit that his games of golf with the CEO of one of their biggest customers, fun as they were, had a negative impact on company profitability.

Tom also realized that certain customers bought products often but in small quantities. They seemed to be waiting for discounts and buying products sold at reduced prices. They often received cash discounts and goods in after-deliveries (additional product deliveries when not all products ordered where shipped at the same time). These customers also returned products more often than others did.

On the basis of this analysis, three alternative relationship strategies emerged: (1) *partnerships*, (2) *contract-dealers*, and (3) *regular* customers. The relationship strategies were described in great detail in terms of offerings for respective customers, the processes necessary to produce the offering, and also how work would be organized with different customer types. A script was also created for each relationship strategy.

The relationship strategies differ in two ways (see Figure 6.12):

- *Service content*, i.e. the degree of service content, i.e. all the support that MOM can give to retailers in terms of training, marketing support, alternative invoicing methods, strategic planning, etc. The service content is greatest for partners and smallest for regular customers, with contract-dealers in between.
- *Flexibility*, i.e. the willingness of MOM to find customer-specific solutions and adapt to retailer processes. The logic here is the same as with the service content. In other words, MOM is willing to make changes to their own processes for partners, whereas they are not interested in creating diverging solutions for regular customers. The regular customers are offered a standardized solution while partners are offered company specific solutions. Contract-dealers are offered some level of customization of the service offering.

Involving Employees in Changing Strategies

Change is always difficult to implement, and changes that aim to improve customer profitability are among the most difficult. This is because change often involves negative aspects from the customer's point of view: prices are raised, delivery terms worsen, less personal service is offered, more self-service is required, etc. For customer contact employees this usually means more complaints from customers and unpleasant customer encounters. As a result, there will be resistance to change from both employees and customers.

It is therefore crucial that the change process is as smooth as possible and that key customer contact people are involved. Employees need to be aware of the profitability data and draw their own conclusions. They have to personally understand the strategic solutions the provider has chosen in order to be able to deal with the complex customer encounters that change often entails.

3. The Implementation Phase

The previous section discussed changing strategies, and ways to make the implementation of change as smooth as possible, for both staff and customers.

Tom decided to involve a large number of the business unit's personnel in the relationship strategy phase. By involving his personnel he hoped that the implementation phase would be made significantly easier.

What was the end result of the work carried out? Tom Peterson is pleased. The company was able to attain several goals at once with the systematic process they created. The business unit no longer incurred losses and personnel had embraced a new way of thinking. There was a much greater awareness of what drives profitability in a company like MOM. Most importantly, MOM had also succeeded in improving customer service as they improved customer profitability.

Unprofitable Customers

It is essential to maintain a positive attitude towards unprofitable customers. Unprofitable customers are not bad customers. Customers are unprofitable because the company's strategies make unprofitable customer behavior possible. There are no bad customers, only bad strategies. Customer profitability is always a function of customer purchasing behavior, and behavior can be influenced in many ways. By changing strategies you can encourage customer behavior, which in turn can have a positive impact on customer profitability.

Many companies dealing with customer profitability issues have drawn too simplistic conclusions from the results of the analyses. As a result, personnel often end up thinking that unprofitable customers are bad customers. This has direct consequences on how customers are handled, which further aggravates profitability problems. It is therefore important for companies to view unprofitable customers in a positive light. Unprofitable customers often represent the greatest profitability potential of a company.

Further Reading

Anderson, J.C. & Narus, J.A. (1995) Capturing the Value of Supplementary Services. *Harvard Business Review*, **73**, January–February, pp. 75–83.

Anderson, J.C. & Narus, J.A. (1998) Business Marketing: Understand What Customers Value. *Harvard Business Review*, **76**, November–December, pp. 53–61.

Anderson, E.W. & Sullivan, M.W. (1993) The Antecedents and Consequences of Customer Satisfaction for Firms. *Marketing Science*, **12**, Spring, pp. 125–143.

Crosby, P.B. (1979) *Quality is Free*. New York: McGraw-Hill.

Grönroos, C. (1990) *Service Management and Marketing. Managing the Moments of Truth in Service Competition*. Lexington, MA: Lexington Books.

Grönroos, C. (1992) Facing the Challenge of Service Competition: The Economies of Service. In Kunst, P. & Lemmink, J. (eds), *Quality Management in Services*. Maastricht, the Netherlands: Van Gorcum Assen, pp. 129–140.

Grönroos, C. (1997) Value-driven Relational Marketing: From Products to Resources and Competencies. *Journal of Marketing Management*, **13**(5), pp. 407–419.

Hart, C.W. & Johnson, M.D. (1999) Growing the Trust Relationship. *Marketing Management*, Spring, pp. 9–19.

Heskett, J.L., Sasser, Jr., W.E. & Schlesinger, L.A. (1997) *The Service Profit Chain: How Leading Companies Link Profit and Growth to Loyalty, Satisfaction and Value*. New York: The Free Press.

Lapierre, J. (1997) What Does Value Mean in Business-to-business Professional Services? *International Journal of Service Industry Management*, **8**(5), pp. 377–397.

Levitt, T. (1986) *The Marketing Imagination*. New York: The Free Press.

Lovelock, C.H. (1994) *Product Plus: How Product + Service = Competitive Advantage*. New York: McGraw-Hill.

Normann, R. & Ramirez, R. (1993) From Value Chain to Value Constellation: Designing Interactive Strategy. *Harvard Business Review*, July–August, pp. 65–77.

Payne, A. & Holt, S. (1999) Review of the "Value" Literature and Implications for Relationship Marketing. *Australasian Marketing Journal*, **7**(1), pp. 41–51.

Pickworth, J.R. (1987) Minding the Ps and Qs: Linking Quality and Productivity. The *Cornell Hotel and Restaurant Administration Quarterly*, May.

Ravald, A. & Grönroos, C. (1996) The Value Concept and Relationship Marketing. *European Journal of Marketing*, **30**(2), pp. 19–30.

Reichheld, F.F. (1996) *The Loyalty Effect. The Hidden Force Behind Growth, Profits and Lasting Value*. Boston, MA: Harvard Business School Press.

Reichheld, F.F. & Sasser, Jr., W.E. (1990) Zero Defections: Quality Comes to Services. *Harvard Business Review*, September–October, pp. 105–111.

Rust, R.T., Zahorik, A.J. & Keiningham, T.L. (1994) *Return on Quality: Measuring the Financial Impact of Your Company's Quest for Quality*. Chicago, IL: Richard D. Irwin.

Rust, R.T., Zahorik, A.J. & Keiningham, T.L. (1995) Return on Quality (ROQ): Making Service Quality Financially Accountable. *Journal of Marketing*, **59**, April, pp. 58–70.

Stauss, B. & Friege, C. (1999) Regaining Service Customers. Costs and Benefits of Regain Management. *Journal of Service Research*, **1**(4), pp. 347–361.

Storbacka, K. (1994) *The Nature of Customer Relationship Profitability*. Helsinki/Helsingfors: Hanken Swedish School of Economics Finland/CERS Center for Relationship Marketing and Service Management.

Storbacka, K. (1997) Segmentation Based on Customer Profitability—Retrospective Analysis of Retail Bank Customer Bases. *Journal of Marketing Management*, **13**(5), pp. 479–492.

Storbacka, K. (2000) Customer Profitability: Analysis and Design Issues. In Sheth, J.N. & Parvatiyar, A. (eds), *Handbook of Relationship Marketing*. Thousand Oaks, CA: Sage Publications, pp. 565–586.

Storbacka, K., Strandvik, T. & Grönroos, C. (1994) Managing Customer Relationships for Profit: The Dynamics of Relationship Quality. *International Journal of Service Industry Management*, **5**(5), pp. 21–38.

Tzokas, N. & Saren, M. (1999) Value Transformation in Relationship Marketing. *Australasian Marketing Journal*, **7**(1), pp. 52–62.

Wikström, S. (1996) Value Creation by Company–Consumer Interaction. *Journal of Marketing Management*, **12**, pp. 359–374.

Wilson, D.T. & Jantrania, S. (1994) Understanding the Value of a Relationship. *Asia-Australia Marketing Journal*, **2**(1), pp. 55–66.

Notes

1 Pickworth, J.R., Minding the Ps and Qs: Linking Quality and Productivity. *The Cornell Hotel and Restaurant Administration Quarterly*, May 1987.

2 Crosby, P.B., *Quality is Free*. New York: McGraw-Hill, 1979.

3 Customer satisfaction studies frequently demonstrate a clear relationship between customer satisfaction and retention. See, for example, Rust, R.T., Zahorik, A.J. & Keiningham, T.L., *Return on Quality: Measuring the Financial Impact of Your Company's Quest for Quality*. Chicago, IL: Richard D. Irwin, 1994 and Anderson, E.W. & Sullivan, M.W., The Antecedents and Consequences of Customer Satisfaction for Firms. *Marketing Science*, **12**, Spring 1993, pp. 125–143. One should, however, remember that there are clear indications that this relationship is often only positive if customers are very satisfied and not merely satisfied.

4 Hart, C.W. & Johnson, M.D., Growing the Trust Relationship. *Marketing Management*, Spring 1999, pp. 9–19.

5 Hart & Johnson, *op.cit.*

6 See Reichheld, F.F., *The Loyalty Effect. The Hidden Force Behind Growth, Profits and Lasting Value*. Boston, MA: Harvard Business School Press, 1996.

7 Reichheld, F.F. & Sasser, Jr., W.E., Zero Defections: Quality Comes to Services. *Harvard Business Review*, September–October 1990, pp. 105–111. Similar results from another study are reported in Heskett, J.L., Sasser, Jr., W.E. & Schlesinger, L.A., *The Service Profit Chain: How Leading Companies Link Profit and Growth to Loyalty, Satisfaction, and Value*. New York: The Free Press, 1997.

8 Grönroos, C., *Service Management and Marketing. Managing the Moments of Truth in Service Competition*. Lexington, MA: Lexington, Books, 1990.

9 Grönroos, C., Facing the Challenge of Service Competition: The Economies of Service. In Kunst, P. & Lemmink, J. (eds), *Quality Management in Services*. Maastricht, the Netherlands: Van Gorcum, 1992, pp. 129–140.

10 Value perception and value formation in relationships have not yet been studied to any considerable extent. See, for example, Ravald, A. & Grönroos, C., The Value Concept and Relationship Marketing. *European Journal of Marketing*, **30**(2), 1996, pp. 19–30, and Lapierre, J., What Does Value Mean in Business-to-business Professional Services? *International Journal of Service Industry Management*, **8**(5), 1997, pp. 377–397. For excellent overviews, see Payne, A. & Holt, S., Review of the "Value" Literature and Implications for Relationship Marketing. *Australasian Marketing Journal*, **7**(1), 1999, pp. 41–51, and Tzokas, N. & Saren, M., Value Transformation in Relationship Marketing. *Australasian Marketing Journal*, **7**(1), 1999, pp. 52–62.

11 Normann, R. & Ramírez, R., From Value Chain to Value Constellation: Designing Interactive Strategy. *Harvard Business Review*, July–August 1993, pp. 65–77, and Wikström, S., Value Creation by Company–Consumer Interaction. *Journal of Marketing Management*, **12**, 1996, pp. 359–374. This is, of course, not an entirely new observation. Theodore Levitt expressed this point of view in the 1980s by noticing that value can only reside in the benefits of customer needs or expectations and that, therefore, only the customer can assign value to a physical product or a service. See Levitt, T., *The Marketing Imagination*. New York: The Free Press, 1986. By and large, Levitt's observation went unnoticed, or received only marginal interest, by practitioners as well as academics.

12 Wilson, D.T. & Jantrania, S., Understanding the Value of a Relationship. *Asia-Australia Marketing Journal*, **2**(1), 1994, pp. 55–66, and Tzokas & Sarin, *op.cit.* Wilson and Jantrania offer a comprehensive discussion of the value concept.

13 Ravald & Grönroos, *op.cit.*, and Grönroos, C., Value-driven Relational Marketing: from Products to Resources and Competencies. *Journal of Marketing Management*, **13**(5), 1997, pp. 407–419.

14 As Christopher Lovelock observes, "creating value requires rigorous analysis of all possibilities on both the cost and benefit sides of the equation" (p. 61). See Lovelock, C.H., *Product Plus: How Product + Service = Competitive Advantage*. New York: McGraw-Hill, 1994.

15 As Anderson and Narus observe, "instead of tailoring their packages of services to customers' individual needs, . . . many suppliers simply add layer upon layer of services to their offerings" (p. 75). By doing so they do not necessarily create more real value for their customers. See Anderson, J.C. & Narus, J.A., Capturing the Value of Supplementary Services. *Harvard Business Review*, **73**, January–February 1995, pp. 75–83.

16 See Anderson, J.C. & Narus, J.A., Business Marketing: Understand What Customers Value. *Harvard Business Review*, **76**, November–December 1998, pp. 53–61. They call such models *customer value models*.

17 Storbacka, K., *The Nature of Customer Relationship Profitability*. Helsinki/Helsingfors: Swedish School of Economics Finland/CERS, 1994.

18 Storbacka, K., Strandvik, T. & Grönroos, C., Managing Customer Relationships for Profit: The Dynamics of Relationship Quality. *International Journal of Service Industry Management*, **5**(5), 1994, pp. 21–38.

19 Rust, R.T., Zahorik, A.J. & Keiningham, T.L., Return on Quality (ROQ): Making Service Quality Financially Accountable. *Journal of Marketing*, **59**, April, 1995, pp. 58–70.

20 Stauss, B. & Friege, C., Regaining Service Customers: Costs and Benefits of Regain Management. *Journal of Service Research*, **1**(4), 1999, pp. 347–361.

21 Storbacka 1994, *op.cit.*

22 Storbacka 1994, *op.cit.* See also Storbacka, K., Customer Profitability: Analysis and Design Issues. In Sheth, J.N. & Parvatiyar, A. (eds), *Handbook of Relationship Marketing*. Thousand Oaks, CA: Sage Publications, 2000, pp. 565–586.

23 See Storbacka, K., Segmentation Based on Customer Profitability—Retrospective Analysis of Retail Bank Customer Bases. *Journal of Marketing Management*, **13**(5), 1997, pp. 479–492. How to calculate customer profitability is discussed in Storbacka 1994, *op.cit.*, and in Storbacka 2000, *op.cit.*

24 This case was developed by Dr Kaj Storbacka, founder and senior partner of the international consultancy firm CRM Customer Relationship Management Ltd and former research director of *CERS* (Center for Relationship Marketing and Service Management) at Hanken Swedish School of Economics, Finland, based on his research on customer relationship profitability and his consultancy experience.

25 See Storbacka, *op. cit.*, 1994, and Storbacka, *op. cit.*, 2000.

Chapter 7

MANAGING THE AUGMENTED SERVICE OFFERING

*Customers deserve more
than just a good service
package. It has to be made
into a functioning service
process too.*

Introduction

Based on discussions of service quality in previous chapters, this chapter presents a conceptual model of how to develop service offerings which are geared to customers' perception of the quality of services. The conceptual model is called the *Augmented Service Offering* model. It takes into account the impact of the outcome of the service processes (the *technical quality* of the service) and the impact of how customers perceive the processes (the *functional quality* of the process). The effects of brand image and marketing communication on the service offering is are also discussed.

The Missing Service Product: Services as a Bundle of Outcome- and Process-Related Features

One of the essential cornerstones in developing service management models is a thorough understanding of the phenomenon to be studied. In other words, what is needed is a good model of services as objects to be produced, marketed and consumed. Physical products are a bundle of features embedded in the ready-made product. However, as discussed in Chapter 3, services are different. Services can be characterized as "no product" services, in that no preproduced object to be marketed and consumed exists.

To understand service management and how to market services it is important to remember that all models and concepts are based on the fact that the service emerges in a process, in which the customer participates, and that the production of a service in a service production process is not separated from the consumption of this service. From the service provider's point of view, some of the service is produced in a back office, but from a quality perception perspective the most critical part of the service is produced at the time when the customer participates, perceives and evaluates the service process.

As discussed in previous chapters, instead of product features embedded in a preproduced physical product, services consist of a bundle of features which are related to the service *process* and the *outcome* of that process. Neither of these exists before the customer initiates the service process in which the service is produced. These characteristics of services have to be taken into account when developing models describing services. We name the bundle of process- and outcome-related features a *service offering*, and the comprehensive model of a service offering described in this chapter is called the *Augmented Service Offering* model.[1]

This chapter will not discuss a new service development process from idea generation to launching.[2] Instead, it will concentrate on the core of such a process, that is, how to understand and manage the object of development itself, the *service offering*. Without a thorough understanding of this core concept, every attempt to design and develop service will fail or at least be less effective.

Any attempt to conceptualize the service offering has to be based on a customer perspective. Far too often internal aspects, too little market research information, or too limited understanding of the customers' point of view guide the process of conceptualizing services to be offered to the market. However, well planned does not automatically mean well executed. The following sections are going to address, in detail, how to develop the service offering so that all aspects are thoroughly covered. This requires, among other things, that service production and delivery issues (that is, the service process), be incorporated as inseparable parts of the process of planning a service offering. Otherwise, well-planned service offerings may remain theoretical, unless the execution of plans is made an integral part of the undertaking to create a service offering.

The Service Package

According to the service package model, which is often used in the literature, the service is described as a package or bundle of different services, tangibles and intangibles, which together form the service.[3] The package is divided into two main categories: the *main service* or *core service* and *auxiliary services* or extras, which are sometimes referred to as peripherals or peripheral services, sometimes also as facilitator services. A hotel service may include the accommodation element as the main or core service, and reception service, valet service, room service, restaurant services, and the concierge as auxiliary services or peripherals in the package. Such extras are often considered to be the elements of the service package that define it and make it competitive.[4]

This is a simple and realistic way of illustrating at least part of the nature of any service. However, it has a few weaknesses if it is to be used for managerial purposes. First, a service is much more complicated than this model would suggest. From a managerial perspective auxiliary services may be used for totally different reasons. This has to be recognized. Second, the main service/auxiliary service (core service/peripherals) dichotomy is not geared to the customer perception of a service and total service quality. Only *what* is supposed to be done for customers is recognized.

How the service process and the process-related features are to be handled (i.e. the *functional quality* aspects of a service), are not included.

A model of the service offering has to be customer-oriented. It has to recognize all the aspects of a service that are perceived by customers. *How* customers perceive the interactions with the service provider (the functional quality of the service process) as well as *what* the customers receive (the technical quality of the outcome) has to be taken into account. In addition to this, the image impact on service quality perception also has to be recognized. What has to be planned and marketed and offered to customers is a comprehensive service offering.

Managing the Service Offering

Based on a well-defined *customer benefit concept*, which states the benefits or bundle of benefits customers appreciate, managing the service offering requires four steps:

1. Developing the *service concept*.
2. Developing a *basic service package*.
3. Developing an *augmented service offering*.

Finally, a fourth step also has to be taken into account:

4. Managing *image* and *communication*.

The *service concept* or concepts determine the intentions of the organization. The package can be developed based on this concept.

The *basic service package* describes the bundle of services that are needed to fulfill the needs of customers in target markets. This package, then, determines *what* customers receive from the organization. A well-developed basic package guarantees that necessary outcome-related features are included, and that the *technical quality* of the outcome will be good. However, even a good service offering can be destroyed by the way in which the service process functions. Therefore, a good service package does not necessarily mean that the perceived service is good, or even acceptable. According to the quality models of services, the service production and delivery process, especially the customer perception of the buyer–seller interactions or the service encounter, is an integral part of the service. This is the reason why the basic service package has to be expanded into an augmented service offering before we have a description of the service as an offering.

In the *Augmented Service Offering* model the service process and the interactions between the organization and its customers are included, that is, service production and delivery. In this way the model of the service offering is geared to the total customer perceived quality of services.

Finally, image has a filtering effect on the quality perception. Therefore, the firm has to manage its corporate and/or local *image* and its *marketing communication* so that they enhance the perception of the Augmented Service Offering.

The Basic Service Package

As noted previously, in the literature a distinction is often made between core services and peripheral services. However, for managerial reasons, it is necessary to distinguish between *three* groups of services:[5]

- core service;
- facilitating services (and goods); and
- supporting services (and goods).

The *core service* is the reason for a company being on the market. For a hotel it is lodging and for an airline it is transportation. A firm may also have many core services. For example, an airline may offer shuttle services as well as long-distance transportation. A mobile phone operator may, for example, offer phone calls as well as an e-mail facility as its core services.

In order to make it possible for customers to use the core service some additional services are often required. Reception services are needed in a hotel, and check-in services are required for air transportation. Such additional services are called *facilitating services*, because they facilitate the use of the core service. If facilitating services are lacking, the core service cannot be consumed. Sometimes *facilitating goods* are also required. For example, in order to be able to operate an automatic teller machine, a customer needs a bank card. However, it is often difficult to say whether the physical things involved in the service offering are goods given to the customer as part of the service production process or are physical production resources. For instance, the bank card can be considered a physical thing (a facilitating physical good), but it can equally be considered a production resource. The ATM equipment, on the other hand, is definitely a physical production resource and not a facilitating good.

The third type of services are *supporting services*. These, like facilitating services, are also auxiliary services, but they fulfill another function. Supporting services do not facilitate the consumption or use of the core service, but are used to increase the value of the service and/or to differentiate the service from those of competitors. Hotel restaurants and a range of in-flight services related to air transportation are examples of supporting services. Games and wake-up calls are examples of supporting services offered by a mobile phone operator. In some cases physical things that can be considered *supporting goods* are used to enhance the service offering. Shampoo and shoeshine in hotel rooms are such goods.

The distinction between facilitating services and supporting services is not always clear. A service which in one situation is facilitating the core service—for example, an in-flight meal on a long-distance route—may become a supporting service in another context, i.e. on a short flight.

From a managerial point of view it is important to make a distinction between facilitating and supporting services. Facilitating services are mandatory. *If they are left out, the service package collapses.* This does not mean that such services could not be designed in such a way that they differ from the facilitating services of the competitors. On the contrary, whenever possible facilitating services should be designed so that they also become means of competition and thus help to differentiate the service. Supporting services, however, are used as a means of competition only. If they are lacking, the core service can still be used. However, the total service package may be less attractive and perhaps less competitive without them.

The basic service package is, however, not equivalent to the service offering customers perceive. This package corresponds mainly to the technical outcome dimension of the total perceived quality. The elements of this package determine *what* customers receive. They only include the outcome-related features of the service. They do not say anything about *how* the process is perceived, which in the final analysis is an integral part of the total service offering customers experience and evaluate. In other words, no process-related features of the service have yet been taken into account.

As the perception of the service process cannot be separated from the perception of the elements of the basic service package, the process has to be integrated into the service offering. Therefore, the basic service package has to be expanded into a more comprehensive model, called the *Augmented Service Offering*.

The Augmented Service Offering

The service process, the buyer–seller interactions or service encounters, are perceived in a number of ways, which differ from situation to situation. Due to the characteristics of most services, there are, however, three basic elements, which from a managerial point of view constitute the process:[6]

- accessibility of the service;
- interaction with the service organization; and
- customer participation.

These elements are combined with the concepts of the basic package, thus forming an *Augmented Service Offering* (see Figure 7.1). It is, of course, essential that these three elements of the service offering are geared to the *customer benefits* which were initially identified to be sought by customers in the selected target segments, and the *service concept* based on these benefits.

The *accessibility of the service* depends, among other things, on:

- the number and skills of the personnel;
- office hours, timetables, and the time used to perform various tasks;
- location of offices, workshops, service outlets, etc.;

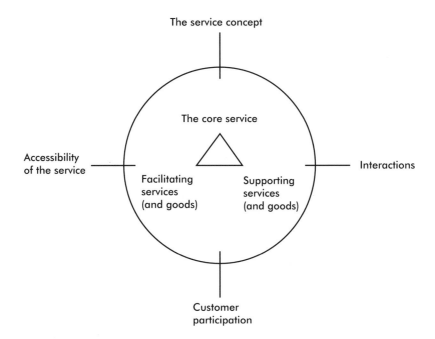

FIGURE 7.1   The augmented service offering. Source: Reprinted with permission from *Add Value to Your Service*, published by the American Marketing Association, Suprenant, C. (ed.), 1987, p. 83.

- exterior and interior of offices, workshops, and other service outlets;
- tools, equipment, documents, etc.;
- information technology enabling customers to gain access to the service provider and the service process; and
- the number and knowledge of consumers simultaneously involved in the process.

Depending on these and other factors customers will feel that it is easy, or difficult, to get access to the services and to purchase and use them. If the telephone receptionist of a repair firm lets the customer wait before answering the telephone, or if he cannot find a service technician for the customer to talk to, there is no accessibility to the service. Even an excellent service package can be destroyed in this way. Even if the service package does not totally deteriorate, the perception of the service may be seriously damaged. Internet sites, help desks and call and contact centers are increasingly becoming accessibility issues for service providers.

For example, in a study of a for-profit laboratory in southwestern United States, the accessibility issue could be broken down into four parts: site accessibility, customer ease of use of the physical resources of the laboratory, contact personnel's contribution to accessibility, and ease of customer participation. The following variables were identified for each of the four aspects of accessibility:

1. *Site accessibility*
   - The convenience and ease of access from a major street.
   - The amount of parking available adjacent to the facility.
   - The number of medical facilities located nearby.
   - The relative ease of locating the laboratory inside the building.
   - Office hours.
   - The ease of getting an appointment.
   - The size of the waiting room
2. *Customer ease of use of the physical resources*
   - The attractiveness and condition of the exterior and interior of the medical building where the laboratory is located.
   - The exterior of the laboratory facility.
   - The waiting room.
   - The patient rooms.
   - The restrooms.
3. *Frontline personnel's contribution to accessibility*
   - The response time to phone calls.
   - The number of employees.
   - The skills of employees.
   - The response time to people walking in the front door.
   - The response time to patients in the waiting room.
   - The professionalism of the employees.
   - The care taken to reduce unpleasantness of drawing blood.
   - The billing procedures.
   - The types of payment accepted.
   - The insurance arrangements available.
4. *Ease of customer participation*
   - The number and difficulty of forms to fill out.
   - The instructions given to patients concerning procedures the patient must participate in or do alone.
   - The difficulty of these procedures.

Interaction with the service organization can be divided into the following categories:

- interactive communication between employees and customers, which in turn depends on the behavior of the employees, on what they say and do, and how they say and do it;
- interactions with various physical and technical resources of the organization, such as vending machines, computers, documents, waiting room facilities, tools and equipment needed in the service production process, etc.;
- interactions with systems, such as waiting systems, seating systems, billing systems, Internet sites and telecommunication systems, systems for deliveries, maintenance and repair work, making appointments, handling claims, etc.; and
- interactions with other customers simultaneously involved in the process.

Customers have to get in touch with employees, they have to adjust to operative and administrative systems and routines of the organization, they may have to use Web sites, and they sometimes have to use technical resources such as teller machines or vending machines. Moreover, they may get in contact with other customers. All these interactions with human as well as physical resources and systems are part of the service perception. Again, if these interactions are considered unnecessarily complicated or unfriendly, the perceived quality of an excellent basic service package may be low.

In the same study interactions between the organization and its customers were broken down into the following parts:

- interactions with medical personnel (their attitudes, attention to the customer, skill in drawing blood);
- interactions with customer service department (attitudes, phone answering promptness, prompt and accurate answers to questions);
- interactions with waiting room environment (space, cleanliness, crowdedness);
- interactions with other customers (communication between patients);
- interactions with payment or billing system (means of payment available to choose from, understandability of invoices and receipts);
- interactions with scheduling systems (waiting time for service); and
- interactions between physicians (referring patients to the laboratory) and customer service department (attitudes, phone answering promptness, prompt and accurate answers to questions, calling results, follow-up).

Customer participation means that the customer has an impact on the service he perceives. Often the customer is expected to fill in documents, give information, use Web sites, operate vending machines, and so on. Depending on how well the customer is prepared and willing to do this, he will improve the service or vice versa. For example, if a patient is unable to give correct information about his problems, the physician will not be able to make a correct diagnosis. The treatment may, therefore, be inappropriate or less effective than otherwise. The service rendered by the physician is thus impaired.

In the study the following questions were asked, to identify aspects of customer participation:

- are patients knowledgeable enough to identify their need or problem?
- do patients have a reasonable understanding of the time constraints involved?
- is the patient willing to cooperate in the process?
- can additional information be obtained quickly from physicians?

Thus, in service encounters the core service, facilitating services and supporting services of the basic service package are perceived in various ways, depending on the accessibility of the services, how easily and well the interactions are perceived, and how well customers understand their role in the service production process.

Finally, in Figure 7.1, the *service concept* is seen as an umbrella concept, to guide development of the components of the Augmented Service Offering. The service concept should thus state what kind of core, facilitating, and supporting services are to be used, how the basic package could be made accessible, how interactions are to be developed, and how customers should be prepared to participate in the process.

The service concept should also be used as a guideline when, in the next phase of the planning process, adequate production resources are identified. In a going concern, there are, of course, a set of human and physical resources as well as functioning systems already in place. They determine to some extent which resources are going to be used. However, the development of an Augmented Service Offering requires a fresh analysis of the types of resources which are needed. Otherwise, existing resources may unnecessarily restrict the implementation of a new service offering. Existing resources must never become a hindrance to the successful implementation of new ideas.

In summary, developing the service offering is a highly integrated process. A new supporting service cannot be added without taking into account the accessibility, interaction and customer participation aspects of that service. On the other hand, the well-planned introduction of an additional supporting service, or an improved facilitating service, may become a powerful source of competitive advantage.

Managing Image and Communication and the Service Offering

As illustrated by the model of Perceived Service Quality, *image* has an impact as a filter on the service experienced. A favorable image enhances the experience; a bad one may destroy it. Therefore, managing image and communication becomes an integral part of developing the service offering. Because of the intangible nature of services, market communication activities not only have a communicative impact on customer expectations, but a direct effect on experiences as well. This latter effect is sometimes of minor, sometimes of major importance.

In the long run, *marketing communications* such as advertising, Web sites, sales and public relations enhance and to some extent form, images. On the other hand, even an advertisement or a brochure (which a customer notices and perceives at the point and time of consumption, or in advance) may have some impact on his quality perception of a service. Moreover, *word of mouth* is essential in this context. Word of mouth communication at the point and time of purchasing and consumption may have a substantial immediate effect as well as a long-term impact. In the same way, a negative comment from a fellow customer may easily change a given person's perception of the service he receives.

The Role of Technology in Service Offerings

The development of information technology and the increase in Internet use has offered new opportunities for firms to develop their service offerings.[7] IT systems and improved databases from which customer information files are easier to retrieve, and which are less complicated to update than before, provide customer contact employees with improved support to help them to be customer-oriented in interactions with customers. More accurate, easily retrievable and available information about customers enables employees to increase the quality of customer interactions. In addition, this use of technology also has a positive effect on the accessibility of services. The Internet may also improve employees' ability to handle customer contacts, for example, when routine interactions can be transferred to an Internet-based help desk.

New technology also give customers the means to access the services of a manufacturer or service firm more quickly and easily. For example, using the Web site of a manufacturer, a customer can easily request supportive information about how to handle a problem with a production machine or make arrangements for the maintenance of the machine. The Internet offers lots of opportunities to make a service more accessible than before, and it may also improve interactions. Of course, customers need to be trained and motivated to use a Web site for such purposes.

However, although some services, such the purchase of movie theater tickets, can be completed on the Internet, in most cases the customer will at some point also interact with employees and more traditional physical resources and technologies of the service provider. It should be kept in mind that well-functioning IT and Internet service interactions have to be supported by the "real," personal interactions that also take place. Quick and easy arrangements to get a maintenance task done using the Internet have to be followed by prompt, skillful and attentive service, otherwise the high-quality perception of the service provider's use of new technology in the mind of a customer is destroyed by a low-quality perception created by traditional means of producing the service offering.

Finally, one should remember that new technologies used in service processes may not be accepted and appreciated by all customers of a given service provider. Some customers can be motivated to accept new technologies, for example after having been informed about their benefits or after having been trained to use them. Others may want to continue to use more traditional means of interacting with the service provider. In any case, the firm has to introduce new technologies carefully, otherwise, their effect may be negative. Also, it is important to market new technologies internally, so that employees are motivated to use them. Employees too have to be properly informed and trained.

Developing the Service Offering: A Dynamic Model

The composition of the Augmented Service Offering in Figure 7.1 is static. The model simply lays out the elements that have to be taken into account and introduces appropriate concepts. In this section the model of the Augmented Service Offering will be placed in a dynamic framework, which illustrates more realistically how the service as a product emerges. Because services are processes in which consumption is inseparable from production and delivery processes, the service offering by definition is dynamic. The service exists as long as the production process goes on. Hence, any model of services, such as the Augmented Service Offering, has to include a dynamic aspect.

The framework can be divided into seven steps.

1. Assessment of customer benefits sought.
2. Defining overall features of an augmented service offering.
3. Defining a service concept which guides the development of the service offering.
4. Developing the core service and facilitating and supporting services and goods of the basic service package.
5. Planning the accessibility, interaction and customer participation elements of the augmented service offering.
6. Planning supportive marketing communication.
7. Preparing the organization for producing the desired customer benefits in the service processes (*internal marketing*).

First, an assessment of the *customer benefits* is needed, so that the development process is geared to customer experiences of total service quality. Next, the desired *features of a competitive Augmented Service Offering* have to be defined as the basis further planning. These features, following the model of Figure 7.1, should be related to the *service concept*, the elements of the basic service package and the various aspects of the service production and delivery process, as well as to corporate and local image and market communication.

The next step is to plan the *basic package*, including the core service, facilitating services and goods, and supporting services and goods, according to the service concept. Then, the *Augmented Service Offering* which materializes through the *service process* has to be developed, so that the service is made accessible in a way that reflects the service concept, and interactions and customer participation meeting the same criterion emerge.

The next step is to plan *supportive market communication*, which not only informs customers about the service and persuades them to try it but also has a positive impact on the consumption of the service and also enhances a desired image.

If all steps so far are properly carried out, the result should be a concrete offering, which—in the basic package elements as well as in the accessibility, interaction, and customer participation aspects of service production and delivery—includes the desired features, which in turn create the benefits customers seek. However, yet another step is required, and that is *preparing the organization* for producing the desired customer benefits through production and delivery of the Augmented Service Offering.

One of the fatal mistakes one can make is to believe that the service, once it has been planned, is automatically produced as planned. The discussion of customer perceived quality, and especially of the Gap Analysis Model, in Chapter 5 demonstrated the problems and pitfalls present in producing excellent perceived service quality and showed how complicated a process it is. Hence, the preparation of the organization has to be made an inseparable part of any development of service offerings, otherwise even sound and customer-oriented plans can easily fail.

The preparation of organizations for a desired performance involves the *creation of sufficient resources* and *internal marketing* of the new offering to the employees, so that they first understand it, then accept it and feel committed to producing it. In Chapter 14 the concept and phenomenon of internal marketing is covered at some length.

To sum up this discussion of the dynamic model of the Augmented Service Offering, the first stage is always an assessment of what benefits target customers are looking for and would appreciate. Proper market research and use of internal information, for example, from the interface between customers and the organization, should provide management with the necessary knowledge of what customers expect, so that corresponding features can be built into the service.

The first three steps of the process, assessing a customer benefit concept, determining the desired features of the service offering to be produced and defining the service concept, are separate processes. However, the next two phases, developing the basic package and planning the interaction, accessibility and customer participation elements of the augmented service offering in the service production and delivery process, as well as the last phase, preparing the organization, are inseparable processes. They have to go together, otherwise there is a risk that a good plan will result in a mediocre service. The basic package may include the correct features, but the crucial importance of the accessibility, interaction and customer participation aspects of service production and delivery to total customer perceived quality will not be fully understood or appreciated. Moreover, the need to actively market the new service internally will be neglected, or not taken care of with sufficient attention to detail.

Next, a case describing a successful development and launching of a new service will be described. The case includes most of the features of the models of the Augmented Service Offering described earlier in this chapter.

Developing an Augmented Service Offering: The Interrent Case[8]

The Company and Its Service Concept

Interrent-Europcar operates nationwide in Sweden in the auto rental market. Although it belongs to an international group, it is managed as an independent Swedish firm. It is one of the main auto rental companies in Sweden. Interrent has operated for a long time as a distinctly service-producing firm. Hans Åke Sand, retired CEO, said:

> When this industry was starting to grow here, we realized that we should not just provide our customers with an automobile, if they ask for one, which our competitors were doing, and still to some extent seem to be doing. Instead we wanted to position our company as a provider of transportation services. We developed a service concept, according to which we *provide immediately accessible transportation solutions to temporary transportation problems.*

This service concept still holds and guides Interrent's new service development and marketing strategies.

Although the firm was doing well, the competition had increased substantially, and continued to do so. Therefore, it was decided that the auto rental service of Interrent should be developed in a more service-oriented direction. Hans Åke Sand said: "The objective was to create a unique position for Interrent, where the most important keywords were trustworthiness and reliability." According to Sand, Interrent wanted to be able to offer customer benefits that were more real and tangible than just "we do it with a smile" or "we try harder."

The Elements of the Basic Service Package

The core *service* was a *transportation solution*. The basic ingredients of the service package were broken down into elements that needed to be designed and planned, so that an "immediately accessible solution to temporary transportation problems" would emerge as required by the service concept. Both *facilitating* services and *supporting* services were needed, and most of the necessary facilitating services were designed so that they simultaneously served as supporting services as well.

The elements considered were as follows (F denotes facilitating service, S denotes supporting service):

- information about terms (S);
- reservation (F and S);
- delivery of auto to customer (F and S);
- customer use of auto (F and S);
- return of car (F and S);
- pricing (S);
- billing (F and S);
- payment (F and S);
- handling complaints (S).

These were the major elements included in the service development process. Three important observations can be made at this point. First, it is interesting to note how elements such as billing and complaints handling, which are normally not considered services, just administrative routines, can be turned into services in a basic service package. Second, most or all facilitating services, even payment and the actual use of the automobile, can also be thought of as supporting services. Lastly, some traditional marketing variables, such as pricing in this case, can be transformed into supporting service elements.

When all the elements of the basic package are there, the necessary outcome-related features of the service offering, that is, the *technical quality dimension* of the total customer perceived quality, have been planned. However, the way in which the basic package functions, that is, *how* the service process functions and is perceived by the customer, is yet to be planned.

Augmenting the Offering: Goals to Be Achieved

At this point, the elements of the *basic service package* have been defined. The next step was to design these elements so that the basic package functions in a service-oriented way, so that the service concept is transformed into a well-functioning service or a successful *Augmented Service Offering*. When this has been done, the *functional process-related quality* dimension of total perceived quality is also accounted for, not just the technical outcome-related quality. In the next phase, *accessibility* issues, *interactions* between customers and Interrent, and the *customers' role during the service process* were looked into. Three general goals, expressed as service guarantees, are *features* the company decided to build into the new service. To plan the augmentation of the service package in the form of developing service guarantees is one way to ensure that a company focuses on the customer and what the customer considers important in the service offering. Moreover, it helps to set standards for employees. Offering guarantees immediately offers service-related goals to employees, which helps management to make the organization perform as planned (close the fourth gap in the Gap Analysis model; see Chapter 5).[9] Of course, offering service guarantees should also have external effects. Research into service guarantees seems to be limited; however, research which has been reported suggests that offering guarantees can reduce the risk customers perceive before purchasing a service. The more variety there is in the quality of services in an industry, the more service guarantees can reduce customers' perceived pre-purchase risk.[10]

The service guarantees Interrent chose to offer were:

1. a *get to your destination* guarantee which addressed the operational security of the service;
2. a *lowest price* guarantee which addressed the issue of cost efficiency *for the customer;* and
3. a *trouble-free service* guarantee which addressed any problems related to the convenience and accessibility of the service.

Get to your destination. To achieve this goal the automobiles must, of course, be in as good a condition as possible; but as there is always a chance of breakdown, a system for taking the customer to his destination if that were to happen had to be designed. It was decided that customers had to be on their way to their final destination not later than 45 minutes after they informed Interrent of the breakdown. Interrent entered into an agreement with a security firm which had a 24-hour telephone answering service. If the customer could not continue his trip without assistance, he was advised to call the security firm's number. The customer was guaranteed that *within 45 minutes he would be on the road again.* If no other solution could be found, a taxi was sent to pick up and transport the customer to his final destination at Interrent's expense, even if this cost could be expected to be high. This, of course, led to substantial internal discussions, but as it turned out, this "rescue service" has not been expensive. It has, however, created a lot of goodwill and positive word of mouth. Hans Åke Sand said: "We wanted to create reliability in our booking and delivery commitment. Our customers have to be absolutely sure that there will be a service available; and we wanted to give our booking center and locations and our partners a strong signal saying that a customer who has a reservation number is entitled to the service, either by car or taxi."

Lowest price. To achieve this goal a well-integrated computer system was required, so that the lowest possible fee, taking into account the various ways of calculating the final price, could always be immediately given to the customer. The system also enabled

Interrent to do this when the automobile was returned to a location other than where it had been picked up. Because of this system, customers did not have to figure out whether they should rent an auto on a daily basis or for a weekend, or whether they should choose a no-mileage fee or not. Before the customer has used the service he will be quoted the lowest possible fee.

Trouble-free service. To achieve this goal, it was decided that picking up the car and returning it must be made as convenient as possible for the customer. First, Interrent decided that an auto could be picked up at any Interrent location, or it could be delivered to company addresses, railway stations or hotels. Interrent also decided to promise that the auto would be delivered *not later than five minutes* after the time agreed upon. If a customer had to wait any longer for a car, he would not be billed by Interrent. Hans Åke Sand said: "The signal to the organization and to the market is clear: it is not acceptable to deliver a car 10 minutes late and offer explanations about unexpected traffic jams." Second, customers are not required to return the car to the same place they got it, but to any Interrent location. They would be guaranteed the "lowest price" quotation at any location, and immediately.

Developing the Augmented Service Offering

Once these goals were decided upon, the next phase was to develop the resources necessary for their implementation. Most of the resources existed already, but some had to be created. For example, the existing computer system could not fulfill the "lowest price" goal, so it had to be further developed. The rescue center did not exist and had to be developed. As mentioned earlier, a partner was engaged here.

The *accessibility* of the service was enhanced by the actions taken to fulfill the "Get to your destination," "Lowest price" and "Trouble-free service" goals. The customers had to be informed about how to react in case of a flat tire, motor breakdown or accident in order to be able to activate the "rescue activities." The *participation of the customers* was ensured by written information on how the three "guarantees" functioned both in the autos and on the accompanying documents, as well as verbally by the employees. Information about these guarantees and the benefits they offered was also included in Interrent's market communication when the new service was launched. Interrent wanted to prepare the customers to be co-producers of the service as well as possible.

In order to make sure that the *interactions* with the systems and physical resources were favorable, the new auto rental service required some specific resources. As far as technology, systems and physical resources are concerned, Interrent already had a nationwide network, where locations operated in isolation from each other and Interrent's headquarters and were therefore used to making decisions on their own. Also, Interrent had its own computer system, but the pricing system had to be developed. Furthermore, the autos used by Interrent were of good quality and dependable, but they had to be maintained as well as possible to avoid unnecessary extra costs due to breakdowns. Support by the garage and the mechanics had to be secured. This was achieved by internal information, oral as well as written, to the mechanics, during the weeks before the new service was launched. The "security alarm system" involving the subcontracted 24-hour telephone reception and rescue system had to be developed and the staff of Interrent's partner had to be trained and motivated to accept the new commitments.

The customer contact people in the reservation center and at the rental locations also had to be trained and motivated to fulfill the goals of the new auto rental service, so that customers experienced favorable and positive interactions with the employees. The "five-minute maximum delay" commitment and the "within 45 minutes on the road again" commitment caused some internal controversy, but the *internal marketing* approach, headed by the managing director, convinced the organization of the rationale behind the new service. Eventually, as the service turned out to function well and without significant extra costs, a total commitment seemed to have been achieved. This internal marketing process had to be squeezed into a 10-day period before the service was launched, so that no information would leak outside the organization ahead of time. Meetings, called "service seminars," were arranged, including oral and written information, where discussion and communication was encouraged. Hans Åke Sand himself, as CEO, took an active part in this process. The new service, the goals, and the rationale behind the promises to the market were explained and discussed. Hans Åke Sand concluded that "the people in the organization perceived the total program we were to offer our customers as a challenge, but they also realized that the firm trusted them, and we achieved a commitment for the new service."

When launching the new service offering, the external marketing campaign was directed at travel agencies, but there was also a short advertising campaign involving leading daily newspapers which focused on the three guarantees. Building upon its previous good image, Interrent wanted to create a *communicated image* of trustworthiness and real value and comfort for its customers.

The Results

Immediately after the service was launched sales increased considerably, improving 15 per cent in the first month, 9 per cent in the second month, and 17 per cent in the third month after launching the service offering. After a year, sales were 23 per cent higher than during the same period the year before.

The costs of operating the new service had not gone up to any significant extent. The fear of enormous extra costs following the three warranties turned out to be unwarranted. Positive and service-oriented standards have also been set for the organization: promises must be kept 100 per cent, no unnecessary (more than five minute) delays will be accepted, no customer must be left without help if a breakdown occurs (on the road not later than 45 minutes after a phone call to the alarm center), and the lowest price must always immediately be quoted. The effects of these and other standards are even greater because of the trust that management showed in the organization. Goals cannot be fulfilled without decentralized decision-making authority. Top management supported this, and provided the employees with sufficient information, guidance and managerial support. The pricing system also produced such support.

As Hans Åke Sand said: "We wanted to get rid of general promises to our customers, such as 'We do it with a smile' or 'We try our best,' and demonstrate real excellence and trustworthiness."

Summary and Questions for Discussion

This chapter discussed the need to develop a service offering in a systematic way. As services are complicated phenomena, service offerings are also complicated. The Augmented Service Offering model was introduced as a conceptual model of the total offering customers perceive when consuming or using a service. The model includes a basic service package and an augmentation of the package into a holistic augmented service offering. The need for supportive marketing communication and positive image as well as for internal marketing to prepare the organization to perform according to the requirements of the augmented service offering was also discussed. The starting point for the process of developing the offering is a clear understanding of the benefits customers want and the formulation of easily understood service concepts. As part of the presentation of how to successfully develop an augmented service offering, the issue of service guarantees were briefly touched upon.

Questions for discussion

1. Why has a service package to be further developed into an augmented service offering in order to be truly customer-oriented?
2. What are the elements of a basic service package?
3. How is the basic service package developed to be an augmented service offering?
4. What is the role of the service concept in the development of service offerings?
5. What can be achieved internally and externally with the introduction of service guarantees?
6. Analyze the services, or a given service, offered by your organization, using the Augmented Service Offering model, or develop a hypothetical service offering using the model.

Further Reading

Bitner, M.J., Brown, S.W. & Meuter, M.L. (2000) Technology Infusion in Service Encounters. *Journal of the Academy of Marketing Science*, **28**(1), pp. 138–149.
de Brentani, U. (1995) New Industrial Service Development: Scenarios for Success and Failure. *Journal of Business Research*, **32**(2), pp. 93–103.
de Brentani, U. & Ragot, E. (1996) Developing New Business-to-Business Services: What Factors Impact Performance? *Industrial Marketing Management*, **25**(6), pp. 517–530.
Edvardsson, B. (1997) Quality in New Service Development: Key Concepts and a Frame of Reference. *Internal Journal of Production Economics*, **52**(1–2), pp. 31–46.
Edvardsson, B. & Olsson, J. (1996) Key Concepts for New Service Development. *The Service Industries Journal*, **16**(2), pp. 140–164.
Grönroos, C. (1987) Developing the Service Offering—a Source of Competitive Advantage. In Surprenant, C. (ed.), *Add Value to Your Service*. Chicago, IL: American Marketing Association.
Grönroos, C. (1990) *Service Managing and Marketing. Managing the Moments of Truth in Service Competition*. Lexington, MA: Lexington Books.
Hart, C.W.L. (1988) The Power of Unconditional Guarantees. *Harvard Business Review*, **66**, July–August, pp. 54–62.

Langeard, E. & Eiglier, P. (1987) *Servuction. Les Marketing des Services*. Paris: John Wiley & Sons.

Lehtinen, J.R. (1986) *Quality-oriented Services Marketing*. University of Tampere, Finland.

Levitt, T. (1983) After the Sale Is Over. *Harvard Business Review*, September–October.

Martin, Jr., C.R. & Horne, D.A. (1993) Service Innovations: Successful versus Unsuccessful Firms. *International Journal of Service Industry Management*, **4**(1), pp. 49–65.

Normann, R. (1991) *Service Management*. 2nd edition. New York: John Wiley & Sons.

Ostrom, A.L. & Hart, C. (2000) Service Guarantees. Research and Practice. In Swartz, T.A. & Iacobucci, D. (eds), *Handbook in Services Marketing & Management*. Thousand Oaks, CA: Sage Publications, pp. 299–313.

Ostrom, A.L. & Iacobucci, D. (1998) The Effects of Guarantees on Consumer's Evaluation of Services. *Journal of Services Marketing*, **12**(6), pp. 362–378.

Storey, C. & Easingwood, C.J. (1998) The Augmented Service Offering: A Conceptualization and Study of its Impact on New Service Success. *Journal of Product Innovation Management*, **15**(4), pp. 335–351.

Notes

1   See Grönroos, C., *Service Managing and Marketing. Managing the Moments of Truth in Service Competition*. Lexington, MA: Lexington Books, 1990. In the service management and service marketing literature, surprisingly little attention has been devoted to the understanding and conceptualization of services or service offerings. An example of one of the few attempts is Storey, C. & Easingwood, C.J., The Augmented Service Offering: A Conceptualization and Study of its Impact on New Service Success. *Journal of Product Innovation Management*, **15**(4), 1998, pp. 335–351.

2   There is a limited but growing number of publications on the design and development of new services. See, for example, de Brentani, U., New Industrial Service Development: Scenarios for Success and Failure. *Journal of Business Research*, **32**(2), 1995, pp. 93–103, de Brentani, U. & Ragot, E., Developing New Business-to-Business Services: What Factors Impact Performance? *Industrial Marketing Management*, **25**(6), 1996, pp. 517–530; Edvardsson, B., Quality in New Service Development: Key Concepts and a Frame of Reference. *Internal Journal of Production Economics*, **52**(1–2), 1997, pp. 31–46; Edvardsson, B. & Olsson, J., Key Concepts for New Service Development. *The Service Industries Journal*, **16**(2), 1996, pp. 140–164; and Martin, Jr., C.R. & Horne, D.A., Service Innovations: Successful Versus Unsuccessful Firms. *International Journal of Service Industry Management*, **4**(1), 1993, pp. 49–65.

3   See, for a few early examples, Normann, R., *Service Management*. 2nd edition. New York: John Wiley & Sons, 1991, Langeard, E. & Eiglier, P., *Servuction. Les Marketing des Services*. Paris: John Wiley & Sons, 1987, and Lehtinen, J.R., *Quality-oriented Services Marketing*. University of Tampere, Finland, 1986.

4   This point of view goes back to the argument put forward by Theodore Levitt: "Having been offered these extras, the customer finds them beneficial and therefore prefers doing business with the company that supplies them." See Levitt, T., After the Sale Is Over. *Harvard Business Review*, September–October 1983, pp. 9–10.

5   Grönroos 1990, *op.cit.*, and Grönroos, C., Developing the Service Offering—a Source of Competitive Advantage. In Surprenant, C. (ed.), *Add Value to Your Service*. Chicago, IL: American Marketing Association, 1987.

6   Grönroos 1990, *op.cit.* and Grönroos 1987, *op.cit.*

7   Bitner, M.J., Brown, S.W. & Meuter, M.L., Technology Infusion in Service Encounters. *Journal of the Academy of Marketing Science*, **28**(1), 2000, pp. 138–149.

8   Although this case is not new, it clearly demonstrates the potential of the Augmented Service Offering Model.

9   Ostrom, A.L. & Hart, C., Service Guarantees. Research and Practice. In Swartz, T.A. & Iacobucci, D. (eds), *Handbook in Services Marketing & Management*. Thousand Oaks, CA: Sage Publications, 2000, pp. 299–313, and Hart, C.W.L., The Power of Unconditional Guarantees. *Harvard Business Review*, **66**, July–August 1988, pp. 54–62.

10 Ostrom, A.L. & Iacobucci, D., The Effects of Guarantees on Consumers' Evaluation of Services. *Journal of Services Marketing*, **12**(6), 1998, pp. 362–378.

Chapter 8

PRINCIPLES OF SERVICE MANAGEMENT

*In services, costs and
revenues are inseparable.
The same resources,
activities and processes drive
both costs and revenues—
and profits.*

Introduction

This chapter will discuss the nature of a strategic approach to service management which is geared to the characteristics of services and the nature of service competition, based on the importance of customer perceived quality to success. This includes a discussion of the pitfalls for service organizations of strategic management from traditional manufacturing, and the development of a service-oriented view of the business logic and the profit equation. Thus, the importance of a service-oriented approach to strategy and management is emphasized. Finally, service management as a management philosophy is defined and principles of this approach to management are discussed. After having read this chapter the reader should understand the pitfalls of a traditional management approach in service contexts and know how to apply a service management philosophy.

Some Traditional Strategy Lessons from Manufacturing

For a manufacturer of goods, conventional managerial thinking generally includes three rules of thumb to follow in order to strengthen the competitive edge of a firm:

1. decrease production and administration costs, to decrease the unit cost of products;
2. increase the budget for traditional marketing efforts such as advertising, sales and sales promotion in order to make the market buy the goods produced; and
3. strengthen product development efforts.

Strategic management includes, of course, a range of other elements as well. However, in this context we will concentrate on these aspects, because understanding them correctly is crucial to managing services.

For manufacturing, these rules of thumb usually make sense, because they are geared to goods. If production costs can be decreased, lower prices can be offered, or higher margins can be obtained. The quality of the goods is the same, because the output of the production process does not change, even though different, more cost-efficient technology or processes are used. The consumption or usage of physical goods can be characterized as *outcome consumption* and, regardless of the new, more effective and efficient production technologies and methods used, the outcome remains the same. Economies of scale normally pay off. Moreover, marketing efforts usually have a positive effect on demand. Continuous product development is of vital importance to manufacturing as well as to services, of course, but misunderstanding the first two rules of thumb may misguide management and cause serious problems.

An improved profit orientation is needed in services, too. However, if lessons from the manufacturing sector are followed unchanged, profits may not be as good. This is due to the different characteristics of services and service production. There is a *strategic management trap*, which management has to observe and avoid.

The Strategic Management Trap

When the rules of thumb outlined in the previous section are followed, the consequences for a service provider may be those illustrated in Figure 8.1. We may assume, for example, that the service firm or service operation either has financial problems, is facing increasing competition or both. Irrespective of the impact of technology, labor costs are high in most service operations. In order to control costs, strategic decisions concerning personnel are often made: personnel reductions, a hiring freeze, greater degree of customer self-service, people are replaced by machines, and so on.

In manufacturing, such decisions should improve production efficiency, lower costs, yet have no effect on the output. They may even improve the quality of the goods produced. A favorable effect on productivity can be expected. In a service context some of this may happen. However, far too often none of these effects will occur, at least not in the long run.

Efficiency is a complicated phenomenon with at least two dimensions, *internal efficiency* and *external efficiency*. The former is related to the way a firm operates and the productivity of labor and capital. It can, for example, be measured by the unit cost of the production output. External efficiency, on the other hand, is the way customers perceive the operations and the output of the firm. External efficiency is a perception of a firm's effectiveness. In this context it is a matter of effectiveness in the mind of customers.[1]

In traditional manufacturing, the interrelationship between internal and external efficiency is less important. Customers only perceive the physical output of the production process. In a service operation the situation is often different. The consumption or usage of services is *process consumption* and, according to the

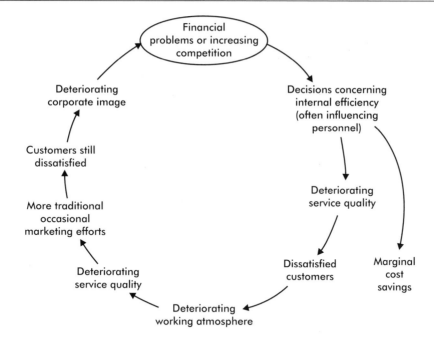

FIGURE 8.1 The strategic management trap. From Grönroos, C., *Strategic Management and Marketing in the Service Sector*, 1983, p. 41. Reprinted with permission of the Marketing Science Institute.

basic characteristics of services, the customer is involved in the production process and perceives not only the output of the process but parts of the process itself. In a service process an efficient manufacturing orientation may easily alienate the customers, make the customers' perception of quality deteriorate and in the end chase customers away. Hence, opportunities are missed to sell more and obtain repeat business in ongoing customer relationships. This is especially true for service encounters where customers are present both as co-producers and consumers. However, in back office processes, where customers are not involved and which are not visible to them, a manufacturer-oriented approach to developing the processes may pay off.[2]

Management decisions concerning the production process in a service context are too often thought of as having an impact only on internal efficiency. This often leads to operations and reward systems supporting the wrong actions. For example, restaurant managers are frequently rewarded for low food costs, which is of no interest to customers, who are looking for good food *and* attentive service. Doing what is important to customers and means value for them should be rewarded instead.

In reality, the external efficiency issue is highly relevant. If only internal efficiency goals are pursued, the perceived service quality changes; too often it deteriorates. Thus, an improved internal efficiency may in service operations lead to a negative shift in external quality. Personnel have less time for a single customer, or for paying attention to the customer, and the customer's problems are not rewarded. This may increase waiting times, decrease the employee's likelihood of penetrating to the problems of a given customer, and leave less time for employee flexibility. Self-service procedures and technology, which may be introduced as a substitute for personal service, may help the customer. Information technology may also improve the service. However, often this unfavorably changes the perceived quality, because the customer either does not accept the new system or is not prepared, trained or motivated to operate it.

Frequently, decisions concerning improvements in internal efficiency lead to a deterioration in quality as perceived by the customers. Usually the technical quality of the outcome of the service process is not critical, but the functional quality dimension of the process is. Customers may feel that they get the same technical quality as before, but that the manner in which the service is provided has deteriorated.

If customers are dissatisfied, they normally show it to the employees and to fellow customers. Employees in contact with such customers are easily affected by such feedback. The result may be a deteriorating working atmosphere, where the employees no longer feel satisfied with their jobs nor as motivated as they may have been initially. Moreover, the direction of decisions taken in the organization, where people are treated mainly as a cost-generating burden, also has a demotivating impact on performance. The decision-making of the employer has a negative effect on the working atmosphere.

This process may be fatal to the service operation. As the atmosphere in the workplace is affected, the functional quality of the service may continue to deteriorate. Employees may have less time to perform well, but they may also be less motivated to do so. Such negative sequences of management decisions easily lead to a *vicious circle*.[3] Once a firm has got into such a circle, its growth potential may be seriously affected.

The destructive process illustrated here and in Figure 8.1 seems to be caused by a lack of understanding of the interrelationship between internal and external efficiency in service competition. Decisions made to help cost savings have an unexpected external effect. The output of the service operation, the service with a technical and functional quality dimension, is not the same as it was, or as it is supposed to be according to traditional management thinking from manufacturing.

At this point the firm sometimes turns to traditional external marketing in order to keep its customers. A temporary boom may be achieved by, for example, heavy advertising, but in the long run the new customers as well as the old ones will observe the decrease in quality and become dissatisfied with what they receive. If marketing campaigns make unrealistic promises, which in situations like this is not uncommon, disappointment will be severe among newcomers who wanted to give the firm's services a try.

Consequently, in spite of traditional marketing efforts, in the long run one often ends up with dissatisfied customers. At the same time the firm's corporate image will change. A decreasing perceived quality and unrealistic promises by external marketing efforts have a negative impact on image. Moreover, a growing number of dissatisfied customers and ex-customers creates a substantial negative word of mouth effect on image, as well as on purchase decisions.

In the end one will probably find that the decisions taken may have caused varying degrees of damage. In the worst case, service quality, especially process-related functional quality, has decreased, the working atmosphere has deteriorated, word of mouth has become a problem instead of a support, the corporate image has been affected, and finally, the problems caused by increased competition have not been solved. In summary, a bad situation has become even worse.

A Vicious Circle: An Example

What is going on in many hospitals with for-profit service providers seems to be an example of such a development, caused, to a greater or lesser extent, by the wrong management approach and a lack of understanding of the characteristics of service. If there are financial problems, doctors are urged to concentrate on professional and technical issues, which they do, and nurses are requested not to interact too much with patients and maybe not at all with family members. The intention here is, of course, to achieve a more effective use of time and, as a consequence of that to cut costs.

The consequences of these actions are a lower level of service quality as perceived by the customers, the patients and their relatives and friends. But this approach from management has a much more severe internal effect, which is eventually perceived by the customers as well. The employees, probably the nurses and staff personnel first, start to feel a role conflict. Patients and relatives demand more, but management says no. They are not encouraged or authorized to give good service. This quickly affects the working atmosphere which in turn leads to a deterioration of the customer perceived quality of the service. At this point, external marketing communication and PR activities communicating a "we care" image have no significant positive effect on customers or potential customers. They know better, or will soon find out what the truth is. Moreover, they will create a substantial amount of bad word of mouth.

However, in one respect, such promotional campaigns clearly have an effect. This effect is not normally recognized by managers, or by communications people. It is an *internal effect*, and it is *negative*. Employees realize that management has deliberately attempted to fool customers and potential customers. It may, in reality, not be deliberate, it may just be a result of bad and thoughtless management, but it is easily perceived as deliberate. For example, nurses know that they cannot fulfill the promise "we care." They just do not have the time, and they are encouraged not to do so. This, of course, by itself hurts morale and damages the internal atmosphere even more. Second, nobody wants to deliberately take part in lies and cheating, which such promotional efforts in this situation are. It goes against the ethics of most people, and increasingly damages the working atmosphere. Consequently, good employees start looking for another job and eventually quit; they have no interest in helping the employer, and quality continues to deteriorate. If the financial problems were initially minor, they grow as the internal crisis deepens and the service quality (the reason for the external crisis) decreases. A few wrong management decisions can easily lead to a downward spiral, a negative trend which *gains momentum once it has started*.

Cost Efficiency and the Risk of Falling into the Trap

Initial cost savings often turn out to be marginal in the long run. Employee absence due to illness or other reasons such as job dissatisfaction tends to increase. Extra personnel, without proper training, have to be hired. The work surroundings and the technology used may not be handled with such care.

The process illustrated in Figure 8.1, and in a sketchy way by the hospital example above, can be called the *Strategic Management Trap* of services. By making the wrong decisions based only on manufacturing know-how, the organization may be thrown into a *vicious circle* or negative downward spiral, which weakens the competitiveness of its operations and causes or intensifies the financial problems that are often the reason for making inappropriate decisions in the first place.

Why did it go wrong? Why do conventional wisdom and guidelines from manufacturing not help? The main reason is the fact that a service organization is not a traditional manufacturing firm, but an organization with characteristics of its own. Service consumption or usage is *process consumption*, not outcome consumption. The nature of services and service competition requires a different approach to strategic thinking and management.

In traditional management thinking the productivity of capital and labor and internal efficiency considerations are the factors that predominantly drive profit. However, a service firm, or any service operation, is different in some vital aspects. As noted earlier in this chapter, external efficiency, how the organization performs and the output of its operations—in short, the perceived service quality with both its process- and outcome-related features—is what customers experience and evaluate. Actions to improve internal efficiency and productivity as traditionally measured can easily have a negative impact on external efficiency and perceived quality. For service organizations, *customer perceived service quality drives profit*, provided of course that customers consume the service in such a way that the cost of producing the service does not exceed revenues from that service.[4] In Chapter 6 the chain of interrelated factors leading from good perceived service quality to profitability was discussed. From this follows, among other things, that productivity conceptually and operationally has to be treated differently in services than in manufacturing. We shall return to this issue in Chapter 9.

However, this does not mean that decisions which are only or predominantly related to internal efficiency always lead to negative consequences. This also does not mean that cost savings and the more effective use of resources are wrong and should not be attempted. On the contrary, improved productivity of resources— labor as well as capital, and information—and better internal efficiency should always be an objective, and new technology and production processes that save costs should be used. The main point here is that such internal developments should be based on the characteristics of services, so *that the interrelationships between the internal and external effects are taken into account*. It should be emphasized that all costs are not equal. On the contrary, there is a difference between various types of costs which has to be taken into account when strategic and operational decisions about efficiency, productivity and cost savings are considered.

Scale Economies or Market Economies?

Internal efficiency and productivity of capital and labor must not, however, remain the predominant goals for managerial actions. Decisions concerning customer perceived quality and external efficiency, and decisions concerning internal efficiency have to go hand in hand. This is a major shift in management focus. Heskett has used the concept of *"market economies,"* as opposed to "scale economies," to demonstrate this shift in management focus.[5] Whereas economies of scale mean that competitive advantage and profit are achieved by the large-scale production of more or less standardized products to keep costs down and productivity up, market economies mean that a competitive edge and profits are accomplished *by a closer customer orientation*. A focus on customer perceived quality and smaller-scale production of solutions that better satisfy customer needs and expectations creates a better competitive position and higher profits than does an orientation toward scale economies.

This approach fits the characteristics of services and the nature of service competition very well. The large and strategically critical interrelationship between external and internal efficiency in service production emphasizes the importance of exploiting market economies. However, there are situations in which large-scale production is profitable; the concept of many fast-food restaurants is an example. But even in large-scale operations where the organization is built up into a network every local outlet is a smaller unit which at least to some extent may face unique market conditions and customer needs. A local orientation toward market economies within the large-scale operation may then be a good solution. In addition, in many cases back office processes can be developed to achieve scale economies and higher internal efficiency without negative effects on external efficiency. For example, banks can develop the processing of accounts in this way.

There is enough evidence to support the potential dangers of poor decision-making, where internal efficiency is treated entirely separately from external efficiency. This tendency is especially obvious in larger firms. On the other hand, as long as the market potential is constantly growing, the negative effects of a manufacturer-oriented approach may not occur. When the situation changes and competition gets tougher, the problems occur; and they may develop very quickly.

Services and the Profit Equation

The rules of thumb from manufacturing described earlier are, of course, intended to improve profitability as defined in a traditional manufacturing context. It is axiomatic to state that profit equals revenues minus costs. What is not axiomatic, however, is to state how and by what means revenues and costs are influenced. Figure 8.2 illustrates, in a simplified way, what the profit equation is traditionally expected to look like.

In the manufacturing of physical goods, production (including the production resources used as well as the production processes) and administration (including general administration, personnel, research and development, training, planning

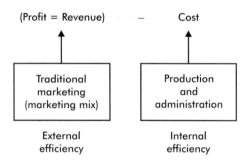

FIGURE 8.2 A manufacturer-oriented view of the profit equation

and budgeting procedures) are thought of as mainly *cost-generating* functions. Their immediate impact on revenues is considered minimal.

Traditional external marketing activities, such as product design and packaging, personal selling, advertising and sales promotion, distribution and pricing, are thought of as functions which *generate revenue*. Since traditional marketing efforts are considered revenue-generating, marketing is given responsibility for successful external impact on the marketplace. Often marketing is thought of as *the* revenue-generating function.

In this way of thinking no interrelationship exists between internal efficiency and external efficiency. As noted previously, in traditional goods manufacturing this assumption often holds true. There, high productivity of labor and capital keeps costs down and thus also drives profit.

In order to avoid the strategic management trap one should realize that in a service context the customer relationships are not influenced as shown in Figure 8.2. According to the characteristics of services and the service quality models, resources and activities that have an impact on future buying and consumption behavior can be found in most departments of the service firm. Production as well as administration, including their various sub-areas, affect customers' behavior. Operations management and management of human resources are related to marketing management in a service context. Peter Drucker's view that marketing, from the customers' point of view, is too important to the result of the firm's performance to be treated as a separate function is very valid indeed.[6]

We demonstrate in Figure 8.3 that decisions concerning production and administration not only affect internal efficiency and costs, but they also have an impact on external efficiency and revenues. *Thus, the formation of the profit equation changes altogether.* The revenue-generating effects of such resources must not be forgotten in the philosophy that guides the strategic planning process and decision-making.

As further shown in Figure 8.3, decisions that simultaneously influence internal and external efficiency should not be made before both the revenue-generating effects *and* the cost-generating effects of such decisions have been taken into consideration and analyzed. Costs which are revenue-generating and costs which predominantly enhance bureaucracy should be kept apart and treated in different ways. The simultaneous occurrence of perceived quality

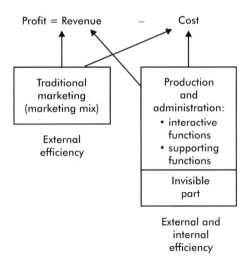

FIGURE 8.3   A profit-oriented view of revenues and costs in a service context

(external efficiency) and internal efficiency considerations is clearly demon-strated in Figure 8.3. Moreover, because customer relationships should be the starting point for planning, according to the relationship marketing perspective, the effects of planning on external efficiency may be considered more important. So, in the final analysis, customer perceived quality drives revenues and profit.

In other words, strategic planning and management should, of course, begin with the revenue-generating implications of a given decision, but as an integ-rated process, cost implications should be considered. This is *not* to say that costs are of minor importance. Although perceived quality drives revenues, profits may suffer if the service is produced with too high costs. Saving costs, in particular costs that do not contribute to the generation of revenues, is necessary in most firms, and monitoring costs is always of crucial importance. Sometimes the cost level can be reduced by encouraging customers to change their consumption habits. For example, banks have recently persuaded customers to use ATMs, computer-based and Internet-based payment of bills instead of withdrawing money and depositing checks at bank counters, which costs more for the bank to administer. However if, for example, a cost-saving decision can be expected to have a negative impact on quality and revenues which is bigger than the cost reduction, it should probably not be made.

Not all production and administration resources and processes can be expected to have effects on revenue. As shown in Figure 8.3, there are interactive functions, with which customers have direct contact, and supporting functions such as warehousing, information processing, and other back office activities which indirectly influence the perceived service quality. Such functions are critical because they have an impact on both revenues and costs. However, there are functions that from the customers' point of view are totally invisible, such as some office production processes and internal book-keeping. These functions are only cost-generating. Here, the occurrence of bureaucracy-enhancing costs should constantly be monitored.

Industrialization of service production in a manufacturer-like manner can be done in the truly invisible part of the organization. In the other parts of the organization, industrialization has to be implemented much more carefully if one wants to make cost savings without damaging service quality and the generation of revenue.

Traditionally, external marketing activities are considered to be more or less solely responsible for revenues. However, this is not true as far as services are concerned, and manufacturers of goods with extensive customer contacts by non-marketing persons face a new reality as well. If the organization produces bad service quality, advertising and selling will not satisfy and make customers buy again from that organization. The scope of marketing will have to be broadened. We will return to this in Chapter 10.

A Service-Oriented Strategy

Figure 8.4 illustrates schematically a favorable process which may occur if a *service strategy* is followed. Figure 8.4 can be compared to Figure 8.1, which demonstrated the strategic management trap. To give an example, if financial problems or problems with increased competition make it necessary to change the strategies of, say, an airline company, cost considerations and internal efficiency should not govern the strategic thinking in the firm. Instead, management should focus upon the interactions with customers and customer relationships. Effects on external efficiency and customer relationships should primarily guide the decisions to be made. Of course, cost considerations and the implications for internal efficiency must not be overlooked. Concern for internal efficiency should be given priority, especially in the part of the organization invisible to customers. Moreover, a distinction between revenue-enhancing costs and other costs should always be made.

External efficiency and service quality concerns should be given top priority in the interactive functions. In an airline, for example, improving buyer–seller interactions in the service encounters, for instance, by increasing seat size in planes, upgrading meals and other in-flight services, and offering the employees appropriate customer contact training, to mention a few possibilities, would probably lead to improved perceived quality from the customers' point of view.

Such decisions may or may not necessitate more personnel, or more advanced technology, but if the effects on revenues make up for the additional costs, such revenue-creating cost increases should obviously be allowed. Here, difficulties in calculating the effects on revenue are no excuse for ignoring the external efficiency effects. It should be noted that improved service quality often does not require additional costs. The only thing that is needed, in many cases, is a better understanding of customer relationships, how quality is perceived, and finally, the importance of the process-related functional quality dimension. Once these points are made clear, internal arrangements for using existing resources in a more systematic and market-oriented way can usually be made.

To return to Figure 8.4, improved quality usually means greater customer satisfaction, which in turn has a twofold effect. Internally, the working atmosphere will probably improve. Increased customer satisfaction is noticed by the

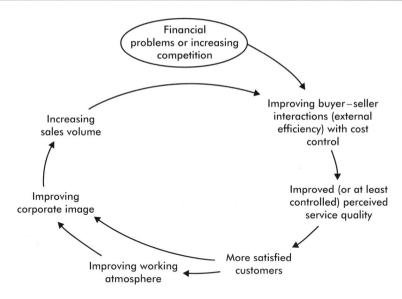

FIGURE 8.4   A service-oriented approach. Source: Grönroos, C., *Strategic Management and Marketing in the Service Sector*, 1983, p. 58. Reprinted with permission of the Marketing Science Institute.

employees. The positive effects are often very obvious. This favorable trend is supported by the service-oriented strategic direction that is chosen by management. Decisions directed toward improving the buyer–seller interactions and service quality imply that management is prepared to accept the revenue-generating power of the employees and to support it. Such a strategic attitude has a considerable positive effect on the internal environment of the firm and on employee motivation. Again, this results in increased internal efficiency. In some situations the service process can of course be improved by introducing technology-based solutions, in which cases fewer personnel may be needed and/ or the role of employees may change. Customers of insurance companies are often requested to ask routine questions over the phone instead of visiting an office in person, whereas service employees are supposed to provide customers with more knowledge-intensive services, such as financial advice. In such situations a critical challenge for management is to maintain and even improve the working atmosphere for personnel.

Improved customer satisfaction also has external effects. Favorable word of mouth is created. Existing customers may increase their business with the service provider and new customers will be attracted to the organization. The corporate image and/or local image is enhanced by positive customer experience and by favorable word of mouth.

Finally, sales volume will probably increase. If internal efficiency, external efficiency and service quality are controlled simultaneously, a larger volume of sales can be expected to have a sound financial effect and to improve the firm's competitive position. Such a positive trend may well continue. The improved atmosphere in the company makes the buyer–seller interactions even better, and the firm will generate more financial resources to be used to back up this trend.

Customer Benefits of a Service Strategy

Good service means certain benefits for the customer. Especially in business-to-business markets, customers may be able to calculate these benefits and see the results on the bottom line. For example, reliable and timely repair and maintenance services may reduce downtime costs which otherwise could amount to considerable sums. Such costs can easily be calculated. Individual consumers may sense these benefits more than see them. Such *relationship costs* were discussed in Chapter 6.

The better the total customer relationship is taken care of, the better the functional quality will be, and the less complicated it is for the customer to maintain the relationship with the service provider. Cooperation between the two parties becomes much easier. For example, the buyer can rely on the seller that deliveries will always be made on time, technical service will be good and non-technical service will be accessible when needed, claims will be handled promptly and with the buyer's interest in mind, and social contacts will be satisfactory. Not only is it more convenient for the buyer to do business with a seller who can be trusted in all respects, in many situations *such a relationship equals a cost reduction for the buyer as well*.

If the level of functional quality is high and cooperation between the two parties is smooth, three sources of cost reduction can be distinguished:

1. *fewer resources/personnel* are needed to maintain contact with the seller;
2. the person involved in contacts with the seller will *need less of their time* for handling these contacts; and
3. it is psychologically less demanding to maintain contact with the seller, which in turn *increases the mental capacity* of personnel to be used for other tasks.

In many cases the relationship cost reductions that can thus be achieved are easy to calculate. The psychological effects of good service may be less so, but the other effects can easily be transformed into euros, pounds sterling or dollars—money that, for the buyer/customer, can be used productively elsewhere. The seller, in turn, can transfer some of this cost reduction to the price. The benefits of improved customer relationships by a service strategy can thus be shared between the buyer and the seller. This should have a favorable impact on profitability.

The Service Concept

Every service provider needs some performance guidelines. Overall, the concept of *business mission* is used to determine in which markets the firm should operate and what kinds of problems it should try to solve. The term *service vision*[7] can be used to indicate a service-oriented business mission. Within the framework of the business mission, concrete guidelines have to be developed. These can be called *service concepts*.

The service concept is a way of expressing the notion that the organization intends to solve certain types of problems in a certain manner. This means that the service concept has to include information about *what* the firm intends to do for *a certain customer segment, how* this should be achieved, and with *what* kinds of *resources*. If there is no service concept agreed upon and accepted, the risk of inconsistent behavior is high. Supervisors do not know what should be achieved and what priorities to set. The same goes for other personnel. A situation would develop in which different parts of the organization perform inconsistently. This, of course, adds to confusion. And in an Internet-based virtual organizational setting with more or less loosely connected network partners a clear and easily communicated service concept is of utmost importance.

The service concept should be as concrete as possible so that it can be understood by everybody. To give an example, in the auto rental company case discussed in Chapter 7 the firm stated their service concept as follows: *"To offer immediately accessible solutions to temporary transportation problems."* This service concept states that since problems are immediate and temporary, therefore the solutions to them must be quick and easy to obtain. This firm has been very successful.

Depending on how differentiated the operations are and how many different customer segments there are, there can be one or several service concepts. It is, however, important that they all fit the overall service vision or business mission. Before a service concept can be determined, careful market research must be carried out, otherwise there is always a risk that there will be an insufficient market for the services produced according to the service concept.

Increasing the Service Impact in Customer Relationships

Implementing a service strategy requires appropriate action at the operational level. Here one should notice that a service strategy can be pursued by actions of many kinds. What is often needed is a new way of thinking. Old rules and ways of thinking may misguide management and leave opportunities unexploited.

The service impact on customer relationships can be increased in three ways:

1. by developing *new services* to offer to the customer;
2. by activating *existing but hidden services or service elements* in a business relationship; and
3. by turning the *goods component into a service element* in the customer relationship.

Too often only the first possibility is taken into account, but there are many additional opportunities for strengthening customer relationships through a better service impact.

Increasing the service impact by adding new services. The first category of activities literally means that new services are added to the offering. *New services* are typically various consultancy services, information services, repair and maintenance services, software development, Web sites, materials administration services, customer training or joint R&D activities. Clearly, this may be a powerful means of differentiating one firm's offering from that of the competition and of adding value to the offering. Such efforts should be used whenever appropriate. However, such new services require new investments and increase the cost level. These must be justified by the additional expected new revenue.

Increasing the service impact by activating existing but hidden services. The second type of activity seems much less dramatic and is therefore frequently not thought of as a strategic issue which should initiate major changes in the customer relationship. It may, nevertheless, have a dramatic impact on the offering, perhaps even more of an impact than the first type. It is a matter of *actively using existing but hidden, often non-billable, service elements in the relationship between the buyer and the seller* in order to differentiate the offering and add value to it and thus make use of these services as a means of competition.

Such service elements in customer relations are, for instance, casual advice, order taking, deliveries, claims handling, invoicing, demonstration of manufacturing processes, technical quality control, help desks and telephone reception services. *Customers do pay for these services, too*, although one seldom thinks about it. However, such service elements are far too often perceived as nuisances rather than as services by most customers. The reason for this is, of course, that they are frequently *handled as mere administrative routines and not as actively rendered services*. If these service elements are thought of as services and the value added that can be created by them is recognized, the firm may improve its position and strengthen its competitive edge.

It is important to realize that these potential services *already exist in the customer relationships*; they only have to be managed in a different way so that their value-creating possibilities are utilized. For example, complaints handling is far too often managed as an administrative task with the seller's interest as the top priority. Instead a complaint could be taken care of in a *service recovery* fashion, quickly, perhaps even before a formal complaint has been made by the customer, with the customer's interest as the first priority. In the former situation, customers consider the complaints-handling process a nuisance, which in addition may cause considerable sacrifice for them. In this situation, the quality problem or service breakdown is recovered in a way which the customer perceives as quality-enhancing and probably also cost-saving.

Many of the services which are managed as administrative routines or in some other way without taking the customer's interests into account are truly *hidden services*. On the one hand, service firms or manufacturers do not see them as potential value-creating services. On the other hand, customers often do not think of them as anything else than a necessary evil. Hence, the firm that manages to turn such hidden services or "non-services" into real services to its customers can easily provide them with a series of positive surprises, and enhance perceived quality in the minds of the customers. From this should follow strengthened customer relationships.

The impact of these elements on a business relationship is normally considered marginal, if thought of as anything other than administrative routines, which are only internal and thus of no concern to customers. However, the service impact of, for example, customer-oriented improved invoicing procedures, call center systems, and complaints handling can be substantial.

Moreover, developing such service elements often does not demand big invest-ments or extra costs. Rearranging existing resources and routines may frequently be all that is needed. In fact, more service-oriented invoicing and complaints handling may ensure that these activities are more effectively handled internally as well, and operating costs can thus be saved. The customer benefits that can be achieved frequently exceed the additional efforts.

Increasing the service impact by turning goods components into services. If the goods component is offered in a flexible manner and tailor-made to fit the needs and wishes of the customer, it is used as a service to the customer. Consequently, it is turned into a service element in the customer relationship. A good salesperson uses such a sales strategy. However, turning the goods component into a service goes far beyond sales. In production, materials administration, installation, IT applications, and so on the same approach is required.

A manufacturer of industrial equipment may try to tailor its goods as much as possible to the specific needs of its customers. A restaurant may cook meals and even add seasoning according to the wishes of a specific customer. In both cases, *the goods component is transformed from being a physical thing to a customized service.*

Service Management: A Service-Oriented Approach to Management

Having demonstrated the nature and characteristics of a service strategy, we now turn to the principles of management which guide decision-making and managerial behavior in service competition. This approach to management has been labeled *service management*.[8] Hence, this is a management approach in which management procedures are geared to the characteristics of services and the nature of service competition. Service management is also very much a market-oriented approach. Often the term "service management" is used instead of the term "service marketing." Sometimes the phrase "service marketing and management" is also used in the literature to describe this field.[9] The use of the term "service management" indicates the cross-functional nature of marketing in service contexts. Marketing is not a separate function, but in the management of all business functions the interests of the customers, i.e. a marketing aspect, has to be taken into account. It is a matter of *market-oriented management*. Chapter 10 discusses marketing in service competition and the relationship between marketing and management.

Service management is understanding how to manage a business in service competition; that is, in a competitive situation where services, defined in a broad sense, are the key to success in the marketplace, regardless of whether the core of the offering is a service or a manufactured product.

Service management can be defined as follows:[10]

Service management is:

1. understanding the value customers receive by consuming or using the offerings of an organization and knowing how services alone or together with information, physical goods or other kinds of tangibles contribute to

this value; understanding how total quality is perceived in customer relationships to facilitate such value and how it changes over time;

2. understanding how an organization (people, technology and physical resources, systems and customers) will be able to produce and deliver this perceived quality and value;

3. understanding how an organization should be developed and managed so that the intended perceived quality and value are achieved; and

4. making an organization function so that this perceived quality and value are achieved and the objectives of the parties involved (the organization, the customers, other parties, etc.) are met.

This means that the firm has to understand the following:

1. the perceived quality and value customers are looking for in service competition;

2. how to create that value for customers; and

3. how to manage the resources available to the organization to achieve such service-based value-creation.[11]

This is an exhaustive description of service management. Shorter definitions lose some of the information content, but may still be clear to readers, and they are easier to remember. According to another definition in the literature "service management is a total organizational approach that makes quality of service, as perceived by the customer, the number one driving force for the operation of the business."[12] Applying service management principles means that service is considered *the* organizational imperative.[13]

"Organization" in these contexts, of course, refers to the bundle of quality-generating resources involved in producing the service, that is, people (personnel and customers alike) as well as technology and physical resources and operating systems, information management and administration. As organizations increasingly move towards being network organizations, many of these resources are outside the boundaries of traditional organizational constructs. It is also important to observe that the definition of service management requires a dynamic approach to management. It is not enough to understand which values or benefits customers are seeking; one must also understand that the benefits customers are looking for will change over time, and that the customer perceived quality and value which is produced has to change accordingly.

A service management perspective changes the general focus of management in service firms as well as in manufacturing firms in the following ways:[14]

1. from product-based value to *total value* in the customer relationship;

2. from short-term transactions to *long-term relationships*;

3. from core product (goods or services) quality (the technical quality of the outcome) to *total customer perceived quality* in enduring customer relationships; and

4. from production of the technical solution (or technical quality of a product or service) as the key process in the organization to *developing total perceived quality and value as the key process*.

Service Management: A Shift in Management Focus

Two basic shifts in focus are implicit in the service management principles when compared to the traditional management approach used in manufacturing. These are:

1. a shift from an interest in the internal consequences of performance to an interest in the *external* consequences; and
2. a shift from a focus on structure to a focus on *process*.

These two shifts are of paramount importance. A service strategy, to be successfully implemented, requires both. As a management philosophy, service management is predominantly related to managing processes in which the underlying structures are of less importance. If the structures take over, the flexibility of operations and the handling of customer contacts suffer. The encouragement and support of managers and supervisors decreases and thus motivation among personnel suffers as well. In the following phase, the perceived service quality decreases and customers are probably lost. The new emphasis on process and external consequences changes the focus on (1) the profit equation and the business logic, (2) decision-making authority, (3) organizational structure, (4) supervisory control, and (5) reward systems; and when there is a shift in the focus on reward systems, other tasks and types of achievement have to be (6) monitored and measured. These *six principles of service management* are summarized in Table 8.1, and discussed below.

The profit equation and the business logic. As discussed in some detail in this chapter, the *general economic focus* or the *business logic* is shifted from managing internal efficiency and the productivity of capital and labor to *managing total efficiency* where customer perceived quality drives profit. However, as discussed in Chapter 6, there are several interrelated factors influencing how, and indeed if, perceived quality leads to sound economic results. Scale economies may or may not be a strategically reasonable objective, but it is never sound, and it is always dangerous to automatically consider economies of scale as a source of profitability. Rather, the pursuit of large-scale production and the potential benefits of scale economies can easily turn an operation into a disaster. Frequently, the opportunities of developing market economies can be used to create a solid competitive advantage and a basis for profitable operations. Because of the nature of services and service competition, some sort of a pursuit of market economies should always be incorporated in the strategic approach.

Service management appreciates the importance to success of managing external efficiency and customer relationships. Internal efficiency needed to function profitably is an inevitable issue, but it is not a top priority *per se*. It must be totally integrated with external efficiency issues and geared to managing customer perceived quality. As soon as the internal perspective begins to dominate, an interest in costs and managing internal efficiency will take over, but without a simultaneous consideration of the quality implications. Issues related

TABLE 8.1 Principles of service management: a summary

Principle		*Remarks*
1. The profit equation and business logic	Customer perceived service quality drives profit	Decisions on external efficiency and internal efficiency (customer satisfaction and productivity of capital and labor) have to be totally integrated
2. Decision-making authority	Decision-making has to be decentralized as close as possible to the organization–customer interface	Some strategically important decisions have to be made centrally
3. Organizational focus	The organization has to be structured and functioning so that its main goal is the mobilization of resources to support frontline operations	This may often require a "flat" organization with no unnecessary layers
4. Supervisory focus	Managers and supervisors focus on the encouragement and support of employees	As few legislative control procedures as possible, although some may be required
5. Reward systems	Producing customer perceived quality should be the focus of reward systems	All relevant facets of service quality should be considered, although all cannot always be built into a reward system
6. Measurement focus	Customer satisfaction with service quality should be the focus of measuring achievements	To monitor productivity and internal efficiency, internal measurement criteria may have to be used as well

to creating and maintaining excellence and revenue generation will then become secondary and receive less or no management attention.

Decision-making authority. Because of the characteristics of services (e.g. the inseparability of critical parts of production and consumption) and the facets of customer perceived service quality (e.g. the demand for flexibility and recovery capabilities), decisions concerning how a service operation should function have to be made *as close as possible to the interface between the organization and its customers.* Ideally, customer contact employees who are involved in service encounters should have the authority to make prompt decisions. Otherwise sales opportunities and opportunities for service recovery, correcting quality mistakes and problems will not be used intelligently. If the moments of truth in the service encounters go unmanaged, service quality deteriorates quickly. Of course, a contact employee, for example, a bank clerk or a service technician, cannot always have the professional knowledge required if a customer wants, for example, a sophisticated financial solution for his international business or an estimate of expected future repair costs. However, the customer contact employee should nevertheless have the decision-making authority to, for example, ask for assistance from office or staff professionals.

If the employees in customer contacts are not given authority to think and make decisions for themselves, they become victims of a rigid system. Customer contact employees may be demotivated by rigid rules and systems which hamper them instead of empowering them to handle deviations from standard operational procedures. "Empowering" personnel is a powerful way of motivating people (empowerment will be discussed in Chapter 14 on internal marketing). It means that employees are encouraged, and trained, to recognize the diversity of customer contact situations and to use their judgment in handling situations and solving problems following on from deviations from standard procedures so that customer satisfaction is created.

Thus, *operational decision-making needs to be decentralized*. However, some strategically important decisions have to be kept centralized; for example, decisions concerning overall strategies, business missions and service concepts. The unique knowledge among contact personnel of aspects of the business that are vital to making such strategic decisions should, however, always be used in central decision-making. First, this improves the quality of decisions, and second, it creates a stronger commitment to these decisions among those who will have to live with them and carry them out.

The "local" manager, whether he is the head of a branch of a multi-outlet organization, such as a bank or hotel chain, or the head of a department in a firm which produces services has, of course, the overall responsibility for his team. The manager is also responsible for the total operation, service consciousness and profitability of his "local" organization. One can say that the manager has dual responsibility, towards the customers and towards the corporation. Svenska Handelsbanken, a retail and commercial bank based in Sweden, has formulated the following ground rule for their local branch managers: "The local manager is responsible for perceived service quality and value for the customers and for profitability for the corporation." This bank is probably the most decentralized and customer-oriented bank in Scandinavia. It is also one of the most profitable banks and has been rated highest by customers in satisfaction studies. This bank and its way of organizing its marketing resources will be discussed further in Chapter 13.

Organizational focus. Traditionally, the *organizational focus* is geared to building up and maintaining a structure in which management decisions are cascaded through processes involving legislative control. This often creates a lack of flexibility, fuels centralization tendencies, and can be a hindrance to the vertical flow of information in the organization. Service management shifts management focus away from structure and control procedures towards improved external efficiency with acceptable internal efficiency. This requires a more flexible organizational solution, where the *mobilization* of resources—management, staff, systems—to support customer contact activities is imperative. The organizational structure that suits this requirement may differ from situation to situation, but some common principles can be identified. Organization for service will be discussed in more detail in Chapter 13.

Supervisory control. In traditional management approaches, supervisory systems are closely related to monitoring the capability of the organization and its various departments in performing their tasks according to predetermined standards. If such standards are met, the employee, or a group of employees, has performed satisfactorily, and may be rewarded.

However, such a supervisory control system does not fit the nature of services and service production very well. By their very nature, services cannot often be completely standardized. Moreover, for employees to deliver quality services, some degree of flexibility is needed to meet the special wishes of customers or to successfully recover negative situations in buyer–seller interactions. Here, guidelines and visions are better than rigidly defined standards. Only the technical quality aspects of services can be monitored by standards; whereas, from a competitive standpoint, the highly important functional quality aspects are not well suited for the development of traditional standards. Functional quality-creating performance cannot easily, if at all, be monitored by comparing it to predetermined standards. Instead, service management requires that the supervisory focus be on the support and encouragement of employees. This may require new management methods. Subsequent chapters on *service culture* and *internal marketing* will touch upon this issue to some extent.

Reward systems. Normally, *reward systems* are geared to the focus of supervisory control. What is monitored can be measured, and what is measured can be controlled and rewarded. Of course, not all, if any, of the tasks and factors that are controlled are geared to reward systems. However, a shift in supervisory focus requires a corresponding shift of focus on rewarding. Generally speaking, service management requires that *producing perceived service quality and value* at some level—excellent or otherwise acceptable—should be rewarded, not just compliance with predetermined standards.

Measurement focus. What is controlled and rewarded has first to be measured. The focus here must of course also be shifted, or at least expanded. The ultimate signs of success are customer satisfaction with total perceived quality, loyal customers and improved profits. Thus, according to service management principles, for service-oriented supervisory approaches and reward systems, customer satisfaction with *service quality* as well as tasks that boost satisfaction and loyalty have to be measured. Measuring how standards are met and the bottom line are not enough. Internal efficiency criteria may have to be used as well, so that internal efficiency is kept under control. However, the external efficiency criteria always dominate.

A Case of Innovative Service Management: easyJet and easyGroup

The main, currently best known activity of the UK-based easyGroup is easyJet, the no-frills discount airline, which at the end of 1999 employed 1,300 people and had 18 airplanes. The business is still very young (less than four years old at the time of writing) and sees itself as a great user of technology and reengineer of the business process.

easyJet

The key characteristics of easyJet are as follows:

- It is a point-to-point flyer and not a network carrier. easyJet flies destination to destination; it does not have a network of alliances with other carriers and is not a member of a reservations group.
- It is a short-haul flyer, covering routes in Europe, often of under two hours flying time, which allows both business and leisure passengers to choose the flights (and the prices) that suit them best.
- It is a no-frills airline, with no on-board meals, no ticketing, no third-party booking channels and no frequent flyer programs.
- It is a low fare operator, selling flights at between one half and a third of the prices charged by the traditional network carriers.
- It is a low cost operator, whose business process has stripped out unnecessary costs and whose emphasis is on continual cost reduction to ensure permanent low fares.
- It is a virtual business, where all communications are paperless and activities are sub-contracted wherever possible: e.g., check-in, baggage handling and in-flight catering.

In developing these characteristics further, it is worth noting that easyJet itself is modeled to a large extent on Southwest Airlines, another very successful no-frills airline based in south-western USA. easyJet has developed a business approach that is European in focus and which offers easyJet the opportunity to create a "cookie cutter" of the business process, which they can duplicate elsewhere.

For example, from their original base at Luton Airport, outside London, they have used the "cookie cutter" approach to establish similar operations in Liverpool in England and in Geneva in Switzerland.

The success of this approach can be judged by the fact that easyJet currently flies five million passengers a year, with an average utilization factor of 80 per cent, making on average a profit of £1.70 per passenger. It is a volume business, with low costs and low margins.

easyJet sells its services via only two channels: telephone and the Internet. The call center in Luton is part of the direct sell culture of easyJet and cuts out the commission of around 10 per cent paid by other airlines to travel agents and other intermediaries. Internet booking was introduced to further reduce costs, and customers are incentivized to book by this channel, with reduced fares as their reward. In October 1999, Internet sales for easyJet for the first time exceeded telephone sales.

easyJet's fares are very flexible. First, the fares are cheaper the earlier you book, and second, fares are set according to demand. For example, a Friday night flight from Liverpool to Nice, Southern France, will be charged at a higher price than a Wednesday evening flight on the same route. The use of secondary airports such as Luton and Liverpool also reduces easyJet's costs, since landing charges are far less than at primary airports such as London Heathrow and Manchester. Moreover, easyJet has a policy of buying aircraft of the same make and model (Boeing 737s) so that their finance, maintenance and crew training costs are also minimized.

In people terms easyJet has a flat hierarchy with only 30 people in "managerial" positions, and it operates a totally paperless office with all mail scanned into their intranet and all communications shared and then stored electronically. The barbecue held every Friday at easyJet's offices in Luton also helps to keep office staff in touch with flight crews, call center staff and ground staff.

Stretching the brand

easyGroup was established to "stretch" the "easy" brand and has already opened easyEverything in London, as the world's largest Internet café. It has 400 terminals and costs £1 per hour for Internet access, which compares with an average price of £6 to £7 elsewhere. easyEverything needs a 60 per cent occupancy to break even on the investment and, since they have bought 2,000 terminals, they are looking to use the "cookie-cutting" approach to replicate easyEverything in other cities with lots of young travelers, such as Amsterdam, Barcelona and Paris. Their aim is to eventually have 25 easyEverythings across Europe.

Further brand-stretching and applications of the use of technology to reengineer the business process can be expected via easyRentaCar, an on-line auto rental service which uses a standard fleet of vehicles and prices them at a basic rate of £9 per day. These rental sites will of course be located at the airports where easyJet fly to. Also being considered is easyMoney, which will offer investment products by cutting out the intermediaries and hence reducing commission and increasing returns for investors.

At the moment easyJet, as the main business unit of easyGroup, has a competitive advantage over the network carriers such as British Airways. This advantage is based on the low cost, low price, low margin, large volume approach described above. There are competitors working off similar, if not the same, model, such as Ryanair, and even the major carriers such as British Airways and KLM have acknowledged the success of easyJet by creating sub-brands in the same image, Go and Buzz. Imitation is the sincerest form of flattery! Time will show how the service management concept of easyGroup and easyJet will work in the long run.

Source: This case example was prepared by Steve Worthington, Staffordshire University.

Summary and Questions for Discussion

There are clear and well-defined customer benefits in pursuing a service strategy. However, doing so requires different knowledge on the part of management as well as those implementing a service strategy. The issues of quality, productivity and profitability have to be addressed differently than in a traditional manufacturing context. This, of course, is due to the characteristics of services and service consumption, and the nature of customer relationships in service contexts. What is standard in managing a traditional manufacturing firm may turn out to be inappropriate for a service business or for a manufacturer pursuing a service strategy. A "service imperative" and the management of service quality is at the heart of service management.

Questions for discussion

1. How could traditional management wisdom from manufacturing become a trap for a service firm?
2. Discuss the profit equation and the factors influencing its components in services and manufacturing respectively.
3. What is meant by a *service imperative*?
4. Discuss how applying the service management principles would change the strategic focus, structure and governance systems of a firm.

Further Reading

Albrecht, K. (1988) *At America's Service*. Homewood, IL: Dow Jones-Irwin.

Chase, R.B. & Haynes, R.M. (2000) Service Operations Management: A Field Guide. In Swartz, T.A. & Iacobucci, D. (eds), *Handbook of Services Marketing & Management*. Thousand Oaks, CA: Sage Publications, pp. 455–471.

Drucker, P. (1973) *Management: Tasks, Responsibilities, Practices*. New York: Harper & Row.

Ekholm, B. (1984) *The Business Idea and Its Lifepath*. Report. Fourth Annual Strategic Management Society Conference, Philadelphia, October.

Fitzsimmons, J.A. & Fitzsimmons, M.J. (1997) *Service Management*. San Fransisco, CA: McGraw-Hill.

Grönroos, C. (1990) Service Management: A Management Focus for Service Competition. *International Journal of Service Industry Management*, **1**(1), pp. 6–14.

Grönroos, C. (1990a) *Service Management and Marketing. Managing the Moments of Truth in Service Competition*. Lexington, MA: Lexington Books.

Heskett, J.L. (1987) Lessons in the Service Economy. *Harvard Business Review*, March–April.

Levitt, T. (1972) Production-line Approach to Service. *Harvard Business Review*, **50**, September–October, pp. 41–52.

Normann, R. (1992) *Service Management*. 2nd edition. New York: John Wiley & Sons.

Schneider, B. & Rentsch, J. (1987) The Management of Climate and Culture: A Futures Perspective. In Hage, J. (ed.), *Futures of Organizations*. Lexington, MA: Lexington Books.

Storbacka, K. (1994) *The Nature of Customer Relationship Profitability—Analysis of Relationships and Customer Bases in Retail Banking*. Helsinki/Helsingfors: Hanken Swedish School of Economics Finland/CERS Center for Relationship Marketing and Service Management.

Notes

1   Following Ekholm, in this context we nevertheless use the *internal efficiency/external efficiency* terminology instead of the efficiency/effectiveness terms. See Ekholm, B., *The Business Idea and Its Lifepath*. Report. Fourth Annual Strategic Management Society Conference, Philadelphia, October 1984.

2   Chase, R.B. & Haynes, R.M., Service Operations Management: A Field Guide. In Swartz, T.A. & Iacobucci, D. (eds), *Handbook of Services Marketing & Management*. Thousand Oaks, CA: Sage Publications, 2000, pp. 455–471. The classical article on the manufacturing orientation of service processes is Levitt, T., Production-line Approach to Service. *Harvard Business Review*, **50**, September–October 1972, pp. 41–52.

3   See Richard, N., *Service Management*. New York: John Wiley & Sons, 1992, where the existence of and internal effects of such vicious circles are extensively discussed.

4   In a major study in the financial services sector in Scandinavia Kaj Storbacka has demonstrated that 20 per cent of the customers do not stand for 80 per cent of profits but for 180 per cent to 200 per cent of profits. Other customers do not contribute to total profits or are directly unprofitable, thus eroding the total profitability accumulated by the group of profitable customers. Moreover, many of the unprofitable customers or customers who do not contribute to profits are what he

calls "satisfied small customers" and sometimes also big customers, that is customers who are satisfied with the perceived service quality but who consume the services in such a way that the cost of producing them exceeds the revenues from those services. See Storbacka, K., *The Nature of Customer Relationship Profitability—Analysis of Relationships and Customer Bases in Retail Banking.* Helsinki/Helsingfors, Finland: Hanken Swedish School of Economics Finland/CERS, 1994.

5   Heskett, J.L., Lessons in the Service Economy. *Harvard Business Review*, March–April 1987.

6   Drucker, P., *Management: Tasks, Responsibilities, Practices.* New York: Harper & Row, 1973.

7   Heskett, *op.cit.*

8   Grönroos, C., Service Management: A Management Focus for Service Competition. *International Journal of Service Industry Management*, **1**(1), 1990, pp. 6–14. This service management concept should not be mixed up with the concept of service management which is used to denote the management of service operations. See, for example, Fitzsimmons, J.A. & Fitzsimmons, M.J., *Service Management.* San Fransisco, CA: McGraw-Hill, 1997.

9   The title of the recently published handbook in the field, *Handbook of Services Marketing and Management*, is a good example. Also, the choice of Center for Services Marketing and Management for a new name of the research center in the area at Arizona State University and the title *Advances in Services Marketing and Management* for the annually published periodical in the service field are indications of the shift from seeing the field of service marketing as a function of marketing management towards an overall service-oriented management process.

10   See Grönroos, C., *Service Management and Marketing. Managing the Moments of Truth in Service Competition.* Lexington, MA: Lexington Books, 1990a.

11   Grönroos 1990, *op.cit.*

12   Albrecht, K., *At America's Service.* Homewood, IL: Dow Jones-Irwin, 1988.

13   Schneider, B. & Rentsch, J., The Management of Climate and Culture: A Futures Perspective. In Hage, J. (ed.), *Futures of Organizations.* Lexington, MA: Lexington Books, 1987.

14   See Grönroos 1990a, *op.cit.*

Chapter 9

MANAGING SERVICE PRODUCTIVITY

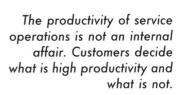

The productivity of service operations is not an internal affair. Customers decide what is high productivity and what is not.

Introduction

In Chapter 8 on service management principles it was noticed that the productivity concept as it has been developed for manufacturing firms cannot readily be used in service contexts. In this chapter this problem in discussed in detail. The shortcomings of a traditional manufacturing-based productivity concept are analyzed, and a service productivity concept is developed. It is observed that decisions based on traditional productivity measurements will almost always lead in the wrong direction. Internal and external efficiency consequences have to be taken into account simultaneously if they are to provide management with meaningful guidance. In the final sections of this chapter the possibility of creating measurement instruments is explored. No final calculation models can yet be offered. The theoretical understanding of service productivity has to be developed further before robust measurement models can be developed. After reading this chapter the reader should understand the problems of a traditional manufacturing-oriented productivity concept in service contexts and the pitfalls of using productivity measurements based on such a concept. The reader should also understand the nature of service productivity and how service productivity measurements could be made.

The Productivity Dilemma: Balancing Revenues and Costs

Productivity as a concept has been largely neglected in research into services.[1] It is often claimed that productivity is low in many service organizations and that services are produced using excess resources and at unnecessarily high cost. With another resource structure the service provider could cut costs and still produce as much as before. For example, banks are urging their customers to use ATMs, PCs and the Internet to take care of regular bank affairs instead of visiting a bank and occupying the bank employees' time. Insurance companies are establishing call centers for customer service, so that customers can interact over the telephone instead of by visiting customer service employees. The reason for these changes in resource structures is of course to shift from expensive resources in the service process to cheaper resources. If customers perceive that they receive the same quality as before, or perhaps even better quality, these changes will have been successful.[2] They have been *cost-effective* and at the same time maintained or improved the firm's *revenue-generating capability*.

However, cost-cutting changes in the resources used may well have the opposite effect. Perceived quality may deteriorate and customers may become dissatisfied and start to look for other options. The service provider's revenue-generating capability thus declines.

The problem with being an effective service organization is that productivity and perceived quality are inseparable phenomena. Improving productivity may have a neutral or positive impact on quality, but equally it may damage perceived quality. If the latter happens, satisfaction with quality declines and the risk that the firm will lose customers increases. Revenues go down, and this may have a negative effect on the firm's overall financial results, even though costs may also have been reduced.

This is the dilemma in service processes. Improved internal efficiency following the introduction of more cost-effective production resources and processes does not necessarily lead to better economic results. In fact, while using a traditional productivity terminology is considered to bring about an increase in productivity, that is, improved internal efficiency, it often has the opposite effect in service organizations. This leads to lost revenue, because of decreasing service quality. The obvious conclusion is that in service contexts productivity cannot be understood without simultaneously considering the interrelationship between productivity and perceived quality. Internal efficiency, which equates to cost efficiency, cannot be managed separately from external efficiency, which in the previous chapter was defined as a firm's capability of producing a certain level of perceived service quality with a given resource structure.[3]

In conclusion, firms are used to treating the management of productivity as an internal issue following a traditional productivity concept. They measure the level of productivity from an internal efficiency perspective, and because of a *constant-quality assumption* take for granted that the external effects on quality and customer value are under control. According to the *constant-quality assumption*, changes in production inputs do not have an impact on the quality produced. However, in service contexts the situation is the opposite. Productivity is not evaluated internally by managers, but externally by the customers, who make external judgements of the productivity of a service operation. This, of course, does not exclude the importance of taking into account the internal efficiency aspects of service productivity as well. However, because the *constant-quality assumption* does not apply in services, the customers have the last word.

To clarify the discussion of service productivity, Table 9.1 describes central concepts and terms as they are used here. Some have been discussed and defined in previous chapters.

TABLE 9.1   Definition and description of central concepts and terms used

Concept/term	Definition and/or description
Productivity	Efficiency in the process of transforming input resources in a service or manufacturing process into customer value
Traditional productivity concept	The conversion of production resources into output, or the ratio between output from the production process and input into that process, given a constant quality level (the *constant-quality assumption*)
Internal efficiency	How efficiently outputs can be produced using a given amount of production resources
Cost efficiency	Synonym for internal efficiency
External efficiency	How efficiently and effectively perceived service quality can be produced using a given amount of production resources
Revenue efficiency	Synonym for external efficiency
Revenue-generating capability	The degree to which the perceived service quality capability enables the service provider to generate sales and revenues
Capacity efficiency	How efficiently the production capacity is used for serving customers (excess supply lowers capacity efficiency; excess demand may affect perceived service quality negatively)
Profit efficiency	How efficiently production resources are used, blending external and internal efficiency, and capacity utilized to produce results (profit efficiency is the ultimate *internal* goal for productivity-improving actions and programs value for customers is the ultimate *external* goal)

Shortcomings Of Manufacturing-Oriented Productivity Concepts

We begin the development of a service productivity concept by discussing the shortcomings of the traditional productivity concept. For the firm managing productivity is a matter of creating *profit efficiency*; in other words *managing the economic results*. By increasing productivity, the economic results are assumed to improve, because an unchanged or even improved customer value is produced using fewer resources or in a more efficient way. As long as this is the case, managing productivity makes sense. If improved productivity does not lead to better economic results, there is no profit efficiency and increasing productivity does not make sense.

The traditional productivity concept has been developed for manufacturers of physical goods. Existing productivity models and productivity measurement instruments are also geared to manufacturing. Moreover, these are based on assumptions that consumption and production are separate processes and that customers do not participate in the production process. In other words, they are developed for *closed systems*. In traditional manufacturing[4] these assumptions make sense of course. In service contexts, where the service (production) process is largely an *open system*, they create confusion, give rise to misleading measurements and guide decision-making in the wrong direction. In Table 9.2 assumptions underpinning the traditional manufacturing-oriented productivity concept and characteristics of services are summarized.[5]

TABLE 9.2   The service productivity dilemma. Adapted from Ojasalo, K., *Conceptualizing Productivity in Services*. Helsinki, Helsingfors: Hanken Swedish School of Economics, Finland/CERS, 1999, p. 59). Reproduced by their permission.

Assumptions included in the manufacturing-oriented productivity concept	Characteristics of services affecting productivity in service concepts
Production and consumption are *separate*; productivity measured in a *closed system* ⇒ perceived quality is dependent on outcome only	Production and consumption are partly *simultaneous processes* with quality-influencing interactions, i.e. an *open system* ⇒ perceived quality is dependent on both outcome and process ⇒ difficulties in separating production input from output
Customers *do not participate* in the production process[6] (closed system) ⇒ perceived quality is not influenced by the production process	Customers *participate* in the service process (open system) ⇒ uncertainty of customer-induced input in the service process; their effects vary ⇒ customer-induced input affects the efficiency of firm-induced input in the process ⇒ perceived quality is influenced by the service (production) process (the functional quality dimension)
Input and output of the production process are *homogenous* ⇒ quality resulting from the production process is constant	Input to and output of the service (production) process are *heterogeneous* ⇒ quality resulting from the service process (both outcome-related and process-related) varies, due to the process-related quality dimension and the effects of customer-induced input into the service process
Productivity can be measured *separately from sales volumes* ⇒ a constant amount of output can be produced	Actual *sales volumes influence* productivity because service cannot be inventoried ⇒ variation in output quantities ⇒ fluctuation in demand affects productivity
Output is *tangible* (although it may be perceived in an intangible way) ⇒ output of the production can be measured and calculated ⇒ easy to relate amount of output (in volume and value) to amount of input (in volume and value)	Output (process-related and outcome-related) is to a considerable extent *intangible* ⇒ output of the service (production) process is difficult to measure and calculate ⇒ difficult to relate amount of output (one unit of service) to input (both in volume and value)

The characteristics of services and the assumption underlying the traditional productivity concept make traditional productivity models and measurement instruments useless for service providers. For example, how raw materials are used in a restaurant to produce a given number of meals can be calculated using manufacturing-oriented productivity methods, and this information is undoubtedly valuable for the restaurant. However, it has nothing to do with the productivity of the total restaurant operations. A totally different approach to productivity has to be taken to measure how well a service provider uses resources to create output in the form of acceptable perceived quality and value for customers. In service processes, where a firm provides customers with a highly standardized infrastructure, such as a telephone operator, and where customers interact with each other only in this environment, the service provider comes close to a manufacturing-resembling closed production system. As long as the infrastructure functions without problems and the customers know how to operate it, traditional assumptions for understanding and measuring productivity apply to a large extent. However, in most service processes, even in high-tech services, the characteristics of services in Table 9.2 apply. There, traditional productivity models and measurement instruments are more misleading than valuable.

Because the service (production) process and consumption are simultaneous processes, where customers actively participate, the resources used to produce services cannot be standardized. It is difficult to relate a given number of inputs, in volume or value terms, to a given number of outputs. Frequently, it is even difficult to define "one unit of service." According to the traditional manufacturing-related productivity concept, productivity is defined as the ratio between output and input, given that the quality of the output is kept constant, or

$$\text{Productivity} = \frac{\text{Output produced}}{\text{Input used}} \mid \text{Constant quality of output}$$

Only if the quality of the production output is constant and there is no significant variation in the ratio between input used and output produced, productivity can be measured using traditional methods. This *constant-quality assumption* is normally taken for granted and not explicitly expressed. Therefore, the critical importance of this assumption is easily forgotten. Traditional productivity measurements only make sense in service contexts when the constant-quality assumption applies. In most service processes it does not apply.

If the constant-quality assumption can be taken for granted in productivity management, *revenue efficiency* is not an issue. A stable quality level is a guarantee of stable revenue streams. This is the case in traditional manufacturing, and that is probably the main reason why the traditional productivity concept is so highly oriented towards managing cost efficiency only. For service providers, however, revenue efficiency considerations cannot be omitted, and therefore they become an integral part of productivity management.

In services, it is not only the input that is difficult to calculate, it is also difficult to measure output. Output measured as a volume is only useful if customers are willing to buy this output. In manufacturing, where the constant-quality assumption applies, customers can be expected to buy an output produced using an altered input or resource structure. In services, where the constant-quality assumption does not apply, we do not know whether customers will purchase the output produced using a different input structure or not. It depends on the effects on perceived process-related and outcome-related quality of the new resources or inputs used. Hence, productivity cannot be understood without taking into account the interrelationship between the use of input or production resources and the perceived quality of the output or services produced with these resources.[7] In other words, the interrelationship between internal efficiency (cost efficiency) and external efficiency (revenue efficiency) is critical for service productivity.

The Interrelationship Between Productivity, Quality, Customer Participation And Demand

As demonstrated in the previous section, productivity and quality cannot be separated in services. The customer's role in productivity is also different in service contexts than in manufacturing (see Table 9.2). This is because customers participate in the service process and influence the progress of the process and its outcome. They may also have an impact on how fellow customers participate in the process and perceive the quality of the service produced in that process. The service provider uses resources in the service process, which are a *provider-induced contribution* to productivity. This can be labeled *provider participation* in the service process. For example, for a hair stylist, his professional and communication skills, time available, the equipment, physical products used in the process, supporting services and goods such as coffee, tea and magazines form the provider participation in the process.

The customer and fellow customers provide some inputs such as information, self-service activities, inquiries and complaints. These are *customer-induced contributions* to productivity. In the hair stylist example, the accuracy of the customer's requests and her ability to provide correct information to guide the hair stylist in cutting her hair are customer-induced contributions to the process. The customers' actions do not only give the input needed to produce the service, they also influence the way the employees and technologies in the service process function. In other words, interactions created by customers influence the efficiency of the service process. This is an *interaction-induced contribution* to productivity. Depending on how well the hair stylist and the customer can relate to and communicate with each other, the interactions that occur will contribute more or less to the perceived quality of the process.

At the same time and as a result of the same resources that contribute to productivity, depending on how these resources perform and interact, there is provider-induced, customer-induced and interaction-induced contribution to quality.[8] *Quality and productivity are thus two sides of the same coin.*

In addition, productivity is influenced by demand. If demand is low, the service provider's resources will be under-utilized, which means that internal efficiency decreases. This of course has a negative effect on productivity. In manufacturing, inventories can be used to offset this effect. In services this is not possible. When there is a demand that meets the provider-induced resources in the service process, internal efficiency improves and a positive effect on productivity is created. When demand starts to exceed what can be managed with existing resources, external efficiency decreases, which has a negative effect on perceived service quality. Hence, demand is also a critical productivity factor. In Figure 9.1[9] the interrelated factors in a service productivity context are schematically illustrated.

The shaded areas of the provider participation and customer participation boxes depict the parts of the provider's resources and the customer's resources that are used in interaction with each other (in buyer–seller interactions and service encounters). Part of provider participation takes place in a back office, where internal services are produced. On the other hand, customer participation

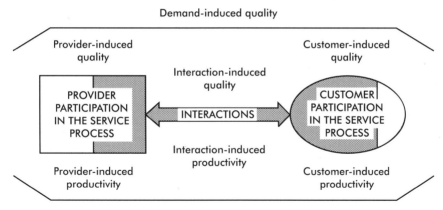

Demand-induced quality

Provider-induced quality

Customer-induced quality

Interaction-induced quality

PROVIDER PARTICIPATION IN THE SERVICE PROCESS

INTERACTIONS

CUSTOMER PARTICIPATION IN THE SERVICE PROCESS

Interaction-induced productivity

Provider-induced productivity

Customer-induced productivity

Demand-induced productivity

Interactive participation by service provider and customer

FIGURE 9.1   Productivity, quality, customer and provider participation and demand as productivity factors in service contexts. Adapted from Gummesson, E., Productivity, Quality and Relationship Marketing in Service Operations. *International Journal of Contemporary Hospitality Management*, **10**(1), 1998, p. 9.

sometimes also takes place outside the interactions with the service provider. For example, when making a telephone call the service is produced by two customers who are interacting with each other. The telephone operator only indirectly supports the service process by providing the telephone infrastructure. For example, IKEA, the Swedish furniture chain, provides its customers with packaged furniture in a box which includes parts, bolts and tools and instructions for assembly. The customer is then expected to continue the service process which started in the shop by assembling the furniture at home. Here again the service provider only indirectly supports the service process in the customer's home by providing tools and instructions.

From a managerial point of view, the following aspects are important in productivity management in services.

- An optimal balance between perceived service quality (external efficiency) and cost efficiency (internal efficiency) must be maintained when the service provider designs its input into the process.
- The service provider's resources (provider participation) must contribute to interactions with customers in the service process in a way that creates an optimal balance between perceived quality and internal efficiency.
- Customers must be chosen, educated and informed in such a way that they, through their participation in the service process, contribute positively to customer-induced quality and productivity as well as to interaction-induced quality and productivity.
- Demand must be managed so that a balance can be maintained between perceived quality and internal efficiency.

The crucial point here is to pay attention to how changes in internal efficiency affect perceived service quality (external efficiency). Improved cost efficiency of resources used in the service process often has a negative effect on perceived service quality and customer value. Longer waiting times and less customer attention from personnel may be the results of a change which increases cost efficiency in the resource structure. These effects can easily have a negative impact on the functional quality of the service process and perhaps also on the technical quality of the outcome. If this is the case, customers may be lost, revenues decline, and in the end the *profit efficiency* of the service provider deteriorates.

On the other hand, actions that improve cost efficiency may have a neutral or even positive effect on perceived service quality. New configurations of inputs may improve cost efficiency and have a positive effect on perceived quality as well. For example, a restaurant may offer a salad bar instead of serving salad to the table, to decrease its input resources. For those customers who appreciate this alternative the perceived quality is maintained or perhaps even improved. For the restaurant this shift has probably led to a more cost-efficient use of resources. In this case, both internal efficiency and external efficiency, and hence also profit efficiency, have improved. And as said previously, improving profit efficiency is the ultimate internal goal for productivity-improving actions.

In conclusion, cost efficiency and managing costs form an important part of the management of productivity in services, as they do in manufacturing. However, because of the characteristics of services, cost efficiency is a more complicated issue in service contexts. In the next section we shall turn to the management of costs in services as one aspect of productivity management.

Managing Costs in a Service Context

In a turnaround process in the 1980s that received a lot of publicity in service management literature, SAS (Scandinavian Airlines System) introduced a useful division of costs. The costs of operating and administrating the firm were divided into *good costs* and *bad costs*.[10] These cost concepts are not related to costs used in the accounting literature, such as fixed and variable costs. Both fixed and variable costs can be good and bad. Recently, Katri Ojasalo added the concept of *mandatory costs* in a large study of service productivity.[11]

Good costs are productive costs, because they improve an organization's capability to produce high-quality services and thus enhance revenue. The costs of maintaining service encounters and back office operations are mostly good costs. Also, the costs of training personnel, goods and service development, and so on are examples of good costs. The connection between such costs and the enhancement of external efficiency is obvious. *Bad costs* are costs that follow from unnecessary bureaucracy, heavy middle and top management layers, large departments and unnecessarily complicated and time-consuming operational and administrative routines. Changes in resource structure that decrease bad costs will have a positive effect on internal efficiency and at the same time on customer perceived quality and external efficiency. *Mandatory costs* are unavoidable, even though they do not have an effect on external efficiency and customer perceptions of the service. Mandatory costs cannot be decreased. Examples of such costs are insurance and maintenance costs.

For example, if management wants to improve productivity, achieve better results, or just cut costs as a means of enhancing the competitiveness of the firm, what is usually done? Far too often the main actions are to save costs of service encounter operations or back office operations. Staff and the management layers are left untouched. It is much easier to cut costs in operations than costs in other parts of the organization. If a firm is facing hard times with poor financial results, personnel training, product development efforts and external marketing activities are also often affected by cutbacks. What management does is to *cut good costs without cutting bad costs*. From this follows, of course, that internal efficiency may or may not improve, but external efficiency and customer perceived quality may be damaged, and the net effect is all too often negative. The firm's situation is not improved, and the competitive position of the firm is worsened.

A clear distinction between good costs, bad costs and mandatory costs has to be made before any cost-saving actions are considered. Even if the firm is suffering from financial hardship, good costs, following from efforts such as improving the skills of customer contact employees or investing in new technology in service encounters, may have to be increased so that its competitiveness is improved or at least not damaged. Good costs should not be cut. Instead, bad costs should be focused on by management. Bad costs not good costs destroy profits. First, bad costs and the sources of such costs have to be identified. Second, actions to eliminate or decrease bad costs should be taken.

Of course, bad costs, for example caused by old-fashioned systems, may occur in operations, in the customer contact activities, or internally, and these should be fought as well as bad costs which create unnecessary bureaucracy. The point is that all costs are not equal wherever they occur. Until a particular cost is identified as good, bad or mandatory, action must not be taken to eliminate or decrease it. Moreover, even if the total cost level has to be decreased, good costs may have to be increased so that the firm stays competitive and can produce good customer perceived quality.

A Service Productivity Model

The discussion so far in this chapter has demonstrated that it is meaningless to develop a service productivity concept based on the management of *internal efficiency (cost efficiency)* and quantity of output only. Because of the characteristics of services and the service process, the management of *external efficiency (perceived service quality)* of the quality of output has to be an integral part of a service productivity concept. Managing external efficiency and perceived service quality is a matter of *revenue efficiency*, because better quality normally means more sales and increased revenues, and vice versa. A third element of a service productivity model is the management of demand or *capacity efficiency*. This is because service providers cannot use inventories to cope with excess capacity or excess demand, as a goods manufacturer can.

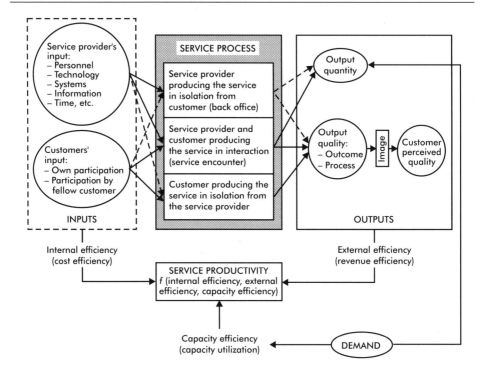

FIGURE 9.2 A service productivity model. Based on Ojasalo, K., *Conceptualizing Productivity in Services*. Helsinki/Helsingfors: Hanken Swedish School of Economics, Finland/CERS, 1999, p. 71.

Hence, a Service Productivity Concept can be described in the following way:

1. Service Productivity = f(internal efficiency, external efficiency, capacity utilization) or
2. Service Productivity = f(cost efficiency, revenue efficiency, capacity efficiency).

In manufacturing, external or revenue efficiency can be eliminated from the productivity function, because quality is considered to remain constant and therefore no revenue effects of changes in input will occur. Within limits, even capacity efficiency can be eliminated, because firms can use inventories as a buffer between excess demand and excess supply. The Service Productivity Model is illustrated in Figure 9.2.[12]

From a productivity perspective the *service process* can be divided into three separate processes:

- the service provider produces the service *in isolation;*
- the service provider and the customer produce the service *in interactions* (service encounters);
- the customer produces the service *in isolation* from the service provider.

The *service provider's inputs* into the service process (personnel, technology, systems, information, use of time, etc.) influence the two first processes *directly* and the third process *indirectly* (as illustrated by the black and dotted arrows respectively), for example by providing the infrastructure for service consumption, as in telephone communication. The *customer's inputs* (customer's own participation and fellow customers' participation) *directly* affect the second and third processes, and *indirectly* affect the first, for example by providing information to back office processes.

The more efficiently the service organization uses its own resources as input into the processes and the better the organization can educate and guide customers to provide process-supporting input to produce a given amount of output, the better the *internal efficiency* or *cost efficiency* of the service process will be. From the provider's point of view, how customers produce services in isolation from the service provider has no direct effect on internal efficiency; but has a decisive impact on service productivity through customer perceptions of service quality.

The *output* of the service process is twofold: quantity of output (volume), and quality of output (outcome and process).

The *quantity produced* is dependent on demand. If demand meets supply, the utilization of capacity or *capacity efficiency* is optimal. If there is excess demand, capacity is utilized to the full extent, but there may be a negative effect on the quality of the output. If demand is lower than potential output, the capacity is underutilized and capacity efficiency will be lower than optimal. For example, if staff in a call center are underutilized the perceived quality of the service that is produced is good, but internal efficiency is low. On the other hand, if the call center is under-staffed, internal efficiency may be high but perceived service quality is probably low, because customers will have to wait for their calls to be served and the employees will have a limited time for each call (low functional quality of the process). In addition, they may not have the time required to solve customers problems or give good advice (low technical quality of the outcome).

Because of the characteristics of services, the quality of the output is partly manifested in the process (interaction-induced quality), and partly in the outcome of the process. As indicated by the Perceived Service Quality model (discussed in Chapter 4), customers experience quality as the *functional quality* of the service process and the *technical quality* of the outcome, and filter the experiences of these two quality dimensions through the *image* of the company, resulting in *Customer Perceived Quality*. The more efficiently perceived quality is produced using a given amount of input (service provider's input and customers' input), the better *external efficiency* or *revenue efficiency* will be, resulting in improved service productivity. On the other hand, if the perceived service quality goes down, because the available input is functioning in a less service-oriented way or the resource structure is altered in a way that decreases quality, external efficiency is reduced and the firm's revenue-generating capability is lowered. This has a negative impact on service productivity.

In conclusion, internal efficiency and the cost-efficient use of resources is one side of service productivity, and external efficiency and the revenue-generating capability following the use of resources is another. In addition, the efficient utilization of resources so that demand and supply meet as much as possible has

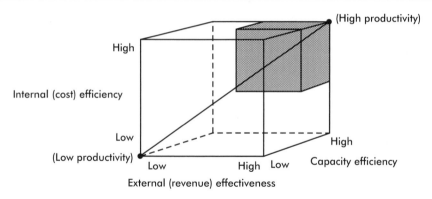

FIGURE 9.3   Service productivity as a function of internal efficiency, external efficiency and capacity efficiency. From Ojasalo, K., *Conceptualizing Productivity in Services*. Helsinki/Helsingfors: Hanken Swedish School of Economics, Finland/CERS, 1999, p. 161.

a positive impact on service productivity. As the service productivity functions shown in the beginning of this section illustrate, high service productivity requires that the three efficiency factors are blended in an optimal way. Increasing (internal) cost efficiency may have the opposite effect on (external) revenue efficiency. On the other hand, improved internal efficiency following new ways of producing a service (for example, using the example given in the beginning of this chapter, going from performing everyday bank services in bank offices to using ATMs, home banking, the Internet and PCs), may very well lead to an improved quality perception and thus to improved revenue-generating capability and external efficiency at the same time as it lowers costs. In addition, how capacity is utilized (*capacity efficiency*) has to be taken into account.

This blending of the three types of efficiency is illustrated in Figure 9.3. The highest possible service productivity is achieved in the shaded area of the figure. However, achieving this may not always be possible, because higher external efficiency and revenue-generating capabilities may require lower internal efficiency and cost efficiency. The optimal combination is dependent on the blend of revenue-generating capability and cost efficiency that optimizes the firm's economic result, also taking into account the effect of the capacity efficiency that can be achieved.

Service Productivity And Marketing

An interesting aspect of service productivity is the fact that because image has an effect on the quality perception, *managing image* is also part of the management of productivity. Keeping in mind that customer perceived quality is a function of the experiences of the service process and its outcome and also of customers' *expectations* (and/or other comparison standards), we realize that service productivity is also influenced by *expectations management*. This is not depicted in the Service Productivity Model, because expectations are included in perceived quality.

External efficiency is dependent on how the service process functions. The way the service functions is an important part of the marketing of a service.

Customer orientation and the performance of the contact employees as *part-time marketers* and of systems in the service encounters form the *interactive marketing process* (these concepts will be discussed in Chapter 10). On the other hand, expectations management is largely a matter of applying traditional external marketing means of competition, such as advertising, sales promotions and pricing. Hence, the total marketing process, including both external and inter-active marketing, has a decisive impact on service productivity.

Is Service Productivity a Productivity Concept?

As the Service Productivity Model shows, productivity is a global concept in service contexts. Is this then a productivity concept? This question can be answered by a "yes" or a "no."

With a narrow definition of productivity, where only the conversion of inputs to outputs is taken into account and the quality effects of this conversion are omitted, the service productivity concept is clearly not a productivity concept. Hence, if only internal efficiency issues are included, as in traditional closed-system manufacturing, the answer is to the above question is "no." However, in services which are produced in open-system processes and where, unlike in traditional manufacturing, quality is not a constant, and when changes in input to the service production process affect quality, it is meaningless to use a productivity concept in which quality is considered constant, when in fact it is not. Hence, if the characteristics of services are taken into account, service productivity is without question a productivity concept, and the answer is "yes."

As has been shown in Chapter 8, production and administrative resources and processes have an impact on both costs and revenues. In that chapter we said that managing productivity is a matter of managing the economic results of a firm or an operation (*profit efficiency*). A narrow, manufacturing-oriented productivity concept where quality is considered a constant is geared to the management of costs and cost efficiency. This makes perfect sense in traditional closed-system manufacturing because there, due to the constant-quality assumption, the revenue-generating capacity is not affected by cost considerations. However, in services managing productivity without including quality aspects simply becomes the management of costs without considering the result-influencing effects. Clearly this is not the sound management of economic results that it is supposed to be.

In conclusion, to manage productivity in service organizations a service pro-ductivity concept including cost (internal) efficiency, revenue (external) effi-ciency, and also capacity efficiency is the only meaningful productivity concept. How to measure productivity based on a service productivity concept is another issue, which we shall turn to in the last section of this chapter.

Long-Term Productivity Counts

Another aspect of productivity management also has to be taken into account. In order to produce acceptable quality, the service provider may have to invest in new technology and in training its personnel to be more customer-oriented. In the short run, say, for the first 12 to 36 months, this may increase costs more than it will generate additional revenue. However, this short-term perspective should never guide management decisions. In American companies, as well as most other Western companies, there is an established inclination to demand quick results and to reject actions that only pay off in the long run and show no short-term benefits. This is a devastating approach, and one of the major reasons why European and American firms have had problems with dealing with Japanese and other Asian competition.

By such an approach the long-term profitability of a firm could be sacrificed in the pursuit of quick revenues, often without management even realizing this. However, a short-sighted outlook can easily lead to deteriorating customer perceived quality, which in turn leads to dissatisfied customers and lost business. If a firm's market share is to be maintained, huge increases in its budget for traditional external marketing are then required, and in the long run even this may not help. A long-term perspective should, therefore, always guide management decisions. If there is ever a conflict between short-term revenue and quality, quality comes first. Focusing too narrowly on finances makes managers lose their long-term perspective and quality improvements that may be needed will not be achieved. By focusing first on quality, better financial results will follow. As Patrick Mene, corporate director of quality and TQM coordinator of the Malcom Baldrige Quality Award-winning Ritz Carlton Hotel Company, says: "You cannot improve a company's financial performance merely by focusing on finances."[13] Such a perspective may mean lost revenue in the short run, but by improving or maintaining a quality level, this pays off well in the long run.

An investment program such as the one illustrated in this section will probably pay off in more internally efficient operations after 12 to 36 months. If a firm, in a bid to achieve quick profits, instead takes actions justified only by internal efficiency aspects to cut costs and in that way increase productivity, the perceived quality will suffer, the firm will lose business, and it may eventually be forced out of business. Applying a service productivity concept including the interrelationship between internal efficiency (cost considerations), external efficiency (revenue-generating capability) and capacity efficiency (utilization of production capacity) to improve productivity requires a long-term approach. Managers who do not realize this may start to apply a manufacturer-oriented productivity concept, which carries a high risk of making the wrong decisions in the long-term survival of the firm.

Applying the Service Productivity Concept: Improving Productivity and Quality at the Same Time

As has been shown here, it is a mistake to believe that improving productivity and increasing service quality cannot be done simultaneously. Modern quality management approaches can improve productivity and increase customer satisfaction at the same time. In services, this is the case as well as in manufacturing. All steps taken to improve service productivity should be based on (1) a thorough understanding of what constitutes good service quality, as perceived by customers, and (2) an equally thorough analysis of how the firm operates to produce that quality; which resources (human, physical, technological and customer), are needed and which are unnecessary, and how effective or ineffective are the systems and routines used. Good costs, bad costs and mandatory costs have to be identified and kept separate. When these two pieces of research (external and internal) are compared, a strong basis will be established for improving productivity and quality simultaneously in a service context. Next, we are going to discuss ways of simultaneously improving service quality and service productivity.

Improving Employee's Technical Skills

High-quality service means, among other things, that employees know how to do things correctly. If they have inadequate skills, the technical quality of the outcome of the service process will be damaged. However, at the same time, customers will probably have to wait longer, and be more proactive themselves, to get an acceptable technical quality. Moreover, they will perceive the lack of skills on the part of the employees. All these aspects of interactions with the firm lower the perception of the functional quality of the interaction process. At the same time, this lack of skills and the need for corrective action and the repetition of activities affect productivity. Consequently, improving the technical skills of a firm's personnel may be a means of simultaneously improving quality and productivity.

Service Orientation of Attitudes and Employee Behavior

Unfriendly and negative attitudes and behavior by personnel has a significant negative impact on the functional aspect of perceived service quality. Moreover, this has a backlash effect on productivity. Angry customers, by their reaction, tend to create problems for employees, which slows down the service process. Moreover, angry and dissatisfied customers may complain either on the spot or later, which creates extra work and lowers productivity. Service-oriented employees, on the other hand, enhance quality perception and thus enhance productivity. Of course, if, for example, employees spend an unnecessarily long time with each customer which does not pay off even in the long run, a productivity problem may occur.

Internal Values Supportive to Good Service Productivity

Internal value systems in organizations that honor conventionality, risk aversion, and behavior inhibition may have an unfavorable impact on service productivity.[14] The development of internal values that support good service; on the one hand, and make employees aware of the need to use resources intelligently, on the other, is a means of improving service productivity. At the same time, employees will have to understand the interplay between internal efficiency (costs) and external efficiency (revenues) effects of their actions and behavior in the service processes. Managers and supervisors have a decisive role in this process of forming internal values and culture (see Chapter 14 on internal marketing and Chapter 15 on service culture).

Making Systems and Technology More Supportive to Employees and/or Customer Participation

If the operational systems and routines used are considered complicated, difficult to handle or to understand, this may create problems for employees, customers or both. For example, if a customer service helpdesk receives too many inappropriate phone calls—for example, requests for general information—productivity and quality problems occur. For employees, this creates barriers to meeting customer service specifications and thus they are unable to care enough for the customers. For customers, it often means a long waiting time for help. Productivity and service quality are damaged. In this situation, a front-end automated device using modern call-center technology that directs phone calls to the correct destination could be an appropriate solution. Thus, both service quality and productivity could be influenced favorably.

Industrializing the Service Operation

Applying manufacturing-like methods of operations as a means of improving services was suggested in the 1970s.[15] Generally, industrializing a service means to substitute technology and automation for people. ATMs, insurance vending machines, Internet banking and Internet shops are examples of such an approach. In some cases industrialization is an appropriate way of improving both service quality and productivity. Today, when retail banks offer ATMs to customers who want to withdraw cash from their accounts with the convenience this offers but offer personal service when they want to discuss financial problems and opportunities, this way of industrializing the service works well. However, problems can arise if industrialization is offered for all types of services to all segments of customers in all situations, which is often the case. Productivity measured by internal measurements may increase, but service quality may decrease, and this may have a negative effect on the firm's economic result, both in the short term and the long term. Hence, industrialization as a means of improving productivity and quality always demands extremely careful internal as well as external quality impact-oriented analyses to avoid errors.

Using the Internet and Information Technology

The Internet and information technology offer many opportunities of creating service processes which demand fewer resources from the service provider and at the same time are perceived as improved service quality by customers. Electronic commerce, Internet shopping and banking are examples of service processes with a different input configuration that lower costs and for many customers provide a high quality service. TV shopping is another example of how an information technology-based resource structure can be used to decrease costs and at the same time provide high-quality services to customers who appreciate this form of shopping. Mobile commerce-based telecommunication and digital TV will probably have the potential to offer similar opportunities.

Increasing Customer Cooperation in the Service Production Process

Another way of improving productivity and quality is to look at customer impact on the service process. There are, in principle, two ways of doing this. First, more *self-service elements* can be introduced. However, it is extremely important that this is not done simply for internal efficiency reasons. Customers have to see that benefits arise from participating in self-service processes. If they do not find those benefits, perceived quality suffers. Customers have to be rewarded for taking part in self-service elements, and they have to be motivated to do so. The other aspect of improving productivity and quality by paying attention to customer participation is to *improve the participation skills* of customers. Sometimes customers do not know exactly what they are supposed to do or say, how documents are to be filled out, and so on. This has a negative impact on the functional quality aspect; it may also affect the technical quality of the outcome. In addition to this, more of the employee's time is required to ensure that customers fulfill their role in the service process. Thus, productivity is affected. Better-informed customers feel more secure, make fewer mistakes, and need less unnecessary attention from employees. Consequently, they are more satisfied with the service. At the same time, there is a twofold effect on productivity. The customers speed up the service production process by their input into the process they improve productivity, and employees can serve more customers, which also enhances productivity.

Reducing the Mismatch between Supply and Demand

Physical goods can be kept in stock, if demand is low; services cannot. If the demand curve has high peaks and corresponding troughs, service quality will probably be good in the latter situations, but at peak times too many customers present at the same time will lead to long lines, longer waiting times, less personal attention, and so on. At the same time, productivity is low, because too often the firm will have idle resources and low capacity efficiency. Hence, reducing the mismatch between supply and demand is a way of making quality more consistent and of simultaneously improving productivity. Using part-time employees may be one way of doing this, but this is not always successful. For example, when retailers replace professional sales clerks with part-time personnel without sufficient training and motivation, service quality suffers permanently, at slow times as well as at peak times. Another way of matching supply and demand is to attempt to manage the flow of customers. Offering better prices during slow periods and making customers change their consumption habits by means of communication are ways of doing this using traditional marketing activities.

In addition to these means of simultaneously improving service quality and productivity, there are other ways that can sometimes be used. Reducing the service level (quantity or quality), introducing new services (smartcards instead of credit cards or bus tickets) and substituting goods for services (new data transfer equipment replacing cable and mail services) are examples.

Service Productivity as a Learning Relationship

Individual customers as well as organizations frequently engage in ongoing relationships with service firms, and manufacturers who face service competition also engage in relationships with customers where a range of services are included in a total offering to them. Hence, service productivity is frequently dependent on how the relationship proceeds. Relationships are *learning experiences* where both or all parties get used to each other and learn how to interact with each other so that errors, service failures, quality problems, information problems, etc. can be minimized. In other words, both the service provider and the customer gradually learn how to avoid errors and problems that create unnecessary costs for both parties and have a negative impact on perceived service quality.[16] These effects of *learning relationships* on service productivity are illustrated in Figure 9.4.

Figure 9.4 demonstrates how the customer (in the upper part of the figure) gains experience of a service provider and the service process (or processes) as the relationship continues. It also shows how this has effects in two directions, on the ability to participate more effectively in the service process, thus improving internal efficiency (to the left in the figure), and on the perception of service quality, thus improving external efficiency (to the right in the figure).

Following the upper part of the figure to the left, one can see an internal efficiency-improving learning process. More knowledgeable customers have what could be called a *narrower competence gap* than customers in earlier stages of the relationship, because their knowledge of how to help to make the service process quicker and smoother is closer to the required competence. This enables more intense customer participation, which in turn results in higher internal efficiency (cost efficiency) and may also lead to improved external efficiency (perceived quality and revenue efficiency). Following the upper part of the figure to the right, one can see external efficiency-improving effects of the same learning process. Customers become more aware of exactly what to expect and this creates a better match between expectations and experiences, which in turn improves external efficiency (perceived quality and revenue efficiency). It may also have a positive effect on internal efficiency (cost efficiency).

In the lower part of Figure 9.4 one can see how the service provider, when it learns more about a customer, becomes more aware of the customer's competence and can allow more intensive customer participation, and learns more about the customer's specific needs, wishes and expectations and therefore can better tailor services for the customer. These processes make it possible for the

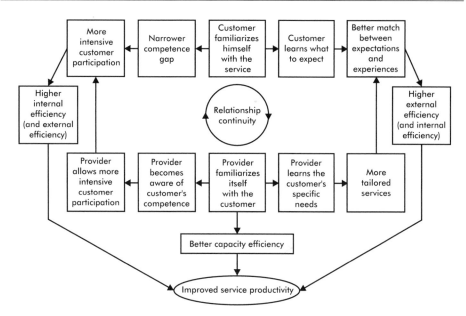

FIGURE 9.4 Effects of learning relationships on service productivity. Based on Ojasalo, K., *Conceptualizing Productivity in Services*. Helsinki/Helsingfors: Hanken Swedish School of Economics, Finland/CERS, 1999, p. 194.

service provider to adjust to the customer and take actions that improve both internal efficiency and external efficiency. At the same time, due to this learning process, the service provider can try to persuade its customers to use its services in a way that levels out demand peaks and troughs, and can adjust its resources to account for customer demand so that capacity better meets demand. In this way the utilization of capacity (capacity efficiency) improves as well. The total result is improved service productivity.

In conclusion, it is important for service productivity that one realizes that customer relationships are *learning relationships*, where both parties learn about each other, and that they last over a long period of time. The more often relationships are broken and lost customers have to be replaced by new ones, the lower service productivity will be. Hence, customer retention is important for service productivity.[17]

Measuring Service Productivity

In the final sections of this chapter, approaches to developing instruments for measuring service productivity will be discussed. No final solutions are provided, because there is not yet enough research on how to measure service productivity available to make this possible. However, suggestions for how to think and in which direction to go will be made.[18]

In traditional manufacturing the *constant-quality assumption* makes it relatively easy to measure productivity. A measure of output is compared to a measure of input. If the ratio grows following alterations in the resources or resource structure used in production, productivity improves. Parts of the total service production process can be measured in a similar way, and this can be used for decision-making. For example, the number of delivery trucks loaded in a warehouse per day or the number of phone calls that a call center can handle in an hour are examples of such partial productivity measures. They give management an idea of how efficiently these processes function from an internal perspective, which may sometimes be a useful piece of information. However, such measures must never be used to judge the productivity of these processes. Instead, measures of, for example, the number of calls received must always be accompanied by measures of the time spent with customers and the quality of the outcome of the call.[19] In services, productivity measurements must always include a measure of how a given input in the form of resources and resource structures affects perceived service quality and the revenue-generating capability of the organization. In addition, considerations of how well capacity is utilized must also be taken into account.

Because service productivity includes both cost and revenue efficiency, the development of a global productivity measure has to incorporate both phenomena. A concept which includes both revenues and costs is, of course, profit. When capacity efficiency is included we get close to the profitability of the service operations. Capacity efficiency influences costs but also revenues where excess demand has a negative impact on quality. The interrelationship between quality, productivity and profit is complicated, but clear. In a previous chapter we discussed the *relationship cost* concept, which demonstrates how improved service quality as perceived by customers can decrease the cost level of the service provider, thus having a positive effect on both revenues and costs. In Figure 9.5 the complicated interrelationship between quality, profit and productivity is illustrated.

The figure is based on the fact that goods and services almost always appear in a symbiotic relationship. As the figure indicates, improved quality can be expected to have a number of internal and external effects, all of which have a positive impact on productivity. The same positive effects of improved quality also lead to a higher profit level. The effects of improved quality on revenues are shown in the left section of the figure, on cost in the middle section and on capital employed in the right section. As Evert Gummesson observes, quality, productivity and profitability form a triplet, the parts of which are all related to the same phenomenon, the welfare of the organization, although they approach this from different perspectives.[20]

Figure 9.5 demonstrates how the effects of quality and productivity improvements eventually lead to improved profit. As was concluded previously, the ultimate goal of productivity management is to achieve better profit efficiency and economic results. Theoretically, the correct way of measuring productivity is to measure how changes in production inputs impact on the level of perceived quality and how this, in turn, affects profits. In traditional manufacturing, due to the constant quality assumption, effects on revenue generation can be excluded from productivity measurement instruments. Therefore, measurements are reduced to cost efficiency calculations. In services, where the constant quality assumption does not apply, effects on revenues have to be included. Hence, measuring service productivity becomes more complicated.

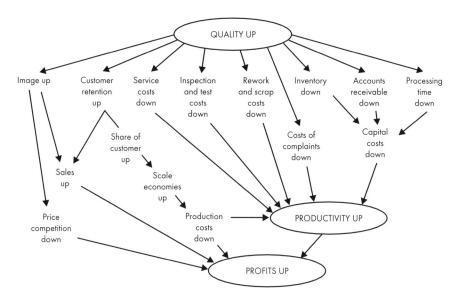

FIGURE 9.5 The interrelationship between quality, productivity and profit. Source: Gummesson, E., Productivity, Quality and Relationship Marketing in Service Operations. *International Journal of Contemporary Hospitality Management*, **10**(1), 1998, p. 6.

The next section will discuss various ways to measure service productivity and will suggest ways to develop service productivity measurement instruments in service organizations.

How to Develop Service Productivity Measurement Instruments

Because external efficiency effects have to be taken into account in service productivity, a measurement instrument for productivity in service operations has to include the customer's perspective as well. It is not enough just to take an internal organizational perspective. This, of course, makes the development of measurement models much more complicated in service contexts than in traditional manufacturing, where paying attention to internal efficiency is sufficient.

As was said before, it can sometimes be useful to measure partial productivity, but only global or total productivity measurements give real information of how a service provider is performing. Table 9.3 gives three basic alternatives for productivity measurements.

Physical measures are the traditional way of measuring productivity in general. The normal way of measuring service productivity has also been to use physical measures. This is natural, but misleading, because there was in the past no theory of service productivity and firms therefore had to borrow the manufacturing productivity concept. In an attempt to cope with the obvious problems of using physical measures in services, combinations of physical and financial measures have also been used. For example, in a restaurant the revenue per

TABLE 9.3   Alternative ways of measuring service productivity. From Ojasalo, K., *Conceptualizing Productivity in Services*. Helsinki/Helsingfors: Hanken Swedish School of Economics Finland/CERS, 1999, p. 133. Reproduced by their permission.

	PHYSICAL MEASURES	FINANCIAL MEASURES	COMBINED MEASURES
PARTIAL PRODUCTIVITY (output/one input)	e.g. $\dfrac{\text{customers served}}{\text{employee – hours}}$	e.g. $\dfrac{\text{revenues}}{\text{labor costs}}$	e.g. $\dfrac{\text{revenues}}{\text{number of employees}}$
TOTAL PRODUCTIVITY	e.g. $\dfrac{\text{customers served}}{\text{total resources}}$	e.g. $\dfrac{\text{revenues}}{\text{cost of resources}}$	e.g. $\dfrac{\text{revenues}}{\text{cost of resources}}$

service employee or restaurant seat has been used to calculate partial productivity of personnel or physical outlets. The ratio between the number of customers served per period and the costs of operating the restaurant have also been used to find total productivity.

Using physical measures by themselves is misleading, because neither cost nor revenue effects are included. Using combination measures is also misleading, because they either omit cost considerations or exclude revenue effects. Other types of combination measures have also been suggested; one proposed measure that comes close to a pure financial measure is calculating "process value productivity," which is the market value of what is produced minus the costs of the resources purchased, divided by the number of employee-hours per period used in the service process.[21]

Purely financial measures are not normally used for measuring service productivity. This is probably because it seems difficult to calculate the value of the output of the service process. First, because of the heterogeneity of production inputs and customer participation in the service process, it is difficult to standardize output and assess a market value. Second, price fluctuations make it harder to use financial measures of output.[22] Table 9.4 shows the pros and cons of physical, financial and combined measures of service productivity.

The only theoretically correct and seemingly practically relevant approach to measuring service productivity is to base productivity calculations on financial measures, regardless of the problems involved. In principle, the correct way of measuring service productivity as a function of cost efficiency (internal), revenue efficiency (external) and capacity efficiency is the following measure:

$$(1)\ \text{Service productivity} = \frac{\text{Revenues from a given service}}{\text{Costs of producing this service}}$$

As a global productivity measure of the operations of a service provider, the following measure can be used:

$$(2)\ \text{Service productivity} = \frac{\text{Total revenues}}{\text{Total costs}}$$

TABLE 9.4   Characteristics of alternatives for measuring service productivity. From Ojasalo, K., *Conceptualizing Productivity in Services*. Helsinki/Helsingfors: Hanken Swedish School of Economics Finland/CERS, 1999, p. 137). Reproduced by their permission.

Physical Measures	– Heterogeneity and intangibility aspects of services make physical measures inappropriate – Physical measures ignore variations in quality – Total productivity is difficult to measure because it is problematic to combine quantities of input resources – Difficult to get precise information on quantities
Financial Measures	– Financial measures signal heterogeneity and intangibility aspects of services – No price indices are needed because both the numerator and denominator of the productivity measure are monetary values of the same period
Combinations of Physical and Financial Measures	– The same problems are experienced as with physical measures – Price indices are needed because neither numerator nor denominator are expressed in monetary values

The perceived service quality following from a given resource structure as inputs in the service process creates sales at a certain level. If the resource structure is changed, the cost level changes along with perceived quality and the revenue-generating capability of the service provider. A change in cost efficiency leads to a change in revenue efficiency, and the result of this can be measured as the ratio between revenues and costs. This is a true measurement of productivity. If revenues increase more than costs, productivity goes up. On the other hand, if a cost reduction leads to lost revenues, but the decline in revenues is less than the cost savings that have been achieved, productivity still improves. However, this may be a dangerous strategy, because in the long term it may lead to a negative image and unfavorable word of mouth, which in turn can have a further negative effect on revenues. Finally, cost reductions may lead to a bigger drop in revenues than is made up for by cost savings. If this is the case, service productivity declines.

Service-oriented productivity measures should be derived from the two formulae above. However, one should bear in mind that there are problems with financial measures that should be observed. Revenue is not always a good measure of output, since price does not always reflect perceived service quality. It may also be difficult to assign capital costs correctly to respective revenues. Table 9.5 summarizes the advantages and limitations of revenue to cost ratios for measuring service productivity.

In conclusion, service productivity is much more complicated than traditional manufacturing productivity, because the constant quality assumption does not apply to services. Hence, quality and revenue effects of changes in input into the production process, such as type and number of resources and resource structures, cannot be excluded from the productivity concept, nor can they be omitted in productivity measurement instruments. In services, it is not possible to make use of the shortcuts for measuring productivity that can typically be used in traditional manufacturing. Examples of such shortcuts are excluding revenue measures from the productivity formula and using physical and

TABLE 9.5   Advantages and limitations of using the revenue/cost ratio for measuring service productivity. From Ojasalo, K., *Conceptualizing Productivity in Services*. Helsinki/Helsingfors: Hanken Swedish School of Economics Finland/CERS, 1999, p. 143.

ADVANTAGES	LIMITATIONS
1. Easy to compute and understand 2. Data from company records are easy to obtain 3. Takes into account all quantifiable output and input factors, and provides an accurate representation of the real economic picture of a service firm on an aggregate level 4. Output quality tends to be *better* taken into account than in volume-based measures (cf. point 2 in the right column) 5. Reflects the level of capacity utilization, since all costs are incorporated in the denominator 6. Shows changes in productivity directly; no price indices are needed for comparisons 7. Easy to compare a firm's productivity at any given moment with its past performance and objectives; and easy to compare separate units of a firm with each other	1. Cannot be used in non-profit service sector 2. Revenues do not always provide a reliable illustration of output quality (cf. point 4 in left column), since prices do not always tend to reflect the perceived quality, especially for services which have been paid for in advance. Also, if the business is subsidized by government, if prices are regulated, or if competition is monopolistic, revenues may be a poor measure of output quality. 3. Does not have the ability to explain reasons for changes in productivity or to show bottlenecks in performance 4. Assigning costs of capital correctly to respective revenues may be difficult, particularly at a detailed level 5. Data for computations are relatively difficult to obtain on service and customer levels, unless data collection systems are designed for this purpose

financial measures. Service organizations have to take the long route to understanding and measuring productivity.

Summary and Questions to Discuss

This chapter concluded that using traditional productivity measurement instruments from manufacturing is not possible in services. Applying a productivity concept geared to traditional manufacturing does not provide management with any useful information. Basically, this follows on from the fact that the *constant-quality assumption* of the traditional productivity concept does not apply in service contexts. When input resources into service processes are altered, the perceived quality of the service changes. Therefore, quality has to be included as an integral part of a service productivity concept. Based on this, a *service productivity concept* including internal or cost efficiency, external or revenue efficiency and capacity efficiency was introduced. A number of ways of improving productivity in services were presented, and finally, problems in measuring service productivity were discussed.

Questions to discuss

1.   What is meant by the *constant-quality assumption* in the traditional productivity concept from manufacturing, and why does this not apply in service contexts?

2. Discuss the differences in measuring productivity in closed and open systems.
3. Why is it more difficult to measure productivity in an open system?
4. What should be taken into account in a service productivity concept?
5. What are the challenges involved in the development of productivity measurement models in services?
6. Discuss the factors that influence the service productivity of service processes in your firm, or in any given service operation.

Further Reading

Bowen, D.E. & Youngdahl, W.E. (1998) "Lean" Service: in Defense of a Production-line Approach. *International Journal of Service Industry Management*, **9**(2), pp. 207–225.

Chase, R.B. & Haynes, R.M. (2000) Service Operations Management: A Field Guide. In Swartz, T.A. & Iacobucci, D. (eds), *Handbook of Services Marketing & Management*. Thousand Oaks, CA: Sage Publications, pp. 455–471.

Coates, R. (1991) Measuring Service Productivity. *Small Business Reports*, **16**(3), pp. 22–25.

Dobni, D., Ritchie, J.R.B. & Zerbe, W. (2000) Organizational Values: The Inside View of Service Productivity. *Journal of Business Research*, **47**(1), pp. 91–107.

Edvardsson, B., Thomasson, B. & Øvretveit, J. (1994) *Quality of Service*. Cambridge: McGraw-Hill.

Filitrault, P., Harvey, J. & Chebat, J.C. (1996) Service Quality and Service Productivity Management Practice. *Industrial Marketing Management*, **25**(3), pp. 243–255.

Grönroos, C. (1990) *Service Management and Marketing. Managing the Moments of Truth in Service Competition*. Lexington, MA: Lexington Books.

Gummesson, E. (1995) Service Productivity: A Blasphemous Approach. In Gummesson, E. (ed.), *Quality, Productivity & Profitability in Service Operations*. Conference Papers from the QP&P Research Program 1992–1994. Stockholm University/Marketing Technique Center, pp. 8–22.

Gummesson, E. (1998) Productivity, Quality and Relationship Marketing in Service Operations. *International Journal of Contemporary Hospitality Management*, **10**(1), pp. 4–15.

Haynes, R.M. & DuVall, P.K. (1992) Service Quality Management: A Process Control Approach. *International Journal of Service Industry Management*, **3**(1), pp. 14–24.

Jones, P.(1988): Quality, Capacity and Productivity in Service Industries. In Johnston, R. (ed.), *The Management of Service Operations*. London: IFS Publications, pp. 309–321.

Levitt, T. (1972) A Production-line Approach to Service. *Harvard Business Review*, September–October.

Ojasalo, K. (1997) *Measuring Service Productivity*. Working Paper 345, Helsinki/Helsingfors: Hanken Swedish School of Economics Finland.

Ojasalo, K. (1999) *Conceptualizing Productivity in Services*. Helsinki/Helsingfors: Hanken Swedish School of Economics Finland/CERS Center for Relationship Marketing and Service Management.

Partlow, C.G. (1993) How Ritz-Carlton Applies "TQM." *The Cornell H.R.A: Quarterly*, August, pp. 16–24.

Reichheld, F.F. (1996) *The Loyalty Effect. The Hidden Force Behind Growth, Profits, and Lasting Value*. Boston, MA: Harvard Business School Press.

Sumanth, D.J. (1997) *Total Productivity Management: A Systematic and Quantitative Approach to Compete in Quality, Price and Time*. Boca Raton, FL: St. Lucie Press.

Truitt, L.J. & Haynes, R. (1994) Evaluating Service Quality and Productivity in the Regional Airline Industry. *Transportation Journal*, **33**(4), pp. 21–32.

Notes

1 Filitrault, P., Harvey J. & Chebat, J.C., Service Quality and Service Productivity Management Practice. *Industrial Marketing Management*, **25**(3), 1996, pp. 243–255.

2   It is often said that quality and productivity cannot be improved at the same time. This may sometimes be the case, but as a general rule this is not true. Quite frequently new technology, a new production system using resources in a new way or an altered customer participation pattern can contribute to better productivity and improved service quality at the same time. For one example, see Truitt, L.J. & Haynes, R., Evaluating Service Quality and Productivity in the Regional Airline Industry. *Transportation Journal*, **33**(4), 1994, pp. 21–32.

3   Grönroos, C., *Service Management and Marketing. Managing the Moments of Truth in Service Competition.* Lexington, MA: Lexington Books, 1990.

4   The phrase "traditional manufacturing," is used because in modern manufacturing, through CAD/CAM techniques and Internet-mediated solutions, the customer is often involved in design and production. In such cases the manufacturing processes become partly open processes and start to resemble service processes. However, the existing productivity concept and measurement instruments are based on a traditional manufacturing context.

5   The table is based on Ojasalo, K., *Conceptualizing Productivity in Services.* Helsinki/Helsingfors: Swedish School of Economics Finland/CERS Center for Relationship Marketing and Service Management, 1999, Sumanth, D.J., *Total Productivity Management: A Systematic and Quantitative Approach to Compete in Quality, Price and Time.* Boca Raton, FL: St. Lucie Press, 1997, and Grönroos 1990, *op.cit.*

6   In modern manufacturing processes this does not always hold anymore.

7   Grönroos 1990, *op.cit.* See also Haynes, R.M. & DuVall, P.K., Service Quality Management: A Process Control Approach. *International Journal of Service Industry Management*, **3**(1), 1992, pp. 14–24, and Chase, R.B. & Haynes, R.M., Service Operations Management: A Field Guide. In Swartz, T.A. & Iacobucci, D. (eds), *Handbook of Services Marketing & Management.* Thousand Oaks, CA: Sage Publications, 2000, pp. 455–471, where the authors demonstrate the interrelationship between productivity and service quality, although they use a traditional manufacturing-oriented productivity concept.

8   See Gummesson, E., Productivity, Quality and Relationship Marketing in Service Operations. *International Journal of Contemporary Hospitality Management*, **10**(1), 1998, pp. 4–15.

9   Figure 9.1 is influenced by a figure in Gummesson, *op.cit.*, p. 9.

10   See Grönroos, *op.cit.*

11   Ojasalo 1999, *op.cit.* See also Ojasalo, K., *Measuring Service Productivity.* Working paper 345, Helsinki/Helsingfors: Swedish School of Economics Finland, 1997.

12   This Service Productivity Model is slightly modified and further developed from a service producitivity concept developed in a large study of the productivity in services by Katri Ojasalo. See Ojasalo 1999, *op.cit.* Her study of service productivity is the largest and most innovative and thoughtful contribution to this field published so far.

13   Partlow, C.G., How Ritz-Carlton Applies "TQM." *The Cornell H.R.A.: Quarterly*, August 1993, p. 22.

14   Dobni, D., Ritchie, J.R.B. & Zerbe, W., Organizational Values: The Inside View of Service Productivity. *Journal of Business Research*, **47**(1), 2000, pp. 91–107.

15   Levitt, T., A Production-line Approach to Service. *Harvard Business Review*, September–October 1972. See also Bowen, D.E. & Youngdahl, W.E., "Lean" Service: in Defense of a Production-line Approach. *International Journal of Service Industry Management*, **9**(2), 1998, pp. 207–225.

16   Ojasalo 1999, *op.cit.*

17   Compare Reichheld, F.F., *The Loyalty Effect. The Hidden Force Behind Growth, Profits and Lasting Value.* Boston, MA: Harvard Business School Press, 1996.

18   Typically, attempts to study productivity in services take only partial productivity into account, and usually only measure internal variables. See, for example, Dobni, R. & Zerbe, *op.cit.*, who in a very interesting study of the productivity impact of employees measure perceived role behavior, organizational commitment, and employee affect.

19   See Coates, R., Measuring Service Productivity. *Small Business Reports*, **16**(3), 1991, pp. 22–25, where the interrelationships of quantity and quality in measuring productivity in services is discussed.

20   Gummesson 1998, *op.cit.* This proposition was originally put forward in a seminal paper on service productivity presented by Evert Gummesson at the 2nd International Research Seminar in Service Management arranged by Institut d'Administration des Enterprises of the Université d'Aix-Marseille in France in June 1992. See Gummesson, E., Service Productivity: A Blasphemous

Approach. In Gummesson, E. (ed.), *Quality, Productivity & Profitability in Service Operations.* Conference Papers from the QP&P Research Program 1992–1994. Stockholm University/ Marketing Technique Center, 1995, pp. 8–22.

21 Edvardsson, B., Thomasson, B. & Øvretveit, J., *Quality of Service.* Cambridge: McGraw-Hill, 1994.

22 For example, in Jones, P., Quality, Capacity and Productivity in Service Industries. In Johnston, R. (ed.), *The Management of Service Operations.* London: IFS Publications, 1988, pp. 309–321, the author argues against the use of financial measures.

Chapter 10

MANAGING MARKETING OR MARKET-ORIENTED MANAGEMENT

Full-time marketing specialists are required to make promises and find customers, but without skilful part-time marketers promises will not be kept, and the total marketing process collapses.

Introduction

This chapter will discuss the nature and content of the marketing process in a service organization. As the chapter title indicates, the traditional view of marketing management may not apply where services are concerned. A relationship approach to marketing is suggested, and the scope and content of the total marketing process is discussed in detail. The concepts of *part-time marketers, interactive marketing* and the *customer relationship life cycle* are discussed. Two types of marketing strategies, relationship marketing and transaction marketing, are analyzed on a *marketing strategy continuum*, and their consequences explored. Finally, it is concluded that for services, marketing is better characterized as market-oriented management than as marketing management in the traditional functionalistic sense. After having read the chapter the reader should understand the role and scope of marketing in a service context, and realize the importance of the interactive marketing process to the total marketing process of a service organization as well as understand the nature of a relationship marketing approach and the consequences of adapting a relationship marketing strategy for a firm.

The Role and Scope of Marketing

The marketing process includes four main parts:

1. *understanding the market and individual customers* by market research and segmentation analysis as well as by using database information on individual customers;

2.   so that *market niches, segments and individual customers can be chosen*;
3.   for *which marketing programs and activities can be planned, implemented and followed up*; and finally,
4.   to *prepare the organization* so that marketing programs and activities are successfully implemented (*internal marketing*).

This approach is based on the so-called *marketing concept*, which describes marketing as a philosophy. This concept holds that the firm should base all its activities on the needs and desires of customers in selected target markets. At the same time, of course, societal restrictions (laws, norms, industry agreements, etc.) have to be recognized. This is also known as a *market-oriented* view, in contrast to a *production-oriented* view, where the firm's activities are geared to existing technology, products or production processes.

The fourth part of the marketing function is traditionally not included. Normally, it is taken for granted that once marketing decisions are made they are executed as planned. However, this may be a dangerous assumption. Marketing programs and activities have to be marketed *internally* to those who are expected to actively implement them *externally*, especially in services.

Traditionally, marketing as a business activity is thought of as a separate function that is taken care of by a group of specialists organized in a marketing department or a marketing and sales department. By and large, the rest of the organization, with the exception of a few people in top management, has no responsibility for the customers or for marketing. Employees in other departments are not recruited or trained to think about marketing; nor are they supervized in a way that would make them feel any marketing responsibilities, or responsibility for customers. Such an approach demands that marketing specialists are the only people who have an impact on the customers' views of the firm and on their buying behavior. In many consumer packaged goods situations, where consumption can be characterized predominantly as *outcome consumption*, this has always been the case. If the product is a preproduced item with no need for service or other contact between a firm and its customers, marketing (and sales) specialists are clearly capable of taking care of customer relationships. Good market research, packaging, advertising campaigns and pricing and distribution decisions by marketing specialists lead to good results.

Figure 10.1 demonstrates the traditional place of marketing according to most marketing textbooks. The arrow pointing up indicates that the marketing specialists acquire information about the market (such as demand and buying behavior analyses) through market research. The downward arrow illustrates the planning and implementation of marketing activities. However, as soon as we leave the area of consumer packaged goods, the situation changes and new elements appear in the relationship between buyer and seller. Many durables need deliveries, installing, complaints handling and service. As soon as this happens, the prerequisites of Figure 10.1 are not valid any more, because more and more *process consumption* characteristics can be seen in the consumption process.

When services are involved, the interface between the firm and the customer grows. This was first pointed out in 1974 in a major services marketing book by John Rathmell.[1] Moreover, the customer no longer acts passively, but takes an

FIGURE 10.1 The traditional role of marketing

active part in the service production process. This is often the case in industrial or business-to-business marketing as well. The more services that are introduced or the more non-services that are actively used as services (e.g. claims handling, billing procedures, etc.) in customer relationships, the more important it is for companies engaged in business-to-business marketing to understand service competition and service management and marketing.

What is Marketing?

Marketing as a phenomenon can be approached in many ways. Far too often marketing is considered to be only a set of tools and techniques. This is a dangerous way of introducing marketing into any organization, but especially into an organization producing services. If marketing is considered to be a set of tools, marketing remains the sole responsibility of a group of marketing specialists who are familiar with these tools and know how to handle them. The rest of the organization (for example, people involved in operations, human resource management, the design and development of technology and systems) are not concerned with marketing, which means that they are not interested in their customers, their desires and wishes.

Marketing has been described variously as a *philosophy* and a *craft*. Focusing on the tools and techniques of marketing is to concentrate on marketing as a craft. However, we have to view marketing in a much larger context. Marketing activities where these tools and techniques are used do not lead to good results if the whole company is not involved. For example, a well designed and executed advertising campaign will not lead to good results if campaign promises are not fulfilled by operations staff or delivery personnel. If this happens, the tool (advertising), may have been used successfully, viewed in isolation from other activities of the organization, but the marketing objective still fails (in the next chapter this particular issue will be discussed in more detail).

Marketing exists on at least three levels:[2]

- marketing as a *philosophy* and an *attitude of mind* or way of thinking;
- marketing as a *way of organizing* the various functions and processes of a firm;
- marketing as a *set of tools, techniques and activities* to which customers are exposed.

Marketing as a way of thinking. Marketing is first and foremost a *philosophy* or a *way of thinking* in an organization. This philosophy, the *marketing concept*, has to guide all people, processes, functions and departments of an organization. It has to be understood and accepted by everyone, from top management to the most junior staff alike. Marketing should, first of all, be an *attitude of mind*. This is the foundation of successful marketing. The marketing philosophy states that customers' and potential customers' (and other stakeholders') opinions of and reactions to the offerings, communications and performance of a firm and people, technologies and systems acting on its behalf (the customer perspective) have to be the starting point for all decisions made by the firm.

However, it should be noted that customer perspective is not the only perspective to take into account in decision-making. For example, the economic realities and demands of other groups of stakeholders are aspects that cannot be forgotten. Also, technological development and what is sometimes labeled "product or production orientation" must not be neglected. Normally product orientation is not good for a firm. However, in some cases this perspective is more important than the customer perspective, because customers cannot always foresee the likely future developments of products and services based on technological advances. Market research does not always give enough input to product development. This is of course most important in situations where rapid or complicated technological advances are taking place. For example, microwave ovens would not have been introduced for common use had firms relied on market research data. No one identified this as a need area. Instead, the skills and innovation of engineers and other specialists gave us this new means of cooking. The ability to send text messages from one mobile phone to another is a similar example. In the long term of course, the customer perspective determines what will be a success and what will be a failure. Not all innovations based on technological advance become successful products or series.

Marketing as a way of organizing. Second, successful marketing requires an appropriate *way of organizing* the firm. Various departments involved in giving and fulfilling promises have to be able to compare notes and coordinate plans, and they have to be willing to do this. Traditional disputes and lack of willingness to collaborate between departments are examples of situations in which firms are not organized for optimal marketing. In firms where such turf fights exist the *marketing attitude of mind throughout the organization* does not exist, and from the customers' point of view successful marketing will probably not be implemented.

Parts of customer relationships, normally traditional marketing and sales efforts, will be taken care of in a customer-oriented way, at least viewed in isolation. Other parts of the relationships, normally those related to interactions with customers, will be less well handled, and hence the total marketing effect, or how well customer relationships are managed over time, will be worse, often disastrous. For example, in a study of the relationship between the pulping industry and suppliers of service and components to firms in that industry, the customers talked about a "taillight or rear light syndrome." They said that as long as negotiations on a deal continued, the supplier, and particularly the sales representative, showed an interest in the customers and their needs and requirements. However, as soon as the deal was closed the customers felt that they only saw the "rear lights" of the salesperson and the supplier as they left. After that they were dealt with by departments such as deliveries, invoicing and claims handling who did not seem to consider them very important.

In today's competitive situation, firms cannot afford to maintain barriers between departments. The marketing philosophy has to be spread throughout the organization, and organizational solutions will have to support the acceptance of this philosophy. *Marketing is a set of ideas which must be integrated throughout the entire organization and overseen by top management.*

In many situations a firm may be dependent on a network of partners to solve the problems of its customers. In such situations the management of this *marketing attitude of mind* often becomes even more complicated. With the growth of virtual or network organizations new challenges to instil this marketing mindset emerge.

Marketing as a set of tools and activities. Finally, marketing is a *set of tools, techniques and activities.* This is, of course, an important aspect of marketing because it is the one to which customers are exposed. But this is also the reason for much of the misunderstanding in many practical situations, where marketing as a phenomenon is predominantly or only thought of as these tools, techniques, and activities: for example, as packaging, promotion, distribution activities and pricing. If marketing is viewed in this limited way, it will probably only lead to limited results.

The Customer Relationship Life Cycle

Far too often people in an organization view customers as an abstract phenomenon or anonymous mass. Customers are seen in terms of numbers. When someone stops being a customer, there are always new potential customers to take their place. From the customers' point of view, however, every single customer forms a relationship with the seller, which the firm should develop and maintain. All business is based on relationships. However, customer relationships do not just happen by magic; they have to be earned. The same goes for relationships with distributors, suppliers and other partners.

It may be useful to view the development of a customer relationship as a life cycle.[3] The concept of the *Customer Relationship life cycle* is illustrated in Figure 10.2. The life cycle consists of three basic phases:

- the initial phase;
- the purchasing phase;
- the consumption (or usage) phase.

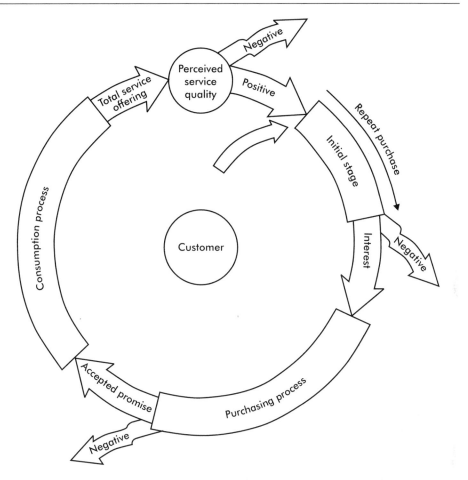

FIGURE 10.2 The customer relationship life cycle. From Grönroos, C., *Strategic Marketing and Marketing in the Service Sector*, 1983, p. 70. Reprinted with permission of the Marketing Science Institute.

A potential customer who is unaware of a firm and its offerings is in the *initial stage* of the life cycle. If this individual, or an industrial customer, has a need which he feels that the firm may be able to satisfy, the customer may become aware of the firm's services and move into the second stage of the life cycle, the *purchasing process*.

During the purchasing process the potential customer evaluates the service in relation to what he is looking for and is prepared to pay for. If the outcome of this process is positive, the customer decides to try the service, so he makes a *first purchase*. This takes the customer into the third stage of the life cycle, the *consumption process* (or *usage stage*, which may be a more appropriate term in a business-to-business context). During this process the customer may observe the firm's ability to take care of his problems and provide services, which the customer perceives have an acceptable outcome-related technical and process-related functional quality. If the customer is satisfied with the perceived quality and considers the value it offers to be good enough, it is more probable that the customer relationship will continue and a new or prolonged consumption or usage process will follow than it would if the customer was unhappy with the service offering.

The customer may leave the circle at any stage, or may stay within the circle and progress to the following stage. After the consumption or usage process the customer may either leave or decide to buy from the same firm the next time he needs a similar service, or may decide to continue using the service provider. Obviously, the marketing efforts of the firm will have an impact on the decision the customer makes. The objectives of the firm's marketing program and the marketing activities to be used depend on which phase of the customer relationship life cycle the customer is in. The firm should therefore recognize (1) where in the customer relationship life cycle a given customer is or its various groups of target customers are, and (2) which resources and activities are effective from a marketing point of view at the different stages of the life cycle, so that the relationship with a given customer is managed as effectively as possible.

The firm should recognize that the position of a customer in the life cycle has substantial marketing consequences. At each stage the marketing *objective* and the *nature of marketing*—the marketing resources and activities that are effective— will be different (see Figure 10.3). At the *initial stage* the marketing objective is to *create interest* in the firm and its services. At the second stage, the *purchasing process*, the general interest should be turned to sales by giving promises which are accepted by the potential customer. The potential customer (an individual customer or an industrial buyer) should realize that *accepting the promises* concerning the future problem-solving offering of the firm is a good option. During the *consumption (usage) process* the customer should receive *positive experiences* of the firm's ability to take care of his problems. At this stage the promises that the customer has accepted should be fulfilled. Thus, resales, cross-sales and enduring customer relationships should be achieved.

Managing the Customer Relationship Life Cycle: An Example

As an illustration of long-range management of customer relationships, let us consider the efforts of a transportation company offering transportation services by sea. The firm operates in a consumer market as well as in an industrial market, offering both transportation services and conference arrangements for businesses and other organizations. This example describes how customer relationships are managed for conference services. This is schematically illustrated in Figure 10.3.

Through advertising and various public relations activities the company attempts to make potential customers interested in it as a possible conference operator. Occasionally, personal selling is also resorted to at this *initial stage*. In addition, the company relies heavily on word of mouth to influence potential customers and on references promoting the idea of using its ships as conference sites. Marketing activities applied at this stage are mostly traditional, supported by indirect promotion drawing on the firm's reputation and word of mouth communication.

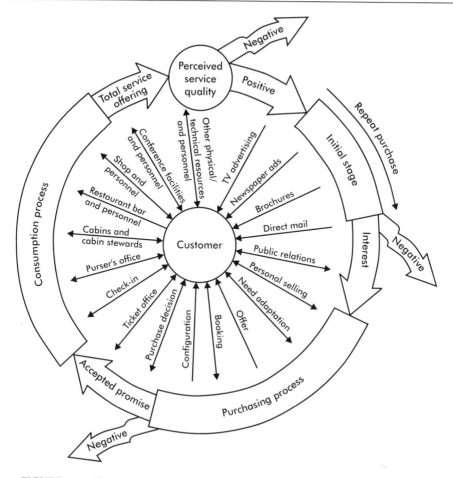

FIGURE 10.3 The customer relationship life cycle of a transportation company. From Grönroos, C., *Strategic Marketing and Marketing in the Service Sector*, 1983, p. 75. Reprinted with permission of the Marketing Science Institute.

When a potential customer contacts the transportation company activities are more specifically directed toward the unique needs of that customer. The *purchasing process* starts. At this stage a conference service that corresponds to the customer's needs and to the customer's conference budget must be designed. Here the output of the process, accepted promises and a first purchase, is to a great extent the result of personal selling efforts. The salesperson will have to find out what the customer really wants. His ability to negotiate is considered critical to success at this point. The customer should be offered a conference design which will satisfy him both during and after the conference, rather than simply a minimum budget design which may seem to correspond to the customer's initial needs but which in the long term will turn out to be a disappointment. The salesperson is, therefore, encouraged to think of himself as a consultant more than anything else.

If the purchasing process is successful, the potential customer will accept the promises made by the transportation firm and buy a conference service. The firm cannot, however, stop considering the customer as soon as the purchase decision is made. The customer relationship has to be managed with equal care throughout the *consumption* or *usage process*. During the consumption process, when the conference service is consumed and experienced and at the same time produced, a number of *moments of truth*, or *moments of opportunity* occur. If the moments of truth go unmanaged, the quality of the service probably deteriorates and the customer may be lost, as well as losing opportunities to create more business.

The company attempts to produce a service that corresponds to the expectations of the customer. The conference facilities, arrangements for meals and accommodation, and the appearance and performance of the personnel on board are of the utmost importance to the success or failure of the company as a conference operator in the mind of the customer.

By appropriately designing the conference facilities as well as other aspects of the serviscape,[4] for example, cabin design, access to the Internet, telephones and computer equipment, and by conducting internal training programs to improve the customer-oriented performance and service-mindedness of its employees, the firm tries to guarantee that the customer, the conference participants and other passengers leave the ship in a state of satisfaction and with a favorable image of the transportation company and its services in mind. The customer and the conference participants will probably return to the transportation company when a need for conference services or other transportation services occurs. It is also expected that they will have a considerable impact on potential customers through word of mouth, resulting in increased interest in the firm and its services.

Defining Marketing: The Marketing Mix Approach

In this and subsequent sections we will discuss how marketing in practice can be managed in service competition. The marketing concept, which was described in the first section of this chapter, is transformed into marketing in practice in the standard literature on *marketing management*. There are dozens of textbooks covering this topic. In this approach to marketing, the core of marketing is overwhelmingly the *marketing mix*. The marketer plans various means of competition and blends them into a "marketing mix,"[5] so that a profit function is optimized. When Neil Borden first introduced the idea of the marketing mix in the 1950s, he offered a list of 12 variables as a guideline and said that they would probably have to be reconsidered in any given situation. The marketing mix was soon reformulated as the "4 Ps" with four standardized categories of marketing variables.[6]

Traditionally, the 4 Ps are *product, place, price* and *promotion*. In a later definition from 1985 marketing, according to the marketing mix approach, is described as follows: "Marketing is the process of planning and executing the *conception, pricing, promotion* and *distribution* of ideas, goods and services to create exchanges and satisfy individual and organizational objectives [emphasis by this author]."[7] During the last two decades marketing researchers have increasingly found that the list of 4 Ps is too restrictive and more categories of marketing variables have been suggested, most often in the form of additional "Ps," such as people, processes and physical evidence[8] as well as public relations and politics.[9]

Defining marketing according to the marketing mix approach is like using a list of objects as a definition. Such a way of defining a phenomenon can never be considered the most valid. A list can never include all relevant elements, it will not fit all situations, and it becomes obsolete. Increasing the number of Ps does not offer a fundamental improvement to the definition. As a matter of fact, the need to add new categories of marketing variables or Ps is a symptom of the weakness of the marketing mix approach, and demonstrates that, as a general marketing model, the marketing mix approach has failed. Still, it may well be helpful in some contexts, such as for consumer packaged goods. In the competitive situation after World War II, with increasing demand and growing markets, the marketing mix and its 4 Ps formed an effective marketing approach. In a relationship-oriented approach to marketing, many elements of the marketing mix toolbox are still highly necessary, because it includes variables, for example promotion and pricing, that are clearly important marketing variables in service competition.

In a situation where service competition dominates, markets are more and more mature and competition more intense, the shortcomings of marketing mix management and its 4 Ps are becoming evident. In practice, the starting point of this approach is a predetermined set of decision-making areas which are considered part of marketing. From this follows, unfortunately, that other decision-making areas are outside the scope of marketing. The process nature of marketing as illustrated, for example, by the *Customer Relationship Life Cycle* model is largely neglected. Marketing activities may be seen as processes, for example when executing a promotional campaign, but the firm's relationship with its customers is not viewed in that way.

Moreover, although it is not inherent in traditional models, marketing has become a function that sits alongside other business functions, delegated to a separate group of marketing specialists and frequently organized in the form of a marketing department. The interface between marketing and production and operations, research and development, human resource management and finance has been neglected, and instead frequent turf battles between marketing and other functions occur. As the marketing department, along with sales, is often the function where customers' interests are given high priority, the customer relationship is managed using a marketing approach only to the extent that the marketing specialists (and salespeople) are involved. The remaining interactions of customer relationships are managed without a clear marketing strategy. The consequences are obvious: low perceived quality, lack of value for the customer and in the end lost business.[10]

It is ironic that the people who by definition have a marketing attitude of mind, the full-time marketing specialists of the marketing departments, are the people who frequently have limited or no customer contact. Those who interact with customers during the consumption or usage stage of the customer relationship life cycle (in deliveries, repair and maintenance, customer training, complaints handling, billing, etc.) normally do not have marketing training or a genuine interest in the customer.

As a consequence of these deficiencies of the marketing mix management approach, the following conclusions can be drawn.

1. Marketing has become a function for marketing specialists, and therefore a marketing attitude of mind is not easily instilled throughout the organization.
2. Because of the lack of marketing training throughout large parts of the organization, the customer's interests are given high priority only in some parts of the customer relationship life cycle (mainly the initial and purchasing phases), whereas during the consumption or usage process the relationship is managed by non-marketing staff and without taking customer considerations properly into account.
3. Finally, because of the decision variable orientation of the marketing mix, marketing and marketing planning have become preoccupied with making and refining decisions which according to the marketing mix are considered to be marketing decisions. At the same time the process of taking customers through the relationship life cycle and ensuring that customers stay in the life cycle, which may require that other decision-making areas are included in marketing planning as well, is neglected.

In service competition, particularly for service providers and in business-to business markets, the marketing mix approach frequently does not cover all resources and activities of the stages of the customer relationship life cycle. As can be seen from Figure 10.3, during the consumption process especially there are a range of contacts between the service firm and its customer which are outside the traditional marketing function as defined by the 4 Ps of the marketing mix. Managing and operating these contacts (for example, the conference facilities, the cabins, the restaurants, and managing the employees on board) are the responsibility of operations and other non-marketing departments. Nevertheless, these contacts—buyer–seller interactions or service encounters—have an immense impact on the future buying behavior of the customers as well as on word of mouth; that is, they have marketing implications, and should therefore be considered as marketing resources and activities and managed as such.

Defining Marketing: A Relationship Approach

In Chapter 2 we discussed the relationship perspective on marketing and the management of customer relationships as marketing. It was noted that this marketing perspective fits service competition well. The *marketing concept* as the basic philosophy guiding marketing in practice still holds, although the customer perspective has to be focused on in a much more customer value-oriented way.[11] In practice, the marketing mix approach to transferring this concept to marketing is, however, considered too narrow in scope to be more than partially useful in most service situations.

A *relationship definition of marketing* can be formulated as follows:

The purpose of marketing is to identify and establish, maintain and enhance, and when necessary terminate relationships with customers (and other parties) so that the objectives regarding economic and other variables of all parties are met. This is achieved through a mutual exchange and fulfillment of promises.[12]

Such relationships are usually long-term, but they do not necessarily always have to be. In this context we are mainly discussing customer relationships, but the same approach can also be used when dealing with other parties, such as suppliers, distributors, co-producers of customer solutions, financial institutions and political decision-makers. It may be necessary for a firm to establish relationships with such parties to supply its customers with appropriate solutions.[13]

In the relationship marketing literature there are several definitions similar to the one presented here. Parvatiyar and Sheth[14] present an excellent overview of the discussion in the literature of relationship marketing definitions as well in the domain of relationship marketing. Evert Gummesson has presented a definition which is somewhat different, but nevertheless has the same process orientation: Relationship marketing is *marketing seen as relationships, networks and interactions*.[15]

This definition points out the central phenomena in marketing according to the relationship perspective (the *relationship* itself) and the key processes in the relationship (the *interactions*) as well as the fact that relationship marketing often takes place in *networks* of cooperating partners.

Finally, from a relationship perspective, the following generic definition of marketing can be offered: *Marketing means to manage the firm's market relationships*.[16]

This definition includes the fundamental notion of marketing as a phenomenon related to the relationship between a firm and its customers and other parties in the market environment.

Long-term customer relationships means that the main objective of marketing is to seek enduring relationships with customers. Of course, in some situations short-term sales based on *transaction marketing* may be profitable. Generally, however, retaining customers in the long term is vital to profitable marketing. In a relationship billable transactions concerning goods, services, knowledge, information or any other asset of value to the customer must take place. Profitability cannot be measured immediately as a result of the first transaction. Profitability is a long-term measurement, which should develop from an ongoing and enduring relationship.

Identifying and *establishing*, *maintaining* and *enhancing* customer relationships implies, respectively, that the process of marketing includes the following:

1. market research to *identify* potentially interesting and profitable customers to contact;
2. *establishing* the first contact with a customer so that a relationship emerges;
3. *maintaining* an existing relationship so that the customer is satisfied with the perceived quality and the value received and is willing to continue to do business with the other party of the relationship;
4. *enhancement* of an ongoing relationship so that the customer decides to expand the content of the relationship by, for example, purchasing larger quantities or new types of goods and services from the same seller; and

5. *terminating* a relationship; sometimes a firm will have to cope with the situation when a customer decides to discontinue the relationship *or* the firm may find it necessary to discontinue a relationship with a customer. Both these situations should be managed so that the relationship can be re-established in the future. We will, however, not discuss this fifth situation here.[17]

These situations are all different from a marketing point of view. In short, establishing the first contact demands good communication and sales skills. Favorable word of mouth and a well-known image help. Maintaining and enhancing customer relationships requires other types of tools and activities. To maintain a relationship the perceived quality of goods, services, information, personal contacts and all other types of service elements present in a given customer relationship have to be good. In addition, good selling skills may be required to enhance a relationship. Good selling does not only, or even mainly, mean good sales performance by professional salespeople, but instead good sales and communication skills by customer contact employees interacting with customers as part of the service process. From the supplier's or service provider's point of view,

- establishing a relationship involves *giving promises*;
- maintaining a relationship is based on *fulfillment of promises*, and finally;
- developing or enhancing a relationship means that *a new set of promises is given with the fulfillment of earlier promises as a prerequisite*.

The Promise Concept

An integral element of the relationship marketing definition is the *promise concept*.[18] According to this, the responsibilities of marketing do not only include making promises and thus persuading customers to act in a given way. A firm that is preoccupied with making promises may attract new customers and build new relationships to begin with. However, if promises are not fulfilled, the evolving relationship cannot be maintained or enhanced. Keeping promises is equally important as a means of achieving customer satisfaction, retention of the customer base, and long term profitability. It is also important to notice that promises are given, and should be fulfilled, mutually. Finally, the firm has to take action to make sure that it, either by itself or together with network partners, has the resources, knowledge, skills and motivation to keep promises. Sufficient efforts to *enable promises* have to be made.[19] This will be discussed in Chapter 14 in the context of internal marketing.

Managing promises is not always an easy task. The promise concept can be complicated. It is helpful to distinguish between *explicit promises* and *implicit promises*. The marketer may plan to give a set of promises, for example by offering an e-mail response opportunity on a Web site. The marketer may have intended to promise that the firm will respond to e-mails as soon as possible, whereas the customer may perceive an *implicit* promise that the firm will respond promptly. Nothing has explicitly been said about how long it will take to answer an e-mail, but a promise of quick response may have been implicitly perceived by the customer. The same may happen with advertisements, brochures and other types of marketing communication. A customer may perceive the promise given differently than the marketer intended. Different customers may perceive different implicit promises in the same communication message. The marketer should always be aware of these problems, and try to minimize the risks of implicit promises.

Marketing Resources and Activities According to the Relationship Definition

The relationship definition of marketing *does not* state that the traditional means of competition of the marketing mix, such as advertising using new or old media, personal selling, pricing and conceptualizing of the product are any less important than earlier. However, it does demonstrate that there is *much more* to marketing. What is important is that it represents a fundamental shift in the way of looking at marketing as a phenomenon as compared to the marketing mix. The relationship approach to marketing is truly *process-oriented*. It views marketing as a process of taking the customer through the customer relationship life cycle and keeping the customer there in order to reach the mutual objectives of the firm and the customer. The exchange of promises indicated in the relationship definition may be of any kind and may concern any type of activities. The resources to which the customer is exposed and interacts with may also be of any type, and they may vary from customer to customer depending on whether the relationship is in the establishment, maintenance or enhancement phase. They cannot be predetermined or categorized, as marketing resources and decision-making areas are according to the marketing mix.

In practical situations, for teaching in classroom settings as well as for marketing planning in organizations, the relationship definition is not as easy to use as the marketing mix. This is natural, because the main virtue of the marketing mix is its simplicity, not its proven capability to capture certain marketing situations. The relationship definition does not provide users with an easy-to-implement list of categories of marketing variables or means of competition. Instead, it forces users to think for themselves and to analyze the marketing situation at hand, as well as develop an understanding of the resources and activities required to establish, maintain, or enhance—and of course, when necessary, to terminate—a relationship with a specific customer or group of customers.

To sum up, according to the relationship approach marketing is a process rather than a function,[20] and it is the concern of every function and department in an organization. A marketing mindset is required by everyone with a direct or indirect impact on how customers perceive the firm, its goods and services and its way of taking care of its customers, regardless of what responsibilities a person may have within the organization. The relationship perspective is, of course, not the only market-oriented way of honoring the marketing concept. It is, though, an approach well suited for understanding, as well as planning and implementing, marketing in service contexts and in service competition.[21]

Case Study: "Better Service for You"

The author of this book was looking for a cordless phone for his son at the Power Buy Company in Bangkok which sold everything from telephones and fax machines to TVs and refrigerators and microwave ovens. When asking about a fairly inexpensive phone, the sales clerk Ms Sumarin, wearing a button saying "Better Service for You," demonstrated for him not only the cordless phone but also the meaning of the message on her button. The phone seemed to be ideal, but it had no international guarantee, so she went out of her way to make sure that the phone functioned without problems. She said, in fluent English, "it will be impossible for you to come back and change the phone when you've left Thailand, so we'd better check everything now." She charged the batteries, connected the phone, and since she was not satisfied with its quality changed it to another one, asked the customer to test the phone and evaluate the sound of his voice when using it. She also prepared all the paperwork for a VAT refund. The customer ended up buying another similar cordless phone for his daughter and an answering machine for himself. The care and concern for the customer showed by Ms Sumarin and her responsiveness to his situation resulted not only in a better outcome for him in terms of the quality of the phones, but also made him feel very good about his purchases. Her impeccable service obviously pays off well for the Power Buy Company too.

Marketing Functions and Processes

As demonstrated by the *Customer Relationship Life Cycle* model, in a service context marketing is by no means only an intermediate function building a bridge between production and consumption or usage. Marketing is an integral part of producing and delivering services, especially during the *consumption (usage) process*. In other words, managing the moments of truth in the *buyer–seller interactions* (service encounters) is a marketing task as well as a responsibility for operations, personnel, human resources management and other departments which have contact with customers. The separation of marketing, production, human resource management and other departments may well be logical in traditional manufacturing where customers order and use the products far away from the place of production. It is not appropriate for service systems where the production of services, delivery, and consumption is simultaneous.[22]

There is, however, a distinct difference between handling the interactions of the moments of truth as a marketing task and executing traditional marketing activities such as advertising, personal selling and sales promotion. Normally the latter are planned *and* implemented by marketing and sales specialists. On the other hand, the former are implemented by specialists in other areas. Moreover, they are frequently planned and managed by non-marketing managers and supervisors; people who are neither aware of their marketing responsibilities nor interested in customers or marketing.

The employees involved in marketing, who are not full-time marketing specialists, are *part-time marketers*, to use a concept introduced by Evert

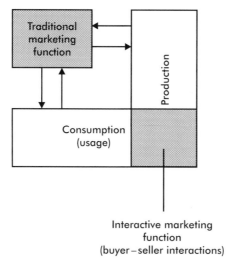

FIGURE 10.4   The two marketing functions of service organizations. From Grönroos, C., *Strategic Marketing and Marketing in the Service Sector*, 1993, p. 62. Reprinted with permission of the Marketing Science Institute.

Gummesson.[23] They are, of course, specialists in their own areas. At the same time, they must learn to perform their tasks in such a way that customers will want to return, thus strengthening the customer relationship. Hence, they will have to learn to act in a marketing-oriented manner, and their supervisors and team leaders too will have to learn to think in terms of marketing and customer impact.

To sum up, the marketing process can be divided into two separate functions or subprocesses: a specialist function, taking care of many traditional marketing mix activities and market research; and a marketing function, related to the buyer–seller interactions of the simultaneous service production and consumption processes, where marketing tasks are performed by part-time marketers, supported by, and sometimes (as in telecommunications or home banking) replaced by, customer-oriented physical resources, technology and systems. The two functions or subprocesses of marketing are the *traditional (or external) marketing process*, and the *interactive marketing process*.

In Figure 10.4 the two marketing functions of service organizations are schematically illustrated. The shaded areas represent the marketing functions. The *traditional marketing function* is separate from other functions. It involves market research, advertising, Internet communication, pricing, sales promotions, public relations and other activities traditionally considered to be part of marketing. This traditional marketing function is also frequently labeled *external marketing*. For consumer services, the traditional marketing function is a *mass marketing function*. However, in business-to-business relationships personal sales contacts by salespeople are also involved.

The interface between production and consumption represents the buyer–seller interactions or service encounters, where the moments of truth or moments of opportunity occur. Because the marketing impact of these interactions occurs in interactive processes, this part of marketing has been called the *interactive marketing function*[24] in the service marketing literature since the late 1970s. Interactive marketing, or marketing outside the marketing department, occurs at the moment when the buyer and seller interact. The service is actually delivered and the foundation for resales laid through activities in the buyer–seller interactions of the service encounters. Traditional marketing efforts may sometimes support the interactive marketing activities performed during these interactions.

The customer's opinion of a service is influenced both by the means of production (i.e. the production facilities, human and non-human production resources and the serviscape) and by the service production process (i.e. the behavior of the employees, the manner in which the production facilities are used, and the way physical resources, technology and systems support the consumption of the service in a customer-oriented fashion.) The interactive marketing function recognizes that every component—human and non-human—in producing a service, every production resource used, and every stage in the service production and delivery process should be handled as a marketing issue, and not considered as merely operations or human resource problems. In addition, customers are not only consumers or users of a service but also *co-producers* of that service. In this respect customers are also a resource in the interactive marketing process. The marketing consequences of every resource and activity involved in interactive marketing situations have to be acknowledged in the planning process, so that the production resources and operations support and enhance the organization's attempts to develop and maintain long-term relationships with its customers.

To sum up, *the marketing resources used in the interactive marketing process are totally different from those used in the traditional external marketing function.* While the latter are "full-time marketing resources," the resources of interactive marketing are only *"part-time marketing resources."* The dual role of the part-time marketers has already been discussed, but the same applies to the rest of the resources as well. Physical resources, technology and systems used in the service process and to build up the serviscape should function well to produce the service in a technical sense and should also keep internal efficiency at an optimal level. However, when investing in these resources and planning how they should be used, a customer-oriented approach simultaneously has to be taken. Resources in the service process should function in interactions with customers in a way that creates good process-related functional quality, and thereby have a good interactive marketing effect. As we have discussed in the context of service management principles, when investing in these resources both internal efficiency (the cost-effective use of resources) and external efficiency (impact on perceived service quality) must be taken into account at the same time. Customers have dual roles, too. They consume or use the service, but they also contribute to how the service process proceeds.

A Serviscape Example: Nike Town Chicago

Nike Town Chicago (NTC) is a three-storey showcase displaying the total range of Nike products. The objective of the concept is to support the Nike brand, rather than achieve immediate sales. Customers entering NTC are invariably struck by the huge assortment of products. The ground floor simulates a small-town shopping district with cobblestone streets. When entering the store the customers or curious visitors encounter statues and framed photos of well-known people as well as large fishtanks and display cases containing Nike products and memorabilia. When moving further into the showcase they are greeted by framed pictures of sports celebrities such as Michael Jordan and Charles Barkley who endorse Nike products. A banner saying "There Is No Finish Line" is clearly visible. On the second floor there is a half-court basketball unit, where the sounds of the Chicago Bulls' team introduction music can be heard in the background. On the third floor cased exhibits show the history of the Nike brand. The whole NTC is designed as a serviscape embodying the Nike brand identity. Through experiencing this serviscape the customer creates his own perception of the Nike brand.

Source: This Nike Town Chicago example of a thoroughly designed serviscape is described in greater detail in Zeithaml, Valarie, A. & Bitner, Mary Jo, *Services Marketing. Integrating Customer Focus Across the Firm.* 2nd edition. Boston, MA: Irwin McGraw-Hill, 2000, p. 264. See also Sherry, Jr., John F., The Soul of the Company Store: Nike Town Chicago and the Emplaced Brandscape. In Sherry, Jr., John F. (ed.), *Serviscapes: The Concept of Place in Contemporary Markets.* Chicago, IL: NTC/Contemporary Publishing Company, 1998, pp. 109–146.

The Internet and Marketing

The Internet, especially the World Wide Web, has become more frequently used in marketing. It is, for example, used for selling, communication, market research and making payments. These are all ways of using it to perform traditional marketing activities. However, *the Internet is also an interactive marketing vehicle*, because a variety of service interactions can be initiated and also performed over the Internet. For example, by providing e-mail connections to helpdesks or other functions of a firm, the Internet becomes part of the service process. The way it functions influences the interactive marketing impact of the firm. This of course requires that the firm manages to assume its role as an interactive partner in the virtual environment. For example, invitations to interact from a customer, perhaps using e-mail, must be responded to, if not immediately, at least as quickly as the customer considers acceptable. Slow responses, or no response, means that no interactions develop, and the interest of the customer will be lost.

The Internet is a service- and relationship-oriented medium, even though it is often only used as a communications and sales tool. It is important to keep in mind, though, that it is not the firm who makes the first contact with a customer over the Internet; it is the customer or potential customer who initiates the contact. If this contact can be developed into a service process with interactions between the firm and the customer, a relationship may emerge. Because it is so easy to jump from one Web site to another, creating a relationship-oriented service interaction with a given customer may be an effective way of maintaining a given customer's interest in the firm and creating ongoing business.

In conclusion, the Internet does not only offer a means of carrying out traditional marketing activities, it is also an interactive process instrument which has an important role in the interactive marketing function.

Case Study of WWOZ Radio—The Sound of New Orleans: The Internet in the Service of Music Broadcasting

WWOZ radio (90.7 FM) is based in the New Orleans Jazz National Historical Park in New Orleans, Louisiana, USA. Playing blues, jazz, calypso, zydeco, gospel, Brazilian, Caribbean, Irish music and a lot more, WWOZ keeps the music and musical heritage of the Crescent City alive. A listener-supported, volunteer-operated, nonprofit radio station, WWOZ uses sophisticated technology to deliver its services to a global audience. In addition to broadcasting live to listeners in the South-eastern Louisiana area, WWOZ broadcasts live on the Internet (http://www.wwoz.org) and can be heard from anywhere in the world.

The New Orleans Jazz & Heritage Foundation, Inc. owns WWOZ and also produces the New Orleans Jazz & Heritage Festival (JazzFest). WWOZ broadcasts start-to-finish coverage of JazzFest. In 1999, six hours of the 56 hours of WWOZ's live JazzFest coverage were uplinked by satellite to a network of public radio stations organized by WWOZ. In addition, they do numerous live broadcasts from music clubs throughout the year via their mobile recording studio. WWOZ also offers selected downloadable MP3 music files from the WWOZ Web site.

Source: This case example was developed by Raymond P. Fisk, University of New Orleans.

The Three-Stage Model

Marketing is a dynamic process, where traditional external marketing activities and interactive marketing resources and activities cooperate so that profitable long-term customer relationships may be developed and maintained. The *Customer Relationship Life Cycle* model illustrated how enduring customer relationships are created through a three-stage process. The *Three-Stage* model demonstrates this long-term marketing approach.

The model, illustrated in Figure 10.5, holds that, in order to satisfy the needs of its target markets, the service organization has to consider the three stages of the *Customer Relationship Life Cycle*, and that recognition of the three stages in the life cycle has substantial marketing consequences. At each stage the *objective* of marketing and the *nature of* marketing—the marketing function to be used—will be different.

At the *initial stage*, when potential customers have no clear view, or perhaps old-fashioned or out of date views, of the firm and its services, the objective of marketing is to *create interest* in the organization and its services. This is best achieved by the *Traditional Marketing Function*. Advertising, Web sites, sales

Stage	Objective of marketing	Marketing function
Initial stage	To create interest in the firm and its services	The traditional marketing function
Purchasing process	To turn general interest into sales* (first purchase)	The traditional and the interactive marketing functions
Consumption process	To create resales, cross-sales and enduring customer relations**	The interactive marketing function

* Giving promises

** Fulfilling promises

FIGURE 10.5 The three-stage model. Source: Grönroos, C., *Strategic Marketing and Marketing in the Service Sector*, 1983. Reprinted with permission of the Marketing Science Institute.

promotions and public relations are appropriate means of competition. Sometimes field selling is also needed, especially in industrial markets. One should also not overlook the potential power of favorable word of mouth communication.

At the second stage, the *purchasing process, general interest should be turned into sales*. More specifically, *promises* about future commitments on the part of the seller are given and should, one hopes, be accepted. Here again the *traditional marketing* activities, including sales, can be used. However, *interactive marketing* activities can also be applied whenever the customer contacts with the firm's production resources before he has made a final purchase decision.

During the *consumption (usage) process*, resales, cross-sales, and enduring customer relationships should be achieved. At this stage, *promises have to be fulfilled*, so that customers realize that the firm can satisfy their needs and that it can be trusted. At this final stage in the life cycle the traditional marketing activities have only a slight chance, if any, of influencing the preferences of the customers toward the service. Here the Interactive Marketing Process is responsible for success or failure. The marketing orientation and service-mindedness of the service process and the resources in the production process are of vital importance if customers are not to be lost at this stage. Traditional marketing activities, such as contacts by salespeople and advertising, have only minor effects, if any, at this point.

Far too often marketing is viewed too narrowly. Only the traditional marketing activities are managed in a marketing context. The firm may be excellent at giving promises, but these promises may be kept in a much less marketing-oriented way, and low perceived quality follows. Marketing may be managed successfully during the two first phases of the customer relationship life cycle, but in the third phase, the consumption or usage process, nobody seems to be responsible for marketing and customers any more.

Marketing has to be planned and implemented throughout the life cycle as a continuous process, otherwise too many customer relationships are broken, which leads to bad word of mouth. Moreover, lost customers have to be replaced by new customers, which requires an increased budget for traditional marketing.

The Marketing Strategy Continuum

As we have seen, relationship marketing means that the firm uses a marketing strategy which aims at maintaining and enhancing ongoing customer relationships. Although getting new customers is still important, the main strategic interest is to market to existing customers. In a relationship marketing strategy, interactive marketing becomes essential. If the moments of truth of the buyer–seller interactions are badly taken care of, thus literally wasting moments of opportunity, no traditional marketing efforts can ensure that the customers will stay with the firm. A relationship marketing approach and excellent interactive marketing capabilities are essential in service competition. Without these elements a service strategy often collapses.

Of course, relationship marketing is not the only marketing strategy option in service competition, although the importance of such a strategy is increasing all the time. It can be useful to think about possible marketing approaches or strategies along a *marketing strategy continuum*.[25] As a strategy, relationship marketing can be considered one end of such a continuum. At the other end of the continuum, the strategy would be to concentrate on one transaction at a time with any given customer, without deliberately trying to develop any enduring relationship with that customer. This type of marketing strategy is often called *transaction marketing* or order-taking marketing. As marketing strategies can be placed on a continuum, where these two types of strategies are the extremes, there are, clearly, situations where firms can combine elements of the two strategies. A relationship type of strategy or a transaction type of strategy may dominate. The *marketing strategy continuum* and its consequences for a number of marketing issues are illustrated in Figure 10.6.

Various types of goods and services can be placed along the continuum. Marketers of consumer packaged goods will probably benefit most from a transaction-type strategy, although this is not necessarily the case. Service firms, on the other hand, would normally be better off by applying a relationship-type strategy. Manufacturers of consumer packaged goods have mass markets but no immediate contact with their ultimate customers, while service firms almost always have such contacts, sometimes on a regular basis, sometimes only at discrete points of time. Therefore, the interface between the service firm and its customers is expanded far outside the departments of marketing and sales specialists. However, the development of information technology has made it possible for marketers of consumer packaged goods to create databases which enable them, too, if they find this effective and justified from an economic standpoint, to treat each and every customer as an individual.

The strategy continuum	Transaction marketing	Relationship marketing
Unit of analysis	Single exchange	Relationship
Time prespective	Short-term focus	Long-term focus
Dominating marketing function	Marketing mix	Interactive marketing (supported by marketing mix activities)
Price elasticity	Customers tend to be more sensitive to price	Customers tend to be less sensitive to price
Dominating quality dimension	Quality of output (technical quality dimension) is dominating	Quality of interactions (functional quality dimensions) grows in importance and may become dominating
Measurement of customer satisfaction	Monitoring market share (indirect approach)	Managing the customer base (direct approach)
Customer information system	Ad hoc customer satisfaction surveys	Real-time customer feedback system
Interdependency between marketing, operations and human resource management	Interface of no or limited strategic importance	Interface of substantial strategic importance
The role of internal marketing	Internal marketing of no or limited importance to success	Internal marketing of substantial strategic importance to success

FIGURE 10.6   The marketing strategy continuum. Adapted from Grönroos, C., From Marketing Mix to Relationship Marketing. Towards a Paradigm Shift in Marketing. *Management Decision*, **35**(4), 1997, p. 329.

In consumer durables the customer interface is broader than for consumer packaged goods, and a pure transaction-type strategy is not the only available option. The durables have to be delivered to customers and often also installed. Industrial goods, ranging from mass-produced components to complex machines and projects, would probably fit best between consumer durables and services. However, in many business-to-business marketing situations the customer relationships are similar to many service situations, and here no distinctions between the industrial marketer and service marketer can be made on the continuum. Even though the discussion here can be seen as a rule of thumb regarding the most appropriate marketing strategy to use, a firm may find it more effective to choose a different strategy, for various reasons.

Consequences for Marketing of the Strategy Continuum

In this section nine different consequences of a relationship marketing strategy and a transaction marketing strategy will be discussed (see Figure 10.6):

1. the unit of analysis;
2. the time perspective;
3. dominating marketing function;
4. price elasticity;
5. dominating quality dimension;
6. measurement of customer satisfaction;
7. customer information system;
8. interdepartmental collaboration;
9. the role of internal marketing.

The unit of analysis and the time perspective. The time perspective of marketing differs depending on where on the continuum a firm is. As transaction marketing means that the firm focuses on single exchanges or transactions at a time, the time perspective is rather short. The unit of analysis is a single market transaction or exchange. Profits are expected to follow from today's exchanges, although long-term image development may occur to support short-term transactions. In relationship marketing the time perspective is much longer. The marketer does not plan primarily for short-term results. His objective is to create results in the long term through enduring and profitable relationships with customers. In some cases, single exchanges that take place in the relationship may even be unprofitable as such. Thus, relationships and how they develop to facilitate transactions which create satisfaction for both parties are the units of analysis.

Dominating marketing focus and price elasticity. Because of the lack of personal contact with their customers and their focus on mass markets, firms pursuing a transaction-type strategy will probably benefit most from a traditional *marketing mix* approach. The 4P model will give guidance in most cases; and this model was originally developed for consumer-packaged goods marketing where transaction marketing is most appropriate.

For a firm applying a relationship strategy the marketing mix is often too restrictive. The most important customer contacts from a marketing success point of view are those outside the realm of the marketing mix and the full-time marketers. The performance of the part-time marketers, the customer orientation of information technology, operating systems, industrialized service routines, such as vending machines, ATMs and home banking systems, and the willingness of customers to perform as co-producers in the service process, are critical ingredients in a relationship-oriented strategy. The marketing impact of the customer's contacts with people, technology and systems and other non-marketing functions determines whether he (or the organizational buyer) will continue doing business with a given firm or not. All these customer contacts are interactive to a certain extent. These resources form the *interactive marketing function.* This marketing function can also be described as all the marketing activities outside the marketing mix and outside a marketing department. In relationship marketing interactive marketing becomes the dominating part of the marketing process. Of course, variables in the marketing mix such as traditional external marketing activities are important here as well, but to a much lesser degree and they merely support interactive marketing activities. In other situations the support of salespeople is needed, for example to close a new deal or to provide continuous attention during the consumption (usage) phase of the customer relationship life cycle.

In transaction marketing there is not much more than the core product (goods or services) and sometimes the image of the firm or its brands, to keep the customer attached to the seller. When a competitor introduces a similar product, advertising and image may help to keep customers, at least for some time, but price usually becomes an issue. A firm that offers a lower price or better terms is a dangerous competitor, because in transaction marketing the price sensitivity of customers is often high. A firm pursuing a relationship marketing strategy, on the other hand, has created more value for its customers than what is provided by the core solution alone. Such a firm develops tighter ties over time more with its customers. If, say, a financial service arrangement is complicated, an Internet grocery store provides its customers with easy-to-use ordering systems, consistent quality of goods, information and deliveries, or a supplier provides its customers with a complex solution, the buyer and seller grow together due to the various ties that have been established over time. Such ties or *bonds* may variously be technological, knowledge-related or information-related, geographical or social in nature. If they are well handled they provide customers with added value; something that is not provided by the core solution itself. Of course, price is not unimportant but is often much less an issue here. Thus, relationship marketing makes customers less price-sensitive.

Dominating quality dimension. The way quality is perceived by customers will typically differ, depending on the strategy used by a firm. In transaction marketing the customers' contact with the firm is limited to the product and exposure to other traditional marketing mix variables. The benefits sought by customers are imbedded in the technical solution provided by the product. The customer will not receive much else that will provide him with value. Hence, the technical quality of the product, or what the customer gets as an outcome, is the dominating quality-creating source in transaction marketing.

The situation is different in relationship marketing. The customer interface is broader, and the firm has opportunities to provide its customers with added value of various types (technological, information, knowledge, social, etc.). Hence, the second quality dimension, how the interaction process is perceived, grows in importance. When several firms can provide a similar technical quality, managing the interactions of the service processes also becomes imperative from a quality perception perspective. Thus, in relationship marketing the functional quality dimension grows in importance and often dominates. Of course, this does not mean that technical quality can be neglected. It is a prerequisite for good total quality, but it is no longer the only quality dimension to be considered.

Measurement of customer satisfaction and customer information systems. A normal way of monitoring customer satisfaction and success is to look at *market share* and to do *ad hoc* customer satisfaction surveys. Market share as a measurement of success is discussed later in this chapter. For a consumer-packaged goods marketing firm, which would typically apply a transaction marketing strategy, there is no way of continuously measuring market success other than by *ad hoc* customer satisfaction studies. A service firm and many industrial marketers, on the other hand, who could more easily pursue a relationship marketing strategy, have at least some kind of interaction with almost every single customer, even if they serve mass markets. Thus, customer satisfaction can be directly monitored. A firm that applies a relationship-type strategy can study customer satisfaction by directly monitoring its customer base.

Managing the customer base means that the firm has at least some kind of direct knowledge of its customer satisfaction levels. Instead of thinking of numbers, or of market share only, management thinks in terms of individuals with personal reactions and opinions. Instead of getting information about marketing success from customer satisfaction studies, the marketer judges success by information direct from customers. This requires a means of gathering the various types of customer feedback that are constantly obtained by a large number of employees in large numbers of customer contacts. In combination with market share statistics, such an intelligence system focusing on customer satisfaction, needs and desires forms a valuable source of information for decision-making. Of course, traditional customer satisfaction studies can be made from time to time to complement the data gathered from daily customer contacts.

Consequently, in a relationship marketing situation the firm can build up an on-line, real-time information system. This system will provide management with a continuously updated database of its customers and information about the degree of satisfaction or dissatisfaction among customers. This can serve as a powerful management tool. In a transaction marketing situation it is more difficult to build up such a database, although thanks to available information technology this is not impossible any more.

The strategic importance of interdepartmental collaboration. The level of inter-dependency between processes and departments in an organization depends on whether the firm has chosen a transaction-type strategy or a relationship-type strategy. In transaction marketing, most or all of the firm's customer contacts are related to the product itself and to traditional marketing mix activities. Marketing and sales specialists are responsible for total marketing; no part-time marketers are involved. Thus, from a marketing point of view the internal interface between functions has no, or very limited, strategic importance to the firm.

In relationship marketing the situation is different. The customer interface is much broader, often involving a large number of part-time marketers in several different departments. This is the case, for example, in most services marketing and business-to-business marketing situations. A successfully implemented interactive marketing performance requires that all parts of the firm involved in taking care of customers can collaborate, cooperate and support each other in order to provide customers with a good total perceived quality. Thus, for a firm pursuing a relationship marketing strategy the internal interface between marketing, operations, human resource management and other departments is of strategic importance to success.

The role of internal marketing. Part-time marketers have to be prepared for their marketing tasks. *Internal marketing* is needed to ensure the support of traditional non-marketing staff. They have to be committed, prepared and informed, and motivated to perform as part-time marketers. This does not apply only to customer contact employees and back office employees. It is, of course, equally important that supervisors, middle-level and top-level managers are equally committed and prepared.

Internal marketing as a process has to be integrated with the total marketing process. The traditional marketing and interactive marketing performance starts from within the organization. A thorough and ongoing internal marketing process is required to make relationship marketing successful. If internal marketing is neglected, interactive marketing in particular will suffer or fail.

Managing the Customer Base and Market Share of Customers

When a transaction marketing strategy is used, exchanges or transactions with a customer are viewed in isolation from other contacts or relations with that customer over time. Customers are numbers that come and go and, the company hopes, come back again. The customers add up to a number of the total amount of exchanges or transactions, measured in volume or sales, called *market share*.

The composition of the market share is unknown, except for a breakdown of any market segments that may exist. Hence, we usually do not know whether a market share is accounted for by a stable customer base offering repeat business or by a large proportion of customers coming and going. In the latter case, new potential customers have to be interested in the firm and its offerings and persuaded to purchase. In the former case, today's customers have to be convinced that it is worthwhile to continue purchasing or doing business with a firm.

If we bear in mind that it is always much more expensive to take a new customer through the customer relationship life cycle to the end of the purchase stage, compared to the cost of making a satisfied customer purchase again, one easily understands that it is better to have as many profitable long-term customer relationships as possible. A highly unscientific rule of thumb suggests that it costs at least five to six times more to get a new customer than to achieve resales to an existing one. It also suggests that if a firm has to win over a dissatisfied ex-customer, it will cost at least 25 times as much to do so, perhaps much more.

In some situations, for example, for consumer packaged goods, some consumer durables, and perhaps some industrial goods, a transaction marketing strategy may be the only possible one. Close relationships with the customers cannot be developed. In such situations, effectively used traditional marketing mix activities, and thorough market research, are the only means of trying to win as many repeat purchases as possible. But even here new information technology makes it possible to create useful customer databases. However, when the size of the business is measured in terms of market share, we really do not know how much of the market share is stable and how much is made up for by new customers replacing lost customers. And the more lost customers that have to be replaced by new ones in order to maintain market share, the more marketing will cost.

In services, and in most business-to-business marketing situations, firms have close contacts with their customers. If, however, a firm pursues a transaction marketing strategy and does not aim at developing long-term and lasting customer relationships, a large proportion of its customer base will probably be new at any given period. This also means that the firm has a number of ex-customers who have decided to quit the relationship for various reasons. When customers come and go, the cost of maintaining a given market share is unnecessarily high because, as we have noticed, marketing to new customers is always much more expensive. If the firm simply measures its market share, it may be very satisfied with its marketing achievements. However, management may fail to see that a substantial proportion of its customer base during a given period has been lost, and has been replaced by potential customers. Management thus feels secure, believing that the firm is doing well. But in such a situation, the firm is *not* doing well. Because of the number of lost and probably dissatisfied customers, a substantial amount of bad word of mouth has been created; moreover, the firm constantly suffers from unnecessarily high marketing costs.

In the situation described above, what the firm is doing is *managing market share only*. This is, however, not enough. Management has to *manage the firm's customer base*, so that both the nature of the resulting market share and the true economic implications of a certain market share are kept under control, otherwise there is no real understanding of how productive marketing efforts are. Managing the *customer base* means that management is focused on customer relationships and their enhancement, not simply on the market share statistics. Customer relationships should be managed in such a way that the firm gets a large *share of its customers* and of their total purchases. Although market share may still provide important information, it is even more important to know how large a share of its customers the firm has—and that this share preferably remains high over time. Monitoring the firm's share of customers is, therefore, more important as a decision-making instrument than simply monitoring market share.

Failure to manage the customer base and the share of customers can be fatal, especially in large corporations. Such firms often have so much capital that the slowly but steadily advancing financial drain caused by a mismanaged or unmanaged customer base is not recognized before a lot of negative word of mouth has been created, the corporate image damaged, and negative economic consequences reached substantial proportions. All of a sudden management is shaken by the fact that the operation is economically unsound, although there have been no problems with the level of market share. But here only the market share figures look good; customer relationships have suffered over time and the customer base is unhealthy.

Marketing Management or Market-Oriented Management?

In traditional marketing literature, which is mainly based on consumer packaged goods experience, the concept of marketing management is used to describe the practical applications of the marketing concept. In a consumer goods context this is perfectly appropriate. However, in situations where the typical customer relationship is extended far beyond the straightforward and impersonal relationship between a marketer and a buyer of consumer breakfast cereals, toothpaste or soap, this straightforward view of how to manage marketing does not hold any more. When marketing is geared to the management of customer relationships, the situation changes.

In business-to-business marketing contexts the marketing management approach becomes awkward. Many customer relationship issues are the concerns of departments other than the marketing department. The interrelationships between departments make planning, coordination, and implementation much more complicated than a traditional marketing and sales department can handle. In a service context the situation is often even more complex. Marketing activities—traditional and interactive marketing activities—are spread throughout the organization; therefore, the whole organizational structure has to be supportive to marketing. Because of the extreme interdependence between the various departments of a service firm and marketing, a *marketing attitude of mind* is needed throughout the organization. Furthermore, as George Day[26] observes, the minds *and hearts* of the entire organization have to be engaged.

Customers have to be considered in planning and implementing most activities in a firm, regardless of whether they are labeled production and operations, human resource management, finance or any other traditional function. In other words, marketing considerations are one aspect, among others, to be observed in decision-making throughout an organization. For the full-time marketers, marketing is the main or only consideration to bear in mind, but for other functions and processes marketing is one of many aspects to take into account. However, in the final analysis it is a firm's success in the marketplace which is crucial. Hence, market-oriented management throughout the organization is needed rather than marketing management as the responsibility of one department only.

Top management alone has the necessary overview of the organization, and the authority, to manage the total marketing process; therefore, ultimate marketing responsibility has to be held sufficiently high up in the organization. A marketing department can plan and implement some marketing tasks, but total management of the marketing process has to be an integral part of overall company management. Hence, even for psychological reasons, market-oriented management is what it is all about, not marketing in the traditional functionalistic sense. Marketing, therefore, becomes an integral part of service management. In fact, because in service contexts it is more a question of market-oriented management than just marketing management, the term "service management" was introduced as a synonym for service marketing.

Summary and Questions for Discussion

In service competition, marketing is not restricted to marketing specialists. It is spread throughout the organization, and *part-time marketers* almost invariably outnumber specialists in, for example, market research, marketing communication and sales. The traditional models of marketing management, therefore, do not fit very well in a service context. The traditional approach to marketing, the so-called marketing mix, is too restrictive and simplistic to be very useful.

Moreover, its approach to marketing as a function with well-defined areas of marketing decision-making guides management interest away from the process nature of customer relationships. Instead a *relationship approach* to marketing was suggested, and a relationship definition of marketing was presented.

The total marketing process is divided into two subprocesses, the traditional marketing process and the interactive marketing process. The interactive marketing process is especially important during the *consumption* or *usage process* of the customer relationship life cycle. Of course, traditional external marketing efforts are still important, but more in the form of support activities and mainly in the *initial* and *purchasing phases* of the life cycle. The concept of a *marketing strategy continuum* was introduced, and two distinct marketing strategy options, relationship marketing and transaction marketing, were analyzed in relation to this strategy continuum. In service contexts, the nature of marketing makes this much more a top management process than it is normally considered to be. Hence, it is actually more accurate to talk about *market-oriented management* than marketing management in the traditional sense of the term. Therefore, marketing becomes an integral part of any theory of service management.

Questions for Discussion

1. Why does marketing have to be a concern of all the departments of a firm in service contexts?
2. What is the difference between traditional external marketing and interactive marketing? Why is interactive marketing considered so critical to the marketing function of service providers?
3. What is the difference between *full-time marketers* and *part-time marketers*? Why are the latter especially important to marketing success in service competition?
4. Define the various groups of *part-time marketers* of your firm, or any given firm, and analyze their importance to the total marketing process. What are the problems with the contribution of the various part-time marketers to the interactive marketing process?
5. In view of the *marketing strategy continuum*, how does a relationship marketing strategy differ from a transaction marketing strategy?
6. Why is "market-oriented management" a better term than "marketing management" in service contexts?

Further Reading

Bateson, J.E.G. (1995) *Managing Services Marketing*. New York: Dryden Press.

Booms, B.H. & Bitner, M.J. (1982) Marketing Strategies and Organization Structures for Service Firms. In Donnelly, J.H. & George, W.H. (eds), *Marketing of Services*. Chicago, IL: American Marketing Association.

Borden, N.H. (1964) The Concept of the Marketing Mix. *Journal of Advertising Research*, June.

Bitner, M.J. (1992) Serviscapes: The Impact of Physical Surroundings on Customers and Employees. *Journal of Marketing*, **56**, April, pp. 57–71.

Bitner, M.J. (1995) Building Service Relationships: It's All About Promises. *Journal of the Academy of Marketing Science*, **23**(4), pp. 246–251.

Calonius, H. (1988) A Buying Process Model. In Blois, K. & Parkinson, S. (eds), *Innovative Marketing— A European Perspective*. Proceedings from the XVIIth Annual Conference of the European Marketing Academy, University of Bradford, pp. 86–103.

Cowell, D. (1985) *The Marketing of Services*. London: Heinemann.

Day, G.S. (2000) Managing Market Relationships. *Journal of the Academy of Marketing Science*, **28**(1), pp. 24–30.

Gordon, I. (1998) *Relationship Marketing*. Toronto: John Wiley & Sons.

Grönroos, C. (1980) Designing a Long Range Marketing Strategy for Services. *Long Range Planning*, **13**, April, pp. 36–42.

Grönroos, C. (1990) *Service Management and Marketing. Managing the Moments of Truth in Service Competition*. Lexington, MA: Lexington Books.

Grönroos, C. (1996) Relationship Marketing Logic. *Asia-Australia Marketing Journal*, **4**(1), pp. 7–18.

Grönroos, C. (1997) From Marketing Mix to Relationship Marketing—Towards a Paradigm Shift in Marketing. *Managing Decision*, **35**(4), 1997, pp. 322–339.

Grönroos, C. (1997) Value-driven Relational Marketing: From Products to Resources and Competencies. *Journal of Marketing Management*, **13**(5), pp. 407–420.

Gummesson, E. (1987) The New Marketing—Developing Long-Term Interactive Relationships. *Long Range Planning*, **20**(4), pp. 10–21.

Gummesson, E. (1999) *Total Relationship Marketing. Rethinking Marketing Management: From 4Ps to 30Rs*. London: Butterworth Heinemann.

Halinen, A. & Tähtinen, J. (1999) *Towards a Process Theory of Relationship Dissolution*. Working Paper No. 9, Turku School of Economics and Business Administration, Finland.

Hoekstra, J.C., Leeflang, P.H. & Wittink, D.R. (1999) The Customer Concept: The Basis for a New Marketing Paradigm. *Journal of Market-Focused Management*, **4**(1), pp. 43–76.

Kasper, H., van Helsdingen, P. & de Vries Jr., W. (1996) *Services Marketing Management. An International Perspective*. Chichester and New York: John Wiley & Sons.

Kotler, P. (1986) Megamarketing. *Harvard Business Review*, March–April.

Lovelock, C. (2000) Functional Integration in Services. Understanding the Links Between Marketing, Operations and Human Resources. In Swartz, T.A. & Iacobucci, D. (eds), *Handbook in Services Marketing & Management*. Thousand Oaks, CA: Sage Publications, pp. 421–437.

Lovelock, C., Vandermerwe, S. & Lewis, B. (1996) *Services Marketing. A European Perspective*. London: Prentice-Hall Europe.

McCarthy, E.J. (1960) *Basic Marketing*. Homewod, IL: Irwin.

McGuire, L. (1999) *Australian Services Marketing and Management*. South Yarra, Australia: Macmillan Education Australia.

Moorman, C. & Rust, R.T. (1999) The Role of Marketing. *Journal of Marketing*, **63**, Special Issue, pp. 180–197.

Rathmell, J.M. (1974) *Marketing in the Service Sector*. Cambridge, MA: Winthrop.

Sherry, Jr., J.F. (1998) The Soul of the Company Store: Nike Town Chicago and the Emplaced Brandscape. In Sherry, Jr., J.F. (ed.), *Serviscapes: The Concept of Place in Contemporary Markets*. Chicago, IL: NTC/Contemporary Publishing Company, pp. 109–146.

Zeithaml, V.A. & Bitner, M.J. (2000) *Services Marketing. Integrating Customer Focus Across the Firm*. 2nd edition. New York: McGraw-Hill.

Notes

1 Rathmell, J.M., *Marketing in the Service Sector*. Cambridge, MA: Winthrop, 1974.

2 See Grönroos, C., *Service Management and Marketing. Managing the Moments of Truth in Service Competition*. Lexington, MA: Lexington Books, 1990.

3 The customer relationship life cycle concept was originally introduced in Grönroos, C., *Strategic Management and Marketing in the Service Sector*. Cambridge, MA: Marketing Science Institute, 1983.

4 Bitner, M.J., Serviscapes: The Impact of Physical Surroundings on Customers and Employees. *Journal of Marketing*, **56**, April 1992, pp. 57–71.

5   The view of the marketer as a mixer of ingredients was first expressed by James Culliton in a study of marketing costs in 1948 and in the 1950s, based on this expression, Neil Borden created the notion of a marketing mix. See Borden, N.H., The Concept of the Marketing Mix. *Journal of Advertising Research*, June 1964.

6   The 4P model was first introduced in a major marketing textbook by McCarthy in 1960 (see McCarthy, E.J., *Basic Marketing*. Homewood, IL: Irwin, 1960). Since then it seems as if marketing textbooks, especially in North America, have had to be organized around the 4Ps of the marketing mix.

7   Definition by American Marketing Association.

8   These are the three new service-oriented categories in a 7P marketing mix for services suggested by Booms and Bitner (see Booms, B.H. & Bitner, M.J., Marketing Strategies and Organization Structures for Service Firms. In Donnelly, J.H. & George, W.H. (eds), *Marketing of Services*. Chicago, IL: American Marketing Association, 1982.)

9   These two additional categories were suggested by Philip Kotler in the context of megamarketing. See Kotler, P., Megamarketing. *Harvard Business Review*, March–April 1986.

10   Some authors go so far as to conclude that a traditional marketing perspective, with the management of the marketing mix and its 4Ps as the central part, had by the end of the 20th century deprived the marketing phenomenon of its importance and made decision-makers in business lose interest in the development of marketing in firms. Only marketers themselves may not have fully realized the need for a reorientation of their discipline. So, for example, says Ian Gordon: "Busy attending to the practice of marketing, marketers may not have noticed that marketing is, for all its practical purposes, dead. . . . Today, marketing attracts neither interest nor patience from the investor community, except to the extent basic marketing skills must be demonstrated by the enterprise. Marketing rarely achieves its promise of differentiating and developing enduring, competitively superior value" (p. 1). He sees a hope for a revitalization of marketing in the relationship marketing philosophy. See Gordon, I., *Relationship Marketing*. Toronto: John Wiley & Sons, 1998.

11   Compare Hoekstra, J.C., Leeflang, P.H. & Wittink, D.R., The Customer Concept: Tha Basis for a New Marketing Paradigm. *Journal of Market-Focused Management*, **4**(1), 1999, pp. 43–76. In this article the authors formulates a new marketing concept, which they label the *customer concept*, which "is mainly based on the realization of superior customer values where the individual customer is the starting point" (p. 43).

12   This definition is further developed from definitions presented in, for example, Grönroos 1990, *op.cit.*, and Grönroos, C., Value-driven Relational Marketing: From Products to Resources and Competencies. *Journal of Marketing Management*, **13**(5), 1997, pp. 407–420.

13   Evert Gummesson has in a relationship marketing context discussed a large number of relationships with various partners. See Gummesson, E., *Total Relationship Marketing. Rethinking Marketing Management: From 4Ps to 30Rs*. London: Butterworth Heinemann, 1999.

14   Parvatiyar, A. & Sheth, J.N., The Domain and Conceptual Foundations of Relationship Marketing. In Sheth, J.N. & Parvatiyar, A. (eds), *Handbook of Relationship Marketing*. Thousand Oaks, CA: Sage Publications, 2000, pp. 3–38.

15   Gummesson, *op.cit.*, p. 1.

16   Grönroos 1996, *op.cit.*, p. 11.

17   Research into the issue of termination on dissolution of relationships is in its infancy. However, it seems to be a topic which will quickly grow. An early study in an business-to business context is reported in Halinen, A. & Tähtinen, J., *Towards a Process Theory of Relationship Dissolution*. Working Paper No. 9, Turku School of Economics and Business Administration, Finland, 1999.

18   Henrik Calonius was probably the first marketing researcher who argued for the explicit integration of promises in marketing models. See Calonius, H., A Buying Process Model. In Blois, K. & Parkinson, S. (eds), *Innovative Marketing—A European Perspective*. Proceedings from the XVIIth Annual Conference of the European Marketing Academy, University of Bradford, 1988, pp. 86–103.

19   The expressions "enabling promises" was in this context introduced by Mary Jo Bitner (Building Service Relationships: It's All About Promises. *Journal of the Academy of Marketing Science*, **23**(4), 1995, pp. 246–251).

20   As Moorman and Rust conclude in an analysis of the role of marketing: "Looking broadly at the marketing literature and practice, it appears that during the past ten years there has been a

movement toward thinking of marketing less as a function and more as a set of values and processes that all functions are participating in implementing" (p. 180). See Moorman, C. & Rust, R.T., The Role of Marketing. *Journal of Marketing*, **63**, Special Issue 1999, pp. 180–197.

21 Service marketing textbooks are typically based on a customer relationship approach. See, for example, Zeithaml, V.A. & Bitner, M.J., *Services Marketing. Integrating Customer Focus Across the Firm*. 2nd edition. New York: McGraw-Hill, 2000. In general, it is interesting to note that full-scale textbooks on service marketing (not just text and reference volumes) now being published in English are more and more organized around a genuinely service-oriented perspective. See, for example, Zeithaml & Bitner, *op.cit.*, Bateson, J.E.G., *Managing Services Marketing*. New York: Dryden Press, 1995, Lovelock, C., Vandermerwe, S. & Lewis, B., *Services Marketing: A European Perspective*. London: Prentice-Hall Europe, 1996; Kasper, H., van Helsdingen, P. & de Vries Jr., W., *Services Marketing Management: An International Perspective*. Chichester and New York: John Wiley & Sons, 1996; and McGuire, L., *Australian Services Marketing and Management*. South Yarra, Australia: Macmillan Education Australia, 1999. The marketing mix approach no longer dominates the structures of these textbooks. An early textbook pioneering such an approach in English is Cowell, D., *The Marketing of Services*. London: Heinemann, 1985, which was organized around the 7P framework. In other languages such genuinely service-based textbooks have existed since the early 1980s.

22 Lovelock, C., Functional Integration in Services. Understanding the Links Between Marketing, Operations, and Human Resources. In Swartz, T.A. & Iacobucci, D. (eds), *Handbook in Services Marketing & Management*. Thousand Oaks, CA: Sage Publications, 2000, pp. 421–437.

23 Gummesson, E., The New Marketing—Developing Long-term Interactive Relationships. *Long Range Planning*, **4**, 1987.

24 See, for example, Grönroos, C., Designing a Long Range Marketing Strategy for Services. *Long Range Planning*, April 1980.

25 See Grönroos, C., From Marketing Mix to Relationship Marketing—Towards a Paradigm Shift in Marketing. *Managing Decision*, **35**(4), 1997, pp. 322–339. An earlier version was introduced in Grönroos, C., The Marketing Strategy Continuum: A Marketing Concept for the 1990s. *Management Decision*, **29**(1), 1991, pp. 7–13.

26 Day, G.S., Managing Market Relationships. *Journal of the Academy of Marketing Science*, **28**(1), 2000, pp. 24–30.

Chapter 11

MANAGING TOTAL INTEGRATED MARKETING COMMUNICATION

Everything communicates something about a firm and its goods and services— regardless of whether the marketer accepts this and acts upon it or not.

Introduction

This chapter addresses the issue of marketing communication and demonstrate the need for a total communication or integrated marketing communications approach where communication messages from a number of different sources are integrated. The *communication circle* concept is described, and the impact of various time horizons on the effects of marketing communication campaigns is analyzed. Some guidelines for managing marketing communications in services are also presented. In the final sections of the chapter we discuss the *relationship dialog* concept and how total integrated marketing communication and relationship marketing relate to each other.

Marketing Communication: A Total Communications Issue

Marketing communication is, of course, a substantial part of the marketing process. In the marketing model in the previous chapter the Traditional Marketing function was shown to include market communication activities such as sales, advertising, sales promotion and communication over the Internet. However, communication is also an integral part of the Interactive Marketing process. What employees say, how they say it, how they behave, how service outlets, machines and other physical resources look, and how they function all communicates something to the customers. The communication effect may be positive, such as "they really care for me here," "they have modern and efficient equipment," "this web site is easy to use and provides useful interactions with the firm" or "the employees are nicely dressed." It may also, of course, be less favorable, such as "how rude their people are," "what a sloppy office they have," or "how can it always take so long to get things done here?"

There is an important difference between the communication of the Traditional Marketing function and that involved the Interactive Marketing process. The latter type of communication is related to reality as customers perceive it. They communicate *what really is* as far as consumers are concerned. The former type of communication, such as advertising, is always on an abstract level for customers. They involve promises and/or information that may or may not be true; however, as far as the customer or potential customer is concerned, the validity of this must still be tested. Testing takes place when the customer meets reality. There is an obvious connection here with how service quality is perceived. Market communication efforts like advertising and sales predominantly impact the *expected* service, whereas the communication effects of the Interactive Marketing process influence the *experienced* service. Of course, advertising and brochures may sometimes have an immediate effect on the perception of the interactions, which probably enhances the customer's opinion of the service.

For example, a retailing chain which advertises a certain product at a special price communicates a positive promise of good value. If the product is not available in the shop from which a customer tries to get it, or if it has already sold out, a negative communication message is created: "They do not advertise honestly" or "They just want me to come to the shop to buy stuff. They probably only had a limited number of the advertised low-price products in stock in the first place." The negative communication impact of the latter is much more forceful, because it is caused by the actual performance of the retailer. Moreover, it changes the favorable effect of the first type of communication into an unfavorable image of the retailing chain.

The size of the gap between expectations and experiences determines the quality perception, as discussed earlier. Hence, here there is a truly *total communication impact*;[1] almost everything the organization says about itself and its performance and almost everything the organization does that is experienced in the service encounters or elsewhere has an impact on the customer. Moreover, the various means of communication and their effects are interrelated. These communication effects, together with other factors such as the technical quality of the services, shape the *image* of the organization in the minds of customers, and potential customers. We shall return to the issue of *image management* and *branding* in the next chapter.

Integrated Marketing Communications

The *integrated marketing communications* notion emerged as an approach to understanding how a *holistic* communications message could be developed and managed.[2] As the *total communication concept*, it is based on the notion that it is not only planned communication efforts using separate and distinct communications media, such as TV, print, direct mail, etc., that communicate a message about the firm and its offerings to customers and potential customers. Although these are communication activities that can easily be planned and implemented by the marketer, other aspects (for example, how the service process functions, what resources are used and what physical products are used in the process) include an element of communication. The messages that these parts of the customer relationship send may be more effective than those that the customer receives from advertisements, brochures and other traditional marketing communications media.

Integrated marketing communications can be defined as follows:[3]

> Integrated marketing communications is a strategy that integrates traditional media marketing, direct marketing, public relations and other distinct marketing communications media as well as communications aspects of the delivery and consumption of goods and services and of customer service and other customer encounters. Thus, integrated marketing communications has a long-term perspective.

According to this definition, *communication messages* can originate from several sources. Duncan and Moriarty distinguish between four kinds of sources of communication messages:[4]

1. planned messages;
2. product messages;
3. service messages;
4. unplanned messages.

Planned messages are the result of a planned marketing communications campaign where separate communications media, such as TV, print, direct mail, the Internet, etc., are used to send a message. Sales representatives also communicate planned messages. Generally, these messages are the least trustworthy, because people know that they are planned by the marketer to persuade customers and potential customers in a certain direction.

Product messages are messages about the firm and its offerings that follow from the physical products in an offering: how a physical product is designed, how it functions, how it can be disposed of, etc.

Service messages are messages that result from service processes. The appearance, attitude and behavior of service employees, the way systems and technology function, and the environment all send service messages. Interactions between customers and service employees in the service process include a substantial element of communication. Not only can the customer get valuable information in these encounters, he may also develop a sense of trust in the firm based on such interactions. On the other hand, the effects may also be negative. How the systems function and how the firm's environment supports the service process also communicate something and may build up trust in the firm. One might say that service messages are more trustworthy than planned messages and product messages, because customers know that it is more difficult to manage the resources that create such messages than it is with planned messages and product messages.

Finally, there are *unplanned messages* which are considered to be the most trustworthy. Unplanned messages about the firm and its offerings are sent by fellow customers who interact with a given customer during the service process or who convey good or bad word of mouth communication, or for example, by articles in newspapers, magazines or in TV programs.

In Figure 11.1 these four types of sources of communication messages as well as examples of the various types of messages are summarized.

Least credible   Most credible

◄───►

PLANNED	PRODUCT	SERVICE	UNPLANNED
MESSAGES	MESSAGES	MESSAGES	MESSAGES
Mass communication	Appearance	Interactions with	Word of mouth
(e.g. advertising)	Design	service processes	referrals
Brochures	Usefulness	Deliveries	References
Direct response	Raw materials	Invoicing	News stories
Sales	Production	Claims handling	Gossip
Web sites	processes	Information	etc.
etc.	etc.	etc.	

FIGURE 11.1   Sources of communication messages. Based on Duncan & Moriarty, *Driving Brand Value*, McGraw-Hill, New York, 1997.

As is illustrated in Figure 11.2 the sources of these four types of messages can be described as *"What the firm says"* (in planned communications messages), *"What the firm does"* (creating product and service messages) and *"What others say and do"* (fellow customers in the service process, word of mouth and media coverage in the form of articles and TV programs).

A major problem in marketing communication is the fact that only the least

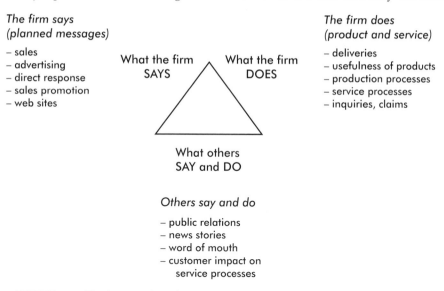

The firm says
(planned messages)

– sales
– advertising
– direct response
– sales promotion
– web sites

What the firm
SAYS

What the firm
DOES

The firm does
(product and service)

– deliveries
– usefulness of products
– production processes
– service processes
– inquiries, claims

What others
SAY and DO

Others say and do

– public relations
– news stories
– word of mouth
– customer impact on
  service processes

FIGURE 11.2   The integrated marketing communications triangle. From Grönroos, C. & Lindberg-Repo, K., Integrated Marketing Communications: The Communications Aspect of Relationship Marketing. *Integrated Marketing Communications Research Journal*, 4(1), 1998, p. 10.

trustworthy source of messages about the firm and its offerings—planned messages ("What the firm says") using separate and distinct communications media—is normally planned as part of the marketing communications program. Product messages may partly be taken into account in such a program, whereas the most trustworthy sources, service messages and unplanned messages ("What the firm does" and "What others say and do") are ignored. Because these types of messages are not part of an organized marketing communications process and not covered by a budget for marketing communications does not mean that their communications impact would be low. However, firms tend to neglect them, because they are difficult to plan. It is much easier to spend even more money on developing planned messages and using advertising, direct mail, sales promotions and other traditional means of marketing communication as well as the Internet and other new media. The effect of such a communications strategy is not guaranteed.

The challenge to a firm is to manage all sources of messages about the firm and its offerings and all the communication media and their effects in an integrated way. Otherwise, customers will receive different, possibly contradictory, signals from the various types of communication. A salesperson may promise one thing while a personalized sales letter may promise something else (both planned communication messages), and a third communication effect may emerge when the customer perceives reality in the buyer–seller interaction when consuming the service (effect of service messages). Furthermore, somewhere along the line there may be an *absence of communication*, either deliberate or accidental, which adds to the confusion of the total communication effect.

On the other hand, the organization which masters total communication management can achieve a powerful market communication impact, which adds substantially to the performance of the total marketing process. It is a way of boosting image and has a significant effect on another communication phenomenon, one that has yet to be disscussed. This phenomenon is *word of mouth*.

The Absence of Communication

In addition to the various types of messages and means of communication discussed above, there is a fifth source of message or type of communication that has to be considered when planning total communication, and that is the *absence of communication*.

The absence of communication may send messages as effectively as planned communication does. When a firm decides *not to inform* its customers about, say, a delay or a quality fault, this is *not* simply a lack of communication. Instead, there is a distinct message involved. This is perceived either immediately or later. It tells the customer that the service provider or supplier does not care about the customer and that the firm cannot be trusted. Absence of communication is frequently perceived as negative communication.

When a customer observes that there is a problem—for example, a flight does not leave on time or delivery of merchandise does not arrive on time—and the firm remains quiet, he loses control of the situation. Customers consider it important to be in control.[5] Even being in control of a negative situation such as a delayed shipment makes a customer more trusting towards the supplier than not knowing what has happened. Also, keeping the customer informed about problems and deviations from what was expected is a way of showing respect. Openly recognizing a service failure is also the a first step in a service recovery process and, as we have discussed previously, successful service recovery is a criterion of good functional quality.

In conclusion, the absence of communication may send a dangerous negative message about the firm. Normally, *even negative information is better than no information.*

Word of Mouth and the Communication Circle

The marketing impact of *word of mouth communication* is usually huge, frequently greater than that of planned communication. Word of mouth means messages about the organization, its credibility and trustworthiness, its ways of operating, its services and so on communicated from one person to another. As services are often based on an ongoing customer relationship, it is useful to understand word of mouth in a relationship context:

> Word of mouth communication from a relational perspective is based on consumers' long-term experiences and behavioral commitment. Their word of mouth communication reflects the nature and value of their perception of relationship episodes or service encounters, as well as psychological comfort/discomfort with the relationship. It varies depending on how strong the relationship is.[6]

In the eyes of a potential customer, a person who has had personal experience with the service provider is an objective source of information. Consequently, if there is a conflict between the word of mouth message and, say, an advertising campaign, advertising will lose.

If a strong relationship develops with a given customer, *advocacy bonds* between the firm and the customer may also develop. Such customers recommend the firm to their friends, colleagues, etc., whereby they thus invite their friends and business associates to share the service experience with them.[7] They become *advocates* of the service offering.

We will not go into word of mouth in any further detail here. Instead, we will turn to the *communication circle*, in which word of mouth plays a critical role. This circle is schematically illustrated in Figure 11.3.

The communication circle consists of four parts, *Expectations/Purchases, Interactions/Service Encounters, Experiences* and *Word of Mouth/References.* A customer or potential customer has developed certain *expectations* and therefore may decide to make a purchase; an ongoing customer relationship thus continues or new business is created, respectively. Having done so, he moves into the consumption stage of the customer relationship life cycle. At this point, the customer gets involved in *interactions* with the organization and perceives the technical and functional quality dimensions of the services rendered. These interactions usually involve a high number of *moments of truth* or *moments of opportunity*. Here the customer is exposed to the *interactive marketing* efforts of the firm and receives service and product messages. The way the employees perform and systems function communicates a number of messages about the firm, its trustworthiness, its interest in customers, etc.

Now, the *experiences* that follow from a customer being involved in interactions in the service encounters and perceiving the quality dimensions multiply several times by means of *word of mouth*. If the message thus communicated is

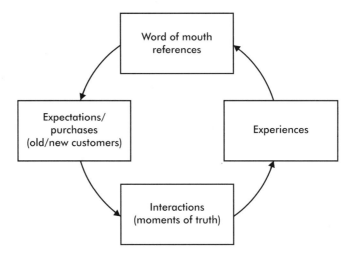

FIGURE 11.3 The communication cycle

positive, customer expectations develop favorably. The customer with positive experiences is more inclined to return or continue to use the services on an ongoing basis. New potential customers get interested in the organization and its offerings as a possible means of satisfying their needs and solving their problems. *References* (and *testimonials*) represent an active way for the firm to use positive word of mouth in its marketing, thus capitalizing more effectively on potential sources of good word of mouth.

The multiplier effect of word of mouth varies between industries and situations. It is frequently claimed that negative experiences tend to multiply by word of mouth quicker and more often than do positive experiences. The multiplier may be any number between, say, three and 30. An often-cited multiplier in service contexts is 12; that bad experiences are communicated to at least 12 other persons, good experiences to fewer. There are no facts to prove this figure, but the trend is clear and sends the marketer a blunt message: *Do not play with word of mouth*. Make it work for you in all situations, and always try to capitalize on it.

Thus, word of mouth has a powerful impact on the formation of *expectations* of existing and potential customers and is an important determinant of future *purchasing behavior*. On the one hand, good word of mouth has a positive effect on expectations and future purchases. On the other, negative word of mouth has, of course, the opposite effect.

Marketing Communication and the Communication Circle

It is extremely important that the existence of the communication circle be understood and its consequences for marketing communication fully appreciated by the marketer. If customer interactions create too many negative experiences and negative word of mouth follows, the customer builds up a *resistance to active marketing communication*. The more negative word of mouth there is, the less effective advertising campaigns, direct communication and sales efforts will be, and the less inclined people will be to look at the firm's Web site. More has to be invested in these types of communication if the negative impact of word of mouth is to be nullified. If too many negative messages are communicated by word of mouth and the image of the organization suffers severely, no increase in the marketing communication budget will be enough to save the situation, at least not in the long run.

Positive word of mouth, on the other hand, decreases the need to spend so much on marketing communication, through, for example, advertising and sales. It also draws customers and potential customers to Internet sites, either because they are looking for solutions to a problem, or simply out of curiosity. Word of mouth takes care of much of the new business that is needed. In theory, *excellent interactions*, including good customer perceived quality and interactive communication, *make mass communication less necessary and allow more freedom in pricing*. Only when totally new services are launched may mass communication such as advertising campaigns be needed. There are numerous examples of small local firms which operate successfully in this way, and larger firms operating in larger areas can do the same. One of the leading banks in Scandinavia, Svenska Handelsbanken, has pursued such a communication strategy for over 20 years, and it has worked well; the profitability of the bank has constantly been well above average.

Whatever communication strategy the organization adopts, the key to successfully executed marketing communication is how the *interactions* between the organization and its customers have been geared to the needs and wishes of customers and to producing excellent perceived quality and building up supportive word of mouth. If the communication aspects of interactions are neglected, the interactive communication impact will not be as good, and could even be negative. As a consequence, more money will be needed for other types of communication, and even this may not be enough.

If marketing communication efforts sending planned messages through, for example, personal selling, mass communication and direct mail are developed without being geared to the communication effects of the service encounter (service messages) and word of mouth, the risk of overpromising and, consequently, of building up quality gaps grows substantially. Customers will then meet a reality that does not correspond to their expectations. This, in turn, destroys the communication circle, and three types of negative consequences may follow:

1. word of mouth and references will become negative;
2. the trustworthiness of the organization's communication messages suffer; and
3. the firm's image is damaged.

On the other hand, if all elements of the communication process and customer perceptions of the buyer–seller interactions of the service encounters are good, the corresponding effect is, of course, the opposite. Good word of mouth is built up, the credibility of the marketing communication efforts increases, and image improves.

To sum up, only a *total communication management* approach where the effects of various sources of communication messages are integrated as well as possible will be effective and justified from a management point of view. The effects of all types of communication, including the absence of communication, have to be taken into consideration and put to work in a *total communication program*. Integrating the different types of marketing communication and sources of messages is not an easy task. This is, however, not a valid excuse for not trying to integrate as much as possible. However, there is sometimes a structural obstacle in firms. Marketing communication is normally managed on a low level in the organizational hierarchy, where for example a marketing communication manager or even a marketing manager cannot integrate more than the planned communication messages, and this sometimes only partially.

Planned and Unplanned Communication

Unplanned messages were discussed in a previous section. These are messages from sources which cannot be planned or which are difficult to plan. There is also another aspect of the planned/unplanned issue. Even planned messages may go partly unplanned. Hence, we can talk about *unplanned communication* as well as planned, depending on how well the marketer manages to plan all aspects of a planned message, or of a product or service message.

Unplanned communication, as opposed to planned communication, has a distinct effect just like the absence of communication.[8] There are often a number of situations where communication effects occur, although these situations have not been planned from a communication point of view. Such unplanned communication effects may be related to planned messages in sales negotiations, advertising or some other distinct communications media, or they may be related to product or service messages.

Unplanned communications can easily have a negative impact on customer perceptions. Therefore, it is important to analyze all sources of communication and their possible effects, planned as well as unplanned. In Table 11.1 examples taken from various situations illustrate how unplanned communication effects may occur.

In practical situations it is, of course, seldom possible to exclude all sources of unplanned communication. However, successful total communications management requires that as many as possible of the potential communication situations be planned and the risk for unfavorable unplanned communication at least minimized.

The Short-, Medium- and Long-Term Effects of Marketing Communication

Frequently marketing communication is only used to achieve short-term goals. Sometimes efforts are made to create more enduring effects, for example, corporate advertising campaigns or image communication programs. Too often,

TABLE 11.1 Planned and unplanned communication

Type of communication	Planned	Unplanned
Personal selling	Good travel plans Good advice	Sloppy dress Uninterested in our values
Mass communication	Target-group directed advertising Informative menus	Communicates values which offend the customer
Direct communication (direct mail)	Correct address Personalized content	Wrong first name Irrelevant information
Web sites	Easy to find Interesting links E-mail contact opportunities	No or delayed answers to e-mails
Communication in service encounters (service messages)	Good manners Pleasant serviscape Effective systems	Snooty Badly maintained premises Complicated technology
Communication by physical products in service processes (product messages)	High-class amenities in a hotel room	Plastic chairs in an outdoor café
Absence of communication	"We don't give any information unless it is correct" "We'll inform you as soon as we know more, and let you know the situation every 10 minutes anyway"	Neglecting to inform customers about delays

however, such long-term efforts are planned separately from other campaigns. Every communication activity, whether short-term or long-term, has effects on *customers*, as well as on *potential customers* and *employees* in a number of different time perspectives.

We are here going to distinguish among three time perspectives and their impacts on how an organization is perceived in the marketplace:

1. a *marketing communication impact* in the short term;
2. a *marketing impact* in the medium term; and
3. an *image impact* in the long term.

Every communication effort, such as an advertising campaign, an Internet site, the behavior of service employees, or the ease with which an ATM is operated, has an instant, *short-term communication impact as a communication activity*. This may be very effective as a means of communication; for example, a well planned and executed advertising campaign that makes potential customers believe in the promises given. However, over a longer period the effects may be less clear, even negative. Another thing that is important to bear in mind is that mass communication has an impact on several target groups, even though it may be planned for and directed at only, say, potential customers. Existing customers and the firm's employees are also exposed to such communication. For example,

TABLE 11.2   Effects of an effectively executed communication campaign involving overpromising in three time periods at three levels

Effect/Period of Time Level	Target Groups		
	Existing Customers	Potential Customers	Employees
Short term: Effect of campaign as *communication*	+ or 0 "Maybe they really mean it!"	+ "This sounds good!"	0 "I doubt it!"
Medium term: Effect of campaign as *part of marketing*	– "I should have known better! Cheated again!"	0 or – "Wasn't it more than this?" or "This is not what I expected!"	– "It's as I thought and I have to explain why we cannot fulfill our promises!"
Long-term: Effect of campaign *on image formation*	– – "They never do what they say they are going to do!"	– – "They just talk and promise."	– – "I'm looking for another employer."

potential customers to whom the firm may promise discounts or special benefits if they make a purchase may be impressed, whereas the firm's existing customers may be annoyed. Such problems should be recognized by the marketer in advance and avoided from the beginning in the planning process.

In Table 11.2 the possible effects of such an effective advertising campaign (or any type of communication effort) are illustrated. "+" denotes a favorable effect, "–" a negative effect and "0" a neutral effect or no effect. Three target groups for this campaign, customers, potential customers and employees, are identified and the impact on these groups indicated. In reality there may be more target groups.

As can be seen from the table this hypothetical advertising campaign obviously includes promises that cannot be fulfilled. For *potential customers* and even for *existing customers* the effects of this campaign may be positive in the short term seen as a communications effect only, if it is well executed. However, *employees*, who know they cannot possibly fulfill such promises, react differently. If this is the first time such overpromising takes place, they will probably react in a neutral way and the campaign will have no effect. However, if such over-promises have been made in the past, their reactions will be negative.

Over a longer period of time, as customers and potential customers get involved in interactions with the organization, the perception of this advertising campaign changes. They realize that reality has not met their expectations and the promises given by the campaign. The combined impact of the advertising campaign as a traditional marketing effort and the interactive marketing effect of the buyer–seller interactions in the service encounters, which are inconsistent with the campaign, thus changes the positive effect of the campaign. This combined effect is the impact of the total marketing process, including traditional as well as interactive activities, and it is probably negative. The customers feel cheated, and justifiably so. Hence, in the medium term, the marketing effect of a campaign, which judged in isolation may seem good and effective, can be poor or directly negative.

TABLE 11.3 Effects of realistic market communication

Effect/Period of Time Level	Target Groups		
	Existing Customers	Potential Customers	Employees
Short term: Effect of campaign *as communication*	+ "They have something new to offer."	+ "I sounds interesting."	+ "We are prepared!"
Medium term: Effect of campaign *as part of marketing*	++ "What a good service!"	+ "They really fulfilled their promises."	+ "It works out well."
Long term: Effect of campaign *on image formation*	++ "That's my service provider!"	++ "You can really trust them."	++ "This is the best employer I've ever worked for."

As far as the employees are concerned, the medium-term effect is definitely negative, because they will have to cope with customers who have unrealistic expectations who may get angry and sometimes even nasty toward the employees. Personnel are put in an awkward position, which damages employee motivation and good interactive marketing performance.

Finally, we can stretch the time perspective even more, and observe the possible *long-term effects* of this advertising campaign. If the campaign runs for a longer period of time, or is followed by other campaigns which also overpromise *customers* and *potential customers* will learn that the organization is not trustworthy. Over the long term single communication campaigns that, again judged in isolation, look like good communication may have a very negative impact on the image of the organization.

Of course, *employees* react as strongly as customers. Dissatisfied customers can normally leave a company with little or no notice, whereas it may be less easy for many employees to find a new employer. In the long run employee motivation suffers badly.

The effects of a trustworthy communication campaign that does not involve overpromising are, of course, totally different. Table 11.3 illustrates the effects that can be expected to occur when, for example, an advertising campaign is run which gives realistic promises. Customers exposed to the messages of this campaign experience a reality that corresponds to the promises, if they decide to buy and consume services provided by the organization.

The effects demonstrated in Table 11.3 are totally different to those in Table 11.2. In the short term, existing and potential customers and employees can be expected to react positively. This initial favorable effect is enhanced by the fact that the service production process is perceived to be in line with the campaign. Interactive marketing in the buyer–seller interactions and the market communication campaign support each other. In the long term, image is improved by the fact that the organization consistently gives a good impression, by marketing communication as well as by reality and interactive marketing performance. The employees react in a similar manner. In the long term, they will probably consider their employer the best possible, if other internal activities or policies do not destroy this impression.

As these examples demonstrate, it is imperative that every communication effort is judged not only on its virtues as a communication effort, but in a much larger perspective, otherwise unwanted effects may occur.

Guidelines for Managing Market Communication

Some general guidelines for managing market communication can be identified.[9] Here nine guidelines are discussed:

1. direct communication efforts to employees;
2. capitalize on word of mouth;
3. provide tangible clues;
4. communicate intangibility;
5. make the service understood;
6. communication continuity;
7. promise what is possible;
8. observe the long-term effects of communication;
9. be aware of the communication effects of the absence of communication;
10. integrate marketing communication efforts and messages.

Direct communication efforts to employees. All advertising campaigns and most other mass communication efforts which are planned for various segments of existing and potential customers are also visible to employees. Employees are therefore an important "second audience" for these campaigns. Promoting the position of employees in external communication campaigns is a way of internally enhancing the employees' roles and adding to their motivation.

Capitalize on word of mouth. As demonstrated by the discussion of the *communication circle* and the vital role of word of mouth and customer references, good word of mouth makes customers more receptive to external marketing communication efforts, and vice versa. Moreover, good word of mouth can be considered the most effective communication vehicle. Therefore, if a firm has created good word of mouth, which is a message from an objective source (satisfied customers), it is a good idea to use the objective nature of word of mouth in marketing communication. Testimonials are examples of this.

Provide tangible clues. As services are intangible, communicating information about a service, especially to an audience of potential customers, can be very difficult. The intangible service can easily become even more abstract. Therefore, it is a good idea to try to make the service more concrete. For example, a firm may illustrate or demonstrate tangible items that are either involved in the service production process or relate to the service. This is a way of demonstrating the quality of the service. Showing the physical comfort of first-class travel on an airline in an advertisement may be a more effective way of giving potential customers something tangible to relate to and remember than an abstract visualization of luxury.

Communicate intangibility. Although it often is possible to offer tangible clues to a service, one should bear in mind that services are intangibly perceived. Emphasizing a tangible component in the service process, such as silverware and flatware for a first-class or business class airline service, may not always differentiate a service in a meaningful way. Instead, the challenge is sometimes to be able to cope with the intangibility of the service, because the differentiating appeal may be found in some aspect of the intangibility of the service. Showing parts of the service process, for example, a customer enjoying his leisure time at a beach while being on an inclusive vacation, or presenting testimonials of satisfied customers are examples of how to communicate intangibility of services.[10]

Make the service understood. Because of the intangible nature of services, special attention has to be paid to making the benefits of a particular service clearly understood. Using abstract expressions and superlatives may not lead to a good communication effect. The service and what it can do for the customer remains unclear. Therefore, it is important to find good metaphors that clearly communicate the service.

Communication continuity. Once more, because services are intangible, and because mass communication about services is difficult for the audience to grasp, there has to be continuity in communication efforts over time. A common tune in a TV or radio commercial or a common layout, picture or phrase in a newspaper ad, which continues from one campaign to the next, may be a way of making the audience realize more quickly what is advertised and what the message is. Typically, marketers feel that a communication theme is out of date and ready to change, just when the target audience has started to realize what the message is all about. In services, the marketer needs more patience than in the communication of physical products.

Promise what is possible. If promises given by external market communication are not fulfilled, the gap between expectation and experience is widened, and customer perceived quality decreases. It is often said that keeping promises is the most important single aspect of good service quality. Clearly, avoiding overpromising is essential in managing marketing communication. This has a clear connection with the next guideline.

Observe the long-term effects of marketing communication. As the discussion in the previous section demonstrated, a communication campaign which seems to be effective may have unexpected, negative effects when viewed over the long term. If promises that cannot be fulfilled are made, the short-term effects on sales may be good, but customers will become dissatisfied as they perceive reality. They will not return but will create bad word of mouth. Over the longest term, the image of the organization is damaged. The effects on employees are similar. Hence, a long-term perspective must always be taken when external marketing communication is planned and executed.

Be aware of the effects of the absence of communication. If there is no information available in a stressful situation, customers often perceive this as negative information because they lose control of the situation. It is usually better to share bad news with customers than to say nothing.[11]

Integrate marketing communication efforts and messages. As a previous discussion in this chapter demonstrated, customers are exposed to a number of different communication messages. These messages may be conflicting, thus creating a confusing impact. If communication messages through, for example, advertising, direct mail and the messages the service process are sending are contradictory, the effect is not trustworthy and the image of the firm may be damaged. Hence, it is important for the marketer to try to integrate all types of communication messages—planned, product, service and unplanned—so that customers know what the firm stands for and can develop a trusting relationship with the firm.

Developing a Relationship Dialog

In an ongoing relationship context it is not only the firm which is supposed to talk to the customer, and the customer who is supposed to listen. It is a two-way street, where both parties should communicate with each other. In the best case a dialog develops. A dialog can be seen as an interactive process of *reasoning together*.[12]

The purpose of a dialog is for two parties to develop a better mutual understanding of a problem and eventually to solve this problem. Hence, two business parties should reason together in order to understand a problem and if possible find a solution to it. The process of reasoning together includes the *willingness of both parties to listen* and an *ability to discuss and communicate* for the sake of achieving a common goal.

A connection between the firm and the customer has to be made, so that they find that they can *trust* each other in this dialog or reasoning process. The intent of this process is to build *shared meanings*, and develop insights into what the two parties can do together and for each other through access to a *common meaning* or shared field of knowledge.[13]

A dialog requires *participation* of the parties involved.[14] Participation takes place not only in interactions between the firm and its customers, but also through one-way messages, such as advertisements, brochures and direct mail as well as one-way Internet communication. Messages through these traditional communication media using old and new technologies should, however, contribute to the development of shared meanings and common fields of knowledge. When such messages through impersonal media *and* interactions between the customer and the firm support each other, *the two parties are reasoning together.*

There is a difference between one-way messages and two-way communication through impersonal media as part of a dialog. One-way messages have a sender and a receiver of those messages. A dialog requires the participation of the parties involved, and hence, in a dialog there are no senders or receivers, only *participants in the dialog process.* Therefore, a dialog resembles a discussion more than communication in a traditional sense.

Frequently marketers send out a direct marketing letter where they invite a response from the receiver. If the receiver reacts by responding, this is taken as the beginning of a dialog or even as the manifestation of a dialog. However, creating a dialog between a firm and a customer takes much more effort than this. A dialog is an ongoing process, where information should be exchanged between the two parties in a way that makes both the firm and the customer ready to start doing or continue doing business with each other. Both parties have to be *motivated to develop and maintain a dialog*, otherwise no real dialog will take place.[15] This, of course, goes for individual consumers as well as for firms.

To maintain a dialog not all communication contacts between the parties have to include an invitation to respond. An informative brochure or even a plain TV commercial may be part of an ongoing dialog, provided that the customer perceives that it gives information which is valuable for him to proceed in the relationship: for example it tells the customer what piece of advice to ask for or gives him information needed to make the next purchase. It is also important to remember that it is not only planned communication through planned communication media (TV commercials, newspaper ads, brochures, direct mail, Internet communication, sales representatives, etc.) that maintains a dialog. In a relationship the other sources of communication messages which were discussed earlier in this chapter (product and service messages, unplanned messages such as word of mouth referrals and public relations and the absence of communication) also send messages which influence the dialog. Products, service processes and interactions with fellow customers during the various service encounters contribute to the firm's total communication message, and thus are all forms of input into an ongoing relationship dialog.

Figure 11.4 illustrates a *Relationship Dialogue Process model*. The two outer circles demonstrate the two distinct communicative processes that are constantly in progress. The *planned communication process* includes communication messages which are planned and where separate and distinct communication media are used. As said above, all types of communication media are effective in this context (for example, TV commercials, newspaper ads, brochures, direct mail, Internet sites and adverts, sales representatives, exhibition stands and sales promotions; in Figure 11.4 a limited number of examples are indicated as illustrations only).

The other communicative process is a real process, where the customers' real interactions with physical products, service processes, customer contact employees, systems and technology, e-commerce processes, administrative and financial routines, etc. occur. This is labeled the *interaction process*. All episodes in this process include an element of communication. For example, a customer calls a helpdesk because he has been advised to do so in a newspaper ad or in a brochure, and he receives attentive service and the required information. This is a good sequence of planned communication (advert or brochure) and service messages (helpdesk support) which favorably supports the development of a relationship dialog. A customer may also have answered a direct mailing and in return received a brochure describing quick and attentive service. Following this sequence of dialog-oriented planned communication messages with the customer's response in between the two messages, the customer decides to purchase the service and enters into interactions with employees and systems in a service process. There he realizes that the service does *not* fulfill the promise of quick and attentive service. There are, for example, too few customer contact

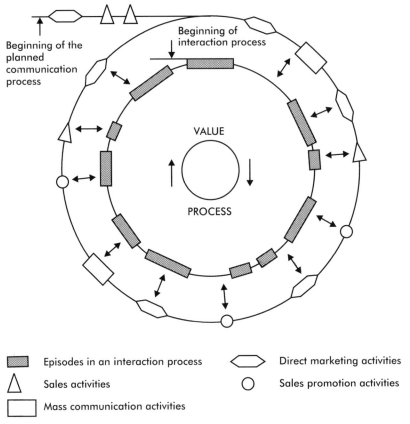

Beginning of the planned communication process

Beginning of interaction process

VALUE

PROCESS

	Episodes in an interaction process		Direct marketing activities
	Sales activities		Sales promotion activities
	Mass communication activities		

FIGURE 11.4   The relationship dialog process

employees and they do not have the time or desire to show a genuine interest in the customer's problem. What started out as a positively developing dialog is seriously damaged by the negative message following the customer's bad experiences with the service encounter. Messages from the planned communication process and the interaction process have not supported each other and, consequently, no favorable relationship dialog developed in the long run.

A successful development of a relationship requires that the two (or more) parties continuously learn from each other. The supplier or service provider acquires a constantly growing understanding of the customer's needs, values and consumption or usage habits. The customer learns how to participate in the interaction processes in order to get quick and accurate information, support, personal attention, well-functioning products and services, etc. This process can be characterized as a *learning relationship*.[16]

An ongoing dialog supports the development of a learning relationship. However, if the collaboration between a supplier and a customer does not include elements of learning, a relationship dialog will not develop. In fact, no real relationship will develop where the parties involved did not feel that a mutual way of thinking exists. The customer may still continue to buy from the same supplier or service firm, at least for some time, perhaps because the seller offers a low price, has a technological advantage over competing firms, or is conveniently located. However, this relationship is much more vulnerable to changes in the marketplace, to new competitors and to new alternative solutions that may become available.

Integrated Marketing Communication and Relationship Marketing

Simply planning and managing marketing communication through distinct communications media, even as a two-way process, is *not* relationship marketing and probably does not create a dialog, although communication efforts may look relational, such as personally addressed letters inviting a customer response. The marketer and the customer are not *reasoning together* to build up a *common meaning. Only the integration of planned communication and interaction processes into one systematically implemented strategy creates relationship marketing.* A true integration of the various marketing communication messages with each other and with the outcomes of the interaction process is required for the successful implementation of relationship marketing. Only in this way can an ongoing relationship between the firm and its customer dialog, which is a key element of relationship marketing, be maintained. This is indicated by the double-sided arrows between the two outer circles in the figure. In such a case customers' perceived value of the relationship is developing favorably, as indicated by the *value process* circle in the middle of Figure 11.4.

In conclusion, planned marketing communication takes place in the planned communication process in the figure. Product and service messages are created in the interaction process. Word of mouth referrals and other unplanned messages are a result of how customers and other parties perceive the two processes and how these support or contradict each other. As the relationship proceeds, the different types of messages develop in a continuous process and their effects accumulate in the minds of customers. If the planned communication process with its planned marketing communication (created in the planned communication process) is supported by the product and service messages (created in the interaction process) favorable unplanned communication *resulting in positive word of mouth communication* will occur.[17]

Both the firm and the customer should be expected to be motivated to communicate with each other. The customer should feel that the firm which sends a message is interested in him and argues convincingly for their products, services or other elements of the total offering. In such a situation the planned communication efforts and the communication aspects of the interaction process merge into one single two-way communication process, i.e. the two processes merge into a relationship dialog with the customer and the supplier or service provider as participants. The nature and content of word of mouth referrals will probably differ depending on how long the customer has been involved in the interaction process. It can be assumed that referrals by a long-standing customer will include more holistic expressions (such as "It's a great company") than detailed experiences and more value-oriented than price-related expressions.[18]

Summary and Questions for Discussion

In this chapter we dwelt upon marketing communications issues, and argued for a holistic integrated marketing communication approach. There are a number of types of sources of communication, but a need exists for a total communication approach where a sufficiently long-term perspective is taken. If this is not done, what is good marketing communication in the short term, may in the long term have a negative marketing impact on customers, because their real experiences with physical products and services are in conflict with the promises given by, for example, an advertising campaign. Furthermore, the effect on company image the longer this continues may be even more negative. A number of guidelines for marketing communication in services were presented. Finally, how total or integrated marketing communication and relationship marketing are related to each other was discussed and the development of a relationship dialog process was explored.

Questions for discussion

1. What is meant by an integrated marketing communication approach? Why is such an approach to marketing communications effective?
2. How can a marketing communication campaign (e.g. an advertisement campaign) which effectively creates awareness and generates sales lead to a negative marketing effect and ultimately damage a firm's image?
3. Discuss how well the planned marketing communication messages given by your firm, or any given firm, are integrated with the product, service and unplanned messages about your offerings to which customers are exposed.
4. What is a dialog? What is a relationship dialog?
5. How can a relationship dialog be created and maintained?

Further Reading

Arndt, J. (1969) *Word of Mouth Advertising*. New York: Advertising Research Foundation.

Ballantyne, D. (1999/2000) Dialogue and Knowledge Generation: Two Sides of the Same Coin in Relationship Marketing. *2nd WWW Conference on Relationship Marketing*, November 1999–February 2000, Monash University and MCB University Press (htp://www.mcb.co.uk/services/conferen/nov99/rm/paper3.html)

Bateson, J.E.G. (1985) Perceived Control and the Service Encounter. In Czepiel, J.A., Solomon, M.R. & Surprenant C.E. (eds), *The Service Encounter: Managing Employee/Service Interactions in Service Businesses*. Lexington, MA: Lexington Books, pp. 67–82.

Bohm, D. (1996) *On Dialogue*. London: Routledge.

Calonius, H. (1989) Market Communication in Service Marketing, In Avlonitis, G.J., Papavasiliou, N.K. & Kouremeos, A.G. (eds), *Marketing Thought and Practice in the 1990s*. Proceedings from the XVIIIth Annual Conference of the European Marketing Academy, Athens, Greece.

Dichter, E. (1966) How Word of Mouth Advertising Works. *Harvard Business Review*, **44**, November–December, pp. 147–166.

Duncan, T. & Moriarty, S. (1997) *Driving Brand Value*. New York: McGraw Hill.

George, W.R. & Berry, L.L. (1981) Guidelines for the Advertising of Services. *Business Horizons*, July/August.

Grönroos, C. (1990) *Service Management and Marketing. Managing the Moments of Truth in Service Competition.* Lexington, MA: Lexington Books.

Grönroos, C. & Lindberg-Repo, K. (1998) Integrated Marketing communications: The Communications Aspect of Relationship Marketing. *Integrated Marketing Communications Research Journal*, **4**(1), pp. 3–11.

Grönroos, C. & Rubinstein, D. (1986) *Totalkommunikation* (Total communication). Stockholm, Sweden: Liber/Marketing Technique Center.

Hui, M.K. & Bateson, J.E.G. (1991) Perceived Control and the Effects of Crowding and Consumer Choice on the Service Experience. *Journal of Consumer Research*, **18**, September, pp. 174–184.

Lindberg-Repo, K. (1999) *Word-of-Mouth Communication in the Hospitality Industry.* Helsinki/Helsingfors: Hanken Swedish School of Economics Finland/CERS Center for Relationship Marketing and Service Management.

Lindberg-Repo, K. & Grönroos, C. (1999) Word-of-Mouth Referrals in the Domain of Relationship Marketing. *The Australasian Marketing Journal*, **7**(1), pp. 109–117.

Mittal, B. (1999) The Advertising of Services. Meeting the Challenge of Intangibility. *Journal of Service Research*, **2**(1), pp. 98–116.

Peppers, D., Rogers, M. & Dorf, B. (1999) Is Your Company Ready for One-To-One Marketing? *Harvard Business Review*, **77**, January–February, pp. 151–160.

Schein, E.H. (1994) The Process of Dialogue: Creating Effective Communication. *The Systems Thinker*, **5**(5), pp. 1–4.

Schultz, D.E., Tannenbaum, S.I. & Lauterborn, R.F. (1992) *Integrated Marketing Communications.* Lincolnwood, Ill.: NTC Publishing Group.

Notes

1 This *total communication concept* was introduced in the 1980s. See Grönroos, C. & Rubinstein, D., *Totalkommunikation* (Total communication). Stockholm, Sweden: Liber/Marketing Technique Center, 1986. In the early 1990s the same notion reappeared in the form of *integrated marketing communications*.

2 See Schultz, D.E., Tannenbaum, S.I. & Lauterborn, R.F., *Integrated Marketing Communications.* Lincolnwood, Ill.: NTC Publishing Group, 1992.

3 Grönroos, C. & Lindberg-Repo, K., Integrated Marketing Communications: The Communications Aspect of Relationship Marketing. *Integrated Marketing Communications Research Journal*, **4**(1), 1998, p. 10. In a definition by the American Association of Advertising Agencies, as in almost every other definition, only traditional means of marketing communication, such as advertising, direct mail, sales promotion and public relations, are included.

4 Duncan, T. & Moriarty, S., *Driving Brand Value.* New York: McGraw-Hill, 1997.

5 Hui, M.K. & Bateson, J.E.G., Perceived Control and the Effects of Crowding and Consumer Choice on the Service Experience. *Journal of Consumer Research*, **18**, September 1991, pp. 174–184. See also Bateson, J.E.G., Perceived Control and the Service Encounter. In Czepiel, J.A., Solomon, M.R. & Surprenant C.E. (eds), *The Service Encounter: Managing Employee/Service Interactions in Service Businesses.* Lexington, MA: Lexington Books, 1985, pp. 67–82.

6 Lindberg-Repo, K. & Grönroos, C., Word-of-Mouth Referrals in the Domain of Relationship Marketing. *The Australasian Marketing Journal*, **7**(1), 1999, p. 115. See also Lindberg-Repo, K., *Word-of-Mouth Communication in the Hospitality Industry.* Helsinki/Helsingfors: Hanken Swedish School of Economics Finland/CERS, 1999. For a classical publication on word of mouth, see Arndt, J., *Word of Mouth Advertising.* New York: Advertising Research Foundation, 1969.

7 Lindberg-Repo & Grönroos, *op.cit.*

8 See Calonius, H., Market Communication in Service Marketing, In Avlonitis, G.J., Papavasiliou, N.K. & Kouremeos, A.G. (eds), *Marketing Thought and Practice in the 1990s.* Proceedings from the XVIIIth Annual Conference of the European Marketing Academy, Athens, Greece, 1989.

9 Many of these guidelines are from George, W.R. & Berry, L.L., Guidelines for the Advertising of Services. *Business Horizons*, July/August 1981, which still today is the best discussion of how to advertise services. Even though they focus on the advertising of services their guidelines are useful in a larger marketing communications context as well.

10 The need to develop advertising and other ways of communicating, based on the intangibility of services has been proposed by Benwari Mittal, who argues that intangibility may often offer better opportunities for differentiating a service in advertising than concentrating on tangible evidence. He discusses various strategies for communicating intangibility in advertising. See Mittal, B., The Advertising of Services. Meeting the Challenge of Intangibility. *Journal of Service Research*, **2**(1), 1999, pp. 98–116.

11 Grönroos, C., *Service Management and Marketing. Managing the Moments of Truth in Service Competition.* Lexington, MA: Lexington Books, 1990.

12 Ballantyne, D., Dialogue and Knowledge Generation: Two Sides of the Same Coin in Relationship Marketing. *2nd WWW Conference on Relationship Marketing*, November 1999–Februry 2000, Monash University and MCB University Press (htp://www.mcb.co.uk/services/conferen/nov99/rm/paper3.html)

13 Schein, E.H., The Process of Dialog: Creating Effective Communication. *The Systems Thinker*, **5**(5), 1994, pp. 1–4, and Bohm, D., *On Dialogue.* London: Routledge, 1996.

14 Bohm, *op.cit.*

15 Dichter, E., How Word of Mouth Advertising Works. *Harvard Business Review*, **44**, November–December 1966, pp. 147–166.

16 Peppers, D., Rogers, M. & Dorf, B., Is Your Company Ready for One-To-One Marketing? *Harvard Business Review*, **77**, January–February 1999, pp. 151–160.

17 These word of mouth effects of ongoing relationships are discussed in Lindberg-Repo & Grönroos, *op.cit.*

18 Lindberg-Repo & Grönroos, *op.cit.* See also Lindberg-Repo, *op.cit.*

Chapter 12

MANAGING BRAND
RELATIONSHIPS AND IMAGE

*If anyone can build a brand,
it is the customer. The
marketer can only create
favorable conditions for a
brand image to develop in
customers' minds.*

Introduction

This chapter discusses two important concepts in marketing, *brand* and *image*. First, the nature of a branding process and a definition of a brand is analyzed. Taking a relationship approach, brands are seen as brand relationships, which are affected by a number of brand contacts that occur during an ongoing relationship between a customer and a supplier or service provider. In the latter sections of the chapter the image concept is discussed. The functions of image on a company are discussed, along with possible reasons for a bad image, and actions that should be taken to improve image are presented. After having read the chapter the reader should understand the importance of branding for service providers and the characteristics of creating service brands, as well as the role of image and how image can be improved in various situations.

What is a Brand—A Traditional View

The *brand* concept is well established in marketing. The first brands in a modern marketing sense were developed a century ago. However, during the second half of the 20th century brands and branding became central issues in marketing. Most discussions of brands are related to physical products, especially consumer packaged goods. Only during the last 10 years or so has an awareness of the importance of creating service brands emerged. Now it is widely recognized that branding is a vital issue for service organizations as well.[1] However, research into service branding is in its infancy.

The American Marketing Association offers the following definition of a brand as "*A name, term, sign, symbol or any other feature that identifies one seller's product or service as distinct from those of other sellers.*"[2]

From a service perspective at least, two objections can be made: this definition misses the key characteristic of services as processes, and it excludes the customer.

First, it points out explicitly issues such as name, term, sign, symbol and feature, but does not address the key characteristic of services, which is that *services are processes* and the consumption of services can be characterized as *process consumption*. Because services are perceived in processes in which the customer normally also participates, this service process undoubtedly creates a distinction between the service of one provider and that of another. Of course, names, terms, signs and so on may also contribute to the brand, but the service process (or service production process) has to be at the heart of service brands, because it is there that the most profound impression on the customer's view of the service is created.

Second, this definition *excludes the customer*. Brands are viewed from the marketer's point of view as things that the firm creates. Much brand development, or brand building as it is often incorrectly labeled, has been based on such a perspective in practice. The marketer uses a number of planned marketing communication efforts to develop a distinct brand, and the customer is expected to form an image of the brand that corresponds to the intended brand.

In reality this is of course not the case, but this view of a brand and branding is due to the normally used branding processes for physical goods, where planned marketing communication is the main instrument used. In a physical goods context this has been a successful way of creating brands, because the good is preproduced and already exists when the branding process starts. The good always includes the same features, and if proper market research has been done customers like or accept these features and they correspond to the benefits the customers are looking for. Because the consumption of goods is *outcome consumption*, the customer does not become involved in the production process and the outcome of that process, the physical good forms a stable base for brand development through planned marketing communication efforts. A bottle or can of soft drink or a breakfast cereal cannot be developed into a successful brand if the customers do not like the taste of the soft drink or the breakfast cereal. Because in the case of physical goods the base for a successful brand already exists in the form of the goods themselves, the central part of the branding process automatically becomes a planned marketing communication issue using distinct communication media, such as television, newspapers, direct marketing and the Internet.

In services, the situation changes and the importance, and involvement, of the customer increases dramatically because a service as a process is a much less standardized base for branding. Second, the customer participates in that process, which is the basis for brand development.

Brand Image and Identity

One of the problems with the discussion of brands and branding seems to be the distinction between brand and brand image that is often made. A *brand* is the identity of a good, or a service, which the marketer wants to create, whereas *brand image* is the image of the good, or service, which is formed in the customer's mind. The term *brand identity* can sometimes be used as a description of the image of the brand that the marketer wants to create. Keeping apart the concepts of a brand and brand image somehow gives the impression that a brand can be created and can exist without the presence of the customer. According to this view, the customers form an image of a readily created brand. Following this line of thought the expression "brand building" has emerged. In reality, customers continuously receives inputs about the brand that is being created, and they relate to these *brand messages* on a continuous basis, to the extent that they observe them and react to them unconsciously, thus forming the brand image in their minds. This is the case with services as well as with physical goods. This can be put another way: a brand is not first built and then perceived by the customers. Instead, every step in the branding process, every brand message, is separately perceived by customers and together add up to a brand image, or brand for short, which is formed in their minds.

When including the customer in the branding process, there is no need to make a distinction between a brand and a brand image. *The brand as a concept is always an image*. Hence, in this book when we talk about a brand we always refer to it as an image in the minds of customers. In this way brand and brand image are synonymous.

The term *brand identity* can be used as a concept which describes the image of the brand that the marketer wants to create in the minds of customers. It is the goal to be achieved. A *brand* is the image that is actually formed in their minds. *Branding* is the process of creating this image.

As we have already noted in this chapter, "brand building" is often used to mean branding. However, this is incorrect and dangerous, because it gives the impression that the marketer can create a brand by himself. From this follows that after the brand has been "built" it can be offered to customers. In reality, as we shall see in the following sections, the customers' role is much more active in the branding process. Whatever the marketer does, it is the customer who decides whether an intended brand is developing or not. *If anybody builds a brand, it is the customer*. The role of the marketer is to create frames for the development of a brand in the minds of customers, by providing an appropriate physical product, service process and supportive communication using various means of planned marketing communication. Thus, the brand is formed. If the marketer has been successful in creating this branding "frame," the intended brand identity is achieved, otherwise it is not.

Brand Relationships and Brand Contacts

When the customer is given an active role in the branding process, our understanding of the brand changes. It is no longer something that exists in a vacuum, something that can be transferred to customers. Rather it is something that continuously develops and changes when the customer relates to the flow of brand messages, originating for example from employees, systems and physical product elements in the service process, from planned marketing communication, word of mouth and Internet chat groups. In this way a *relationship* between

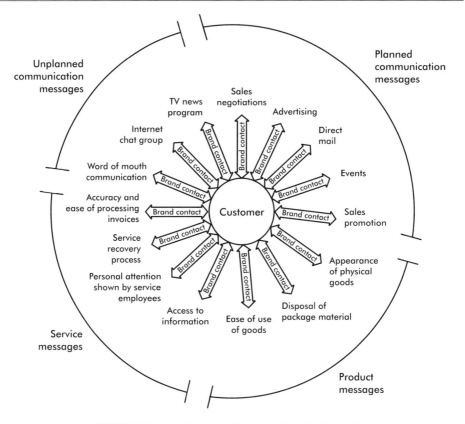

FIGURE 12.1   Brand contacts forming a brand relationship

the customer and the brand emerges and develops. *This brand relationship gives the goods, services or combinations of the elements of a solution meaning in the minds of the customers.*[3] Therefore, the brand, or brand image, is the consequence of how a given customer perceives his relationship with a brand, or *brand relationship*, over time.

Schultz and Barnes[4] state that a brand relationship develops in a series of *brand contacts* experienced by customers. They define a brand contact as an image and information-bearing experience had by a customer or a potential customer, regardless of where this experience takes place or what kind of experience it is. In Figure 12.1 examples of such brand contacts are illustrated.

In the figure a number of brand contacts are depicted to illustrate the concept. Depending on the situation, the types of brand contacts experienced by a customer will differ. For a soft drink messages and planned communication messages dominate, but service messages and unplanned communication messages may occur in the brand relationship. The marketer may, for example, develop a waste management system to collect empty cans. This system sends a service message to consumers of this canned soft drink. For some people this message adds favorably to the brand in their minds, for others it does not. For bank services, service messages and planned communication messages dominate, but product and unplanned communication messages may occur in the brand relationship. For

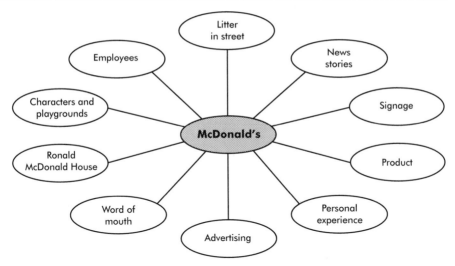

FIGURE 12.2   Sources of brand contacts in services: McDonald's. From Schultz, D.E. & Barnes, B.E., *Strategic Brand Communication Campaigns*. Lincolnwood, IL: NTC Business Books, 1999, p. 47.

example, gold credit cards signal prestige which for some consumers creates a positive extra to the bank brand in their minds. For others such cards do not have that branding effect. In an ongoing relationship the customer experiences various kinds of brand contacts on a continuous basis.

In Figure 12.1 the time perspective is missing. In the previous chapter we discussed the *planned communication process* (consisting of planned communication messages) and the *interaction process* (communicating product and service messages) and how, following a successful integration of the elements of these two processes a relationship dialog can be developed and maintained (see Figure 11.4). The elements of the two processes shown in Figure 11.4 are brand contacts forming the brand relationship at the same time as they are instrumental in the creation of a dialog. Hence, the value process in the center of that figure can also be termed a *brand value process*.

In Figure 12.2 sources of brand contacts of a service, McDonald's fast food, are illustrated. Customers' brand relationship is based on a variety of brand contacts. Managing some well and neglecting others, thereby perhaps letting them communicate negative brand messages, creates a unfavorable brand relationship where the brand value declines. As the figure clearly demonstrates, a service brand is a function of a large number of communication messages originating from a variety of brand contacts.

Brand Value, Customer-Based Brand Equity and a Relationship-Oriented Definition of a Brand

In this context *brand value* is the customer's perception of how valuable a given good, service or solution is to him in comparison with other alternatives. If the brand value declines over time, the customer will be more open to other solutions and more interested in communication messages from other firms. On the other hand, if the brand value increases, the likelihood that the customer will stay loyal can be expected to increase. In the same way it can be seen that brand value is important to suppliers, distributors and other network partners. They also perceive a brand value of a given supplier or service firm with which they do business or may do business.

A brand also provides value to the firm. The more customers consider a brand valuable, the more sales can be expected to be achieved. However, it is the value of the brand to the customer that is most important, because this is a basis for creating a brand value to the firm. The term *customer-based brand equity* is used to describe the brand value to customers. It is defined as follows:

> The differential effect that brand knowledge has on the customer response to the marketing of that brand. Equity occurs when the customer is familiar with the brand and holds some favorable, strong and unique brand associations in memory.[5]

Based on the ongoing development of the brand relationship the customer accumulates a specific *brand knowledge*, or *image of the brand*, which differentiates one physical good, service or solution or relationship, from others. This differential effect can be either positive or negative.

Finally, a brand can be defined as a brand image based on the notion of the customer's brand relationship:

> A brand is created in continuously developing brand relationships where the customer forms a differentiating image of a physical good, a service or a solution including goods, services, information and other elements, based on all kinds of brand contacts that the customer is exposed to.

According to this brand relationship definition it is meaningless to try to develop a brand without taking into account the relevant customers' and potential customers' ways of relating to branding activities. Also, in a relationship context, the expression "to build a brand" is inaccurate, because it implies that the marketer can initiate and implement activities which create the brand. This of course is not true. The brand is created in the mind of a customer following a flow of brand contacts—interactions between customer and supplier or service provider, including physical products, service processes, information, etc., and planned marketing communication elements—in the ongoing relationship between the two parties. Hence, when taking a relationship approach to marketing *creating brand relationships* is an accurate and descriptive term for the process of developing and maintaining a brand in the minds of customers, potential customers and other stakeholders.

If a brand relationship has been created and nurtured so that a customer feels attached to a given service and that this service, or any other type of offering, is different from competing services, active and favorable word of mouth can be expected to follow. The customer will feel motivated to talk about this service and will do so, thus keeping the total communication circle in Chapter 11 going. The marketer has achieved *brand involvement* from the customer.[6] Strong brand involvement means that a customer feels positively involved with the service process of a given supplier or service provider. This often makes the customer himself an effective marketer of the service.

How to Create Service Brand Relationships

When branding a service two circumstances have to be kept in mind:

- there is no ready-made, standardized product to be taken as a starting point for the creation of brand relationships. Instead the service (production) processes themselves are at the heart of the branding process.
- the basis for the branding process is most often the company itself and its service processes, not separate services (although firms may sometimes create services which are separable from the company itself).

In the context of physical goods the key issue in the branding process is usually planned marketing communication efforts using distinct marketing communication media (planned communication messages) implemented by the marketer, whereas the product itself is a supporting element. It should include features and benefits that the customers are interested in and relate to. Designing the product is of course a part of the branding process here, too, but in practice, it is often taken for granted that the product is readily designed to support the intended brand identity. Marketing communication (planned communication messages) is then the big most important aspect which a brand manager spends time and money on.

In the context of services, because of the process nature of services, planning and managing the service process is at the heart of the branding process. Planned marketing communication is only a supporting element in the branding process. If the service process leads to a negative brand value, no planned communication efforts can compensate for that. A service marketer who concentrates on planned communication as key branding activities is always at risk of failure. If the service process is not part of the branding process, it may easily provide negative brand contacts which effectively counteract the planned communication efforts. As will be discussed in Chapter 15, a customer-oriented service process that consistently includes favorable brand contacts is largely dependent on the existence of a supportive service culture in the organization. If such a culture exists, the service process will effectively contribute to a planned brand identity. Thus, an intended brand emerges when the values of the customers and the values of the organization do not conflict with each other, but complement each other.

We can summarize the branding of services in the following way. When creating brand relationships, bear the following in mind:

- the main task in the branding process is to manage the service (production) processes so that they provide the customers with positive brand contacts, which create a favorable brand relationship; whereas
- the planned marketing communication efforts are only supportive activities in the creation of brand relationships.

Furthermore,

- even a good service brand concept can and will be destroyed by a malfunctioning service process;

- the service process will not contribute to the emergence of an intended brand, if the brand identity that the firm is aiming at is in conflict with the corporate culture; and
- if the service process does not create a positive brand in the minds of customers, this cannot be compensated for by planned marketing communication supporting a brand identity that is not manifested in the service process and in the organizational culture.

Very few researchers have focused on how to create service brands. Leonard Berry presented a systematic view of how to "cultivate service brands" in order to develop customer-based brand equity.[7] His suggestions, which are based on an in-depth study of a number of firms providing excellent service, include four strategic viewpoints that should be taken into account in order for the firm to cultivate brand equity and to create brand relationships that pay off:[8]

- be different;
- determine your own fame;
- make an emotional connection;
- internalize the brand.

In Table 12.1 these four viewpoints are briefly described.

So far in this chapter we have discussed brand relationships and brands as brand images. In the rest of the chapter we will turn to another aspect of image,

TABLE 12.1 How to create successful service brand relationships. From Berry, L.L., *Discovering the Soul of Service*. New York: The Free Press, 1999, Chapter 10.

Viewpoint	Comments
Be different	Firms with good brands never offer their services as commodities. They innovate rather than imitate. Their service is presented differently (brand relationships different from those of competitors are created). Hence, the brand is distinct in the minds of the customers
Determine your own fame	Firms with good brands develop something that is important and valuable to customers. Differentiating the service from that of the competitors is not enough; the service has to be a valuable offering to the market. Branding is a way of demonstrating the firm's mission to the market. Therefore, such firms perform their services better than competitors. In this way good word of mouth communication is also created
Make an emotional connection	Services always have an emotional string attached. Therefore, firms with good brands always attempt to reach beyond the logical and economic aspect of the service. They create feelings of trust, affection and closeness. Brands should reflect customers' core values which often go beyond the logical
Internalize the brand	The brand relationship is to a large degree created in the service encounters of the service process, where customer contact employees often have a central role. In the service process they can support or destroy the branding process. Firms with good service brands internalize the brand relationships inside the firm. Internal marketing is important for service firms with good brands

the image of a company as an organization not directly related to the brand image. However, there is always a connection between the company image and the brand as an image. According to the model of Perceived Service Quality, the perception of the quality of a service is filtered through the image of the service provider. Hence, it should be remembered that company image and brands as images are closely related.

Managing Company Image

The image of an company or any other organization, international, nationwide, or local, represents the values customers, potential customers, lost customers and other groups of people connect with the organization. The image may vary depending on which group is being considered, and may even vary between individuals. However, there is some common perception of the organization, which may be very clear and well-known to some groups and unfamiliar to other groups.

Image exists on several levels. A large network organization, such as a restaurant chain, has an overall company image. In addition to this, a local organization, such as a local restaurant, has a local company image. If many outlets or offices belong to a local organization (for example, a range of auto rental locations belong to the same local franchise-holder, which, in turn, is part of a nationwide auto rental organization), each individual outlet may very well have an image of its own, in addition to an overall local image.

Company images on different levels are interrelated. The overall image influences the perception of the local organization (i.e. the local image) and the image of an individual office or outlet to some extent depends on the local image. Moreover, the various images can affect each other in different ways. Very large customers, such as financial organizations, are more inclined to be influenced by company image. Smaller and local customers are more interested in local image. For a local firm, overall company image and local image may be virtually the same thing.

It is important from a management point of view to note that a local unit is inevitably affected by the company image of the bigger organization of which it is a part. On the other hand, service operations in many respects are local, which presents a good opportunity for a local organization to develop an image of its own among its local customers. For example, if a hotel has a bad reputation on the corporate level, a specific hotel in that chain may nevertheless develop a strong and favorable local image, which helps to attract customers. This is probably most effective from a local perspective and in relation to enduring customer relationships, whereas customers who are tourists or just passing through town are more likely to be influenced by corporate, national image when making their purchasing decisions.

From the company's point of view, a distinct local image may be tolerated within limits, whereas too-different local images may be harmful as far as the pursuit of a corporate strategy is concerned. If the images of local hotels are too diverse, it may be difficult to maintain a clear company image. This, of course, is a very industry-specific, and even company-specific, issue.

However, again, services are local, and most customer relationships are local. Therefore, corporate-level management should not automatically try to stream-line the images of all hotels. Local business environments and societies are different, and a too-streamlined local image may damage business. The issue of streamlining or differentiating local images in relation to a desired corporate image is a management concern, where the strengths of disparate local images should be compared to the need for a clear corporate image. Sometimes there is a conflict involved, sometimes not.

The Importance of Image

A favorable and well-known image, overall company image and/or local image, is an asset to any firm, because image has an impact on customer perceptions of the communication and operations of the firm in many respects. The role of image is at least fourfold. For the sake of simplification, no distinction between overall organizational image and local image is made here.

- Image communicates expectations.
- Image is a filter influencing perceptions.
- Image is a function of expectations as well as of experiences.
- Image has an internal impact on employees as well as an external impact on customers.

First, *image communicates expectations*, together with external marketing cam-paigns such as advertising, personal selling and word of mouth communication. Here we will only consider customer relationships, but image works in a similar manner in relation to other organizations as well. Furthermore, image has an impact on expectations, and it also helps people to screen information, marketing communication as well as word of mouth. A positive image makes it easier for a firm to communicate effectively, and it makes people more perceptive to favor-able word of mouth. Of course, a negative image has a similar effect, but in the opposite direction. A neutral or unfamiliar image may not cause any damage, but it does not increase the effectiveness of communication and word of mouth either.

Second, *image is a filter* which influences the perception of the performance of the firm. Technical quality and functional quality are both seen through this filter. If the image is good, it becomes a shelter. Minor problems, even occasional more serious problems of a technical or functional quality nature, can be overlooked due to this sheltering effect. However, this only works for a short period. If such problems often occur, the effect of this shelter diminishes, and the company image will change. This filter has the opposite effect as well. An unfavorable image makes customers feel more dissatisfied and angrier with bad service than they would otherwise be. A neutral or unfamiliar image does not cause any harm in this respect, but it does not provide a shelter either.

Third, as briefly mentioned already, the *image is a function of the experiences as well as of the expectations of customers*. When customers develop expectations and experience reality in the form of the technical and functional quality of the service, the resulting perceived service quality changes the image. If the perceived service quality meets the image or exceeds it, image is reinforced or even improved. If the firm performs below image, the effect will be the opposite. Also, if the image is not clear or well-known to customers, it is developed and given distinct features by customer experience.

There is a fourth effect of image which is important to management. *Image has an internal impact on employees as well as the external effect on customers*. The less clear and distinct the image is, *the more this may affect employee attitudes* toward the organization as an employer. This, in turn, may have a negative influence on the employees' performance and thus on customer relationships and quality. On the other hand, a positive image, say, of a firm with excellent service, communicates clear values internally and may thus strengthen positive attitudes toward the business among its employees. Such a firm easily attracts good employees, too.

Developing Image

Frequently we hear managers say that the image of their firm is poor or unclear or old-fashioned. Far too often they try to solve this problem without analyzing it and the reasons behind the unfavorable image. This, in turn, leads to poor decisions and actions. For example, cosmetic actions, such as corporate image advertising campaigns or actions involving other means of mass communication, are often turned to in situations where they will not solve the actual problem. Such actions have a limited positive effect, or they may even have a negative effect.

There is a well-known saying that *image is reality*.[9] Therefore, image development or image improvement programs have to be based on reality. If the company image is unknown, but the firm performs well, there is a need for planned marketing communication. But if its image is bad and the firm does not perform well, the basic problem is different. The organization faces a serious problem, not only a communication problem.

First, one has to analyze why there is an image problem. Basically, there are two possible reasons: the organization is known but has a bad image; or the organization is not well known and, therefore, has an unclear image or an out-of-date image based on old customer experiences.

If the image is negative in one way or the other, *the experiences of the customers are probably bad*. There may be problems with technical and/or functional quality. In such a situation if management calls upon an advertising agency to plan an advertising campaign offering the message that the firm is service-oriented, customer-conscious, modern or whatever the message may be, the result will be disastrous. At best, the campaign will be a waste of money; however, there are cases where such actions have had much more serious consequences. A national retail chain in a European country suffered from a poorly service-oriented image. It invested extensively in a corporate advertising campaign which communicated good service, customer-conscious employees, a pleasant shopping atmosphere in its retail outlets, and so forth. In the short term, sales improved, but in the long term, sales decreased again to where they had been and even fell below this level. The organization's already bad image was further damaged.

The lesson is that because image is reality, if market communication does not fit reality, reality normally wins. An advertising campaign that is not based on reality only creates expectations that will not be fulfilled. If expectations are higher than they used to be, but reality has not changed, the perceived service quality is affected in a negative way, and the company image will be damaged.

If the image problem is a real problem, only real action will help. Real problems with the performance of the firm, its technical and/or functional quality, cause an image problem. Internal actions to improve the performance of the firm are needed if the poor image is to be improved.

If the company's image is unknown, there is a communication problem. The firm may be entering a new market, where it is unknown, or the nature of its business may lead only to sporadic customer contacts, which means that customers never develop an in-depth image of the firm based on experience. Also, the firm's reality may have changed so that it is, say, more customer-conscious and service-oriented than before, but this has not yet been fully appreciated by its customers. Therefore, the image is still negative or not as good as it should be. The image will improve eventually, when enough customers become sufficiently experienced with the new reality. However, if the firm communicates this change to the market by using an advertising campaign, this process will probably take less time. In these situations an image problem is really a communication problem, and improved marketing communication offers a solution.

Furthermore, it is always possible to support a company's image using various means of planned communication. The layout of Web sites, advertisements, brochures, packages and letterheads and the design of offices and delivery trucks may support a given image if they are in line with it. On the other hand, modern office design and advertisement layouts do not improve a firm's image if the performance of the firm is perceived as being old-fashioned and bureaucratic.

In summary, it is important to realize that image portrays what exists in reality; image is not what is communicated through planned marketing communication if the communicated image does not correspond with reality. When there is an inconsistency between real performance and communicated image, reality wins. The planned communication of the firm is perceived as untrustworthy, which damages image even more. If there is an image problem, management should analyze the nature of the problem thoroughly before taking action. A communication problem can and should be solved by improved communication. However, if there is a real problem, if the negative or otherwise unfavorable image is due to bad performance, the image can be improved only by internal action, the objective of which is to improve performance. Only in a second phase can planned communication be used, when the real performance-related reason for the poor image has been removed.

Summary and Questions for Discussion

In this chapter the issues of *branding* and *image* in service contexts were discussed. A brand develops in the minds of customers as a result of accumulated experiences of various brand contacts. In services, the service processes are at the heart of branding. Unlike physical products, planned marketing communication does not form a central instrument in the development of brands. Such communication can be seen as supportive activities in a branding process. If service processes do not function in a way that customers want to relate to, planned marketing communication cannot compensate for this. It was noted that customers can be understood to have *brand relationships* with ongoing service processes or relationships with a supplier or service provider including on-going interactions related to physical products, service processes, information, etc.

In the second part of the chapter the concept of image was discussed. It was noted that image exists on an overall organizational level as well as on a local and branch office level. When managing an image in services, it is important to realize that planned communication efforts cannot improve the image if a poor image is caused by problems in the service processes. Only actions that improve the quality of the service can improve the image.

Questions for discussion

1. What is a brand? What is the difference between brand, brand image and identity?
2. Which are the most critical aspects in the development of service brands?
3. What characterizes the branding processes of excellent service providers?
4. Identify brand contacts, analyze the brand in the mind of customers, and discuss customer-based brand equity for a given service offering provided by your organization, or any organization.
5. What is the relationship between a brand and a company image?
6. What could be the reasons for a poor image? How should a poor image be improved?
7. What are the functions of a company image and a local image?

Further Reading

Aaker, D.A. (1996) *Building Strong Brands*. New York: The Free Press.

Bennet, P.D. (1995) *Dictionary of Marketing Terms*, 2nd edition. Chicagol IL: American Marketing Association.

Bernstein, D. (1985) *Company Image & Reality*. Eastbourne: Holt, Rinehart and Winston.

Berry, L.L. (1999) *Discovering the Soul of Service*. New York: The Free Press.

Berry, L.L. (2000) Cultivating Service Brand Equity. *Journal of the Academy of Marketing Science*, **28**(1), pp. 128–137.

Duncan, T. & Moriarty, S. (1997) *Driving Brand Value*. New York: McGraw Hill.

Keller, K.L. (1993) Conceptualizing, Measuring and Managing Customer-Based Brand Equity. *Journal of Marketing*, **57**, January, pp. 1–22.

Lindberg-Repo, K. & Grönroos, C. (1999) Word-of-Mouth Referrals in the Domain of Relationship Marketing. *Australasian Marketing Journal*, **7**(1), pp. 109–117.

Schultz, D.E. & Barnes, B.E. (1999) *Strategic Brand Communication Campaigns*. Lincolnwood, IL: NTC Business Books.

Notes

1   Berry, L.L., Cultivating Service Brand Equity. *Journal of the Academy of Marketing Science*, **28**(1), 2000, pp. 128–137.

2   Bennet, P.D., *Dictionary of Marketing Terms*, 2nd edition. Chicago, IL: American Marketing Association, 1995.

3   See Schultz, D.E. & Barnes, B.E., *Strategic Brand Communication Campaigns*. Lincolnwood, IL: NTC Business Books, 1999, where the brand is also seen as a brand relationship.

4   Schultz & Barnes, *op.cit.*, p. 46.

5   Keller, K.L., Conceptualizing, Measuring and Managing Customer-Based Brand Equity. *Journal of Marketing*, **57**, January 1993, pp. 1–22.

6   See Lindberg-Repo, K. & Grönroos, C., Word-of-Mouth Referrals in the Domain of Relationship Marketing. *Australasian Marketing Journal*, **7**(1), 1999, pp. 109–117.

7   Berry, L.L., *Discovering the Soul of Service*. New York: The Free Press, 1999.

8   Berry 1999, *op.cit*. See also Berry 2000, *op.cit*.

9   See Bernstein, D., *Company Image & Reality*. Eastbourne: Holt, Rinehart and Winston, 1985.

Chapter 13

MARKET-ORIENTED ORGANIZATION: STRUCTURE, RESOURCES AND SERVICE PROCESSES

The firm should turn the organizational pyramid upside down—mentally and structurally. Its customers have done so long ago.

Introduction

This chapter discusses how to structure a service organization and manage service processes so that the service provider becomes customer-oriented. The first half of the chapter concentrates on structural issues, such as the use of marketing departments or other organizational solutions, so that a total marketing process can best be facilitated. The rest of the chapter discusses how to plan and manage the service (production) process so that the interactive marketing process of a service provider is successful. A *Service System Model* is presented. After having read the chapter the reader should understand the problems involved with organizing marketing in a traditional way in service contexts, and know how to develop the service process so that a good marketing impact is achieved.

The Marketing Process and the Marketing Department

In standard marketing thinking, which is based mainly on experience from consumer packaged goods, a marketing department is the organizational unit responsible for planning and implementing marketing activities. The logic behind this solution is, of course, that marketing can best be planned and implemented if all marketing activities are concentrated on and taken care of by a group of specialists. If marketing is seen as a function, as usually has been the case in the past, this also makes sense.

However, such logic requires that marketing as a function be separated from the other business functions and activities of the firm in a logical and manageable way. In mainstream marketing this way of organizing for marketing is considered appropriate. At the same time, however, an increasing amount of criticism of this has emerged over the last 20 years.[1] According to this criticism, in the emerging business environment marketing cannot remain a specialist function or be delegated to one department where the specialists plan and implement all marketing activities of the firm. This need for marketing to break free from the marketing department was recognized very early in service marketing research, especially in the Nordic school of service marketing thought.[2] The traditional military model with its hierarchical charts-and-box structure is seen as old-fashioned in today's business environment. Process organizations and project organizations have been used as a way of overcoming the problems in these functionalistic organizational solutions.

The development of *virtual* or *network organizations* also shows how traditional rigid solutions are becoming less effective. Such an organization[3] includes a nucleus which puts together and manages a network of other organizations and actors, and its assets, processes and people critical to the success of the business exist and function both inside and outside the conventional borderlines of the organization. In such organizational solutions, relationships and the process nature of marketing are natural ingredients.[4] Achrol and Kotler define a network organization in the following way:

> A network organization is an independent coalition of task- and skill-specialized economic entities (independent firms or autonomous organizational units) that operates without hierarchical control but is embedded, by dense lateral connections, mutuality, and reciprocity, in a shared value system that defines "membership" roles and responsibilities.[5]

However, a brief look at standard marketing textbooks and journals reveals that the traditional marketing department is still most often offered as the standard solution. The same is true for the practice of marketing. However, when moving the focus from the established areas of marketing, such as consumer goods marketing, to newer areas, such as industrial marketing and services marketing, one can see another picture, where marketing departments are less dominating or there are no formal marketing departments at all; where network organizations are developing. The long-term marketing perspective and the recognition of the characteristics of long-term customer relationships of service firms and business-to-business marketing demonstrate that marketing is not solely the responsibility for marketing specialists, but that *marketing activities are carried out throughout the entire organization.*[6] We thus have an organizational dilemma created by the fact that those who produce and deliver services carry out marketing activities for that service as part-time marketers, whether they know it or not and whether they accept it or not.

Figure 13.1 illustrates the position of marketing in a professional services firm, as in any service organization. The dotted areas indicate the marketing responsibilities of various functions. For example, the President, divisional and regional directors, consultants and assistants as well as all other employees have marketing responsibilities as part-time marketers, because what they say and do

Firm   Environment

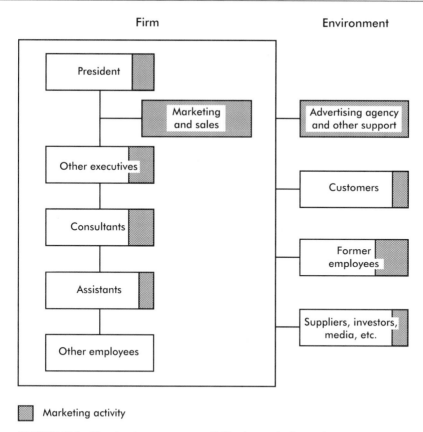

☐ Marketing activity

FIGURE 13.1 The simultaneous responsibility for marketing and operations among the personnel of a service provider. From Gummesson, E., *Total Relationship Marketing. Rethinking Marketing Management From 4Ps to 30Rs.* Oxford: Butterworth-Heinemann, p. 49, 1999.

and how they do it may have an important impact on the future buying and consumption behavior of customers. Simultaneously, they have responsibility for operations as well. In addition, people outside the formal organization may also make a marketing impact on behalf of the service provider. In the figure, clients and former employees are examples of such people. To take a bank as an example, the managing director, regional directors, loans director and tellers are employees who have similar marketing duties as part-time marketers.

The status of most employees in service operations is complicated. They have dual responsibilities because clearly a cashier, bank teller, waiting staff, hotel receptionist or maintenance engineer must first be able to take care of his technical duties. However, at the same time they all have to realize that the way in which they do their duties is a marketing task. Marketing activities are carried out by every employee who influences the customer relationships of the organization directly or indirectly. In every service organization there is a large number of *part-time marketers* who have *dual responsibilities*: to perform their tasks well in a technical sense and at the same time in such a way that they create a good marketing impact. In many service organizations these part-time marketers outnumber marketing specialists in the marketing department many times over. In the words of Evert Gummesson, this is because "marketing and sales departments (full-time marketers) are not able to handle more than a limited portion of the marketing *as their staff cannot be at the right place at the right time with the right customer contacts*" (my emphasis added).[7]

The main problem in most situations is the fact that the *marketing department* is mistaken for the much larger concept of a *marketing process* or *marketing function* as it is more often labeled. *The marketing process includes all resources and activities that have a direct or indirect impact on the establishment, maintenance and strengthening of customer relationships, irrespective of where they are in the organization.* The marketing department, on the other hand, is an organizational solution which aims at concentrating some parts of the marketing process into one organizational unit. Introducing and using a marketing department as an organizational solution to handling marketing may at some stage be an acceptable step. By doing so, management may be able to create an interest in and at least a theoretical understanding of the importance of marketing to service providers. The introduction of a marketing department may, however, also have a negative effect, because it may become an excuse for the employees to forget about the customer and concentrate on their "real" job. In the long term a marketing department, especially a dominating one, can easily become a trap, which in practice makes it difficult for the whole organization to think and perform in a true customer-oriented manner.

The Marketing Department as an Organizational Trap

In a consumer goods context, mixing the two concepts of the marketing function and the marketing department is not a serious mistake, because most of the contacts between the firm and its customers can be taken care of by the marketing department. The preproduced product, sales, advertising and other planned marketing communication efforts, price and distribution channels, is what the customers see and are influenced by. A very limited number of customer-influencing activities take place outside the marketing department.

Figure 13.2 shows the differences between the coverage of a marketing department in a consumer goods context and in a service context. The circles in the figure denote the total marketing process, and the dotted areas illustrate the proportion of total marketing that can be handled by a marketing department. As can be seen, the difference between consumer goods and services is remarkable.

In most service contexts the situation is the opposite of that characterizing consumer goods. Normally only traditional marketing tasks such as advertising, pricing and sales promotion can be handled by a typical marketing department, whereas other marketing activities carried out as part of operations and other functions are outside the realm of this department. In a service firm a large part of the marketing process is carried out by part-time marketers outside the marketing department. Nevertheless, growing service firms have, in the best consumer goods tradition, often been inclined to establish a marketing department, in order

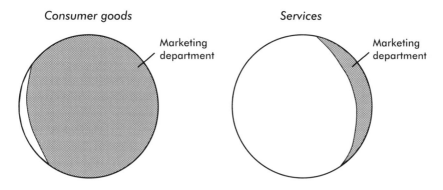

FIGURE 13.2   The marketing department versus the total marketing process

to maintain or even strengthen the market orientation of the firm. However, the long-term effect of this may easily be the opposite of that intended.

A traditional marketing department cannot usually be responsible for the total marketing process of a service provider. The introduction of such departments, on the contrary, easily influences the organization in an unfavorable direction. People working in other departments performing, for example, operational or administrative tasks stop worrying about their customer-related responsibilities and concentrate on handling what they see as their "real" job. The reason for this is clear. The firm now has marketing specialists in the marketing department; why should people in other departments bother any longer to do a marketing job? There is someone else to blame if things go wrong. The result is an increasing inward orientation and a less customer-oriented performance. The marketing department solution becomes *an organizational trap*.[8]

The above problem is very real. As one executive of a large insurance company recognized:

> Our corporate marketing department has become an organizational trap. Employees working in various operational departments and account servicing and administration concentrate on handling operations rather than focusing on their customer influencing activities. These customer influencing activities are thought of as being the responsibility of the corporate marketing department. Although these employees realize that they do have responsibility for maintaining customer satisfaction, they tend to focus on the technical aspects of their job. Performance is measured quantitatively and quality is enforced by penalties for mistakes.

If the negative effects of a marketing department are further reinforced by performance measurement systems and rewarding systems that focus on aspects of jobs other than customer relationship building and maintaining, the problems increase. In such situations these negative effects are not only psychological, but actual. Concentrating solely on the technical aspects of a job instead of paying attention to customer relationship aspects gives more credit to the employee; the reverse discredits the employee in the eyes of his superiors. Internal efficiency is seen as being more important than external efficiency and the delivery of good service quality and value to customers.

In summary, in service organizations marketing departments should not be introduced as *the* ultimate solution to problems where a market orientation is lacking or insufficient.[9] Sometimes they can, however, be used as an intermediate solution. There are good examples of firms that have either closed down or drastically reduced the size of their marketing departments and become very successful in the marketplace. In a later section a case study illustrating such a development is described.

Marketing departments may be helpful for planning, market research and executing corporate campaigns. As much marketing effort as possible should, however be planned and implemented in the line organization, where the immediate responsibility lies for rendering the service. A marketing department should always be introduced very carefully, so that no one in the organization misunderstands its role. Furthermore, it should never be given a dominant position. If and when such departments are introduced, careful attention should always be paid to the measurement and reward systems used for the *part-time marketers* outside the marketing department. *A marketing department is not an excuse for the rest of the organization to stop being responsible for customers.*

Organizing for Market Orientation: Inverting the Pyramid

A service organization should not be unnecessarily bureaucratic or have a large number of hierarchical levels. Customer orientation requires thoroughly understood and accepted responsibility for customers and the authority to take action to serve them. Large staff with substantial planning and decision-making authority may not have sufficient knowledge and/or the ability to make decisions quickly enough to serve customers well. The organizational hierarchy or pyramid should therefore have as few layers as possible between the customers and top management.

The customer contact personnel create value for customers. The rest of the organization, the back office functions, management and staff, form a support for buyer–seller interactions in service encounters. This support creates the necessary back-up for service production and delivery of the service encounters, i.e. for the successful handling of the numerous moments of truth so that they become well-utilized moments of opportunity which reinforce the customer relationships.

Management should not be directly involved in operational decision-making on an everyday level, but it should give the strategic support and resources necessary to pursue a service strategy. In a traditional "military structure" top management is often far removed from reality. In addition, top management is often surrounded by a staff organization which seals it off from the rest of the organization including the service encounters and the customers. This of course may have a harmful effect on strategic decision-making. Among other things it tends to draw attention away from external efficiency aspects and make top management overemphasize internal efficiency instead.

The old traditional view of the organization and the modern service-oriented organizational framework are schematically illustrated as pyramids in Figure 13.3. The transition in organizational thinking which is the result of a change in

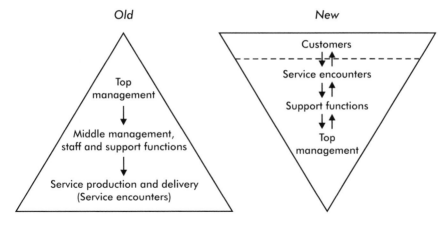

FIGURE 13.3   Serivce-oriented organizational structure

strategic thinking according to the principles of service management, means three things. First of all, priorities are changed. This is demonstrated by the fact that the organizational pyramid is turned upside down.[10] Top management is not the apex of the pyramid and thus the part of the organizational structure that immediately determines whether the strategy of the firm will be a success or failure. Instead, buyer–seller interactions involved in service encounters, including personnel, physical resources, information technology and operational systems, interacting with customers, are at the top of the organizational hierarchy. The organization's performance in service encounters determines whether it will be successful and profitable or not. Staff, other support functions and management are a prerequisite for success.

Second, the responsibility for customers and for operational decisions is moved from management to staff involved in the service encounters and thus those immediately responsible for the moments of truth. Third, the new thinking means that the organizational pyramid has to be flattened. This follows from the transition of responsibilities and authority from departments to service encounters. Fewer intermediate levels are needed.

The Relative Size of Organizations

Flattening the organizational pyramid and the decentralization of decision-making authority are necessities if service organizations are to become truly customer-oriented. Strategic decisions should be taken by top management at the bottom of the pyramid. Another rule is that decision-making should not be transferred from the service encounters in the pyramid. Some operational decisions have to be taken by middle management, but as much as possible decisions should be taken where the reason for a decision occurs.

It could be argued that a small service firm is frequently more customer-oriented than a big firm. In a smaller organization operational decisions are made more quickly and closer to the market. It is easier to develop good interactive marketing performance and to give better functional quality in such situations.

Internal marketing is less time-consuming and troublesome. On the other hand, there is more potential strength in large firms. In a bigger firm more resources can be used in order to develop technical quality.

Invisible systems and support functions, to which local branches can easily gain access, can often be developed centrally. This may give economies of scale as well as improve the efficiency of the total service system. It is also sometimes easier to attract better trained people to leading positions in a larger organization, although this is not always the case. Economies of scale can be achieved in production, administration, finance departments and so on, which are invisible to the market.

In summary, one may argue that *a growing service firm, in order to remain customer-oriented and be successful, will have to combine the strengths of being a small firm with the strengths of belonging to a large organization.* However, there is much evidence that demonstrates that this may be difficult to do. As an organization grows and tries to achieve the advantages of being a large company, far too often it destroys the potential strength of being a small company.

Successful Organizational Development: A Bank Case Study

The SCB Bank is a major bank operating nationwide in Scandinavia. In the past it suffered from low profitability and production-oriented attitudes among its personnel including branch managers and other middle management. Marketing was handled by a large marketing department at head office. In order to turn the bank into a customer-oriented and profitable firm, it was decided that it should concentrate on profitable services and market segments. An organizational development process was also initiated. This process included several stages, where each stage followed on from customer orientation problems perceived at the previous stage.

At the first stage, the central marketing department was closed down and a *customer contact development office* established. This office was only staffed by a few people, and reported directly to the managing director. The bank was divided into regional banks, and responsibility for marketing, including selling to individual households and organizational, was delegated to local branch managers. Marketing consultants were located at the regional level, to give marketing assistance to local managers. At the same time the bank stopped all national advertising, because management felt that purchase decisions should be made locally and are influenced by the performance of the local branch offices.

However, the local branch offices remained production-oriented, and did not actively take over marketing tasks. When the branch manager felt he should do some marketing, he called upon the regional marketing consultant. When the regional marketing consultants left the local office, interest in customer-oriented activities decreased again. Nevertheless, the situation had improved because the customer contact development office created guidelines for local planned marketing communication and sales campaigns and developed training programs for employees. These training programs were intended to help employees handle customer contacts and communication with customers.

In order to improve further customer orientation on the local level, the regional marketing consultants were removed, and the total responsibility for marketing was given to local branch managers. The local offices operated as profit centers. When the regionally located marketers were gone, and there was no central marketing department to turn to, the interest in marketing and customer consciousness among the branch managers increased; they had no choice but to start focusing on their customers. The profit center responsibility, accompanied by a higher decision-making authority, obviously supported this change of attitude.

The customer contact development office supported the branch office managers in training their personnel and in developing planned marketing communication and local sales efforts. Slowly, customer-orientation improved. The bank also became one of the most profitable in Scandinavia and has remained so.

Internal Service Providers and Internal Customers

Traditionally, customers are thought of as people or organizations external to a company. Such *external customers* have to be served in such a fashion that their needs are fulfilled and they are satisfied with the firm's performance. However, there are user-service provider relationships inside an organization as well and also between network partners. The customer contact employees and departments in a firm have to be supported by other people and departments in the firm, if they are to give good service to customers. For example, goods cannot be delivered in a service-oriented way if the warehouse does not supply the truck driver with the correct items, in good condition, and on time.

Every service operation is full of such *internal service functions* which support one another and the customer contact employees and departments interacting with external customers. Frequently, there may be many more internal service functions than external customer service functions.

To sum up, if internal service is poor, the externally rendered service will be damaged. However, it is often difficult for people involved in internal service functions supporting other departments to realize the importance of their performance to the final service quality. They never see "real" customers, and they can easily feel that those whom they serve internally are somehow just fellow employees and that the service they get does not affect external performance in any way.

A way of tackling the attitudinal problem of those who should serve "somebody else" (other than the ultimate customers) is to introduce the concept of *internal customers*.[11] This concept brings customer–service provider relationships inside the organization, as illustrated by Figure 13.4. There may be one or a whole range of internal service functions, each illustrated by a box within the larger box in the figure. These functions are *internal customers* to other internal service providers; they are also *service providers* to other internal customers. Finally, in the service process, the ultimate output is the external service received and perceived by the ultimate external customer. In a network context or in an

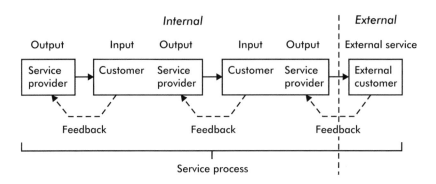

FIGURE 13.4   Internal service functions and internal customers

virtual organizational constellation the difference between what is internal and what is external becomes blurred. However, the same type of service provider–internal customer chains exist and have to be managed in the same customer-oriented manner, so that the final, ultimate external customer receives good service.

When the existence and importance of internal customer relationships are realized by personnel, it is much easier to change attitudes among employees. The concept of internal customers gives a totally new dimension to the tasks performed inside an organization. It is more easily realized that "a satisfied customer" should not only refer to individuals or organizations external to the firm.

Sometimes the internal customer–service provider relationships may be straightforward. However, frequently they can be complicated, with relationships in which both parties serve each other, or when the outcome of one department depends on the internal service provided by two or more other departments. It is mandatory that *such internal customers are served as well as external customers are expected to be served*. This means that generating quality into services is not the exclusive duty of departments visible to external customers. For example, the perceived quality of delivery services depends just as much on the performance of the warehouse as it does on the performance of the delivery function. Therefore, *the responsibility for producing good service quality is spread throughout the organization as well as in a network of cooperating organizations throughout the network*.

A Systems Model of Service Production

In many cases two or more departments may be directly involved with customers. Then it is of vital importance that these parallel processes are coordinated and perceived by customers as one single service process, otherwise service quality will deteriorate. If there is no one responsible for the customer in such situations, the customer may be sent from one person to another in an disorganized way. The organization does not take responsibility for the service,

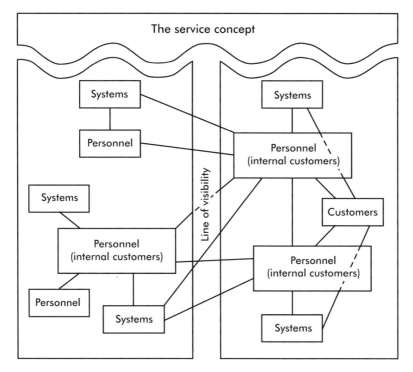

FIGURE 13.5 The service production system as a function of subprocess

and the customer is forced to take over the responsibility for getting service. This is bad quality.

Figure 13.5 shows how the service production process is built up by inter-relationships and interdependencies between a number of subprocesses. The external customer only gets in touch with part of a company's subsystems. As indicated in the figure, there is a *line of visibility*[12] dividing those parts of the process that customers immediately see and perceive from those parts that only indirectly influence the service quality perception. Psychologically, this sometimes causes internal problems.

Staff who do not deal directly with external customers may misunderstand their role in the service process. They may feel that what they do and how they do it is less important than the performance of those who are visible to customers. They do not see themselves as internal service providers. This is a mistake, of course, because the importance of servicing internal customers is forgotten. However, such a mistake is often understandable, because in many cases these interdependencies are not discussed and stressed enough by management. Figure 13.5 demonstrates the range and impact of the internal customer phenomenon. *Almost all staff have customers to serve, although customers may be internal ones.*

When developing the service production system various strategies can again be used. The part of the total system that is on the visible side of the line can be limited to, say, only one or two persons. Customers only contact them, and most of the service production process is taken care of internally. For example, an insurance company that directs all of its contacts through one single agent uses such a strategy. Such a strategy is applied, of course, to make it as easy as possible for customers to deal with the firm. In other situations the visible side of the line consists of a system or physical resources only, as in Internet shopping where the customer interacts with a Web site. Another strategy is to expose customers to many subprocesses. A restaurant, for instance, is normally forced to apply such a strategic approach. In this case the customer relationship is broader and more vulnerable. Mistakes that may occur do so under the eyes of the customer. Fewer problems can be taken care of as internal affairs. Of course, there are an unlimited number of options between these two examples. The main thing is that the service production process is designed so that perceived service quality can be monitored and kept at an intended level. Again, the needs and wishes of target customers should guide strategic decisions concerning where the line of visibility is drawn.

Where Is Marketing in the Organization?

To conclude the discussion about organizational structures, it is appropriate to ask "Where is marketing in the organization?" As marketing is what a firm does to get customers and to keep customers on a profitable basis, there is only one logical answer to this question:

> Marketing is definitely not only carried out in a marketing department of full-time marketing specialists. Marketing is everywhere in the organization, wherever brand contacts occur and wherever the customers' quality and value perception is formed as a basis for their willingness to continue their relationship with the service provider. Marketing is also wherever internal customers are served in internal office operations.

From this one could draw the conclusion that if marketing is everywhere and is the responsibility of no one department, then it is nowhere and nobody's responsibility. Indeed, service providers in practice often establish functionalistic marketing departments to take care of the marketing process, so that they can see where marketing is concentrated. Soon enough they realize that this does not work. *Marketing is everywhere in the sense that there has to be a marketing aspect in all roles, tasks and departments of a service organization*; in other words there has to be an appreciation of the customer in all tasks that are performed in the organization. *Part-time marketers* can be found in operations, finance, administration, research and development, human resource management, and all other departments. Furthermore, technology and systems that have an interactive marketing impact are also all around the organization and should be treated as *part-time marketing resources*, for example, when investment decisions are made.

   Of course, service providers also need someone who takes responsibility for market research, planned marketing communication (to the extent this is needed), pricing issues and other traditional marketing activities. Therefore, most service organizations need some *full-time marketers* to take care of the *traditional external marketing processes*. Full-time marketers should also be instrumental in internal marketing processes, normally working closely with human resource management. However, to organize them into a "marketing department" may be detrimental and ineffective. Such a department can give promises, and can do so effectively, but it cannot contribute to the fulfillment of promises. Finally, the better the organization takes care of its customers and provides them with good service quality and value, the less work there is for full-time marketers.

The only person who can be responsible for the total marketing process is the managing director, or locally the regional director, and more locally the outlet/branch manager. A marketing manager who is responsible for a department of full-time marketers can only be responsible for this department. However, a marketing manager is a customer specialist and should have an active role in the total marketing process as an internal consultant to top management.

Another conclusion to be drawn is that marketing cannot be organized in a service firm. *Marketing can only be instilled in the organization.* However, it has to be systematized in some way. Here are a few guidelines:

1. instilling a *marketing attitude of mind* in people in all departments and enabling customer-oriented performance as well as supervisory and reward systems that reinforce such performance is one aspect of how to organize marketing in a service firm;
2. clarifying the responsibility for the customer of top management and all line managers is another aspect of marketing;
3. the service provider may of course also need to use traditional external marketing efforts to some extent, and to do market research. Therefore, resources for doing this internally and/or externally should be secured. Many traditional marketing activities can be taken care of by the local line organization, but a central marketing group or staff with full-time marketers may be required as well;
4. it is important to make sure that that this central group does not become a dominant marketing department; and
5. full-time marketers have an important role in the marketing process, but it is the part-time marketers and the interactive marketing process that are at the heart of marketing services.

In conclusion, when organizing marketing in a service firm the following should be kept in mind.

- Successful marketing requires a *marketing attitude of mind* throughout the organization, because the central part of marketing services takes place in the service encounters and in administrative support to service encounters through customer-oriented *part-time marketers* and service-oriented systems and technologies (the *interactive marketing process*).
- Responsibility for marketing lies within the line organization, and the managing director has to accept the ultimate responsibility for marketing.
- Many of the traditional external marketing activities that may be needed can be handled locally in the line organization, but a central marketing staff of *full-time marketers* may sometimes also be required to take responsibility for centrally implemented marketing activities as well as to act as internal consultants to top management in customer-related issues and in internal marketing.

The following sections of this chapter shall look more closely at the service process and discuss how it can be developed so that a good interactive marketing effect can be achieved.

The Consumption Process from the Customer's Point of View

To identify the resources required to produce a service, an *analysis of the consumption process* of the customers can be carried out. Because of the basic characteristics of services, the service process includes a range of activities and subprocesses. Because service consumption can be characterized as *process consumption*, the customer perceives these. Some production subprocesses, for example, administrative activities, are not perceived directly by the customer, since only the results of these activities are consumed. However, often a substantial part of the service production process takes place simultaneously with the consumption process. Moreover, part of consumption may take place afterward, as is the case with hairdressing or laundry services.

From a service quality point of view, the observation that production and consumption are simultaneous processes is of vital importance. In this way the vital functional quality of the process is perceived. As pointed out earlier, excellent functional quality is a necessity in service competition. The perception of very good technical quality of the output of the process is easily destroyed by a bad functional quality impact.

First, however, it is essential that the firm knows who its customers really are and understands how they make their decisions. It is not enough to have a fair knowledge of the composition of customer segments; a more detailed understanding of individual customers is required.

The Customer as an Individual and Part of a Group

The customer concept, consumer behavior, or organizational buying behavior will not be discussed here in any detail. Instead, a few important issues in connection with the customer concept will be addressed. First, it is important to realize that the customer may either be an individual or a member of a group. For many consumer services, such as hairdressers, airline travel and restaurants, the customer is a single person who purchases and consumes the service. Sometimes the customer is a group of individuals. The service may be purchased by one person, a *purchasing agent*, but will actually be used or consumed by other persons.

The services and the performance of the organization should, of course, be geared to the needs and wishes of the customer. However, if many people are involved in the role of customer in the relationship between the service provider and buyer, *the whole group is the customer*. All these agents of the buyer—purchasing agent, users, formal decision-maker and others—together form what is often called a *buying center*.[13] Every individual involved in the relationship is equally important. Frequently, the purchasing agent, with whom the salesperson interacts, is considered *the* customer. The other people involved, for example, when the service is used by the buying organization, are often considered less important.

For example, when a sales representative from a cleaning company negotiates with a buying firm, he most often only negotiates with a purchasing agent. If the potential customer is a smaller firm, the sales representative may be in contact with an office manager or even the managing director. In any case, he hears the views of a person who is not involved in using the service of the cleaning firm. There may be internal differences in the buying firm concerning what is needed. The purchasing agent, however, may not represent all these opinions, and probably not the view of the users. He may be more interested in the technical specifications of the service and in price than in how the cleaning firm functions in reality. The sales representative gets the views and perspectives of the purchasing agent, and gives promises that satisfy that individual. However, when the cleaning firm starts to operate the assignment, the users of the service in the offices, factories or service locations may be dissatisfied with the firm. They may dislike the way the firm functions, or they may be dissatisfied with the technical specifications of the service, or they may like their employer to pay more for a higher level of service. For one reason or another, the service is considered less good than anticipated. This opinion eventually spreads to the decision-maker and the purchasing agent. The customer is a group, although the salesperson may not meet anyone other than the purchasing agent. Those providing the service will be in contact with many more representatives of the buyer, and they, too, have an impact on the future purchasing and usage behavior of the customer. The development of *key account management*[14] principles is a way of coping with these kinds of problems as far as important customers are concerned.

Viewing the customer too narrowly may turn out to be a serious mistake. The users of the service are the people who perceive the quality of the services. If they are not satisfied with what they get, the whole group, including the purchasing agent, may eventually become discontented with the service provider. If and when this happens, it will be difficult, probably impossible, for the salesperson to keep the customer relationship alive. The customer will be lost. Replacing a lost customer with a new customer is almost always more expensive than reselling and cross-selling to existing customers. Marketing to a new, potential customer may be five or six times more expensive than marketing to an existing customer; another way of saying this is that to get repeat business from an existing customer it costs only 15–20 per cent of what it costs to acquire a new customer.

What Do We Need to Know About Our Customers?

What makes a given customer want a certain type of service? What makes the customer purchase it from a certain service provider? The reactions of customers are based on their *expectations*, but these are a function of a whole range of internal and external factors.

The *needs* of a customer form a basic factor, which directs expectations toward a certain type of solution. An organization may form its needs in a more complicated way than a single customer or a household. In principle, however, an organization or a person's need is some sort of a problem that requires a solution. This solution may be solved in a number of ways. For example, house cleaning can be managed by buying proper equipment and by a do-it-yourself approach, or one can take care of it by purchasing a service. In both cases there are a number of options available in relation to what to buy, and where to buy the necessary equipment or service.

It is, however, essential to realize that needs alone do not determine what kind of service a person looks for. Needs determine *what* the potential customer wants, and many service providers can usually produce an acceptable solution in this respect. In addition, customers also have certain *wishes* in relation to *how* they want the service provider to treat them. This normally narrows the scope of options available. For example, almost any retailing bank can provide an individual with banking services, but not every bank manages to treat customers in a way they are pleased with (compare the *technical* and *functional* dimensions of customer perceived service quality.) This is also related to the *value system* of the customer, which determines what kinds of solutions to a problem are considered acceptable and what is considered out of the question. Environmental concerns are examples of aspects in the value system that exclude some otherwise possible need-satisfying solutions. Some consumers do not want to use cosmetics which have been developed using animal testing, and they will not buy such products.

Furthermore, the service or physical product purchased has to fit the *customer's internal value-generating processes*, so that it creates value for him (or for the organization he represents). For example, a firm that looks for a sales supporting database system wants a solution that makes it possible to easily find out, save, change and retrieve information about customers in order for the sales representatives to develop an understanding of the needs, values and internal processes of customers and offer them services that suit their needs. Any solution that does not fit this process will not interest the firm, because it will not create the value they want.

To sum up, in order to thoroughly understand customers and potential customers the marketer needs to acquire information about the following:

- customer needs;
- the value systems of customers;
- the internal value-generating processes of customers.

Needs, wishes, value systems and internal value-generating processes of customers are of vital importance for the development of *customer expectations*. However, expectations are also formed by external factors (this was discussed in more detail in previous chapters). For example, what family acquaintances and business associates say about a given service provider (word of mouth communication) has an impact on the formation of the expectations as well as what newspapers and trade magazines write about the service firm and its services.

This is often of great importance. Moreover, planned marketing communication activities, such as personal selling and advertising campaigns, influence expectations. Finally, the overall company image and local image also influence expectations.

Case Study: Selling ¼-Turn Fasteners, but Not Any ¼-Turn Fasteners

Dennis Holmlund, sales representative of Unilink Co, marketing Fairchild Fastener products and specialty fastening systems to industrial markets, had negotiated for some time with a major customer in the industrial freezer market about fastening solutions to the customer's freezers for supermarkets. The machinery of the freezers is accessible through a small door which should be easily opened and closed. He had offered ¼-turn fasteners which were very easy to operate. The buyer was not convinced that this was a good solution, which puzzled Mr Holmlund, because he knew that an easier-to-use fastener did not exist on the market, and that price should not be a problem. The fastener he suggested clearly fulfilled the needs of the customer.

Then he accidentally overheard a discussion between the buyer and another executive of the freezer manufacturer when they were talking about the safety of toddlers and small children. It turned out that the customer did not feel that they could offer freezers to supermarkets where the freezer door could be opened by mistake and which could therefore be hazardous to small children, who opened the door out of curiosity. An easy-to-operate fastener was an excellent solution but nevertheless did not fit the value-generating process of the customers. The values of the freezer manufacturer focused on concern for the safety of the small children accompanying their parents in the stores, and did not accept the fastener, regardless how well it fulfilled the basic need.

When these values and value-generating processes of the customer were revealed, Mr Holmlund asked Fairchild Fastener to make a change to the basic fastener, so that it was still an easy-to-operate ¼-turn fastener, but was impossible to open by mistake. Hence, the values of the customer, i.e. not to offer solutions that could be hazardous to toddlers and small children in supermarkets and grocery stores, were met.

Customer Segments and Target Groups

Customers have differing needs and/or wishes about how they want to be treated. An organization can, therefore, very seldom satisfy the needs of every potential customer in a similar manner. It should not even try to solve everyone's problems. Customers have to be divided into homogeneous *segments* which are sufficiently different from each other. One or a few such segments are then chosen as *target groups* of customers. In service contexts it is often difficult to satisfy target groups of customers with too widely varying needs and wishes. Because customers frequently meet and interact with each other, they influence fellow customers' perception of the service. For example, a family having a picnic on a Saturday afternoon in the park does not mix well with a bunch of beer drinkers. If the firm goes for segments that are very different from each other, it is usually a good idea to keep them apart. Finally, it should be noticed that a service production system cannot usually take care of satisfying too diverse needs and wishes. This follows from the fact that services are complicated phenomena and service production is a complicated task.

It is also important to remember that customers in a relationship with a service provider often want to be recognized and treated as individuals, even though they are part of a larger segment. Therefore, the firm should not be blinded by the fact that it may have mass markets and may use the segment concept for analytical purposes. Customers often want to be treated as *segments of one*.[15] Direct customer contacts occur naturally in most services and they give a good starting point for the individual treatment of customers. In addition, the information technology available to firms today also supports individualistic treatment of customers.

Relating the Service Package to the Consumption Process

Having discussed the nature of customers in previous sections, we now turn to the issue of how the customer and the consumption process can be incorporated into the service process. Doing this is of utmost importance because of the nature of services and the inseparability of large and critical parts of production and consumption. The service consumption process can be divided into three phases.[16]

1. The joining phase.
2. The main consumption phase.
3. The detachment phase.

The *joining phase* is the first stage of the consumption process, where the customer gets in touch with the service provider in order to buy and consume a core service, for example, elevator maintenance. In this phase facilitating services are mainly required, for example, telephone contact to the elevator maintenance firm in order to get hold of a service technician. Some supporting services may be used, for example a toll-free number or an easy-to-use Web site which makes it easy for the customer to get in touch with the maintenance firm.

The *main consumption phase*, or simply *consumption phase*, is the main stage of the total service consumption process. In this phase the needs of the customer have to be satisfied, or his problem has to be solved.

Hence, the core service or services are consumed at this stage. For example, the elevator is serviced. Furthermore, there may be some facilitating services (for example, a shelter surrounding the work space) and supporting services (for example, instructions to people normally using the elevator directing them to the stairs and telling them when the job is expected to be finished). In the *detachment phase* the customer leaves the service process. This often requires some facilitating services (for example, the service technician fills in a report and hands it over to the caretaker or another representative of the customer). Supporting services may be used here, too.

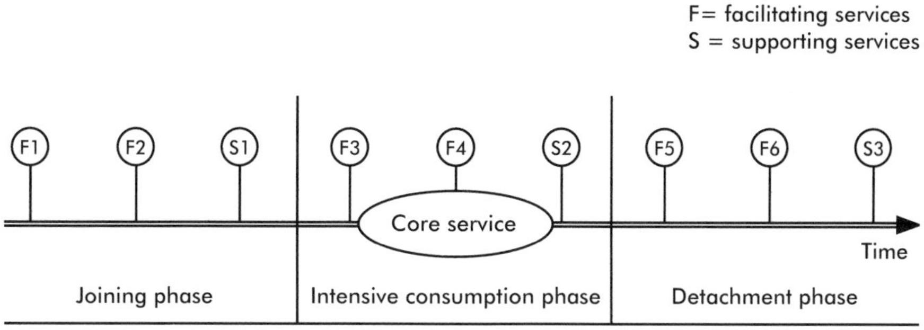

F= facilitating services
S = supporting services

FIGURE 13.6   The service package and the service consumption process. Based on Lehtinen, J., *Quality Oriented Services Marketing*. University of Tampere, Finland, 1986, p. 38.

In Figure 13.6 the service consumption process and the types of services related to the three phases of the process are schematically illustrated. If, for example, we look at a full-service restaurant, the *joining phase* may include table reservations (F1) and cloakroom services (F2) as facilitating services, and valet parking (S1) as a supporting service. During the *main consumption phase* the core service, which may be a three-course dinner, is consumed. The table setting (F3) and the performance of the waiting staff (F4) are facilitating services, and live music (S2) may be a supporting service. In the *detachment phase* when the customer leaves the restaurant, some facilitating services are needed, for example, paying the check (F5) and again the cloakroom services (F6). Valet parking (S3) may be used as a supporting service again at this stage.

It should be observed, however, that this model only takes into account the components of the basic service package (core service as well as facilitating and supporting services and goods). The next step is to take the components of the Augmented Service Offering (see Chapter 7); that is, *accessibility*, *interactions*, and *customer participation*, into account so that the functional quality dimension of the process is also covered.

The Service System Model

The Service System Model illustrated in Figure 13.7 can be used for analyzing and planning the service process or system.[17] In this figure the various quality-generating resources are combined in a systematic way. The large central square illustrates the service-producing organization from the customer's perspective. From the producer's point of view there may be several functions or departments involved, but the customer sees it as one integrated process or system. The customer is located inside the square because he is a resource participating in the service process and therefore an integral part of the Service System Model. Yet, in most service processes, customers are treated as an outside factor only. This, of course, is due to a manufacturing-oriented view of the role of the customer. Customers are not distant and outside the organization as they are in a mass manufacturing context. Instead, they interact with parts of the organization in the service process and are a service production resource.

The *line of visibility* divides the part of the organization that is visible to customers from the part that is invisible. To the right, outside the main square, the means of influencing the *expectations* of customers are illustrated, such as their needs and wishes, their previous experiences, overall company and local image, word of mouth, external planned marketing communication and absence of communication.

To the left of the square are the *business mission* and the corresponding *service concepts* which, like umbrellas, should guide planning and managing the Service System. At the bottom of the main square is the *corporate culture*; that is, the shared values that determine what people in the organization think and appreciate. This culture is always present. Sometimes it has a substantial impact on the employees, sometimes it is more vague. If the culture is not service-oriented, it creates problems for an organization providing services. This issue will be returned to later in Chapter 15.

The Interactive Part

The visible or *interactive part* of the Service System Model (see Figure 13.7) corresponds to the service encounter where the customer meets the service organization. It consists of customers and the rest of the quality-generating resources which the customers interact with directly. Here the *moments of truth* take place. The quality-generating resources in the interactive part are as follows:

- customers involved in the process;
- customer contact employees;
- systems and operational routines; and
- physical resources and equipment.

Customers are directly involved in the service system as a quality-generating resource. Because of the nature of service production and consumption, customers are not simply passive consumers. At the same time they consume the service, they also take part in production of that service in an active way; sometimes more (as when at the hairdressers or having a three-course dinner at a gourmet restaurant) sometimes less (as when using a freight forwarder's service). In some cases customers interact with a large service system when staying at a hotel, but in other situations they are in touch with only a limited subsystem, as when operating an automatic teller machine. Sometimes several customers are present simultaneously in the process interacting with each other. In other situations, as in the case of telephone communication, the service concept is to provide technology and a system that make it possible for customers to contact each other. Irrespective of the nature of the situation, customers, however, actively take part in the process and in service production.

Employees directly interacting with customers are called *customer contact employees*. Anyone can be a contact person, irrespective of which position or job he may have in the hierarchy. Interactions that take place may be face-to-face contacts or interactions over the telephone or even by e-mail, fax, or letter. A manager or supervisor may also be a contact person if direct customer contacts,

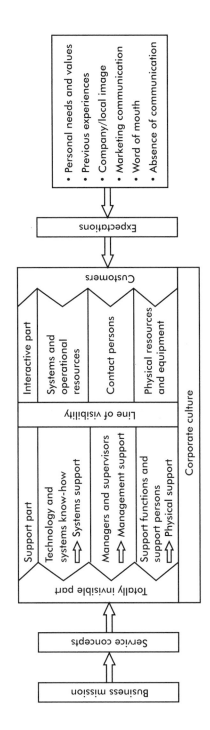

FIGURE 13.7 The service system model. From Grönroos, C., *Service Management and Marketing. Managing the Moments of Truth in Service Competition.* Lexington, MA: Lexington Books, 1990, p. 208.

on a regular or irregular basis, are part of his job. Frequently, contact personnel are the most crucial resource for a service provider. Systems, technology and physical resources are a valuable support, but most service organizations depend more on their contact staff than on other resources. Contact staff are in a position to recognize the wishes and demands of customers in the moments of truth by watching, asking questions and responding to the customers' behavior. Furthermore, they are able to instantly follow up on the quality of the service rendered and undertake corrective action as soon as a problem is observed. However, more and more service processes are designed so that no contact staff are present, at least not on a regular basis. This makes the process more vulnerable when service failures occur.

Systems and routines consist of all operational and administrative systems as well as work routines of the organization. Queuing systems, call center systems, how to cash a check in a bank, how to operate a vending machine or how to make purchases on a Web site are examples of such systems. There are a vast number of systems and routines that influence the way of consuming the service and performing various tasks. The systems can be more or less service-oriented. A complicated document which customers are supposed to fill in forms a system that is not service oriented. This normally means that the perceived service quality is poorer than it otherwise would be. A manufacturer of goods has a range of such systems, which may be performed as administrative tasks without taking the customer into account or turned into service-oriented procedures. Such systems include research and development, the installation of machines and equipment, deliveries, customer training, quality control at the customer's premises, claims handling, billing or the services of telephone receptionist.

These systems and routines have a double impact on service quality. First, they *directly influence the quality perception of customers*, because customers have to interact with systems. If they feel comfortable with a certain system, it is probably service-oriented. If they feel that they are forced to adjust to a system, however, there is room for improvement. Quality is destroyed or damaged by the system. Second, the systems and routines have *an internal impact on employees*. If a certain system is considered old-fashioned, complicated or not service-oriented, employees who have to live with the system will get frustrated. This, of course, influences motivation in a negative way.

Physical resources and equipment include all kinds of resources used in the service system. Computers, documents and tools belong to this category. Some of these physical resources are a prerequisite for the good technical quality of the output. They also influence, however, functional quality because customers may find it more or less easy to use them in self-service tasks and they give a favorable or less favorable impression on customers. Other physical resources only have an impact on functional quality. The interior of waiting rooms is an example of such physical resources. Physical resources and equipment used in the service process have an internal effect on employees similar to that of the systems. Physical resources and equipment form the *serviscape*[18] of the service process, where customers, contact staff and systems and resources work together. The serviscape can also include objects, music and even aromas that support a positive perception of the ambience and physical elements of the service encounter. All these elements form the visible part of the service process.

Every single part, including the customers, has to match the total system if good quality is to be perceived.

The Impact of the Support Part

Behind the interactive part, where the customer directly encounters the service organization, there is the *line of visibility* (see Figure 13.7). Customers seldom see what is going on behind this line, and they often do not realize the importance of the service production that takes place there. This causes at least two types of problems for the service provider. First, what takes place behind the line is not always appreciated as much as it should be by customers. Because of this, customers do not realize how much the service production there contributes to service quality. Irrespective of whether good quality, especially good technical quality, is produced here, customers probably perceive a bad service quality if the interactive part adds mediocre or worse quality. What often happens is that good technical quality produced behind the line of visibility is damaged by bad functional quality produced in the Service System in front of this line.

Second, customers may not understand why a given service has a certain price, because they do not realize how much is done behind the line of visibility. It may be difficult to explain why the price is so high, when the visible service production process may seem uncomplicated and therefore in the minds of customers should not justify the real cost and price level.

The service provider, on the other hand, may interpret the importance of the supporting back office in another way which is equally wrong. Because the service provider knows how much of the total value of a service is produced in the back office invisible to customers, he can assume that customers also know and appreciate this, and consequently enough attention is not paid to the customer orientation of the visible and interactive part of the service process. This may turn out to be a serious mistake.

Components of the Service System Behind the Line of Visibility

What happens in the supporting and invisible part of the organization has an impact on what can be accomplished by the interactive part. This support is sometimes a major prerequisite for good service. There are three kinds of support to the interactive service production (see Figure 13.7):

- management support;
- physical support; and
- systems support.

The most important type of support is *management support* which every manager and supervisor should provide to their staff. Managers and supervisors maintain corporate culture, and if the firm wishes to be characterized by a *service culture* (this concept is discussed in detail in Chapter 15), they will have to support the values of such a culture. They are responsible for shared values and ways of thinking and performing in their work groups, teams and departments. If employees are to be expected to maintain service-oriented attitudes and behaviors, managers are the key to success. The manager is the leader of the troop. If the boss does not provide his team with a good example, and if he is not capable of encouraging them to be service-minded and customer-conscious, the organization's interest in its customers and in giving good service will decrease. From this follows deteriorating functional quality of the service production process and perhaps even difficulties in maintaining the technical quality of the outcome of the process.

Contact staff often have to rely on *physical support* provided by functions and departments invisible to the customers. These *support employees* have to consider customer contact staff as their *internal customers*. In the supporting part there may be a range of support functions, for example, behind each other as discussed previously in this chapter. Support staff have to be treated as internal customers by support functions further behind in the service system. Internal customers have to be treated as well as external customers. *Internal service* has to be as good as the service to ultimate customers, otherwise the perceived service quality will be damaged. Processing checks in bank offices and loading trucks in warehouses are examples of physical support.

The third type of support is *systems support*. This is of a somewhat different nature. Investments in technology, for example, computer systems, information technology, buildings, offices, vehicles, tools, equipment and documents, form the systems support from behind the line of visibility. If the organization invests in an unreliable slow computer system which does not permit prompt answers to customers' questions or rapid decision-making or which regularly crashes, or a database which does not provide contact staff with easily and quickly retrievable information about customers, the service system lacks good systems support. If a contact person cannot provide good service because of existing management regulations, there may be another type of inadequate system support—rules and regulations that are too rigid.

There is also another kind of systems support. The knowledge employees have of operating various systems is *systems knowledge*. The organization must invest in employees who know how to operate and make best use of the company's systems and technology, and should provide training.

Behind the support part is the *totally invisible part* of the organization. This part is in a way outside the service system. It consists of functions that do not influence the service offering or service quality, either directly or indirectly. Internal bookkeeping is an example. Frequently, analyzing an organization shows that there are surprisingly few parts that are totally invisible.

The Service System Model: An Elevator Repair and Maintenance Case Study

Here is presented the development of the service system in a major elevator repair and maintenance operation. These services are provided by one of the major manufacturers, the service, maintenance and modernization operations of which count for more than half of their total invoicing. The first part of this case was presented in Chapter 3 to illustrate customers' perception of service quality. In that context it was observed that customers, although they were satisfied with the technical quality of the outcome of the firm's service processes, did not appreciate the functional quality of the process, and therefore considered the total quality of the service to be low. Customers did not like that almost every time the elevator needed maintenance or there was a need for repair a new service technician arrived to take care of the job. The successive technicians did not develop a hands-on knowledge of the elevators and did not get to know the customers. The customers, in turn, did not get to know the service technicians, which made communication difficult. Moreover, the customers did not understand why the service technician often left an unfinished job, especially as no information on the reasons for this and when the technician could be expected to return was given. Moreover, problems were experienced with the punctuality of the service and the flexibility of the firm.

The technology already existed to create a good outcome of the repair and maintenance processes. However, the systems (as well as the attitudes and skills of the employees) necessary for implementing the process were lacking. Hence, a new service system was developed and implemented. The subsequent changes in the interactive and support parts of the service system and their impact on the service process are presented and discussed in this part of the case study.

Systems and operational resources. Previously the supervisor of a regional or local service group (covering a smaller city or part of a bigger city) allocated each day's repair and maintenance jobs to the service technicians available that morning, without considering the previous history of the various customers or whether a given service technician had any previous experience of the customers and elevators that were assigned to him. In this way no relationship between a given customer and a given service technician could develop. Moreover, service technicians did not develop a knowledge of or responsibility for any of the customers. This was now changed, so that every service technician was given long-term responsibility for the same set of customers. A back-up system to be used in case the regular technician was sick was also developed.

In order for the company to change its operational system, specific systems knowledge had to be developed. This was not an easy process because of the history of organizing workflow in the company. However, by developing a new understanding of how operational systems should function, a *systems support* was created that enabled the service technicians to get a far better knowledge of the history of the elevators they were responsible for as well as to feel more responsible for the customers to which they had been assigned.

Physical resources and equipment. Previously the service technicians had had a limited stock of spare parts and a limited assortment of tools in their vans. If they needed a tool they did not carry, they had to leave the job and get the missing spare part or tool from a central depot. This was one of the reasons why customers were left wondering where the service technician had gone and why he had left the job unfinished. Now the decision to invest in new and bigger vans and to keep more spare parts and tools in stock was taken (a decision to renew the car park had already been taken, but instead of purchasing the vans that originally had been planned, the company bought bigger vans.) This made it possible for service technicians to finish almost all jobs without interruption. Hence, this decision not only increased the usefulness of the physical resources used in the service process, it also had a favorable impact on the operational systems used in the process.

By changing the technology used the company created an additional *systems support* that made it possible for the service technicians to perform in a more customer-oriented fashion.

Contact staff. It was obvious that service technicians concentrated on the outcome of the repair and maintenance tasks, and were much less concerned with the way they did their jobs and with their interactions with the customers. Operational systems and management support from supervisors had been outcome-oriented and had not encouraged an interest in the process itself. An *internal marketing* process was initiated, where the objective was to focus the interest of service technicians as well as their supervisors and managers on the quality perceptions of the customers, especially on the importance of the functional quality perception of the process. The reasons for these changes in systems and equipment were explained. By this internal marketing process management wanted to achieve a change in all employees' attitudes towards the customers and towards their jobs, so that a more customer-oriented performance would be achieved.

Traditionally supervisors and managers had focused on the outcome of the service process, while the understanding of how to support and manage the process of repair and maintenance from a quality perspective had been neglected. Elevator repair and maintenance had been thought of as solely outcome consumption. However, in reality it was process consumption. Now a process perspective was taken, supported by the internal marketing process. Hence, *management support* by supervisors and managers was created.

A support function responsible for information about customers already existed. Through more customer-oriented market research, more accurate *physical support* in the form of better customer information was achieved.

Customers. The new service system was intended to make it easier for the customer to interact with the service technicians. Customers would feel that their viewpoints were recognized and that they more easily got answers to their questions. Their time could be expected to be used more effectively, because unnecessary breaks in the repair and maintenance jobs could be avoided in future.

The results of the development of the service system were positive. Fewer customers left the company, while the company managed to maintain its premium price level. The business became profitable.

The Service System in a Network of Systems

In previous sections the service system model has been viewed as a single organizational unit. This is, of course, not always the case. Frequently a total system is built up through a network of separate service systems. This, in the minds of customers, is normally perceived as *one* service system.

For example, a hotel chain may have a hotel reservation system, which is geographically located away from the hotels. Customers who make their reservations themselves through this system on one date and stay at a hotel at a later date judge the two service processes (the reservation system and the hotel's service production system) separately, but they also view the reservation system as a part of the hotel's system. If the reservation system fails, the customer will not make a reservation at the hotel, and consequently, the total service process system (reservation and hotel together) fails. In principle, the same holds true if the customer makes his reservation through a travel agent not affiliated with the hotel chain. From a management point of view, it will probably be more complicated to manage the total service system, since the other system of this *network*, reservation through an independent travel agent, is an independently managed organization.

Often the situation becomes even more complicated because the relationships between the parties in a network are often mutual. In the previous case, the hotel's service system depends on that of the travel agent. But the service system of the latter also depends on that of the hotel. If the travel agent directs a customer to a hotel that turns out to be unsatisfactory, the customer will blame not only the hotel but also the travel agent. In this situation the travel agent can be considered a subcontractor of the hotel. However, they are both part of a network that consists of the service systems of both parties, and the customer will judge not only the systems of the two parties separately, but the total service system of the network.

In manufacturing, firms often use various types of subcontractor to carry out service activities. For example, independent delivery firms transport goods to customers, and independent firms are used to handle installation, technical service and repair and customer training. In these situations, similar networks emerge, where the manufacturer is often judged by the performance of the service system of its subcontractor.

From a management point of view, it is essential to observe the existence of these networks of independent or affiliated service systems, and to realize the impact of one system on another and on the success of the total system. For example, bad performance by one party, say an insurance broker, in the network may damage, or even destroy, the other party, in this case the insurance company. On the other hand, excellent service provided by a partner in the network, say, by a delivery and transportation firm, may substantially enhance the image of the manufacturer in the minds of its customers.

Fitting Resources in the Service System to the Service Consumption Process

The quality-generating resources—personnel, systems, technologies and physical resources, and customers—have to be carefully planned so that a competitive functional quality is produced in the service process. If good quality is produced, an excellent interactive marketing impact is also created. In Figure 13.8 the nature of this issue is schematically illustrated.

The model demonstrates the need for achieving a balance between the resources involved. As we look at the buyer–seller interface and its moments of truth, *contact personnel* emerge as one critical resource. Every contact person has a

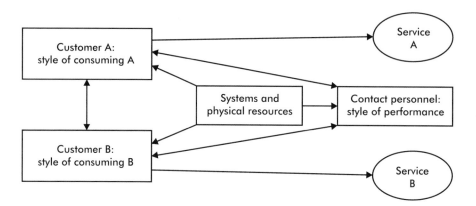

FIGURE 13.8   The content of the buyer–seller interaction. Source: Derived from Lehtinen, J., *Asiakasohjautuva palveluyritys* (Customer-oriented service firms). Espoo, Finland: Weilin & Gröös, 1983, p. 81.

specific way of performing, which can be called their *style of performance*.[19] For example, a dental receptionist and a dentist have their own way of doing and saying things and of performing their tasks. This style is, of course, partly due to their professional skills, but partly also due to their attitude toward patients.

This style of performance has to be geared to the corresponding *style of consuming* of the customers, here the dentist's patients. If there is a misfit between these two styles, perceived service quality will probably be damaged. Since many different customers are frequently present at the same time, their styles of consuming must also fit. For example, a nervous patient in the waiting room may scare other people waiting to see the dentist. In a restaurant, a group of young men drinking beer and a family having lunch may not get along well in the same place. The perceived service quality deteriorates.

The *systems and physical resources* used in the service production process will also have to fit the style of performance of contact staff as well as customers' style of consuming. Inappropriate systems make this unnecessarily complicated and even frustrating for contact persons to do their job. Also if there is a misfit between the systems and the customers' style of consuming, they will not want to adjust to the systems and they will find it awkward to take part in the process. The perceived service quality is again damaged. For example, the treatment procedures and the equipment of the dentist, as well as registration and recall systems and waiting room facilities, have to fit the dentist and the other contact staff as well as the patient. The circles "Service A" and "Service B" in Figure 13.8 indicate that Customers A and B may perceive slightly different services, irrespective of whether or not the basic service package is the same. In conclusion, the availability of quality-generating resources as such does not automatically lead to good customer perceived service quality. Sufficient and properly designed resources are a prerequisite, whereas the fit between them determines success.

Figure 13.8 illustrates a case involving external customers. The same applies for internal customers too. The style of performance of supporting staff will have to match the style of consuming of contact staff as internal customers. If there is a misfit, the internal climate will suffer and contact staff will feel that they get bad support—that is, insufficient internal service—from the support function. Moreover, the systems and physical resources of the support function will have to fit into the service process in a similar manner.

Summary and Questions for Discussion

This chapter discussed how to organize marketing in a service organization. It was observed that in a service firm marketing cannot really be organized. *Marketing has to be instilled by creating a customer-oriented or marketing mindset in everyone throughout the organization at every hierarchical level.* Most of the marketing process takes place outside the responsibility and reach of a traditional marketing department and is implemented by *part-time marketers* who belong to other departments and functions. The role of marketing specialists or full-time marketers is more of a supportive nature. In the latter part of the chapter a Service System Model was presented and discussed. Depending on how well such a system is designed, interactive marketing will be more or less successful.

Questions for discussion

1. What does "marketing cannot be organized in a service firm, but instead has to be instilled in the organization" mean?
2. Why does a service organization have to be able to combine the strengths of a large and small company? What results can be achieved by doing so effectively?
3. Why is there a difference between the marketing process and the marketing department?
4. How can a service package be related to the consumption process?
5. How should a service system be designed so that a good interactive marketing impact is created?
6. Analyze, using the service system model, a service of your organization, or a service of any organization, in order to detect the strengths and weaknesses of the system. What are the marketing effects of such strengths and weaknesses? How should the system be developed in order to create a better marketing effect?

Further Reading

Achrol, R.S. & Kotler, P. (1999) Marketing in the Network Economy. *Journal of Marketing*, **63**, Special Issue, pp. 146–163.

Bitner, M.J. (1992) Serviscapes: The Impact of Physical Surroundings on Customers and Employees. *Journal of Marketing*, **56**, April, pp. 57–71.

Carlzon, J. (1987) *Moments of Truth*. Cambridge, MA: Ballinger.

Grönroos, C. (1983) *Strategic Management and Marketing in the Service Sector*. Cambridge, MA: Marketing Science Institute.

Grönroos, C. (1990) *Service Management and Marketing. Managing the Moments of Truth in Service Competition*. Lexington, MA: Lexington Books.

Gummesson, E. (1979) The Marketing of Professional Services—An Organizational Dilemma. *European Journal of Marketing*, **13**(5), p. 308.

Gummesson, E. (1991) Marketing-orientation Revisited: The Crucial Role of the Part-time Marketer. *European Journal of Marketing*, **25**(2), pp. 60–75.

Gummesson, E. (1999) *Total Relationship Marketing. Rethinking Marketing Management: From 4Ps to 30Rs*. Oxford: Butterworth-Heinemann.

Haller, T. (1980) Strategic Planning: Key to Corporate Power for Marketers. *Marketing Times*, 2.

Hedberg, B., Dahlgren, G., Hansson, J. & Olve, N.-G. (1997) *Virtual Organizations and Beyond: Discovering Imaginary Systems*. Chichester: John Wiley & Sons.

Lehtinen, J. (1983) *Asiakasohjautuva palveluyritys (Customer-oriented service firm)*. In Finnish. Espoo, Finland: Weilin & Göös.

Lehtinen, J. (1986) *Quality Oriented Services Marketing*. The University of Tampere, Finland.

McDonald, M., Millman, T. & Rogers, B. (1997) Key Account Management: Theory, Practice and Challenges. *Journal of Marketing Management*, **13**, pp. 737–757.

Peppers, D. & Rogers, M. (1997) *Enterprise One-to-One*. London: Currency/Doubleday.

Piercy, N.F. (1985) *Marketing Organization. An Analysis of Information Processing, Power and Politics*. London: George Allen & Unwin.

Piercy, N.F. (1992) *Market-Led Strategic Change*. Oxford: Butterworth Heinemann.

Piercy, N.F. & Cravens, D. (1995) The Network Paradigm and the Marketing Organization. *European Journal of Marketing*, **29**(3), pp. 7–34.

Shostack, G.L. (1984) Designing Services That Deliver. *Harvard Business Review*, January–February.

Simon, H. (1996) *Hidden Champions*. Boston, MA: Harvard Business School Press.

Webster, Jr., F.E. & Wind, Y. (1972) *Organizational Buying Behavior*. Englewood Cliffs, NJ: Prentice-Hall.

Zeithaml, V.A. & Bitner, M.J. (2000) *Services Marketing. Integrating Customer Focus Across the Firm*. 2nd edition. Boston, MA: Irwin McGraw-Hill.

Notes

1 In the 1980s, Haller and Piercy predicted that marketing as a separate function and marketing departments as organizational solutions would disappear. See Haller, T., Strategic Planning: Key to Corporate Power for Marketers. *Marketing Times*, No. 2, 1980, and Piercy, N.F., *Marketing Organization. An Analysis of Information Processing, Power and Politics*. London: George Allen & Unwin, 1985.

2 See, for example, Gummesson, E., The Marketing of Professional Services—An Organizational Dilemma. *European Journal of Marketing*, **13**(5), 1979, and Grönroos, C., *Strategic Management and Marketing in the Service Sector*. Cambridge, MA: Marketing Science Institute, 1983.

3 See Hedberg, B., Dahlgren, G., Hansson, J. & Olve, N.-G., *Virtual Organizations and Beyond: Discovering Imaginary Systems*. London: John Wiley & Sons, 1997. Also, see Piercy, N.F. & Cravens, D., The Network Paradigm and the Marketing Organization. *European Journal of Marketing*, **29**(3), 1995, pp. 7–34.

4 See, for example, Achrol, R.S. & Kotler, P., Marketing in the Network Economy. *Journal of Marketing*, **63**, Special Issue 1999, pp. 146–163. The authors distinguish between *internal*, *vertical*, *intermarket* and *opportunity networks*.

5 Archol & Kotler, *op.cit.*, p. 148.

6 The first researcher to point this out in the context of service marketing was Evert Gummesson. See Gummesson, *op.cit.*

7 Gummesson, E., Marketing-orientation Revisited: The Crucial Role of the Part-time Marketer. *European Journal of Marketing*, **25**(2), 1991, p. 72.

8 The notion of marketing departments as organizational traps for service providers was first introduced in Grönroos, *op.cit.*, based on a large study in the service sector in Scandinavia.

9 Grönroos, *op.cit.* See also Simon, H., *Hidden Champions*. Boston, MA: Harvard Business School Press, 1996; and Piercy, N.F., *Market-Led Strategic Change*. Oxford: Butterworth Heinemann, 1992.

10 Jan Carlzon, former managing director and president of SAS (Scandinavian Airlines System) who in the 1980s successfully turned around this airline to a highly service-oriented and profitable firm, used the notion of inverting the organizational pyramid. See Carlzon, J., *Moments of Truth*.

Cambridge, MA: Ballinger, 1987. The title of the Swedish original of this book was "Tear Down the Pyramids."

11 The concept of *internal customer* was introduced to the service and relationship marketing context by Gummesson. See Gummesson, E., *Total Relationship Marketing. Rethinking Marketing Management: From 4Ps to 30Rs*. Oxford: Butterworth-Heinemann, 1999.

12 The *line of visibility* concept was introduced in the service marketing literature by Lynn Shostack as part of her service blueprinting model. See Shostack, G.L., Designing Services That Deliver. *Harvard Business Review*, January–February 1984.

13 Webster, Jr., F.E. & Wind, Y., *Organizational Buying Behavior*. Englewood Cliffs, NJ: Prentice-Hall, 1972.

14 See McDonald, M., Millman, T. & Rogers, B., Key Account Management: Theory, Practice and Challenges. *Journal of Marketing Management*, **13**, 1997, pp. 737–757.

15 See Peppers, D. & Rogers, M., *Enterprise One-to-One*. London: Currency/Doubleday, 1997, who discuss the issues of identified individual one-person segments by creating interactive interfaces with customers and by mass customizing solutions to them.

16 See Lehtinen, J., *Quality-oriented Services Marketing*. The University of Tampere, Finland, 1986, which introduced this three-stage approach.

17 Grönroos, C., *Service Management and Marketing. Managing the Moments of Truth in Service Competition*. Lexington, MA: Lexington Books, 1990.

18 Bitner, M.J., Serviscapes: The Impact of Physical Surroundings on Customers and Employees. *Journal of Marketing*, **56**, April 1992, pp. 57–71.

19 This approach to understanding the balance between resources in the service process was developed by Jarmo Lehtinen. See Lehtinen, *op.cit.*

Chapter 14

MANAGING INTERNAL MARKETING: A PREREQUSITE FOR SUCCESSFULLY MANAGING CUSTOMER RELATIONSHIPS

Without good and well-functioning internal relationships, external customer relationships will not develop successfully. Managing employees—on all levels—is a true test of managing an organization.

Introduction

This chapter will discuss a phenomenon that has been highlighted by the research into service marketing, that is *internal marketing*. Throughout this book, the issue of internal marketing has emerged in several contexts. The term was coined as an umbrella concept for a variety of internal activities and processes which are not new, but which, focused upon in this way, offer a new approach to developing a service orientation and an interest in customers and marketing among an organization's personnel. Internal marketing starts from the concept that employees are a first, internal market for the organization. If goods, services, planned marketing communication, new technologies and operational systems cannot be marketed to this internal target group, marketing to ultimate, external customers cannot be expected to be successful either. Internal marketing is a prerequisite for successful external and interactive marketing. The latter part of the chapter will focus upon two concepts which are closely related to internal marketing, *empowering* and *enabling employees*. After reading the chapter the reader should understand the role of internal marketing in service management and know how to develop an internal marketing process, as well as understand the opportunities of empowerment and the risks related to half-hearted empowerment processes.

Internal Marketing: A Summary

Internal marketing is not a new phenomenon, and it was not new when the term was first used in the service marketing literature in the 1970s.[1] Firms have always used morale-boosting activities and campaigns, and employees' attitudes and motivation have long been a concern of personnel management and human resources staff. However, the notion of internal marketing has brought three new aspects to human resources management in a firm:

- the employees are a first market, an internal market, for the firm's offerings as well as for its external marketing programs;
- an active, coordinated and goal-oriented approach to all employee-oriented efforts which combines these internal efforts and processes with the external efficiency of the firm (that is, interactive marketing performance in customer relationships); and
- an emphasis on the need to view people, functions and departments internal to the firm as internal customers, to whom internal services have to be provided in the same customer-oriented manner as to external customers.

The first observation is important, because it points out the fact that everything the service provider does for its customers (planned marketing communication, service offerings, etc.) is first perceived and evaluated by its own personnel. If employees do not believe in the promises given by external marketing activities and campaigns, do not know how to implement a service offering or how to make use of technology or systems in the service process; if they do not accept them, or feel that they do not have the skills to perform according to what is required of them, they will not "buy the offering." In that case they will not be able or willing to perform as effective *part-time marketers* and contribute to a good *interactive marketing* impact. The employees form an internal market which should be attended to first.

The second notion is equally important, because it emphasizes the fact that all internal efforts, programs and processes have to be geared towards maintaining or improving the external performance of the firm. The management of human resources is not only an internal matter, but is also a matter of making sure that employees contribute to the external performance of the service provider. Such efforts and processes have to be planned and implemented with a similar approach as external marketing, i.e. in a *coordinated*, *active* and *goal-oriented* way.

The third observation that internal customers exist and that they have to be treated in the same way as external customers has an important impact on the internal relationships of an organization.[2] Fellow employees must not be provided with slow, inattentive and careless service and support, because if this is the case their ability to provide the firm's "real" customers with good service and to create high perceived service quality for them is seriously jeopardized.

The new interest in internal marketing among researchers that emerged in the 1990s has revitalized the concept from a relationship-oriented and network organization-based perspective. Here organizations collaborate in networks of firms with traditional boundaries or, increasingly, in networks of relationships between firms. This has brought two more new aspects to the management of human resources: a need to view individuals on the internal markets as relationship partners; and a need to create internal marketing processes that do not only include the personnel of one organization but reach out to people in relationships with other organizations in the network.[3]

The first observation emphasizes the need to view employees not as subordinates but from a win–win partnering perspective, where people feel that they are working for an organization that provides them with something in return, such as opportunities to develop, an encouraging environment, access to skills, information and support from a knowledge-generating team, and of course an acceptable salary.[4]

The second observation demonstrates that the borderline between what is inside an organization and what is outside it becomes blurred. Furthermore, it also points out that the distinction between relationships with employees internal to a firm or a network and relationships with customers, and for example, with suppliers, distributors and financial institutions, which are traditionally considered to be on the outside, become blurred as well. Suppliers, service providers and their customers become one interactive organization, where value for customers is created jointly in interactive relationships.[5]

Internal Marketing: A Strategic Issue

The term *internal marketing* was originally derived from the notion of the internal market of employees, and the need for the marketer to first make sure that employees understand and accept external marketing programs and efforts and offerings before these are launched on to the external market of customers and potential customers. It can be argued that this term is not very appropriate. Employees who have no marketing training and who do not consider themselves to be involved in marketing, and often who have not been appointed as part-time marketers, have a negative view of marketing and do not want to be involved in anything labelled marketing. Why should they want to be involved in something called "internal marketing?" If the term becomes a problem internally, one can always choose another name for this phenomenon for internal use. Many firms have done so, and any term or slogan that functions well will do. However, the term *internal marketing* is used to describe the concept *in principle*, what it includes and how it can be implemented.

Human resources form a strategic resource for any firm. With employees who are inadequately trained, have poor attitudes towards their job and towards internal and external customers and who get inadequate support from systems, technologies, internal service providers and their managers and supervisors, the firm will not be successful. Therefore, *internal marketing is a management strategy*.[6] It is a strategic issue, in spite of the development of information technology and the growth of high-tech services. *If top management does not understand the strategic role of internal marketing, money invested in internal marketing efforts and processes will not pay off.* In that case money invested in information technology and systems often does not pay off very well either. The active and continuous support of top management, not merely lip service to the importance of employees, is a necessity for successful internal marketing, and also therefore for the successful external marketing and successful management of customer relationships.

In internal marketing the focus is on good internal relationships between people at all levels in the organizations, so that a service-oriented and customer-oriented mindset is created among customer contact employees, support employees in internal service processes, team leaders, supervisors and managers. However, such a mindset is not enough. Adequate skills (for example, for how to interact and communicate with customers) and supportive systems are also required. This is also part of internal marketing.

Top management, human resource management and marketing all contribute to the implementation of internal marketing processes. However, they do so in close collaboration with service operations and other departments, where part-time marketers work.[7] As will be seen later in this chapter, many of the activities of internal marketing already exist in firms. It is only a matter of refocusing, coordination, and active and goal-oriented implementation.

Internal marketing thus operates as a holistic management process to integrate multiple functions of the firm in two ways. First, it ensures that employees at all levels in the firm (including management) understand and experience the business and its various activities, campaigns and processes in the context of an environment that supports customer consciousness. Second, it ensures that all employees are prepared and motivated to act in a service-oriented manner. The premise of internal marketing is that internal relationships between the organization and its employee groups must operate effectively before the firm can be successful in achieving its goals regarding its external markets.

The Internal Marketing Concept

The increasing need for internal marketing is due to the human factor in business. In service competition the manufacturer logic has to be replaced by a new service logic. The emerging importance of services to almost every business has enhanced the notion that a well-trained and service-oriented employee, rather than raw materials, production technology or the products themselves, is the most critical resource. These employees will be even more critical in the future in an increasing number of industries. The more information technology, automated and self-service systems are introduced in service processes, the more important will be the service orientation and customer-consciousness of the employees who remain. The customer contacts that occur from time to time will have to be consistently perceived favorably by the customers. In such service processes, the high-tech processes are largely taken for granted, whereas contacts with service employees, when they occur, either make or break the customer relationship.

Hence, in interactive marketing processes and in handling customer relationships the role of employees is vital. Marketing specialists in the marketing department are not the only human resource in marketing; often they are not even the most important resource. In customer contacts, these full-time marketing specialists are almost always outnumbered by employees whose main duties are production and operations, deliveries, technical service, claims handling or other tasks traditionally considered non-marketing. However, the skills, customer orientation, and service-mindedness of these persons are all critical to customers' perception of the firm and to their future patronage. Hence, customer orientation and a willingness to serve customers in a marketing-oriented fashion and to provide customer satisfaction has to be spread throughout the organization, to every department and work group.[8]

The *internal marketing concept* states that:

> . . . the internal market of employees is best motivated for service-mindedness and prepared for customer-oriented performance by an active, goal-oriented approach, where a variety of activities and processes is used internally in an active, marketing-like and coordinated way. In this way internal relationships between people in various departments and processes (customer contact employees, internal support employees, team leaders, supervisors and managers) can best be enhanced and geared towards service-oriented management and implementation of external relationships with customers and other parties.

Internal marketing is the management philosophy of treating employees as customers.[9] They should feel satisfied with their job environment and relationships with their fellow employees on all hierarchical levels as well as with their relationship with their employer as an organization. Human resource management (HRM) and internal marketing are not the same thing,[10] although they have a lot in common. HRM offers tools that can be used in internal marketing, such as training, hiring and career planning. Internal marketing offers guidance on how these and other tools should be used, i.e. to improve interactive marketing performance through customer-oriented and skillful employees. Successfully implemented internal marketing requires that marketing and HRM work together.[11]

As we have said before, the need for and existence of internal marketing is not new. What is new with the internal marketing concept as described in this chapter is the introduction of a unifying concept for more effectively managing a variety of interfunctional and well established activities as part of an overall process aiming at a common objective. *The importance of internal marketing is the fact that it allows management to approach all of these activities in a more systematic and strategic manner.* Internal marketing is not legitimated by its methods—any activity could be part of internal marketing—but by its purpose of gearing internal personnel-oriented processes towards their external customer-oriented effects (or internal customer-oriented effects).[12]

Two Aspects of Internal Marketing: Attitude Management, and Communications Management

Internal marketing means two types of management processes, *attitude management* and *communications management*. First of all, the attitudes of employees and their motivation for customer consciousness and service-mindedness has to be managed. This can be called the *attitude management* aspect of internal marketing. This is often the predominant part of internal marketing for an organization that strives to develop a competitive edge by pursuing a service strategy.

Second, managers, supervisors, contact people, and support staff need information to be able to perform their tasks as leaders and managers and as service providers to internal and external customers. They need information about job routines, goods and service features, promises given to customers by, for example, advertising campaigns and salespersons, and so on. They also need to communicate with management about their needs and requirements, their views on how to improve performance, and their findings of what customers want. This is the *communications management* aspect of internal marketing.

Both attitude management and communications management are necessary if good results are to be expected. Too often only the communications management aspect is recognized, and perhaps only as a one-way information task. In such cases, internal marketing typically takes the form of campaigns and activities. Internal brochures and booklets are distributed to personnel, and personnel meetings are held where written and oral information is given to the participants and very little communication occurs. Also, managers and supervisors typically take limited interest in their staff and do not recognize their need for feedback information, two-way communication, recognition and encouragement. The employees receive an abundance of information but very little encouragement.

This, of course, means that much of the information they receive has no major impact on the staff. The necessary change of attitudes and enhancement of motivation for good service and customer consciousness is lacking, and employees are, therefore, not receptive to the information.

If the need for and the nature of the attitude management aspect of internal marketing is recognized and taken into account, *internal marketing becomes an ongoing process* instead of a campaign or series of campaigns, and the role of managers and supervisors, on every level, is much more active. Also, much better results are achieved.

In conclusion, a successful internal marketing process requires an *attitude management impact* as well as *communications management support*. Attitude management is a continuous process, whereas communications management may be more of a discrete process including information activities at appropriate points in time. However, these two aspects of internal marketing are also intertwined. Naturally, much or most of the information shared with employees has an effect on attitudes. For example, contact staff who are informed in advance about an external advertising campaign develop more positive attitudes toward fulfilling the promises of that campaign. The tasks of managers, supervisors and team leaders include, as integral and often inseparable parts, both communications management aspects and attitude management aspects.

Overall Objectives of Internal Marketing

From a relationship perspective, the objective of internal marketing is

> . . . to create, maintain and enhance internal relationships between people in the organization, regardless of their position as customer contact staff, support staff, team leaders, supervisors or managers, so that they first feel motivated to provide services to internal customers as well as to external customers in a customer-oriented and service-minded way, and second have the skills and knowledge required as well as the support needed from managers and supervisors, internal service providers, systems and technology to be able to perform in such a manner.[13]

Such internal relationships can only be achieved if employees feel that they can trust each other, and above all trust the firm and its management to continuously provide the physical and emotional support required to perform in a customer-oriented and service-minded way.[14] This feeling of trust can be described as a *psychological contract* in the form of an implicit agreement between management and employees and between, for example, support employees and customer contact employees regarding what each party gives and gets in internal relationships.[15]

As observed at the beginning of this chapter, the difference between relationships inside an organization and between the organization and its customers becomes rather blurred. A similar *psychological contract* should exist in the relationship between a firm and its customers as well.[16] One could say that it may be easier to manage internal relationships. However, as noted before, in a virtual organizational context with several cooperating network partners, the difference between what is internal and what is external becomes more blurred.

From the relationship-oriented objective of internal marketing, four more specific overall objectives can be derived:

1. to ensure that employees are motivated for customer-oriented and service-minded performance and thus successfully fulfill their duties as *part-time marketers* in the interactive marketing process;
2. to attract and retain good employees;
3. to ensure that internal services are provided in a customer-oriented manner in the organization or between partners in a network context; and
4. to provide people who render service internally or externally with adequate managerial and technological support which enables them to fulfill their responsibilities as *part-time marketers*.

The main objective is, of course, to create an internal environment and implement internal action programs so that employees feel motivated to carry out part-time marketing behavior. However, the second objective follows on from the first one. The better its internal marketing works, the more attractive the firm is considered as an employer. The third objective is of course only an extension of the first one, and the fourth objective is a requirement for maintaining a motivation for customer orientation as well as for making it possible to perform well in a practical situation as a part-time marketer. These overall objectives can be developed into more specific goals depending on the situation at hand. In the following sections we will discuss internal marketing situations where the goals are different. Of course, in any specific situation such general goals have to be made more specific to meet the requirements of that situation.

The Three Levels of Internal Marketing

In principle, three different types of situation can be identified where internal marketing is called for:

1. when *creating a service culture* in the firm and a service orientation among personnel;

2. when *maintaining a service orientation* among personnel; and
3. when *introducing new goods and services or external marketing campaigns and activities or new technologies, systems or service process routines* to employees.

These situations represent three levels of internal marketing. Each of the situations will be discussed below.

Developing a Service Culture

As will be discussed in more detail in Chapter 15, a *service culture* exists when a service orientation and an interest in customers are the most important norms in the organization.

In many firms a service culture is lacking or weak. In such cases internal marketing is often seen as a means of achieving such a culture. However, internal marketing alone is not sufficient. Chapter 15 will discuss what else is required. It is important to realize that internal marketing programs in a vacuum cannot establish a service culture. Internal marketing can, however, be a powerful means of developing a service culture in connection with other activities. In general, internal marketing goals in this situation are:

1. to enable employees—managers, supervisors, customer contact employees and support employees—to understand and accept the business mission, strategies and tactics as well as the goods, services, external marketing campaigns and processes of the firm;
2. to create positive relationships between people in the organization;
3. to develop a service-oriented management and leadership style among managers and supervisors; and
4. to teach all employees service-oriented communications and interaction skills.

It is essential to achieve the first goal, because one cannot expect employees to understand why services, service orientation and customer consciousness are important and why they have responsibilities as part-time marketers unless they are aware of what the firm wants to achieve. The second goal is important, because good external relationships with customers and other parties are dependent on the internal climate in the organization. The third and fourth goals are important because service-oriented management methods and communication and interaction skills are fundamental requirements of a service culture.

Maintaining a Service Culture

The second situation where internal marketing can be useful is when a service culture should be maintained. Once such a culture has been created it has to be maintained in an active manner, otherwise employees' attitudes will easily revert back to a culture where non-service norms dominated. Internal marketing goals for helping to maintain a service culture include:

1. to ensure that management methods are encouraging and enhance the service-mindedness and customer orientation of employees;
2. to ensure that good internal relationships are maintained;
3. to ensure that an internal dialog is maintained and employees get continuous information and feedback; and
4. to continuously market new goods and services as well as marketing campaigns and processes to the employees before they are launched externally.

The most important internal marketing issue here is the management support of every single manager and supervisor. Management style and methods are of extreme importance at this point. Employees seem to be more satisfied with their jobs when supervisors concentrate on solving problems for customers rather than enforcing existing rules and regulations. There are, of course, other factors involved as well.

Because management does not have the ability to directly control service processes and the moments of truth of the service encounters, it has to develop and maintain *indirect control*. Such indirect control can be established by creating the corporate atmosphere which makes employees feel that service should guide their thinking and behavior.[17] In this continuous process, every single manager and supervisor is involved. If they are able to encourage their staff, if they can open up communication channels—both formal and informal—and if they make sure that feedback information reaches employees, an established service culture can be expected to continue. Managers and supervisors are also instrumental in maintaining good internal relationships.

Introducing New Goods, Services, External Marketing Activities, Campaigns, and Processes

Internal marketing initially emerged as a systematic way of handling problems when firms planned and launched new goods, services or marketing campaigns without properly preparing their employees. Contact employees especially could not perform well as part-time marketers when they did not know what was going on, did not fully accept new goods, services or marketing activities, or learned about new services and advertising campaigns from newspaper ads or TV commercials or, even worse, from their customers.

It should be noted that this third level of internal marketing is interrelated to and reinforces the other two. These introductions, however, form an internal marketing task in their own right. At the same time, they enhance the maintenance of an established service culture or support the establishment of such a culture. The internal marketing goals for helping with these introductions of new goods, services, and external marketing campaigns and processes include the following:

1. to make employees aware of and accept new goods and services being developed and offered to the market;
2. to make employees aware of and ensure their acceptance of new external marketing campaigns and activities; and

3. to make employees aware of and accepting of new ways—utilizing new or renewed technologies, systems, routines, etc.—in which various tasks influencing internal and external relationship and interactive marketing performance of the firm are to be handled.

Prerequisites for Successful Internal Marketing

If internal marketing activities are implemented purely as a campaign, or, even worse, as separate activities without connections to other management factors, the risk that nothing enduring will be achieved is overwhelming. The organizational structure and the strategy of the firm have to support the establishment of a service culture. Moreover, management methods and the management and leadership style of managers and supervisors have to be supportive if they are to be expected to fulfill their tasks in internal marketing.

The three prerequisites for successful internal marketing are:

- internal marketing has to be considered an integral part of strategic management;
- the internal marketing process must not be counteracted by the organizational structure of a firm or by lack of management support; and
- top management must constantly demonstrate active support for the internal marketing process.

In order to be successful, internal marketing starts with *top management*. Next, *middle management* and *supervisors* have to accept and live up to their role in an marketing process. Only then can internal marketing efforts directed toward contact employees and support employees be successful. Employees' ability to function as service-minded *part-time marketers* depends to a large extent on the support and encouragement they get from supervisors. Genuine leadership at all levels in the organization is a necessity if customer contact and support employees are expected to be committed to good service.

Finally, all other categories of employees have to be involved as well. The *contact staff* form a natural target market for internal marketing. They have the immediate customer contacts and are instrumental in the interactive marketing process. However, they often depend on support from other employees and departments in the firm. Often there is a large number of employees who do not come in contact with customers themselves, but who nevertheless indirectly influence the service received by customers. The ability of contact employees to perform their interactive marketing tasks depends to a large extent on their service-mindedness. Such groups of employees, the *support personnel*, should perform in a customer-oriented manner when they serve their *internal customers*. They are *part-time marketers* as well, although their customers are internal and not external. Thus, support employees should also be included in the target audience for internal marketing programs. In summary, the four main target groups for internal marketing are:

- top management;
- middle management and supervisors;

- customer contact personnel; and
- support personnel.

It should be noted that the same person may occupy several positions. A support person may sometimes be a contact person. A supervisor who, for example, is supposed to support and encourage contact people may be a contact person serving customers, or a support person serving internal customers, regularly or occasionally. Middle or top management may also have customer contacts. When they have such contacts they, too are *part-time marketers* in the firm's marketing process.

Internal Marketing Activities

There is no exclusive list of activities that should belong to an internal marketing process. Almost any function or activity that has an impact on internal relationships and on the service-mindedness and customer consciousness of employees can be included. This, of course, follows from the notion that internal marketing, first of all, is a philosophy for managing internal relationships in an organization, or a network of interrelated organizations, and a systematic way of developing and enhancing a service orientation.

However, typical internal marketing activities can be identified. The following list is not intended to be inclusive, nor does it distinguish between activities to be used in developing or maintaining a service culture or in introducing new goods, services and marketing campaigns internally. Many of the activities are mutual for two or three of these situations.

Training

A lack of understanding of the firm's strategies and of the existence and import-ance of part-time marketing responsibilities is almost always present. "Service knowledge" is lacking in strategic thinking as well as on an operational level. This is partly due to insufficient or nonexistent knowledge of the content of a service strategy, of the nature and scope of marketing in a service and relationship context, and of the employees' role with dual responsibilities in the firm. This goes for contact and support employees as well as for managers and supervisors.

Partly, this is an attitude problem. Indifferent or negative attitudes have to be changed. On the other hand, attitude problems normally follow on from a lack of understanding of facts. Therefore, the tasks of improving employees' knowledge and changing attitudes are intertwined.

Training, either internal or external, is most frequently needed as a basic component of an internal marketing program. Three types of training tasks can be included:

- developing a *holistic* view of a service strategy and of the total marketing process as well as of the role of each individual in relation to other indi-viduals and processes in the firm, and in relation to customers;

- developing and enhancing *favorable attitudes* toward a service strategy and *part-time marketing* performance; and
- developing and enhancing *communications, sales,* and *service skills* among employees.

Training, together with internal communication support, is the predominant tool of the communications management aspect of internal marketing. However, to some extent they are also part of the attitude management process. If the first type of training goal is overlooked, it will be very difficult or impossible to create conditions for favorable attitudes towards service and part-time marketing responsibilities or to make employees interested in getting the skills required to perform as good part-time marketers. An individual who does not recognize and appreciate the whole picture will not understand why he should change his behavior towards fellow employees and customers and bother to acquire new skills unrelated to his traditional tasks. Because employees need to feel that there is a trusting relationship between themselves, fellow employees and management (or the existence of a *psychological contract*), training programs must also include elements focusing on the fair treatment of both employees and customers.[18]

Management Support and Internal Dialog

No training program alone is enough in an internal marketing process. In order to achieve continuation in such a process, the role of top management, middle management and supervisors is paramount. Managers, supervisors and team leaders have to show leadership, not only administrative "managing and controlling."

Management support can be of various types, for example:

- *continuation* of formal training programs by everyday management actions;
- active *encouragement* of employees as part of everyday management tasks;
- *involving* employees in planning and decision-making;
- *feedback* to employees and flow of *information* and *two-way communication* in formal and informal interactions; and
- establishing an open and encouraging *internal climate.*

Normally, people returning from a course have no follow-up on the course material. Their supervisor is not interested in what they have learned or how to make use of new ideas and factual knowledge. Employees are usually left alone to implement new ideas. Sometimes employees get the impression that the fact that they have been away for training has only created problems, for example with undercapacity. Nobody seems to care about any positive effects of the course. In such situations, any new idea and favorable attitude effects are rapidly destroyed.

Instead, the manager or supervisor should encourage employees to implement new ideas and help them to realize how they could be applied in their specific environment. Recognition is a critical part of management support. Some in-house training is often helpful and encouraging as a continuation of the course or training program. The management style demonstrated daily by managers and supervisors has an immediate impact on the job environment and internal climate, thus management style is an internal marketing issue.

Joint planning and decision-making with the employees involved is a means of achieving commitment in advance to further actions that emerge from the planning process. Customer contact employees have valuable information and knowledge for the needs and desires of customers, so that the involvement of these employees in the planning process leads to improved decision-making.

The need for information and feedback has been discussed already in this book. Here, managers, especially supervisors, have a key role. Moreover, they are responsible for creating an open climate where service-related and customer-related issues can be raised and discussed in a relationship-enhancing internal dialog.

Management support and the internal dialog are the predominant tools of the attitude management aspect of internal marketing, but they are also key ingredients of communications management.

Internal Mass Communication, and Information Support

Most managers and supervisors realize that there is a need for them to inform employees about new service-oriented strategies and new ways of performing in internal and external service encounters, and to make them understand and accept new strategies, tasks and ways of thinking. However, many people do not know how to do this. Therefore, it is important to develop various kinds of supporting materials. Computer software, videotapes and other audio-visual and written material explaining new strategies and ways of performing can easily be used by managers during staff meetings.

Brochures, internal memos and magazines, as well as other means of mass-distributed communications material can also used in internal marketing.

Human Resource Management

It is essential to get and keep the right kind of employees in a firm. Successful internal marketing starts with recruitment and hiring. This, in turn, requires proper job descriptions where the part-time marketing tasks of contact and support employees are recognized. Job descriptions, recruitment procedures, career planning, salary, bonus systems and incentive programs as well as other HRM tools should be used by the organization to pursue internal marketing goals.

None of these tasks is new. However, they are often used passively, more like administrative procedures than as active marketing tools to achieve internal objectives. The external marketing implications of these tasks are also all too often neglected, either for cost efficiency reasons or because management is not aware of them. Because of the traditional management approach, most employees are considered as costs only, and not as revenue-generating resources.

Rewarding employees for good service is also an important internal marketing instrument.[19] People should know that good service is appreciated by the firm and this should be recognized in the reward system. Far too often cost efficiency achievements and other internal efficiency factors are the basis for reward systems. If a high number of phone calls dealt with is considered good and rewarded in spite of the fact that customers may be dissatisfied because they feel that they got too little attention, good service is not encouraged and good service will not be rendered.

In many service businesses, the important customer contact jobs are placed in the hands of the newest, least trained employees, who are often hired on a part-time basis only. Quite often they are unskilled and paid little. Their job can be monotonous. No positive relationships with the employer can develop under such circumstances, although such employees can have a major influence on customer experiences of service quality. Their impact on profits can be equally important.[20] If the firm faces service competition, this is, of course, a dangerous way of managing customer relationships. Another less effective strategy which is often used is to promote employees who are successful in customer contacts to supervisory or staff positions where their customer contact abilities are not utilized. Such good contact employees may turn out to be less effective supervisors or managers. The lack of logic of this type of staffing and career development strategy is all too evident, yet, it is frequently applied.

External Mass Communication

The internal effects of any external mass communication are seldom fully recognized. However, employees almost always form an interested and responsive target audience for advertising campaigns, Internet communication, and other means of mass communication. Advertising campaigns, brochures and commercial should be presented to employees before they are launched externally. This may create commitment and decrease confusion. One step further would be to develop such campaigns in cooperation with the employee groups affected by the external communication effort. This can be expected to commit employees to the fulfillment of promises given in planned external marketing communication.

Developing Systems, and Technology Support

The development of customer information databases, systems for effective internal service support from support persons and systems, and other types of systems and technologies that make it possible for the contact employees to give good service are important parts of internal marketing. If such support is lacking, even the most customer-oriented and service-minded employees will eventually start to feel frustrated and lose interest in being good part-time marketers.

Information technology and the development of intranets have had a tremendous impact on internal processes and provided an effective support system in internal marketing. Through easy access to databases, Web sites and e-mail, people and internal processes can reliably and quickly connect to each other. The feeling of being connected to the same body of information as everyone else may create a commitment to a mutual cause among employees which has a positive influence on internal relationships.[21] However, there is also a risk that the use of e-mail and intranets may alienate employees from each other and from the work community. It is too easy to be antisocial and only communicate using information technology. Such negative aspects of this technology are also enhanced by a surplus of information, of which much may be totally irrelevant.[22] From an internal marketing point of view such risks with intranets have to be considered and, if necessary, attended to by management.

Internal Service Recovery

From time to time customer contact employees and support employees face service encounters where a service failure has occurred, or have to interact with customers who are having a bad day. The situation may be frustrating and sometimes also humiliating for the contact person. Furthermore, the less empowered they are, the more they may experience feelings of low perceived control of the tricky situation and helplessness in dealing with the service failure. The customers may have been emotionally upset, frustrated or angry. Internal customers may react in similar ways. Contact staff who have had to cope with situations like these may need help to recover from the mental stress they suffer following such encounters and from the pressure that they have been under. The firm must actively address these issues to help employees to recover. Bowen and Johnston call this *internal service recovery*.[23] Managers and supervisors have a decisive role in handling such internal recovery situations. Support from the whole work group can be valuable for fellow employees in such stressful circumstances. Management may need to a create system which guarantees that a support network exists and functions.

Market Research and Market Segmentation

Both internally and externally, market research can be used to find out, for example, attitudes toward part-time marketing tasks and service-oriented performance. Market segmentation can be applied in order to find the right kind of people to recruit for various positions in the organization.

In summary, a continuous internal marketing process can be divided into three stages:

1. Analysis of the nature of a service strategy and of attitudes among employees and customers.
2. Getting people to understand the concept of customer consciousness and an interactive marketing process.
3. Achieving and nurturing continuous customer-oriented and service-oriented performance.

Case Study: HG Hardware

In the Scandinavian market, computer hardware competition has been fierce, and many firms have suffered. Forced to stay out of his office because of a broken leg, Mr Sam Hardman, marketing director of HG Hardware, a regional chain with some 15 stores, a central warehouse, and some 120 employees, took the time to develop an internal marketing concept to increase employee commitment to the employer and to good service. According to this concept, the attention of everyone in the firm—e.g. managers, office personnel, sales clerks, drivers of delivery trucks, warehouse workers, and cleaners—should be drawn to the economic performance of the firm, and everyone should be rewarded if its financial result exceeded a set level.

An easy-to-understand chart showing how costs and revenues lead to a Return of Investment (ROI) measure was developed, and an equally easy-to-read booklet about how everyone's performance contributed to costs and revenues was distributed to employees. In this booklet it was demonstrated how the level of service to customers over the counter contributed to revenues, how the work of office employees in the warehouse and in stores deliveries affected costs, on one hand, and, and the opportunity of serving customers well and creating revenues, on the other. The expected impact on costs and revenues of employees paying increased attention to their tasks and to serving internal and external customers was explained in detail and in an understandable way. Each and every employee, regardless of his position in the firm and area of responsibility, could see how the way he did his job influenced costs and revenues, and eventually had an effect on ROI. They could also see how changes in ways they did their job had an impact on ROI, either positively or negatively.

The firm invested in an extensive training program, the objective of which was to teach employees to understand the economic consequences of the way they did their jobs and to help them realize how they all contributed to ROI, regardless of their tasks.

HG Hardware's management set a modest ROI target of 15 per cent for the first year, and informed the employees that, provided that this target was achieved, the owner would take 7.5 per cent to cover their ROI objectives and for future investment in the business, and the rest of the achieved ROI would be split equally between the owners and the employees. On the 15th of every month the ROI figure for the end of the previous month was displayed in all luncheon and coffee rooms and other social areas, so that everyone could follow how their performance had paid off. This created interest in the firm's financial results. After the first year the target had been exceeded. Mr Hardman said "It worked. People became interested in the economic consequences of how they took care of their tasks, and we got a commitment to good service. Our customers seemed to have noticed it, too."

Empowering and Enabling Employees

Two concepts which are closely related to internal marketing are *empowering* and *enabling*. An understanding of both concepts and their meaning is important for the effective implementation of internal marketing.

Empowering employees means to give, for example, customer contact employees the authority to make decisions and take action in a large number of potential problematic situations.[24] There will probably be limits to how far this authority can go, and these limits must be carefully determined. For example, decisions where legal matters have to be considered and/or large sums of money are at stake probably need to be taken to a higher management level. Management must set clear and acceptable boundaries for frontline employees' service recovery latitude.[25] The main thing is that the contact (or support) employee knows his responsibilities and is encouraged to perform more effectively and in a more customer-oriented fashion. The ultimate goal is, of course, to improve the part-time marketing performance of the customer contact and support employees.

Correctly implemented empowerment as part of an internal marketing process can have a decisive impact on the job satisfaction of employees, which in turn may improve the part-time marketing impact of employees in customer contacts. Through improved customer retention and more cross-sales this can be expected to have a positive effect on profit.[26]

The empowerment concept has, however, also been criticized. Chis Argyris[27] claims that over the last 30 years little real empowerment has taken place. He argues that change programs which aim at empowering employees are full of inner contradictions which have a negative impact on motivation. He also claims that, based on his observations, managing directors consciously and unconsciously by their actions and attitudes counteract efforts to empower personnel. Although they say they are in favor of empowerment and less traditional control systems, in practice they rely more on standardized processes that steer the performance of the employees in a predetermined direction. This does not create an environment for self-governance or motivated employees to take responsibility for their actions, especially for actions that deviate from the normal route. Clearly, empowerment is a complicated issue, and it takes serious and whole-hearted support from management to succeed. However, if it is successfully introduced, the results can be very favorable.

Empowerment demands a continuous nurturing of trusting relationships between management and employees.[28] Managers must show that they respect employees' authority to analyze situations and make decisions. In this way a mutual trust between management and employees can be instilled. It is also important to realize that empowerment cannot happen overnight. Rather management must create and maintain the conditions needed so that an employee can feel that he has power and can use his power in customer interactions.[29] The *enabling* concept is part of the process of creating the conditions required for empowerment.

Bowen and Lawler[30] put empowerment in a larger context. They claim that empowering employees means (1) providing them with information about the performance of the organization, (2) rewarding them based on the organization's performance, (3) creating a knowledge base that makes it possible for employees to understand and contribute to the performance of the organization, and (4) giving employees the power to make decisions that influence organizational directions and performance.

Empowerment cannot function without simultaneously *enabling* employees so that they are prepared to take the responsibility that goes with the new authority.

Enabling means that employees need support to be able to make the independent decisions effectively in the service process. Without such support, proper conditions for empowered employees do not exist. Enabling includes:

1. *Management support,* so that supervisors and managers give information and also take over decision-making when needed but do not interfere unnecessarily with the decision-making authority of employees.
2. *Knowledge support* so that employees have the skills and knowledge to analyze situations and make proper decisions.
3. *Technical support* from support staff, systems, technology and databases that provide contact employees with information and other services required for handling situations.

It is important to realize that *empowerment without enabling creates more confusion and frustration.* People who are required to take responsibility for customers but who are not enabled to do so will feel ambiguity, frustration and anger, and they will probably make bad decisions. The connections between empowerment and internal marketing can easily be seen. Among the objectives of internal marketing is the development of management support, knowledge support and technical support so that empowered employees have the tools and assistance they require and will feel motivated to perform effectively as part-time marketers.

The benefits of empowerment of service employees are as follows:[31]

1. *Quicker and more direct response to customer needs in the service process,* because customers will not have to wait for a decision until a supervisor can be found in unusual situations. At the same time customers will experience a feeling of spontaneity and willingness to help which has a positive effect on perceived service quality.
2. *Quicker and more direct response to dissatisfied customers in service recovery situations,* again because customers will not have to wait for a decision until a superior can be found, or will not have to file a formal complaint in situations that do not warrant such a complicated procedure.
3. *Employees are more satisfied with their job and feel better about themselves,* because they take ownership of their job and know that they are trusted employees. This may also decrease absenteeism and employee turnover.
4. *Employees will treat customers more enthusiastically,* because they are more motivated to do their job. This of course requires that they have been made aware of their part-time marketing responsibilities.
5. *Empowered employees can be a valuable source of new ideas,* because they have direct customer contacts, see the problems and opportunities experienced in service encounters, and the customers' needs, wishes, expectations and values. As empowered employees they are more inclined to notice these problems and opportunities and to share the findings and the ideas they get from them with supervisors and managers.
6. *Empowered employees are instrumental in creating good word of mouth referrals and increasing customer retention,* because they can be expected to serve customers

in a quick, skillful and service-oriented manner, thus surprising customers and making them more inclined to spread the word and stay with the same service provider.

Empowerment does not mean that managers and supervisors should have less managerial responsibility.[32] The nature of this responsibility will differ, however: there will be more leadership orientation instead of mere managing, more independent judgment instead of managing by the book, and a clear understanding when decisive action on the part of the manager or supervisor is required.

Sometimes empowering employees may incur some extra costs. Additional employee training may be required and it may be necessary to pay empowered employees better. There is also, of course, the risk that empowered customer contact employees will make bad decisions which may cost the firm money and perhaps also have a negative effect on customers. This can, however, be avoided by recruiting and enabling personnel carefully. It should also be remembered that not all employees can be empowered, because everyone will not want to have the responsibility that goes with it. Some seemingly unnecessary costs that make customers happy, for example in service recovery situations, will probably pay off in the long run. Generally speaking, the positive revenue-boosting effects of empowered and enabled employees can be expected to be much greater than the extra costs. In addition, cost reduction can be expected due to decreased absenteeism and lower employee turnover.

Case Study: Empowerment at Nordstrom

Nordstrom, the North American department store chain whose headquarters are in Seattle, Washington State, has a long-established reputation for empowering its sales associates. In turn, the chain also has a phenomenal reputation for fervently loyal customers.

Nordstrom's sales associates have an "empowered state of mind," and they feel more *control* over how to perform the job; more *awareness* of the business context in which the job is performed and more *accountability* for performance outcomes. Nordstrom accomplishes this through management practices that confer significant amounts of power, information, knowledge and rewards upon them. As to power, the associates have the discretion to do whatever it takes to please the customer. The Nordstrom policy manual essentially consists of two sentences: "Use your good judgement in all situations. There will be no additional rules." Information on products and sales performance is widely shared. Knowledge refers to training, and Nordstrom relies on extensive on-the-job training, rather than formal classroom training. Finally, as to rewards, sales associates can earn well above the industry average through commissions on sales. There are also numerous status rewards such as being elected as Employee of the Month or being nominated to the V.I.P. Club. It is this empowerment that industry analysts claim accounts for the high level of employee sales, customer satisfaction and profits that make Nordstrom a benchmark in retailing.

Source: This case example was developed by David E. Bowen, Thunderbird, The American Graduate School of International Business.

Different Approaches to Motivating Employees

Based on their experience, Katzenbach and Santamaria propose five different approaches to motivating employees.[33] They only discuss contact employees, but their suggestions are valid for people in most positions in an organization. All of these approaches require the use of the internal marketing tools discussed in the previous section. The five approaches or paths are as follows:

1. Create a collective pride in the mission and values of the firm among employees (the mission values. and pride path).
2. Make everyone's tasks, why they are important and how performance is measured, clear to employees and follow up on results in a consistent manner (the process and metrics path).
3. Give employees personal freedom and opportunities for earnings, but also significant personal risks, with few rules about behavior (the entrepreneurial spirit path).
4. Show respect for the individual achievements of employees and recognize quality performance (the individual achievement path).
5. Offer reward and bonus systems to support accomplishments (the reward and celebration path).

Figure 14.1 illustrates the content of these five approaches, or paths as the authors call them, as well as their intended effects on employees. In the figure examples of firms which follow these approaches are also included.

Berry and Parasuraman[34] offer a number of guidelines for firms which want to practice internal marketing effectively:

1. Compete for talented employees.
2. Offer a vision that brings purpose and meaning to jobs.
3. Make sure that employees have the skills and knowledge needed to do their job excellently.
4. Create teams of people who can support each other.
5. Leverage the freedom factor.
6. Encourage achievements through measurement and rewards.
7. Base job design decisions on research.

These seven guidelines make good sense; however, it is not always easy to implement them.[35] Employees need to be empowered to perform, but they also need the support of good management, support systems, technology and information. They also need training so that they have the skills needed to perform effectively. Most people feel motivated to perform better if they have the freedom to think, analyze, make decisions and act. To be able to do that they need knowledge and skills, so that they feel secure in an empowered position. It all starts with recruitment procedures. The better people the firm can hire from the outset, the more effectively they will perform as part-time marketers and in their other duties. In spite of all its technology, a firm is only as good as its people. However, how often do firms violate some or all of these guidelines when hiring and managing customer contact employees or support employees and their supervisors and managers?

	Emotional energy generated by	Reasons employees are committed to the organization	Organizations that follow this path
The Mission, Values, and Pride Path	Mutual trust, collective pride, and self-discipline	They are proud of its aspirations, accomplishments, and legacy; they share its values	U.S. Marine Corps, 3M, New York City Ballet
The Process and Metrics Path	Transparent performance measures and standards; clear tracking of results	They know what each person is expected to do, how performance is measured, and why it matters	Johnson Controls, Hill's Pet Nutrition, Toyota
The Entrepreneurial Spirit Path	Personal freedom, the opportunity for high earnings, and few rules about behavior; people choose their work activities and take significant personal risks	They are in control of their own destinies; they savor the high-risk, high-reward work environment	Hambrecht & Quist, BMC Software, Vail Ski and Snowboard School
The Individual Achievement Path	Intense respect for individual achievement in an environment with limited emphasis on personal risk and reward	They are recognized for the quality of their individual performance	FirstUSA, McKinsey & Company, Perot Systems
The Reward and Celebration Path	Recognition and celebration of organizational accomplishments	They have fun and enjoy the supportive and highly interactive environment	Mary Kay, Tupperware

FIGURE 14.1 Five approaches to motivating employees. From Katzenbach, J.R. & Santamaria, J.A., Firing up the Frontline. Reprinted by permission of *Harvard Business Review*, May–June 1999, p. 109.

How to Implement an Internal Marketing Strategy

When starting to plan and implement an internal marketing strategy, a few guidelines should be observed. First of all, the *internal focus* of internal marketing has to be recognized and fully accepted by management. Employees sense that management considers them important when they are allowed to participate in the process; both in an internal research process and in planning their work environment, the goals and scope of their tasks, information and feedback routines and external campaigns. When employees realize that they are able to involve themselves in improving something that is important to them, they will be more inclined to commit themselves to the business and the goals of the internal marketing strategy.

However, the *external focus* of an internal marketing strategy and of any internal marketing process should never be forgotten. Improving the work environment and tasks for the employees is, of course, an important objective in its own right. It is, nevertheless, the external marketing impact of every employee that is the ultimate focus of internal marketing. The ultimate objective is to improve customer consciousness and service mindedness, and thus, in the final analysis, the *interactive marketing* abilities and the *part-time marketing* performance of the employees. Consequently, *the internal and the external focus of internal marketing go hand in hand*.

Furthermore, it should always be remembered that the internal marketing process will fail if it is viewed as being simply tactical and initiated only at the customer contact level involving only contact employees. This level alone cannot breed a service culture for the organization, nor reach the many support employees who also have to function as part-time marketers internally. Only in a situation where a solid service culture has been established can the internal marketing of, for example, an advertising campaign or a new service be directed toward a specific target group of, say, contact employees in a certain department. In all other situations, internal marketing has to involve, and start with, top management, and include middle management and supervisors. As has been said, continuous management support, not only by paying lip service to internal marketing, but by active involvement in the process, is an absolute necessity.

Finally, internal marketing is a continuous process. The organization needs constant attention from management. Changes in strategy, in technologies used in service processes and in external marketing must always be carefully introduced to the organization. Changing a corporate culture in a service-oriented direction takes time, and management must understand that it has to be given the time it takes. After that the service culture has to be continuously nurtured.

Summary and Questions for Discussion

Internal marketing is an umbrella concept for a range of internal activities and processes, the objective of which is to develop a service orientation, service-minded attitudes and an interest in part-time marketing behavior among the personnel. It is, therefore, first a management philosophy, and second a set of tools. As a management philosophy it emphasizes the pivotal role of the employees as a first internal market. The importance of internal relations were emphasized. Three levels of internal marketing were discussed; (1) developing a service culture, (2) maintaining a service orientation among the personnel, and (3) introducing new goods, services, marketing campaigns and activities, systems and technologies in service processes to the personnel. A number of typical activities which can be part of an internal marketing process were also discussed. In the final part of the chapter the concepts of *empowerment* and *empowering* and *enabling employees* were presented and discussed at some length.

Questions for discussion

1. Why has a need for internal marketing emerged in service firms?
2. What does it mean to take a relationship approach to internal marketing?
3. Which are the levels of internal marketing? Which processes and activities can be expected to function well as part of internal marketing at each of these levels?
4. What is empowerment? What is the role of empowerment in internal marketing?
5. Why is it dangerous to empower employees without simultaneously considering the need for enabling employees?
6. Analyze the level of service orientation in your firm, or in any given firm, and determine the need for internal marketing. Also, discuss which internal marketing processes and activities might function well for your firm.

Further Reading

Argyris, C. (1998) Empowerment: The Emperor's New Clothes. *Harvard Business Review*, **76**, May–June, pp. 98–105.

Ballantyne, D. (1997) Internal Marketing for Internal Networks. *Journal of Marketing Management*, **13**(5), pp. 343–366.

Ballantyne, D. (2000) The Strengths and Weaknesses of Internal Marketing. In Varey, R.J. & Lewis, B.R. (eds), *Internal Marketing*. London: Routledge.

Berry, L.L. (1981) The Employee as Customer. *Retail Banking*, March.

Berry, L.L. & Parasuraman, A. (1991) *Marketing Services: Competing Through Quality*. New York: The Free Press.

Bowen, D.E. & Johnston, R. (1999) Internal Service Recovery: Developing a New Construct. *International Journal of Service Industry Management*, **10**(2), pp. 118–131.

Bowen, D.E. & Lawler III, E.E. (1992) The Empowerment of Service Workers: What, Why, How, and When. *Sloan Management Review*, Spring, pp. 31–39.

Bowen, D.E. & Lawler III, E.E. (1995) Empowering Service Employees. *Sloan Management Review*, **36**(4), pp. 73–84.

Bowen, D.E. & Schneider, B. (1988) Service Marketing and Management: Implications for Organizations. *Research in Organizational Behavior*, 10.

Bowen, D.E., Gilliland, S.W. & Folger, R. (1999) HRM and Service Fairness: How Being Fair with Employees Spills Over To Customers. *Organizational Dynamics*, **27**(3), pp. 7–23.

Bowen, D.A., Schneider, B. & Kim, S.S. (2000) Shaping Service Cultures Through Strategic Human Resource Management. In Swartz, T.A. & Iacobucci, D. (eds), *Handbook of Services Marketing & Management*. Thousand Oaks, CA: Sage Publications, pp. 439–454.

Cahill, D.J. (1996) *Internal Marketing. Your Company's Next Stage of Growth*. New York: The Haworth Press.

Eccles, T. (1993) The Deceptive Allure of Empowerment. *Long Range Planning*, **26**(6), pp. 13–21.

Eiglier, P. & Langeard, E. (1976) *Principes Politique Marketing pour les Enterprises des Services*. Working paper, Institute d'Administration des Enterprises, Université D'Aix-Marseille, December.

Edvardsson, B., Larsson, G. & Setterlind, S. (1997) Internal Service Quality and the Psychosocial Work Environment: An Empirical Analysis of Conceptual Interrelatedness. *The Service Industries Journal*, **17**(2), pp. 252–263.

Gilmore, A. & Carson, D. (1995) Managing and Marketing to Internal Customers. In Glynn, W.J. & Barnes, J.G. (eds), *Understanding Service Management*. Chichester: John Wiley & Sons, pp. 295–321.

Grönroos, C. (1978) A Service-orientated Approach to the Marketing of Services. *European Journal of Marketing*, **12**(8), pp. 588–601.

Grönroos, C. (1990) *Service Management and Marketing. Managing the Moments of Truth in Service Competition*. Lexington, MA: Lexington Books.

Gummesson, E. (2000) Internal Marketing in the Light of Relationship Marketing and Virtual Organizations. In Lewis, B. & Varey, R.J. (eds), *Internal Marketing*. London: Routledge.

Hallowell, E.M. (1999) The Human Moment at Work. *Harvard Business Review*, January–February.

Harari, O. (1997) Stop Empowering Your People. *Management Review*, **86**(2), pp. 48–51.

Herriot, P., Manning, W.E.G. & Kidd, J.M. (1997) The Content of the Psychological Contract. *British Journal of Management*, **8**(2), pp. 151–162.

Johnson, P.R. (1994) Brains, Heart and Courage: Keys To Empowerment and Self-Directed Leadership. *Journal of Managerial Psychology*, **9**(2), pp. 17–21.

Katzenbach, J.R. & Santamaria, J.A. (1999) Firing up the Front Line. *Harvard Business Review*, May–June.

Khan, S. (1997) The Key To Being a Leader Company: Empowerment. *Journal of Quality and Participation*, **20**(1), pp. 44–50.

Ling, I.N. & Brooks, R.F. (1998) Implementing and Measuring the Effectiveness of Internal Marketing. *Journal of Marketing Management*, **14**, pp. 325–351.

Lovelock, C. (2000) Functional Integration in Services. Understanding the Links Between Marketing, Operations, and Human Resources. In Swartz, T.A. & Iacobucci, D. (eds), *Handbook of Services Marketing & Management*. Thousand Oaks: CA: Sage Publications, pp. 421–437.

Normann, R. & Ramírez, R. (1993) From Value Chain to Value Constellation. *Harvard Business Review*, July–August, pp. 65–77.

Oakland, J.S. & Oakland, S. (1998) The Links Between People Management, Customer Satisfaction and Business Results. *Total Quality Management*, **9**(4/5), pp. 185–190.

Piercy, N.F. & Morgan, R.A. (1991) Internal Marketing—the Missing Half of the Marketing Program. *Long Range Planning*, **24**(2), pp. 82–93.

Pitt, L.F. & Foreman, S.K. (1999) Internal Marketing's Role in Organizations: A Transaction Cost Perspective. *Journal of Business Research*, **44**(1), pp. 25–36.

Rafiq, M. & Ahmed, P.K. (1993) The Scope of Internal Marketing: Defining the Boundaries between Marketing and Human Resource Management. *Journal of Marketing Management*, **9**, pp. 219–232.

Reynoso, J.F. & Moores, B. (1996) Internal relationships. In Buttle, F. (ed.), *Relationship Marketing: Theory and Practice*. London: Paul Chapman Publishing, pp. 55–73.

Sasser, W.E. & Stephen, P. (1976) Selling Jobs in the Service Sector. *Business Horizons*, **19**(3), pp. 61–65.

Schneider, B. & Bowen, D.A. (1995) *Winning the Service Game*. Boston, MA: Harvard Business School Press.

Smith, S. (1997) Internal Affairs. *Marketing*, August 7, pp. 24–25.

Varey, R.J. (1995) Internal Marketing: A Review of Some Interdisciplinary Research Challenges. *International Journal of Service Industry Management*, **6**(1), pp. 40–63.

Varey, R.J. & Lewis, B.R. (1999) Beyond the Popular Conception of Internal Marketing. In Fisk, R. & Glynn, L. (eds), *Jazzing into the New Millennium: 1999 SERVSIG Services Research Conference*. Chicago, IL: American Marketing Association, pp. 44–51.

Voima, P. (2000) Internal Relationship Management—Broadening the Scope of Internal Marketing. In Lewis, B. & Varey, R.J. (eds), *Internal Marketing*. London: Routledge.

Voima, P. & Grönroos, C. (1999) Internal Marketing—a Relationship Perspective. In Baker, M.J. (ed.), *The IEBM Encyclopedia of Marketing*. London: International Thomson Business Press, pp. 747–751.

Wasmer, D.J. & Bruner II, G.C. (1991) Using Organizational Culture to Design Internal Marketing Strategies. *Journal of Services Marketing*, **5**(1), pp. 35–46.

Wikström, S., Lundkvist, A. & Beckirus, A. (1998) *Det interaktiva företaget. Med kunden som största resurs* (The interactive firm. With the customer as the greatest resource). In Swedish. Stockholm, Sweden: Svenska Förlaget.

Notes

1   The observation of the existence of an internal market and of the need for service firms to market their campaigns and offerings internally was probably first made by Eiglier and Langeard in France in a working paper published in 1976 (Eiglier, P. & Langeard, E., *Principes politique marketing pour les enterprises des services*. Working paper, Institute d'Administration des Enterprises, Université D'Aix-Marseille, December 1976), although they did not explicitly use the phrase "internal marketing." In the same year Sasser and Arbeit address the issue of "selling

jobs to the employees" and discuss recruitment, training, motivation, internal communication and retention of service-minded personnel as aspects of this internal task (Sasser, W.E. & Stephen P., Selling Jobs in the Service Sector. *Business Horizons*, **19**(3), 1976, pp. 61–65). In the 1970s Christian Grönroos also pointed out the need for internal marketing (Grönroos, C., A Service-orientated Approach to the Marketing of Services. *European Journal of Marketing*, **12**(8), 1978, pp. 588–601). Leonard Berry was another early proponent of internal marketing (Berry, L.L., The Employee as Customer. *Retail Banking*, March 1981).

2 In some publications on internal marketing the relationship between internal suppliers and internal customers (that is, the marketing of goods and services internally in the organization) is considered the main or only domain of internal marketing. See, for example, Ling, I.N. & Brooks, R.F., Implementing and Measuring the Effectiveness of Internal Marketing. *Journal of Marketing Management*, **14**, 1998, pp. 325–351, and Reynoso, J.F. & Moores, B., Internal Relationships. In Buttle, F. (ed.), *Relationship Marketing: Theory and Practice*. London: Paul Chapman Publishing, 1996, pp. 55–73. In this book, the authors have a much broader perspective.

3 Varey, R.J., Internal Marketing: A Review of Some Inter-disciplinary Research Challenges. *International Journal of Service Industry Management*, **6**(1), 1995, pp. 40–63; Voima, P. & Grönroos, C., Internal Marketing—a Relationship Perspective. In Baker, M.J. (ed.), *The IEBM Encyclopedia of Marketing*. London: International Thomson Business Press, 1999, pp. 747–751; Gummesson, E., Internal Marketing in the Light of Relationship Marketing and Virtual Organizations. In Lewis, B. & Varey, R.J. (eds), *Internal Marketing*. London: Routledge, 2000, and Voima, P., Internal Relationship Management—Broadening the Scope of Internal Marketing. In Lewis, B. & Varey, R.J. (eds), *Internal Marketing*. London: Routledge, 2000.

4 Gummesson, *op.cit*. See also Ballantyne, D., Internal Marketing for Internal Networks. *Journal of Marketing Management*, **13**(5), 1997, pp. 343–366.

5 The notion of joint value creation in value constellations instead of in traditional value chains has been discussed in Normann, R. & Ramírez, R., From Value Chain to Value Constellation. *Harvard Business Review*, July–August 1993, pp. 65–77. Solveig Wikström and her colleagues have studied the effects of bringing customers into the suppliers' or service providers' organizations to jointly develop offerings and service systems with higher value for the customers and better profit potential for the supplier or service provider. See Wikström, S., Lundkvist, A. & Beckérus, Å., *Det interaktiva företaget. Med kunden som största resurs* (The interactive firm: With the customer as the greatest resource). In Swedish. Stockholm, Sweden: Svenska Förlaget, 1998.

6 Grönroos, C., *Service Management and Marketing. Managing the Moments of Truth in Service Competition*. Lexington, MA: Lexington Books, 1990, and Piercy, N.F. & Morgan, R.A., Internal Marketing—the Missing Half of the Marketing Program. *Long Range Planning*, **24**(2), 1991, pp. 82–93.

7 Bowen, D.A., Schneider, B. & Kim, S.S., Shaping Service Cultures Through Strategic Human Resource Management. In Swartz, T.A. & Iacobucci, D. (eds), *Handbook of Services Marketing & Management*. Thousand Oaks, CA: Sage Publications, 2000, pp. 439–454. Also from an HRM perspective, the internal marketing requirement of close collaboration with other business functions is an opportunity which according to Schneider and Bowen, helps HRM to "avoid the HRM trap." See Schneider, B. & Bowen, D.A., *Winning the Service Game*. Boston, MA: Harvard Business School Press, 1995.

8 Compare Gilmore, A. & Carson, D., Managing and Marketing to Internal Customers. In Glynn, W.J. & Barnes, J.G. (eds), *Understanding Service Management*. Chichester: John Wiley & Sons, 1995, pp. 295–321, where internal marketing is defined as the task of spreading the responsibility for marketing across all departments in a firm.

9 Berry, L.L. & Parasuraman, A., *Marketing Services: Competing Through Quality*. New York: The Free Press, 1991, p. 151.

10 Rafiq, M. & Ahmed, P.K., The Scope of Internal Marketing: Defining the Boundary Between Marketing and Human Resource Management. *Journal of Marketing Management*, **9**, 1993, pp. 219–232. Pitt and Foreman claim that the question of whether internal marketing is synonymous with good human resource management has not been studied thoroughly enough. See Pitt, L.F. & Foreman, S.K., Internal Marketing's Role in Organizations: A Transaction Cost Perspective. *Journal of Business Research*, **44**(1), 1999, pp. 25–36. Varey and Lewis suggest that internal marketing should incorporate organizational development (see Varey, R.J. & Lewis, B.R., Beyond the Popular Conception of Internal Marketing. In Fisk, R. & Glynn, L. (eds), *Jazzing into the New*

Millennium: 1999 SERVSIG Services Research Conference, Chicago, IL: American Marketing Association, 1999, pp. 44–51).

11 Compare Bowen, Schneider & Kim, *op.cit.*

12 Ballantyne, D., The Strengths and Weaknesses of Internal Marketing. In Varey, R.J. & Lewis, B.R. (eds), *Internal Marketing*. London: Routledge, 2000.

13 This relationship-oriented definition of internal marketing is adapted from Voima & Grönroos, *op.cit.*, p. 748. In the latter part of the 1990s, following intense interest in relationship marketing there has been a revival in research into internal marketing, but from a relationship perspective.

14 A lack of trust internally has been shown to have a negative effect on internal relationships. See Herriot, P., Manning, W.E.G. & Kidd, J.M., The Content of the Psychological Contract. *British Journal of Management*, **8**(2), 1997, pp. 151–162.

15 Bowen, D.E., Gilliland, S.W. & Folger, R., HRM and Service Fairness: How Being Fair with Employees Spills Over To Customers. *Organizational Dynamics*, **27**(3), 1999, pp. 7–23.

16 *Op.cit.*

17 See Bowen, D.E. & Schneider, B., Service Marketing and Management: Implications for Organizations. *Research in Organizational Behavior*, 10, 1988.

18 Bowen, Gilliland & Folger, *op.cit.*

19 See Lovelock, C., Functional Integration in Services. Understanding the Links Between Marketing, Operations, and Human Resources. In Swartz, T.A. & Iacobucci, D. (eds), *Handbook of Services Marketing & Management*. Thousand Oaks: CA: Sage Publications, 2000, pp. 421–437. As Lovelock observes, "*reward systems* send powerful messages to all employees as to what kind of organization management seeks to create and maintain, especially as to desired attitude and behavior" (p. 426).

20 Katzenbach, J.R. & Santamaria, J.A., Firing Up the Front Line. *Harvard Business Review*, May–June 1999.

21 Smith, S., Internal Affairs. *Marketing*, August 7, 1997, pp. 24–25.

22 As Gummesson points out, technology is only supportive when put to constructive use. See Gummesson, *op.cit.* See also Hallowell, E.M., The Human Moment at Work. *Harvard Business Review*, January–February 1999.

23 Bowen, D.E. & Johnston, R., Internal Service Recovery: Developing a New Construct. *International Journal of Service Industry Management*, **10**(2), 1999, pp. 118–131.

24 Pamela Johnson claims that brains, a heart and courage are three requirements of empowered people. See Johnson, P.R., Brains, Heart and Courage: Keys To Empowerment and Self-Directed Leadership. *Journal of Managerial Psychology*, **9**(2), 1994, pp. 17–21.

25 Bowen, D.E. & Lawler III, E.E., Empowering Service Employees. *Sloan Management Review*, **36**(4), 1995, pp. 73–84.

26 Oakland, J.S. & Oakland, S., The Links Between People Management, Customer Satisfaction and Business Results. *Total Quality Management*, **9**(4/5), 1998, pp. 185–190.

27 Argyris, C., Empowerment: The Emperor's New Clothes. *Harvard Business Review*, **76**, May–June 1998, pp. 98–105.

28 Khan, S., The Key To Being a Leader Company: Empowerment. *Journal of Quality and Participation*, **20**(1), 1997, pp. 44–50.

29 Harari, O., Stop Empowering Your People. *Management Review*, **86**(2), 1997, pp. 48–51. The author expresses concerns about empowering when used without proper care. See also Edvardsson, B., Larsson, G. & Setterlind, S., Internal Service Quality and the Psychosocial Work Environment: An Empirical Analysis of Conceptual Interrelatedness. *The Service Industries Journal*, **17**(2), 1997, pp. 252–263, where the authors show that the psychosocial work environment has an impact on the service orientation of employees.

30 Bowen, D.E. & Lawler III, E.E., The Empowerment of Service Workers: What, Why, How, and When. *Sloan Management Review*, Spring 1992, pp. 31–39.

31 Bowen & Lawler, *op.cit.*

32 Eccles, T., The Deceptive Allure of Empowerment. *Long Range Planning*, **26**(6), 1993, pp. 13–21.

33 Katzenbach & Santamaria, *op.cit.*

34 Berry & Parasuraman, *op.cit.*

35 Cahill, D.J., *Internal Marketing. Your Company's Next Stage of Growth*. New York: The Haworth Press, 1996.

Chapter 15

MANAGING SERVICE CULTURE: THE INTERNAL SERVICE IMPERATIVE

A functioning service culture requires that providing good service is second nature to everyone within that organization.

Introduction

In this chapter the concept of service culture will be discussed. First, are presented two broader concepts, corporate culture and climate, and their importance to the attitudes and behavior of people in an organization. Next, the issue of a service culture and the need for such a culture is covered. Prerequisites for a service culture are analyzed and ways of creating such a culture are described. Finally, barriers to and opportunities for developing such a culture are discussed. After reading the chapter the reader should understand the importance of a service culture for service providers, know the prerequisites for a service culture and know how such a culture can be created.

The Importance of Corporate Culture

The concept *corporate culture* is used to describe a set of common norms and values shared by people in an organization. Hence, culture is an overall concept that explains why people do certain things, think in common ways, and appreciate similar goals, routines, even jokes, just because they are members of the same organization. Corporate culture can be defined as *the pattern of shared values and beliefs that give the members of an organization meaning, and provide them with the rules for behavior in the organization.*[1] Culture represents values that can be thought of as residing deep in the organization. It is not easy to see it, but it is always present.[2] The existing culture in a firm is a result of its organizational past, and it provides stability, meaning and predictability in the organization.[3]

Corporate culture can be seen as an internal *climate* in the organization. As discussed in the previous chapter, the organizational climate is partly dependent on how internal relationships function between people in the organization. The climate is the employees' accumulated sense of what is important in an organization.[4] This is a result of what goals employees are given to pursue in their jobs and how daily routines are handled in the organization.[5] Service providers have to manage their internal climate so that employees who serve internal or external customers develop positive attitudes towards giving service. Such attitudes and a service-oriented climate can be expected to exist, if the employees feel that organizational routines, directions for action given by policies and management and reward systems indicate that focusing on giving good service is important.[6] Because of this, the culture and climate of a firm have a vital impact on how service-oriented its employees are. The terms *culture* and *climate* are often used interchangeably to means more or less the same thing, because they are so closely related to each other.

Culture is an important phenomenon to study and understand, because it is considered a potential basis for competitive advantage.[7] Therefore, managing the company culture is always important in any type of business. For service firms and manufacturers facing service competition the development and management of a service culture is a critical task.

Internal activities or projects, such as training programs or courses, do not lead to expected results if they do not fit the existing culture in the firm. For example, a service-oriented training program alone would probably have no significant impact on the thinking and behavior of employees of a manufacturer where goods-oriented industrial norms are highly regarded, or the employees of a service firm where sales and cost-efficient operations are the only visible management priorities. A much more strategically oriented and comprehensive process would be needed if any results are to be achieved.

A weak corporate culture, where there are few or no clear common shared values, creates an insecure feeling concerning how to respond to various clues and how to react in different situations. For example, what to do when a customer has unexpected requests may be self-evident, when a company has a strong culture. On the other hand, if there is a weak culture, such a situation frequently results in inflexible behavior by contact employees, long waiting times, and a feeling of insecurity on the part of the customer. This, of course, damages customer perceived service quality. In such a culture, employees do not have any clear norms to relate, for example, sales training or service skills courses to, and hence they do not know how to respond to such activities.

A strong culture, however, enables people to act in a certain manner and to respond to various actions in a consistent way. Clear cultural values seem particularly important for guiding employee behavior, especially in service organizations.[8] In many cases new employees are easily assimilated into the prevailing culture.[9] A customer-conscious and service-minded person with a favorable part-time marketing attitude who is recruited for a service job may quickly be brought down to earth by his new colleagues who share strong values which do not honor interest in customers or in giving good service. Again, a strong service-oriented culture easily snowballs. Service-oriented employees are attracted by such an employer, and most new employees are influenced in a favorable way by the existing service culture.

When employees identify with the values of an organization, they are less inclined to quit, and customers seem to be more satisfied with the service provided. In addition to this, when there is a minimal employee turnover, service-oriented values and a positive attitude toward service are more easily transmitted to newcomers in the organization.[10]

The modern views of quality and productivity are related to corporate culture. Improving productivity and quality requires a new way of thinking in the culture of the organization.

A strong culture is not, however, always good. In situations where the surrounding world has changed and new ways of thinking are called for, such a culture may become a serious hindrance to change. It may be difficult to respond to new challenges. In such a situation a strong culture does not only affect the responsiveness of employees in a negative fashion, but may also paralyze management. For example, a strong manufacturing-oriented or sales-focused culture may develop into a serious problem for a firm that should obviously respond to service-related changes in the market, or to a situation where keeping existing customers has become the most important way of doing profitable business. A service strategy is perhaps the obvious solution, but the management team may be too restricted by their inherited way of viewing the business. If only marginal internal activities to introduce a service strategy are implemented, old-fashioned ways of thinking among middle management and the rest of the personnel do not permit any major attitude change.

A Case Study of Culture-Driven Success: Nokia

Nokia, the Finland-based telecommunications and mobile phone giant, can attribute its success to innovative management, leading-edge technological knowledge and the innovative development of mobile phone technology, products and designs. However, this firm technology base combined with innovation has created a strong corporate culture that drives the organization in a certain direction and in an innovative fashion, and second, surprisingly quickly assimilates new employees. In this way a coherent and vision-oriented team is reinforced and even created by the culture. External observers note that the corporate culture may be the major driver behind success.

The firm is clearly managed by visions and milestones to achieve. The Nokia culture is a major instrument in directing the efforts of research and development, new ventures, production, administration, sales and marketing, and other business functions towards these milestones. It even involves outside business partners.

The Importance of Climate and Culture in Service Organizations

In a service context a strong and well-established culture, which enhances an appreciation for good service and customer orientation, is extremely important, perhaps more so than in a traditional manufacturing environment. This follows from the nature of service production and consumption. Normally service production cannot be standardized as completely as an assembly line, because of the human impact in the buyer–seller interactions of the service encounters. Customers and their behavior cannot be totally standardized and predetermined. Situations vary, and therefore a distinct service-oriented culture is needed which tells employees how to respond to new, unforeseen and even awkward situations.[11]

It has been argued that a strong culture is especially important in service organizations, because the attitude and performance of the employees is so visible to customers. If employees experience a service-oriented climate, the customers' experience of service quality will probably be better than otherwise expected. There seems to be a clear interrelationship between employee experiences and customer experiences.[12]

Since service quality is a function of the cooperation of so many resources— human as well as technological—a strong culture which enhances quality is a must for successful management of quality in a service context. Moreover, since it is more difficult to control quality in a service context than in manufacturing, very service-oriented and quality-conscious values are necessary in the organization. In this way management can execute *indirect control by culture*.[13]

Managing Relationships Requires a Service Culture

Customer relationships (as well as relationships with suppliers, distributors and other types of network partners) include a large number of services. Some of these services, such as over-the-counter personal services, goods deliveries, maintenance, and consulting services can easily be seen by management as what they are in the minds of customers; that is, as value-creating services. Other types of services such as invoicing, complaints handling, answering phone calls or e-mails, and a host of similar activities, which were earlier labeled hidden, unbillable services in relationships are not as easily recognized by management or by those who are implementing these activities as value-adding services.

If the culture in a firm which has decided to give priority to the management of customer relationships (and relationships with other parties) does not honor services and a constant attention to giving good service to the other party, it will be difficult to implement the relationship-oriented strategy. The non-service culture will keep people (managers, supervisors and customer contact employees alike), from realizing the importance of all the "hidden services," and even the more visible service elements will not be given enough attention. The values which dominate in the firm will direct people's attention elsewhere. Therefore, managing customer relationships, and relationships with other parties, requires a service-oriented culture.

Profitability through a Service Strategy Requires a Service Culture

Implementing a *service strategy* requires the support of all employees in the organization. Top management, middle management, customer contact employees and support employees will all have to get involved. An interest in service and an appreciation of good service among managers and all other employees is an essential requirement. What is needed is a corporate culture that can be labeled a *service culture*. Such a culture can be described as

> . . . a culture where an appreciation for good service exists, and where giving good service to internal as well as ultimate, external customers is considered by everyone a natural way of life and one of the most important values.

Hence, service has to be the *raison d'être* for all organizational activities. This, of course, does not exclude other values from being important, too. Instilling a service culture in an organization does not mean that other values have to lose their importance altogether. For example, attention to internal efficiency and cost control is still important, as well as an appreciation of sales and getting new customers. However, the service-oriented values should have a dominating position in the organization. They must not remain a marginal or lower priority concern, but a top-priority concern in strategic as well as operational thinking and performance.

A service culture means that the employees of an organization can be characterized as being service-oriented. Service orientation can be described as shared values and attitudes that influence people in an organization so that interactions between them internally and interactions with customers and representatives of other parties are perceived favorably. Internally, a service orientation can be expected to enhance the internal climate and improve the quality of internal services and support. Externally, a service orientation should create good perceived quality for customers and others as well as lead to strengthened relationships with customers and other parties.

Clearly, a service orientation enhances the functional quality dimension of customer perceived service quality, and probably also supports the production of good technical quality. As Figure 15.1 illustrates, service orientation among personnel fuels an important positive process within an organization. A service orientation that is a characteristic of a service culture improves service quality as perceived by customers.

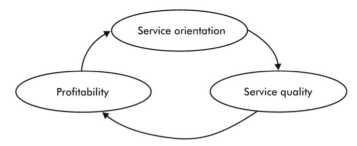

FIGURE 15.1 Effects of a service orientation

Service-oriented employees who take an interest in their customers do more for the customers, are more courteous and flexible, try to find appropriate solutions to customers' wishes, and go out of their way to recover a situation where something has gone wrong or an unexpected situation has occurred. Furthermore, we know that customer perceived quality is a key determinant of profitability, although it is not the only one. Hence, service orientation improves service quality which, in turn, positively affects profitability. This favorable process continues as an upward spiral, because better profitability provides means to maintain and further improve service-oriented attitudes among personnel. The process fuels itself.

However, a word of warning is important here. Although good perceived quality can be expected to improve profitability, this requires that the service offerings provided to customers are put together in such a way that customers are prepared to pay a price which matches the cost of producing the service. There are situations where customers may be very satisfied with the perceived service quality, but they are still not profitable over time.[14] Furthermore, the positive connection between culture and profitability is often claimed to exist, and a clear service-oriented culture probably has a favorable impact on the financial performance of the firm. However, it is difficult to show that this is the case, because there are always so many external factors involved that it is difficult to isolate the effects of culture.[15]

Shared Values

The values shared by people in an organization and the prevailing norms are the foundation of the culture. The shared values constitute guidelines for employees in performing their everyday tasks. In an organization with strong shared values three common characteristics are often present:[16]

- the shared values are a clear guideline for task performance;
- managers devote much of their time to developing and reinforcing the shared values; and
- the shared values are deeply anchored among the employees.

It has also been found that performance is improved by strong shared values in an organization. Managers and employees devote themselves more to issues and ways of performing that are emphasized by the shared values. Performance is better, because people are more motivated. Strong shared values may, however, become a problem, too; for the following reasons:

- the shared values may have become *obsolete* and are therefore not consistent with current strategies and service concepts; and
- strong shared values may lead to *resistance to change*, which makes it difficult for the organization to respond to external challenges.

In many firms these are highly relevant problems. Even though there may be no service culture, there may be a strong corporate culture. The existing culture may emphasize manufacturing ideals or bureaucratic routines, or emphasize short-term sales instead of the importance of concentrating on keeping customers. In many manufacturing firms and institutions within the public sector, a strong culture that does not appreciate service is a major hindrance to change.

Challenges from the market and from society may go unnoticed or the organization may not be capable of adjusting to the need for change. The results are sometimes fatal. The effects of a single internal activity, for example, a training program that does not have a strategic foundation will probably be counteracted by the hostile culture. Internal marketing efforts may easily fail if they are not in line with the prevailing culture, or if the objectives of the internal marketing efforts are contradictory to it. On the other hand, a long-term internal marketing process is one ingredient in a process that aims at changing an existing culture. A strategic approach to internal change is needed.

Requirements for a Service Culture

Introducing and implementing a service strategy requires a service culture. In many firms or organizations within the public sector a cultural change is called for. Such a change is a *long-range process*, which demands extensive and long-range activity programs. In the previous chapter we discussed one major ingredient in such a process, *internal marketing*. This chapter will look at general prerequisites for achieving a service culture.

The *requirements for good service*[17] are strategic requirements; organizational requirements; management requirements; and knowledge and attitude requirements.

If the four kinds of requirements are not all recognized, the internal change process will suffer and the result will be mediocre at best. The four different requirements above are intertwined. For example, a complicated organizational structure may make it impossible to implement a good service concept; or a service-minded and motivated contact employee becomes frustrated and loses interest in giving good service because he gets no support or appreciation from his boss, or finds it impossible to be service-minded because the service orientation is not derived from a strategic foundation, and therefore sufficient resources are not granted and continuous and consistent top management support is lacking. The following sections will discuss the four requirements above in some detail.

Developing a Service Strategy

The *strategic requirements for good service* are fulfilled by developing a service-oriented strategy. This means that top management *want* to create a service-oriented organization; the management team is not just paying lip service to service orientation. Here top management may be the managing director and his management team, but it may also be the head of a regional or local organization or a profit center which can operate sufficiently well independently.

The *business mission* is the foundation of strategy formulation. Strategies are developed based on the scope and direction of the business indicated by the mission. A service strategy means that the mission includes a *service vision*. It demands that a service orientation, which of course means different things in different industries and even firms, is to be achieved. This will not be discussed here.

However, a service strategy requires that *service concepts* related to the business mission and the strategy be defined. If service concepts are not clearly defined, the firm lacks a stable foundation for discussion of goals, resources to be used, and performance standards. As previously stated, the service concept states *what* should be done, to *whom, how,* and with *which resources,* and *what benefits* customers should be offered. If these issues are not clarified, personnel will not understand what they are supposed to do. Moreover, goals and routines do not form a clear and understandable pattern, because there is no clear and well-known service concept to relate them to. If the service concepts are not clearly understood at the middle management level, it will be difficult to perform supervisory duties consistently.

Human resource management is an important part of strategic requirements. Recruitment procedures, career planning, reward systems and so on are vital parts of a service culture. Good service performance has to guide HRM. The more aspects other than skills and service-orientation dominate, for example recruitment procedures and reward systems, the less inclined toward service-mindedness employees will be, and a service culture will be difficult to achieve.

Good service has to be rewarded and accomplishments have to be measured in such a way that employees realize the importance of service. However, able employees are sometimes forced to do dumb things, because measurement and rewarding systems are wrong. Quite often only internal efficiency issues, such as the number of meals served in a restaurant or the number of phone calls dealt with, are measured and reward systems developed accordingly. If this is the case, and employees feel they are rewarded for accomplishments other than excellent service quality, any attempt to develop a service culture is bound to fail.

Developing the Organizational Structure

Development of the organizational structure creates the *organizational prerequisite for good service.* All aspects of organization design have to be geared to the service process, if high service quality is to be achieved and consistently maintained. The more complicated the formal structure is, the more problems related to giving good service will occur. The organization of a firm can be a serious obstacle to a service culture. Good service means, among other things, easy access to services and quick and flexible decision-making. It requires cooperation between various departments in designing, developing and executing services. If the organizational structure does not allow employees to perform in this way, values characterizing a service culture cannot be developed. Good intentions, even when they are based on strategy, cannot be implemented without the structure being in place. This makes people frustrated and may have a counter-effect. Employees may feel that management demands the impossible, and this only achieves negative effects as far as service-oriented attitudes are concerned.

There is also an informal organizational structure. People create a value structure and personal contacts, good or bad which make the formal structure either less or more complicated. In the former case, positive attitudes among the employees involved may make it possible to solve the problems created by a complicated structure. In the latter case, on the other hand, even a service-oriented structure may be an obstacle to good service. If people do not want to collaborate, a service culture is harder to accomplish.

Normally, a service-oriented firm requires a relatively flat organizational structure with few hierarchical levels. Decisions have to be made by employees who are close to the customers. The roles of managers change. The customer contact and support employees get more responsibility and they are expected to perform more independently. However, this does not mean that the supervisory level loses power, only that the role of supervisors changes. They are not just technical managers and decision-makers anymore; instead, they are supposed to be coaches and demonstrate leadership. They will have to assist and encourage their staff and create an open climate where good service is a leading shared value.

The role of supervisors in support functions must also be clarified. Often employees who do not have immediate customer contacts regard themselves as carrying out passive functions with some administrative duties. In fact, their role in most support functions is much more active. As we have noted in previous contexts, they should see people in customer contact functions as their *internal customers*, whom they will have to serve as well as they serve the ultimate (external) customers.

In many firms, the customer contact functions are understaffed, whereas back office and staff functions departments are overstaffed. The obvious conclusion is to strengthen the customer contact processes and streamline and redesign other departments so that they support the buyer–seller interactions in a more effective and service-oriented way.

Another aspect of organizational development is the development of operational systems, routines and work flows. Good service normally requires simplified ways of doing things, so that unnecessary delays and information breakdown are avoided. The effects of this are twofold. First of all, *customers* perceive such a development as better functional quality of the service. Second, *employees* feel that their job has become more meaningful and motivating when routines and work flows have been simplified, and unnecessary or time-consuming elements of the operational systems have been eliminated.

Information technology also provides opportunities to make changes in internal information systems and operational systems. The introduction of *intranets* can create a feeling of belonging and strengthen corporate identity among personnel. An intranet makes everyone a member of the same information system and makes it possible, for example, for every customer contact and support employee to share the same, relevant information about a given customer at the same point in time. If the information is easily retrievable, constantly updated and relevant, such a system supports good and timely interactions with customers and helps employees to give good service. This can contribute to a positive service culture.

Developing Leadership

The management prerequisite for good service is promoted by establishing a *service-oriented leadership*. This includes managers' and supervisors' attitudes toward their role, their teams, and how they act as managers. Management must be supportive, inspirational and attuned to the individuals they manage. Without active and continuous support from all managers and supervisors, the values that characterize a true service culture cannot be spread throughout the organization and maintained once they have been established. Such a managerial impact is of vital importance if service-oriented values are to be communicated to the employees, strengthened, and made an integral part of the everyday life of the organization.

Managers are leaders in an organization, and by leading they also contribute to the culture. In this way managers, and supervisors, have a key role in the development of a service culture. On the other hand, a manager who is not aware of this, will be led by the culture.[18] This can be a problem in a situation when the culture needs to be changed, for example towards a more service-oriented direction. Hence, it is very important for every manager and supervisor in the organization to be aware of the corporate culture.

Simply being a technical manager without taking on the role of coach and leader does not do much for the pursuit of a service culture. A more whole-hearted devotion to the service concepts and the employees is called for. Service is still to a large extent a human business and the result of interactions between humans internally as well as externally. Inhumane management styles do not fit in here.

Communication is a critical ingredient of leadership. The manager and supervisor will have to be willing to, and know how to, communicate with their staff. Communication is a two-way street, where the ability to listen to others is an important aspect. A leader should be able to create a dialog with his staff, and also be able to give clear direction and guidance, and make decisions when he is expected to take a firm stand.

One of the biggest risks involved in a process toward a service orientation is the risk of ambiguity. If the manager talks about the need of service-mindedness and customer consciousness, but in reality does not pursue a service strategy, he *and* the service culture lose credibility. A sense of uncertainty among personnel is easily created, and the concept of service orientation and a service culture will not be taken seriously anymore. Performance that is in line with good quality and the nature of a service culture as expressed by management has to be measured and rewarded. Internal efficiency and manufacturing-oriented productivity measures must not be given priority. Hence, management has to talk about the importance of good service and of pursuing a service culture, *and demonstrate by their actions* their belief in this. Otherwise, serious damage may easily be done to a service-orientation process that may have been initiated in good faith.

The top person in the organization, which may be a firm, a local unit, a profit center, a strategic business unit, or another well-defined organizational unit, will constantly have to give the service strategy top priority and continuously and actively give it his strong support. Furthermore, every manager and supervisor will have to accept the role of a coach. They have to be able to encourage employees and strengthen their motivation for service-oriented performance.

Monitoring performance and results is, of course, still an integral part of management. However, the traditional role of management is shifting from controlling toward guiding employees. Many managers feel that their authority is eroding as a consequence of such a shift, and they cannot effectively "manage" their people anymore. This is not the case. The leadership-oriented management philosophy does not mean that management abdicates, but instead that it sets up goals and guidelines and delegates operational responsibility in a clear manner. Hence, the traditional role as mere technical manager is changed to a new role characterized by *leadership* and *coaching*. Another aspect of a service-oriented management style is the development of a positive internal communication climate. On the one hand, employees need information from management to be able to implement a service strategy; on the other, they have valuable information for management about customers' needs and wishes, any problems and opportunities, and so on. Feedback is required so that they see the results of their job and their actions. If there is a lack of feedback, employees easily lose interest in what they are doing.

It is a good idea to get contact employees involved in the planning process and in decision-making concerning, say, what new services to offer and how they should be produced and delivered. Overall objectives for a group or a department can be broken down into subgoals for that unit in cooperation with the employees who are supposed to accomplish those goals. This process is, first, a way of communicating the strategy and objectives of the firm to the employees, and second, a way of achieving employee commitment to the service strategy and to the goals.

Finally, as noted in the previous chapter, management methods and the attitudes of managers and supervisors toward their employees are of pivotal importance to the long-term success of an internal marketing process.

Service Training Programs

By training employees, the *knowledge and attitude requirements for good service* can be achieved. Training employees is also an integral part of internal marketing. In organizations where existing values are not service-oriented, an attitude of resistance to change can be expected. A large portion of this resistance can be removed by creating the previously discussed strategic, organizational and management prerequisites for good service. However, this resistance is also at least partly a question of attitude and a lack of knowledge. If the firm has always operated in say, a, manufacturer-oriented or bureaucratic way, it is not easy to make people think in new directions. This goes for management as well as for other employees.

If top management, middle management, and support and customer contact employees are expected to be motivated for service-oriented thinking and behavior, they will need to know how a service organization operates, what makes up customer relationships, what their role in the operation and in customer relationships is, and what is expected of the individual. A person who does not understand what is going on and why cannot be expected to be motivated to do a good job as a contact person or an internal service provider in support functions behind the line of customer visibility.[19]

Moreover, every person should be aware of the firm's business mission, strategies and overall objectives as well as the goals of his own department and function and his own personal goals. Otherwise, it would be unrealistic to think that an employee understands why he is told that it is important to perform in a certain way. This is even more important for employees in support functions than for contact employees.

In training programs, knowledge-oriented training and attitude training are intertwined. The more knowledgeable a person is, the easier it is for that person to have positive attitudes toward a specific subject. It is essential to realize that attitudes can seldom be changed without knowledge. Pep talks may help on some occasions, but they will never create enduring service-oriented attitudes if people do not have the facts: employees need to know why the firm is a service business, or why as a manufacturer it adopts a service strategy; which requirements for performance follow from this; what my role is in relation to other functions and people, and in relation to customers; what is demanded of me as an individual, and why.

Service training can be divided into three categories:

- developing a *holistic* view of the organization and its subfunctions as a service organization of how it functions in a market-oriented manner;
- developing *skills* concerning how various tasks are to be performed; and
- developing specific *communication and service skills*.

All three types of training are needed. The first type gives a general foundation for understanding a service strategy and how to implement it. It puts every function, department and task into perspective, and demonstrates how the processes in the organization and the people performing these processes are related to each other and to a common goal of servicing customers well and creating support for their internal value-generating processes. The second type, vocational training, provides the skills required so that employees can perform their tasks, which may have been changed after the introduction of a service strategy, efficiently. The third type of training provides employees, especially customer contact employees but also support employees, with specific skills as far as communication tasks are concerned. Courses which address service-mindedness belong to this group, too. A serious mistake, which is all too common, is to believe that only the third type of training is needed to change employee attitudes. Such an approach is hardly ever successful. It may be the easiest, but at the same time it is the least strategic way of addressing the issue of attitude change. Doing this is a pitfall which should be avoided.

In the present chapter the nature and importance of a service culture is discussed as well as the framework for developing such a culture. When the organizational and strategic prerequisites are present, the rest is a matter of human resource development. Managers and other personnel will have to be motivated to pursue a service strategy in strategic and operational planning as well as in implementing the strategy. Here substantial help can be provided by the concept of *internal marketing*.

Developing a Service Culture: Barriers and Opportunities

Clearly, the task of changing the corporate culture and creating a service culture is a huge one. Getting started is often a substantial problem. There is an initial barrier to starting the process, and there is a threshold to cross on the way. Before this threshold has been crossed, no major changes can be seen in the internal value systems. However, once the process develops far enough, it usually gains pace, provided it is constantly supported and enhanced, especially by top management. A service culture has to be maintained once it has been achieved, otherwise there is always the risk that the interest in service and in servicing internal as well as external customers will start to deteriorate.

It is not easy to get started, but in some situations it is easier than in others. Favorable conditions for a change process are:

- *environmental pressure*, such as increased competition, changes in customer needs and expectations, the introduction of new technologies, or deregulation or regulation of the business;
- *new organizational strategies*, which differ from the previous ones; and
- *new structural arrangements*, such as new management or a major change in the organizational structure.

All or some of these things could, of course, occur simultaneously, which would probably help the process. When times are good, and problems seem to be too far into the future or are invisible to most people in the organization, it is much more difficult to start to change the existing corporate culture. However, when changing an organization's culture, it is critical to preserve some of what has gone before and build on it to make the change. Honoring and learning from the past is important and does not have to mean that it slows down the process or counteracts it.[20] It is probably a good idea to move slowly, to set intermediate goals and to make change gradually. Sometimes, however, there is no time for that. In most cases there is though, and trying to implement change too rapidly may lead to bad results. A cultural change means that the mindset of people have to change. The process has to be planned and executed in the same way as any important organizational task.

Summary and Questions for Discussion

The phenomenon of corporate culture and service culture is extremely complicated. Developing a specific culture, therefore, requires that a whole range of internal issues be addressed. Culture is a holistic phenomenon. It cannot exist in isolation from or side by side with, for instance, the organizational structure, management approaches and methods, or the business mission and strategies of the organization. It is the result of these and other aspects of organizational life.

Hence, culture becomes a strategic matter. It does so in two ways, which are related to each other. First of all, creating a service culture requires a holistic view of the company by the decision-makers and those responsible for developing the culture; only top management holds that position. Therefore, it becomes a strategic issue that internal requirements for the creation of a service culture be developed. Second, implementing a service strategy requires, among other things, the kind of people who believe in service and who consider that it is essential in business to provide internal as well as external customers with good service. Therefore, if an organization intends to implement a service strategy, it is of vitally important that it aims for the achievement of a service culture.

Questions for Discussion

1. Why is culture of strategic importance for the performance of an organization?
2. What is the difference between organizational climate and culture?
3. Which are the strategic requirements for a service culture?
4. Discuss the possible relationship between a service culture, service quality and profitability in a service organization.
5. Analyze how well the strategic requirements for a service culture are fulfilled in your firm, or in any given organization. What should be done to improve or strengthen the culture?
6. What are the problems related to starting to change the corporate culture?

Further Reading

Barney, J. (1986) Organizational Culture: Can It Be a Source of Sustained Competitive Advantage? *Academy of Management Review*, **11**(3), pp. 656–666.

Bowen, D.E. & Schneider, B. (1988) Service Marketing and Management: Implications for Organizational Behavior. *Research in Organizational Behavior*, 10.

Bowen, D.A., Schneider, B. & Kim, S.S. (2000) Shaping Service Cultures Through Strategic Human Resource Management. In Swartz, T.A. & Iacobucci, D. (eds), *Handbook of Services Marketing & Management*. Thousand Oaks, CA: Sage Publications, pp. 439–454.

Carlzon, J. (1987) *Moments of Truth*. Cambridge. MA: Ballinger.

Davis, S.M. (1985) *Managing Corporate Culture*. Cambridge, MA: Ballinger.

Deal, T.F. & Kennedy, A.A. (1982) *Corporate Cultures: The Rites and Rituals of Corporate Life*. Reading, MA: Addison-Wesley.

Gorbachev, M. (1987) *Perestroika—New Thinking for Our Country and the World*. New York: Harper & Row.

Grönroos, C. (1990) *Service Management and Marketing. Managing the Moments of Truth in Service Competition*. Lexington, MA: Lexington Books.

Schein, E.H. (1992) *Organizational Culture and Leadership*. 2nd edition. San Fransisco, CA: Jossey-Bass.

Schneider, B. (1986) Notes on Climate and Culture. In Venkatesan, M., Schmalensee, D.M. & Marshall, C. (eds), *Creativity in Services Marketing. What's New, What Works What's Developing*. Chicago, IL: American Marketing Association.

Schneider, B. (1990) The Climate for Service: An Application of the Climate Construct. In Schneider, B. (ed)., *Organizational Climate and Culture*. San Fransisco, CA: Jossey-Bass, pp. 383–412.

Schneider, B. & Bowen, D.E. (1995) *Winning the Service Game*. Boston, MA: Harvard Business School Press.

Schneider, B., Brief, A.B. & Guzzo, R.A. (1996) Creating a Climate and Culture for Sustainable Organizational Change. *Organizational Dynamics*, **24**(4), pp. 7–19.

Schneider, B., White, S. & Paul, M.C. (1998) Linking Service Climate and Customer Perception of Service Quality: Test of a Causal Model. *Journal of Applied Psychology*, **83**(2), pp. 150–163.

Siehl, C. & Martin, J. (1990) Organization Culture: A Key to Financial Performance? In Schneider, B. (ed.), *Organizational Climate and Culture*. San Fransisco, CA: Jossey-Bass, pp. 241–281.

Storbacka, K. (1994) *The Nature of Customer Relationship Profitability*. Helsingfors, Swedish School of Economics Finland/CERS Center for Relationship and Service Management.

Zemke, R. (1988) Creating Service Culture. *The Service Edge*, No. 8.

Zerbe, W.J., Dobni, D. & Harel, G.H. (1998) Promoting Employee Service Behavior: The Role of Perceptions of Human Resource Management Practices and Service Culture. *Revue Canadienne des Sciences de l'Administration*, **15**(2), pp. 165–179.

Notes

1. Davis, S.M., *Managing Corporate Culture*. Cambridge, MA: Ballinger, 1985.

2. Bowen, D.A., Schneider, B. & Kim, S.S., Shaping Service Cultures Through Strategic Human Resource Management. In Swartz, T.A. & Iacobucci, D. (eds), *Handbook of Services Marketing & Management*. Thousand Oaks, CA: Sage Publications, 2000, pp. 439–454.

3. Schein, E.H., *Organizational Culture and Leadership*. 2nd edition. San Fransisco, CA: Jossey-Bass, 1992.

4. Schneider, B. & Bowen, D.E., *Winning the Service Game*. Boston, MA: Harvard Business School Press, 1995.

5. Schneider, B., Brief, A.B. & Guzzo, R.A., Creating a Climate and Culture for Sustainable Organizational Change. *Organizational Dynamics*, 24(4), 1996, pp. 7–19.

6. Schneider, B., The Climate for Service: An Application of the Climate Construct. In Schneider, B. (ed.), *Organizational Climate and Culture*. San Fransisco, CA: Jossey-Bass, 1990, pp. 383–412.

7. Barney, J., Organizational Culture. Can It Be a Source of Sustained Competitive Advantage. *Academy of Management Review*, **11**(3), 1986, pp. 656–666.

8. Schneider, B., Notes on Climate and Culture. In Venkatesan, M., Schmalensee, D.M. & Marshall, C. (eds), *Creativity in Services Marketing. What's New, What Works What's Developing*. Chicago, IL: American Marketing Association, 1986.

9. Schein, *op.cit.*

10. Bowen, D.E. & Schneider, B., Service Marketing and Management: Implications for Organizational Behavior. *Research in Organizational Behavior*, **10**, 1988.

11. Schneider, *op.cit.*

12. Schneider, B., White, S. & Paul, M.C., Linking Service Climate and Customer Perception of Service Quality: Test of a Causal Model. *Journal of Applied Psychology*, **83**(2), 1998, pp. 150–163.

13. For example, in a study of the airline industry it became clear that the service culture had a direct effect on service behavior. See Zerbe, W.J., Dobni, D. & Harel, G.H., Promoting Employee Service Behavior: The Role of Perceptions of Human Resource Management Practices and Service Culture. *Revue Canadienne des Sciences de l'Administration*, **15**(2), 1998, pp. 165–179.

14. In a large study of the profitability of customer bases in retail banks in Scandinavia, Kaj Storbacka showed that a large number of satisfied customers had a substantial negative effect on the overall profitability of the bank. See Storbacka, K., *The Nature of Customer Relationship Profitability*. Helsingfors, Finland: Swedish School of Economics Finland/CERS, 1994.

15. Bowen, Schneider & Kim, *op.cit.* See also Siehl, C. & Martin, J., Organization Culture: A Key to Financial Performance?. In Schneider, B. (ed.), *Organizational Climate and Culture*. San Fransisco, CA: Jossey-Bass, 1990, pp. 241–281.

16. Deal, T.F. & Kennedy, A.A., *Corporate Cultures: The Rites and Rituals of Corporate Life*. Reading, MA: Addison-Wesley, 1982.

17. Grönroos, C., *Service Management and Marketing. Managing the Moments of Truth in Service Competition*. Lexington, MA: Lexington Books, 1990.

18. Schein, *op.cit.*

19. Jan Carlzon, the former managing director and president of SAS, illustrates in his book about the turnaround process of SAS in the 1980s (*Moments of Truth*. Cambridge. MA: Ballinger, 1987) the impact of a holistic understanding of the tasks people are involved in by the following anecdote:

> There is no better way to sum up my experience than with the story about the two stone cutters who were chipping square blocks out of granite. A visitor to the quarry asked what they were doing. The first stone cutter, looking rather sour, grumbled, "I'm cutting this damned stone into a block." The second, who looked pleased with his work, replied proudly "I'm on this team that's building a cathedral."

This anecdote is still often told in similar contexts. It is interesting to note that, in slightly different words, Mikhael Gorbachev, the last leader of the Soviet Union, told it as an illustration of the *perestroika* process. See Gorbachev, M., *Perestroika—New Thinking for Our Country and the World*. New York: Harper & Row, 1987.

20   Zemke, R., Creating Service Culture. *The Service Edge*, No. 8, 1988.

Chapter 16

CONCLUSIONS: MANAGING RELATIONSHIPS AND THE SIX RULES OF SERVICE

Good intellectual analysis and thorough planning of a service-oriented business is value-less unless management has the determination, courage and strength needed to implement their visions and plans.

Introduction

This final chapter will summarize the essence of a service strategy. First, the scope of *service management and marketing* are summarized. Then, six "rules" of service are presented and, finally, the barriers to achieving results in an organization are presented.

An Overview of a Market-Oriented Service Strategy

In Figure 16.1 the essence of service management and marketing is summarized. The core of the process is the series of *moments of truth* of service encounters, where the employee and the customer, supported by systems and technology and physical resources, meet and interact. These service encounters create value for customers. If they are not well taken care of, the *Perceived Service Quality* (service quality as perceived by the customer), is damaged, and the service provider may lose business. *The main focus in service competition is the continuous management of the series of moments of truth in service processes, as well as adequate support from managers and supporting functions and from investments in technology, operations and administrative systems.* If the ongoing moments of truth are well taken care of the service encounters will turn out well, and the relationship will probably develop satisfactorily and lead to continuous business.

Value for customers is not, of course, entirely produced in the service encounters. Much may have been preproduced by the supporting part of the organization. The final value for the customers emerges in the consumption or usage of the service. *From the customer's point of view, however, what happens in the*

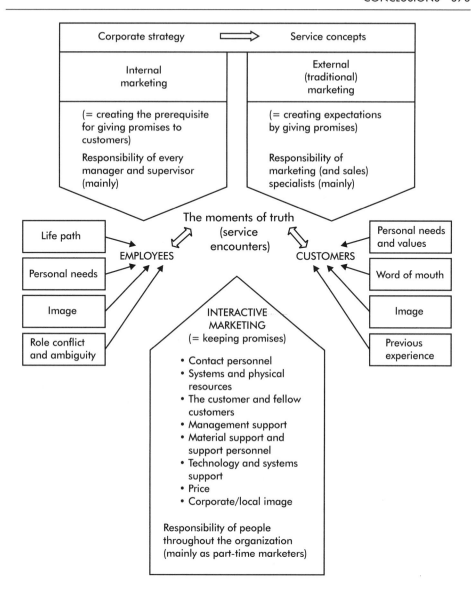

FIGURE 16.1   An overview of a market-oriented strategy

service encounter counts. If the customer is not satisfied with what he experiences, then the preproduction efforts in back offices, or by manufacturers in factories, have been in vain.

Giving Promises: Traditional External Marketing

Customers' experiences of service encounters do not take place in a vacuum. They go into them with certain *expectations*, which are partly created by the service provider itself. By its *external marketing* process, involving *traditional marketing* efforts, such as market research, personal selling, advertising, Internet communication, direct mail, sales promotion and pricing the organization *gives promises*, which should correspond with the personal needs, values and wishes of the target group of customers. The *full-time marketers* inside the organization or outside of it (for example, in advertising agencies and market research firms) are usually responsible for this type of traditional external marketing.

These promises are enhanced or counteracted in the minds of the customers by their *previous experiences*, if they have had any, by *word of mouth communication*, and by customers' conception of the *image* of the service provider.

Enabling Promises: Internal Marketing

Employees' abilities and motivation to meet the expectations of customers are backed up by *internal marketing efforts*. By creating and maintaining a service culture, as well as by actively marketing new goods and services, and by marketing campaigns and activities directed toward the employees, the organization can prepare its employees for *part-time marketing* responsibilities. Thus, internal marketing is a must for *creating the prerequisite conditions for keeping promises*.

Internal marketing is a *top management* responsibility, but it is also the responsibility of *every* manager and supervisor. Of course, personal needs of jobs and supervisors' encouragement of employees, as well as their life path and their image of the employer, also have an impact on the employees' performance as part-time marketers. Moreover, employees are influenced by *role ambiguity*; related to, for example, what they perceive customers and the organization expect them to do. Employees are also influenced by *role conflicts*; for example, when what management says the employees should consider important in their jobs conflicts with the opportunities to live up to these intentions that management provides them. Grocery retailers sometimes give promises in their advertising about cooking advice that customers can get in the store. If the employees, a large proportion of whom may be working on a low-pay, part-time basis, do not have the cooking knowledge or interest needed to give such advice to customers who may often be better cooks than they are, they will be put in an awkward situation which they cannot handle. If they get information from customers about what they are supposed to do, which is not uncommon, the situation is even more frustrating for the employees. Bad internal relationships and bad external relationships with customers follow from this.

Another aspect of how well promises are enabled is the *support of systems and technology*—information technology and other—gotten by the employees. If information about customers is difficult to retrieve from databases, or if customer information files are not properly updated, customer contact employees have difficulty in providing customers with attentive, prompt and accurate service. Moreover, a lack of *systems support* also has a negative impact on internal marketing processes in the organization.

Empowering employees is another key aspect of enabling promises. Employees who have the authority to handle customer contact situations themselves, and who have the technical skills and the motivation to take this responsibility will fulfill promises effectively and in a customer-oriented manner. Here again, a lack of systems support can seriously diminish the potential positive effects of empowerment.

Keeping Promises: Interactive Marketing

What actually happens in the moments of truth of the service encounters, where customers and employees meet and interact, determines whether customers' experience meets their expectations. If experiences are equal to or are higher than expectations, the perceived service quality is probably good; otherwise there may be a quality problem. Good quality is a strong basis for a long-term customer relationship, including resales and cross-sales, as well as for favorable word of mouth and image.

Thus, *fulfilling promises* in the buyer–seller interactions of the service encounters is one major aspect of the *Interactive Marketing process*. The customer contact employees are most often the key to success. However, information systems, operational systems and physical resources, and the customers all influence interactive marketing performance. Although the role of the employees is most often paramount, it should not be over-emphasized. First of all, there are a range of situations in which customers interact only with systems and physical resources. Using an ATM, making a local telephone call, sending a text message from a mobile phone or making a purchase on the Internet are examples of such situations. Second, employees need a service-oriented operational system and proper computer technology, customer databases and other physical resources to be able to create positive moments of truth. However, one should never forget that if the technology or automatic service production system does not work, breaks down or cannot be operated, the key to recovering the situation is a service-minded and customer-conscious employee.

The material support of support personnel and functions, as well as management support, are critical to the service orientation of the customer contact employees and systems of the visible part of the service process. Furthermore, customers' experiences in service encounters are influenced by the corporate and/or local image of the service provider. Finally, the price level and possible price offerings have an impact on the level of customer satisfaction. This is not always altogether true, however. For example, if a manufacturer needs service and spare parts in order to keep its machines running, and if every hour of delay means thousands of euros, pounds or dollars of lost production, he is probably willing to pay almost anything to get the service.

Interactive marketing and keeping promises is almost entirely the *responsibility of operations and other traditionally nonmarketing functions*. Therefore, employees involved in such functions are called *part-time marketers*, with dual responsibilities—for operations, or whatever their tasks concern, and for the marketing impact of their performance as well. To some extent, full-time marketers are also involved, but their role is marginal. Of course, in most business-to-business relationships the sales personnel have continuous responsibility for their customers. They cannot, however, do much to rescue a customer relationship if the organization has made a customer sufficiently dissatisfied with the service quality. In the short term the organization may be able to hold on to the customer's business; in the long term it loses customers.

From Transactions to Relationships in Marketing

Service processes are inherently relationship-oriented. Normally, interactions between the customer and the service provider occur and continue for some time. In many cases, services are consumed or used on a continuous basis. The same customer meets the same service provider over and over again. Marketing of services has often been difficult and considered less effective because service firms have not recognized that services are inherently relationship-oriented and have instead taken a transactional approach in their marketing strategies and programs.

There are certainly situations where a transaction marketing approach leads to good results, and there are customers who do not appreciate relationships in commercial contexts, but as a principle a relationship approach can be expected to lead to better results in service competition. Because markets are maturing and new customers are difficult to get, other than by poaching them from competitors, long-lasting relationships with existing customers become exceedingly important. It is much more difficult to compete with a core solution, whether it is a physical product or a service, than before. Firms have to develop total service offerings to provide competitive value for their customers. This means that more and more businesses have become service businesses and that *service competition* has taken over. Sometimes a transaction approach can work, but generally speaking these developments require a relationship approach to managing customers (and other parties).

Guidelines for Managing Service Competition

In this last part of this concluding chapter a set of guidelines for service management is going to be presented. The situation differs, of course, between firms and industries. However, some general guidelines for implementing a service strategy can be put forward. These guidelines start from the idea that people are the critical resource and the bottleneck in most service businesses. However, information technology, the Internet, operational systems and physical resources are increasingly important. Hence, technology and an understanding of how to use it may also be the bottleneck in a service process. As business is a social phenomenon, it is, of course, incorrect to talk about any rules of services in a strict sense. Nevertheless, in order to emphasize the common characteristics of the customer relationships in most organizations in service competition, these concluding guidelines have been labeled *the six rules of service*. The reader is asked to bear in mind that these rules are general and overemphasize the role of the employees for some situations. The Fifth and Sixth Rules, however, focus on other aspects of service management.

The *six rules of service* are as follows:

First Rule: The general approach.
Second Rule: Demand analysis.
Third Rule: Quality control.
Fourth Rule: Marketing.
Fifth Rule: Technology.
Sixth Rule: Organizational support.

The First Rule: The General Approach

The importance of service elements in customer relationships grows over time and customers—business customers as well as individuals—increasingly demand individual and flexible responses from the service provider. Success in the market requires that the firm can offer advice and guidance; for example, technical advice needed to start operating a printer, as well as small details, for example, a quick response on the phone about airplane departure times. If employees are authorized to make their own judgements and have the knowledge needed to do that, and in addition have a service-oriented approach to their job and to their customers, and if the firm is competitive in other respects, this will give good results in the marketplace. In spite of automated service systems, the increased use of information technology and the Internet, the creativity, motivation and skills of people are still the drivers behind successful development of new services, the implementation of service concepts and recovery of service failures that are occur from time to time. Hence, the first rule of service can be expressed as follows:[1]

> People develop and maintain good and enduring customer contacts. Employees ought to act as consultants, who are prepared to do their duty when the customer needs them and in a way the customer wants. The firm which manages best to do this strengthens its customer relationships and achieves the best profitability.

The Second Rule: Demand Analysis

Services are either rendered directly to people or organizations, or they are services on equipment owned by people (or organizations). In all cases representatives of the customer are present, extensively or occasionally, when the service is produced and delivered. Direct interactions between customer contact employees and customers occur, and in such situations immediate actions may have to be decided upon and taken by the contact person, or the contact person may have to give some information or change his way of doing the job according to the needs of the customer. Such a reaction may be, for example, changing the level of a customer training seminar to better meet the requirements or level of knowledge of the attendees, or a quick decision by a telephone receptionist about whom to put on the phone when the person a customer is asking for is absent. Nobody other than the person who produces the service can recognize the perhaps unexpected shift in the needs or wishes of the customer, if corrective actions are to be taken immediately. As has been discussed in previous chapters, in such situations prompt action is called for.

Market demand can, of course, be measured in advance using standard market research, and should be done in this way. However, the changing needs and wishes of customers at the point and time of service production and consumption cannot be measured in advance. Nor can this be reacted to later on, when somebody else has detected the changes that took place. The customer relationship was affected long ago, if a quick reaction did not occur at the time. Only customer contact personnel can do this in a satisfactory manner. Hence, the second rule of service can be expressed as follows:

> The customer contact personnel producing the service in contact with customers will have to analyze the needs, values, expectations and wishes of the customers at the point and time of service production and consumption.

The Third Rule: Quality Control

According to traditional manufacturing quality control models, the quality of a product is controlled by a separate unit, which checks the preproduced goods. This view is not valid anymore in modern quality management. Everyone, in manufacturing as well as in service production, has a responsibility for quality, and producing good quality is based on a notion that things will have to be done correctly the first time. Because of the characteristics of services and the nature of service production and consumption, postproduction control cannot prevent failure; it can only be observed that bad service quality has been produced *and* consumed by the customer. Moreover, if things are not done correctly the first time, the cost of correcting quality problems, which have occurred either in the back office or in the buyer–seller interface, is frequently high. As the quality goal is often less than 100 per cent and mistakes are therefore tolerated, these costs easily become "hidden costs" which are taken for granted and considered a necessary evil. Consequently, it is not possible to have a separate quality control unit following every production step; instead, everyone has to control the result of his job.

In service operations this is very true. Services are to a large extent the result of cooperation or interactive relationships between representatives of the customer and the service provider, which makes quality management even more complicated than in manufacturing. In manufacturing, one has to do things right the first time according to static specifications. In service production, *the specifications may change during the service process*, as was demonstrated by the discussion of the second rule. The customer may change his mind. Technology may break down, or almost anything may happen to change the situation and demand new or unforeseen actions.

The one who renders the service in contact with the customer, the customer contact employee, will have to check the quality of the service at the time it is produced and delivered. For example, when goods are delivered to a customer, an elevator is repaired, a customer in a restaurant is being served, or a telephone receptionist handles a call made by a customer, the quality of that service operation cannot be controlled and managed by anyone other than the person who has contact with the customer. Normally, there are no supervisors physically present in employee–customer interactions who can monitor quality on a continuous basis. Afterwards the quality can, of course, be checked, for example, by market research, but then the mistake has already been made and the customer relationship may have been damaged.

On the other hand, the contact person must not be left totally alone. "Common sense" may not be sufficient guidance. Management must provide employees with the knowledge, skills and directions needed to manage quality on their own with their customer contacts (internal or external). Moreover, management has to enhance the attitudes and mental capabilities of the employees to manage quality. Hence, the third rule of service can be expressed as follows:

> The customer contact person producing the service in contact with customers will have to control the quality of the service at the same time he produces the service.

The Fourth Rule: Marketing

In service competition the nature of marketing changes as well. Although traditional external marketing activities, such as market research, advertising campaigns, personal selling by a professional sales force and sales promotion, are as important as ever, they are not the only activities to be performed as marketing activities. The *marketing process* is much larger and is spread throughout the organization. Traditional means of competition are used mainly to establish new customer relationships, but these are of less importance, when ongoing relationships are to be maintained and strengthened. In order to develop existing customer relationships, the exchange of goods, services, and information, as well as financial and social exchange, are of critical importance. Personal selling, advertising and sales promotion activities are, of course, used in such situations, too, but their impact is often minor. Price is important at all stages of the Customer Relationships Life Cycle.

In service competition every contact between a contact person and a representative of a customer includes an element of marketing. These contacts are the moments of truth or the moments of opportunity where the success of the service provider is determined, and resales and cross-sales opportunities can be utilized. If these moments of truth give the customer a favorable impression of the contact person, of the systems and resources used, and thus of the total organization, the customer relationship is strengthened. The probability that it will last longer and lead to further business increases. However, the opposite is also true. Badly handled service encounters—that is, negatively experienced moments of truth—damage customer relationships and lead to lost business.

Thus, as noted earlier, any service organization has a large number of *part-time marketers*. Their main responsibility is the task they are set to perform. Marketing is only their second responsibility. However, if the marketing aspect of their job is missing, customers will perceive the quality of the service more negatively. Furthermore, in almost every service organization the part-time marketers outnumber the full-time marketers and salespeople several times over.

However, the marketing impact of what they do and how they perform their tasks has to be recognized by management, because their role in the total marketing process is critical. *If the interactive marketing performance of the part-time marketers fails, the marketing process fails, irrespective of whether the efforts of the salesforce or the advertising campaigns or other means of competition have been successful or not.* This is the essence of services marketing.

Marketing the service as a part-time marketer in the interactive marketing sense does not necessarily mean that the contact person would have to actively sell or offer the service, although this may also occur. Normally good part-time marketing behavior means that the job is done skillfully, in a flexible manner, without unnecessary delays, and with a service-oriented attitude. Hence, the fourth rule of service can be expressed as follows:

> The customer contact person has simultaneously to be a marketer of the service he produces.

The Fifth Rule: Technology

Information technology is becoming exceedingly important for more and more service processes. If a Web site is designed so that users find it complicated or uninteresting, or if people using a Web site do not get a quick response to their inquiries, they quickly lose interest in the firm and its offerings; it is so easy to jump to the next Web site. However, it is not only the Internet that is critical here. Information technology should also enable contact employees to get easily retrievable and reliable information about the customers they are serving. If that is not the case, interactions between contact employees and customers are affected and bad perceived quality created.

Other kinds of technology and physical resources used in services processes must also be customer-friendly and reliable. As previously concluded, technology is no less important in the service economy than it was before. On the contrary, it is more important. A technological solution, or a physical resource that is geared to the needs and wishes of the user and that fits the situation in which it is to be used, may well enhance the quality of the service. It can improve the efficiency of operations and profitability as well. Even more frequently, technological support enables personnel to produce a better service. Appropriate technology and physical resources, such as computer systems, documents, tools and equipment, may at the same time improve working conditions and enhance the motivation of the employees to give good service. On the other hand, technology that employees do not understand or are not willing to use has a negative effect both on internal relationships in the organization and on external customer relationships. Employees need adequate *technological support*.

Hence, the fifth rule of service can be expressed as follows:

> The impact on customers' ability and willingness to use technology, systems and physical resources (of any kind), as well as the impact of such resources on the employees in interactive and supporting parts of the organization, and on their ability and willingness to serve customers have to be taken into account when investments in such resources are made, so that the service quality perceived by customers is not affected in a negative way.

The Sixth Rule: Organizational Support

The current organizational structure of many firms does not support customer-oriented and high-quality service operations. Contact employees or departments which have to interact with each other in order to produce a service may be geographically or physically far apart in the organization. Often decisions concerning even minor details are made too far away from the service encounter, which, of course, can have a negative impact on the perceived service. Internal regulations may restrict the flexibility of the contact staff. For example, hotels frequently have their employees say, "No, sir, we cannot do that—management regulations, sir" to customers who ask for a service outside the normal procedures. Pants cannot be ironed on a Sunday, or pyjamas cannot be supplied for a guest whose luggage has been left behind by an airline. Management does not trust employees to think for themselves and make sensible decisions.

In many manufacturing firms, service elements are considered to be low priority. This means that services are not, like goods, an integral part of the total offering to the market. They receive fewer resources and less of management's time.

The employees, managers and their subordinates often feel that services are not important. A company's organizational structure may not be geared to the demands of the new service competition. The result is inevitable, of course. Employees involved in the firm's variety of service operations feel no pride in their job, nor do they feel motivated to give good service to customers. In order to develop their services into powerful means of competition, firms will have to adjust their organizational structure so that the organization supports employees in their efforts to give good service. An *organization structure support* is needed.

There is a second type of support that is given to employees and that is essential to good service; *management support*. It is well known that managers and supervisors get the staff they deserve. They have an important effect on the values that guide the overall way of thinking and behaving in the organization. In service competition this is as true as it ever was, and even more important to realize than before, because of the enormous and immediate impact that contact staff have on demand analysis, quality control and marketing.

Managers and supervisors have to be true *leaders*, not simply technical managers. There are too many rules and restrictions which managers and supervisors use as managing devices. This not only damages the service for the customer, but in the long term it destroys the employees. People are normally able to think for themselves, act spontaneously and flexibly, and still make good judgements, if they are well informed. Such service-oriented attitudes are effectively damaged by too much rules-and-regulation management and too little leadership.

Managers have to be able to motivate their people to be service-oriented and customer-conscious, by, for example, their leadership style, their way of sharing information and giving feedback to people in their organizational unit, and their way of encouraging, supporting and guiding employees. They will have to demonstrate, by the way they do their job, that they, too, consider that good service and satisfied customers are important. It goes without saying that this attitude is required of every manager in the firm, irrespective of their hierarchical position and their own involvement in service operations.

Unclear visions and/or badly defined or undefined *service concepts* (one or several) make it difficult for managers and their subordinates to decide in which direction they should go, what leads to fulfilling goals, and what is contradictory to the objectives of the organization. If service concepts are not well stated, no clear goals can be set. In such situations there will be chaos both in planning and in the everyday implementation of plans. To sum up, the employees need the support of the organizational structure, as well as the encouragement of their managers and supervisors, in order to be able to successfully meet the new service competition. Moreover, clearly defined service concepts are a necessity, if the organization is to avoid a chaotic situation where nobody knows what to do in certain situations or how to react to changes in the environment and to unexpected customer behavior. Hence, the sixth rule of service can be expressed as follows:

The organizational structure and managers, and explicitly defined service concepts have to provide the guidance, support and encouragement needed to enable and motivate customer contact personnel and support personnel alike to give good service.

Creation of New and Innovative Service Systems Through Employee Initiative: The Hospital Maternity Ward Case Study

There are significant opportunities for services and relationship marketing in the UK healthcare sector. However, realizing measurable success here is fraught with difficulties, some due to its corporate culture. However, a recent tragic event has had the effect of inspiring a radical turnaround in one maternity ward in a major regional hospital. This event was the theft of a baby from another hospital maternity ward. The subsequent public outcry made finding a solution of the utmost importance. What catalyzed service improvements in this particular organization was *a series of employee-driven changes* that had the effect of significantly changing both procedures and the way in which patients were treated. What was the most significant change, however, is who actually made it happen.

In almost all UK hospitals, it is the responsibility of the Estates department to take care of such matters as gardens, car parking, building maintenance, cleaning and security. Since baby theft was clearly a security matter, the Estates department acted promptly in implementing new procedures and systems. CCTV, security passes, visitor screening and so on all had the effect of making the obstetrics ward appear to be under siege. One of the new work practices was to cease rotating the cleaning staff whose additional tasks were to help with security maintenance. As people became used to new working practices, certain problems arose. Nursing staff felt pressurized under the greater administrative load caused by the heightened security procedures. Because they were no longer regularly reassigned to different groups, cleaning staff had by then acquired, for the first time, a team ethos. This moved them to suggest ways in which they might help. Cleaners began undertaking nonmedical tasks, such as serving meals to patients, managing visitor traffic and helping with admission of patients. The "siege mentality" induced by the security regime, engendered a supportive enclave of teams who expressed this support by regularly meeting to discuss ways in which their service might improve. The Estates managers were keen to give them autonomy since they were also learning—and significantly, they wanted to avoid another public relations disaster. Two small but significant changes occurred—patients were now called *mothers*, and the cleaners now called themselves the *domestic staff*. The first change was in response to the way in which the domestic staff viewed their clientele. They reasoned that unlike other hospital patients there was nothing "wrong" with their patients, they were not ill; they freely entered into pregnancy, but did need medical support services. Mothers did not need "fixing;" instead of *commiseration* there should be a *celebration*, and so the mindset of service providers was positive. Mothers, in turn, did not see such caring and supportive service providers as simply cleaners, and the term "domestics" was felt more appropriate to the mindset of the customer.

Domestic staff made significant strides in freeing the medical staff from the pressure of the security environment. Nursing staff, in turn, were highly supportive of their internal suppliers, expressing confidence by giving the domestics more freedom in assisting them. Domestic staff for the most part were mature women, with much experience. First time mothers and difficult birth mothers were routinely isolated, which may have made medical sense but made little human sense. Domestics organized their work around ensuring that no such mother was ever isolated, each spending as much time with the mothers as needed to support them psychologically, advising, alleviating fears, and simply listening. Thus, the level of service, both in terms of efficiency and effectiveness had the effect of achieving a virtuous circle of self-sustaining benefits available to each member of the obstetrics department. More effective planning could be observed, administrative efficiency was optimized, staff morale was high, management input was minimal and mothers expressed far more satisfaction than at any time previously. At the heart of these beneficial effects was the emergence of a relatively autonomous empowered workforce, none of whom were very well qualified, and certainly not sophisticated intellectuals. The lucky induction of a simple Hawthorne effect impelled a highly complex series of events, the momentum of which created the conditions for a continuous improvement quality strategy.

Source: This case example was developed by Peter Murphy, Dundee University.[2]

Five Barriers to Achieving Results

The fifth and sixth rules can be made more explicit by adding five additional statements which follow directly from the discussion about these rules. These statements all concern major *barriers to successfully implemented service management*. Most of these are due to an outdated management philosophy and old organizational structures, which hamper the development of sound and effective management of firms in the post-industrial society of the 21st century.[3] They are:

- organizational barrier;
- systems and regulations-related barrier;
- management-related barrier;
- strategy-related barrier; and
- decision-making barrier.

Barrier 1 (organizational barrier). *Good service, and sound change processes toward a service culture, are effectively destroyed by an old fashioned and obsolete organizational structure.* If an unappropriate organizational structure is left outside a change program, much of the effort to achieve better services may be in vain. The organization simply is not suitable for services and, thus, becomes a barrier to change.

Barrier 2 (systems and regulations-related barrier). *Employees would normally like to treat their customers well and provide a good service, but internal rules and regulations, the systems of operating, and the technology used may make this an impossible task.* It is only natural that most people would prefer to treat their customers well and give them good service, but if management regulations, operations or administrative systems, or the technology used is counteracting good service, they cannot do this. The internal infrastructure of the organization becomes a barrier to change. This typically happens when training efforts are used by themselves as the predominant means of developing a service culture in an organization, and no attention is given in the change process to this infrastructure provided by regulation, systems and technology.

Barrier 3 (management-related barrier). *How managers treat their staff is the way the customers of the organization will be treated.* If a change process focuses predominantly or only on contact and support personnel and top and middle management are left outside, there is a high risk that the superiors of those involved in customer contacts will not be fully aware of what should be emphasized in these contacts and how the moments of truth should be handled and managed. Supervisors can easily encourage the wrong aspects of a role, and a role conflict emerges for the employees. They would like to implement new ideas, but their bosses have become a barrier to doing this.

Barrier 4 (strategy-related barrier). *If well-defined and easily understood service concepts are lacking, chaos will reign in the organization, and managers and customer contact and support employees alike will be uncertain about how to act in specific situations, in planning as well as in implementing plans.* If the organization throws itself into a change process without first clearly analyzing the benefits sought by the customers in the organization's target segments, and decides what it should do, and how corresponding goals should be accomplished, there is no solid foundation for a consistently pursued change process. A number of projects are initiated and programs started without anyone really knowing why this is being done and what the ultimate objectives are. In short, there is no strategic approach, and this becomes a barrier to change.

All of the four barriers above, as well as the six rules, are easy to accept, and generally it is not difficult for managers to admit that these rules have been broken and/or several barriers are present in their organizations. However, there is a big step from understanding a phenomenon and accepting that a problem may exist to doing something to change the situation. Therefore, a fifth barrier is finally offered as the key to success:

Barrier 5 (decision-making barrier). *Good intellectual analysis and thorough planning is of no value unless there is the determination, courage, and strength needed in the organization to implement new visions and intellectually sound plans.* To put this another way, weak management is always a barrier to implementing change processes.

Conclusion

This chapter has illustrated the essence of management and marketing in service competition. The first sections summed up the market-oriented service management framework, and in the following sections six general guidelines for service management, the six rules of service, were described.

The conclusions in this chapter hold true not only for so-called service firms such as hotels and restaurants, banks and financial institutions, insurance companies, transportation firms, and a variety of public services. *They are equally valid for any type of organization*. This follows from the fact that in most industries the importance of service has grown dramatically. Everybody is now part of the service economy. Hence, *every firm faces some kind of service competition*. Services can be found in any industry, and they should be an integral part of any firm's offering, irrespective of whether goods or services are the core business of the firm.

The traditional ways of handling demand analysis, quality control and marketing are not sufficient anymore. The new *service competition* requires a new way of thinking, a *service knowledge*. If management cannot adjust its ways of thinking and its actions according to the new situation, the risk that the firm will suffer and lose market share will grow. *Service knowledge is a strategic issue as well as an operational one*. The ways in which demand analysis, quality control and marketing have been carried out in the past are not necessarily totally outdated today. Traditional activities may still be efficient and effective, and they should be applied whenever appropriate. The main thing is that they are not sufficient anymore. They have to be accompanied by new efforts, and they should be viewed from a new, much more holistic perspective.

In service competition, if the firm fails to understand the characteristics of services and the critical importance of the successful management of customer relationships, the firm's operations will deteriorate and be less successful. A number of moments of truth will become wasted moments of opportunity. On the operational level, every employee has to meet the demands that competition makes on them all the time. The support of the fifth and sixth rules of service must always be present. Of course, this may be impossible to achieve in practice. Mistakes happen. However, *the objective must be to achieve 100 per cent excellence*. Otherwise, the battle is lost before it has even begun; customers will get inconsistent service, bad word of mouth is created, and the organization's image is damaged.

Inconsistency of services is perhaps the most serious problem facing service operations today. Most parts of a service process may function well, but if one or two interactions with a customer are handled badly, all the good that has been developed may be destroyed by these elements of bad service. Or the customer may be pleased with the service he receives from all the normal departments of a service firm, but if he has an unexpected request or a service failure has occurred, no service can be obtained. This means that his opinion of the firm's service will be revised. Whether the customer experiences bad service or a lack of willingness to give good service, the total *perceived service quality* will collapse in the mind of the customer on that occasion. The inconsistency of the service process caused by one or more badly handled moments of truth has an immense negative impact on the customer relationship. Successful service management requires an appreciation for the customers' perspective throughout the organization and consistency in the way that every part of the customer relationship is handled.

Questions for discussion

1. Discuss the importance of the six rules of service.
2. In your organization, or in any organization, which of the barriers to achieving results are present? What are the reasons for the existence of these barriers? How can they be removed?

Further Reading

Grönroos, C. (1999) Företagsledningens tvångströja (The management straitjacket). In Swedish. *Ekonomiska Samfundets Tidskrift* (The Journal of the Economic Society of Finland), **52**(3), pp. 115–116.

Mickwitz, G. (1985) Arbetstid och service (Working hours and service). *Ekonomiska Samfundets Tidskrift* (The Journal of the Economic Society of Finland), **38**(4), p. 163.

Murphy, P. (2000) *Front Stage Transactions Lead to Back Stage Relationships: A Study of Role Repertoires in Hospital Service Provision.* Unpublished research paper. Dundee University, Scotland, UK.

Notes

1   The logic underpinning this general rule of service was discussed by Gösta Mickwitz in an essay on the role of service in business. See Mickwitz, G., Arbetstid och service (Working hours and service). In Swedish. *Ekonomiska Samfundets Tidskrift* (The Journal of the Economic Society of Finland), **38**(4), 1985, p. 163. Gösta Mickwitz is a former professor of marketing and economics at Hanken Swedish School of Economics and Helsinki University in Finland and my mentor, who taught me to think laterally and seek solutions outside the limits set by the prevailing opinion.

2   Murphy, P., Front Stage Transactions Lead to Backstage Relationships: A Study of Role Repertoires in Hospital Service Provision. Unpublished research paper. Dundee University, Scotland, UK, 2000.

3   Grönroos, C., Företagsledningens tvångströja (The management straitjacket). In Swedish. *Ekonomiska Samfundets Tidskrift* (The Journal of the Economic Society of Finland), **52**(3), 1999, pp. 115–116.

INDEX